# THE COMPLETE BOOK OF
# PRUNING

### DUNCAN COOMBS
B.Sc. (Hons), M.Hort., Cert. Ed., C.Biol., M.I.Biol.

### PETER BLACKBURNE-MAZE
M. Hort., M.I. Hort

### MARTYN CRACKNELL
B.Tech. (Hons), Cert. Ed., G.I.Biol.

### ROGER BENTLEY
B.Sc. (Hons)

Edited by Duncan Coombs

**CASSELL**PAPERBACKS

## ACKNOWLEDGEMENTS

The publishers are grateful to the following for granting permission to reproduce the following colour photographs: Martyn Cracknell (pp. i, ii, iii, xiv & xv); Duncan Coombs (pp. iv, v, vi, vii, viii, ix, x, xii, xvi, xvii & xx); and Peter Blackburne-Maze (pp xviii, xix, xxi, xxiv, xxvi, xxvii, xxviii (top) & xxix). All the remaining photographs were taken by Bob Challinor.

All the line drawings were drawn by Michael Shoebridge.

First published in the United Kingdom in 1992 by Ward Lock

This paperback edition first published in 2001 by
Cassell Paperbacks,
Cassell Illustrated
2-4 Heron Quays
London E14 4JP

Distributed in the United States of America by
Sterling Publishing Co., Inc.
387 Park Avenue South,
New York, NY 10016-8810

A CIP catalogue record for this book is available from the British Library

ISBN 1-84188-143-0

Printed and bound in Slovenia by DELO tiskarna by arrangement with Prešernova družba, Ljubljana

# Contents

# Preface

Pruning should always give a deep sense of satisfaction. Sometimes the improvement produced is immediately apparent as in the removal of a competing leading shoot from a young tree. In other cases we prune with a more distant end in view, for example when pruning wisteria in early summer to stimulate the production of flowers the following spring.

The book aims to be encyclopaedic, covering the pruning of trees, shrubs and fruits of Northern Europe and the United States.

The Introduction explains the various reasons for pruning a plant. Plant physiology is touched upon to clarify the plant's response to pruning – vital knowledge if the desired result is to be achieved. Details are given in accordance with modern practical and research findings of how and when major limbs should be removed and correct subsequent treatment.

Part 1, Ornamental Plants Outdoors, starts with the necessary pruning to produce a well-shaped young tree or shrub. The reader will then find specialist chapters devoted to pruning trees, shrubs, hedges, topiary, climbers and roses. Each group is dealt with comprehensively, giving full practical details and supported by illustrations for each plant.

The cultivation of plants in conservatories is enjoying a surge in popularity. Part 2, Ornamental Plants Under Glass, recognizes that an important key to success is the knowledge of how to manage the often very vigorous growth of such plants. You will discover a full explanation of how to prune this diverse group of plants.

The pruning of trees and soft fruits, whilst based upon the same plant physiological responses common to all plants, has developed into a detailed specialist subject. Part 3, Fruit Trees and Bushes, forms a major part of this book. You will find the same developmental sequence from plant propagation to mature fruiting plants being used as a basis for the chapters, as with the propagation and pruning of ornamental plants. Again, as with the rest of this book, the aim is to be comprehensive and the range of plants is very wide. For example, a complete chapter is devoted to the important, but seldom written about, topic of pruning cultivated nuts.

Specially commissioned line drawings, many taken from life, are used to show details and stages in pruning clearly. Colour photographs have been specially taken and included to illustrate the methods and results of good pruning.

Written in a light, easily understood manner, the requirements of the amateur gardener, student and professional horticulturalist have all been kept clearly in mind, and each should find a wealth of useful information.

D.J.C., P.B-M., M.J.C., R.B.

# INTRODUCTION

## CHAPTER 1
# *The Reasons for Pruning*

### The plant's response to pruning

Pruning is the selective removal of part of a plant's top growth, namely branches and shoots, or part of its bottom growth, the roots, so as to control subsequent plant growth and behaviour. The response of a plant to pruning is due to the alteration of the root:shoot ratio. If branches are removed, the hormones and complex metabolites, made by leaves and buds, will not be as plentiful and this will reduce root growth. If roots are removed, the flow of nutrients from the soil and the supply of hormones and storage compounds from the roots will all be reduced. If these are not so readily available to buds on the shoot system their growth will be controlled.

It is clear from this that the effects of pruning are dependent upon the transport of materials up and down the stem between the root and the shoot systems. It is sometimes useful to control this transport by making incisions in the stem, called 'nicking and notching,' or to impede the downward flow of nutrients by ring-barking or girdling. Bending branches down (festooning) and planting at a shallow angle to the ground, such as with cordons, also impede transport in the stem.

A more recent method of exerting influence over the plant growth is to use chemical plant growth regulators instead of, or in conjunction with, pruning. These may suppress the natural hormone production within the plant, or may artificially supply hormones to mimic normal production after a part of the plant has been removed, or they may have an independent overriding effect on growth.

During the growth of a plant, from the seedling stage through to maturity, the root and shoot systems will have been mutually regulating each other through the production of hormones and the supply of nutrients. A great deal of further work is required to unravel the amazingly complex interactions which occur and to understand the role of some of the chemicals which plants produce. However, much progress has been made and it is possible to explain many of the observed responses of plants in terms of the interactions between the root and shoot systems.

In an intact shoot, the apical bud usually grows with greater vigour and is larger than lateral or axillary buds occurring on the stem below. This observation has led to the suggestion that the apex exerts a controlling influence over the shoot, and suppresses the growth of lateral buds. The term 'apical dominance' has been used to describe it. If the tip is removed the apical dominance is broken and one of the buds below the apex will begin to grow and become the new leader; this one establishes its own dominance over the other buds. In this way, a plant which loses its principal growing point can produce a replacement in a very short space of time.

In some situations, such as when clipping a hedge or in topiary, it is desirable that removal of a shoot tip should promote the breaking and growth of several lateral buds, resulting in a very close texture to the hedge surface. In other situations, for example when shaping a young fruit tree, the breaking of numerous buds might be undesirable. It is essential to understand how the root and shoot systems communicate, so that they can be managed to obtain the desired results.

The apex consists of a small dome of actively dividing cells, called the apical meristem, which produces hormones called auxins. One auxin which is widely distributed in the plant kingdom, is called indole-3-acetic acid (IAA).

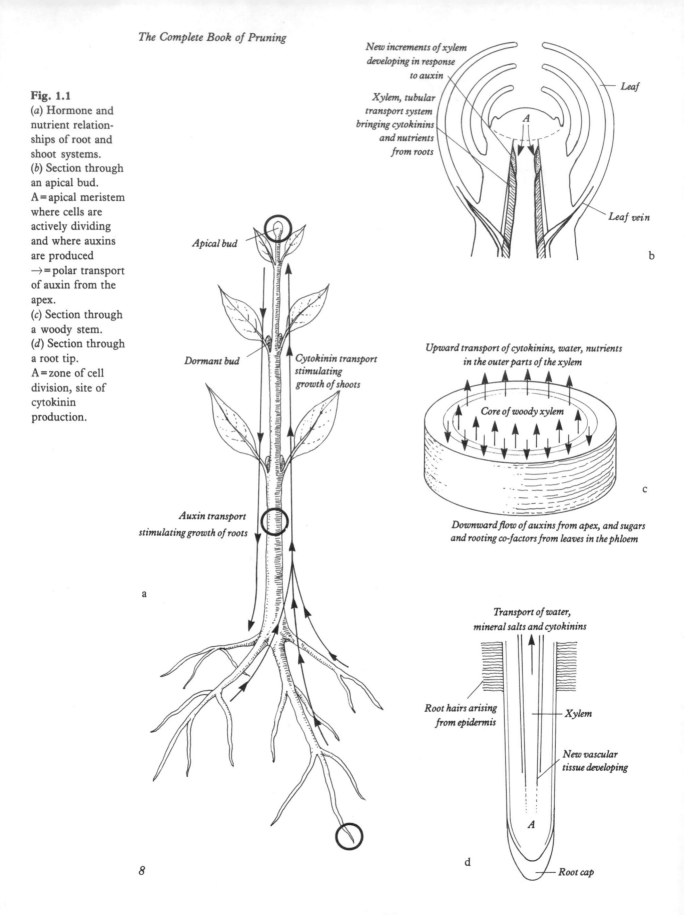

**Fig. 1.1**

(*a*) Hormone and nutrient relationships of root and shoot systems.
(*b*) Section through an apical bud.
A = apical meristem where cells are actively dividing and where auxins are produced
→ = polar transport of auxin from the apex.
(*c*) Section through a woody stem.
(*d*) Section through a root tip.
A = zone of cell division, site of cytokinin production.

New increments of xylem developing in response to auxin

Xylem, tubular transport system bringing cytokinins and nutrients from roots

*A*

Leaf

Leaf vein

b

Apical bud

Dormant bud

Cytokinin transport stimulating growth of shoots

Auxin transport stimulating growth of roots

a

Upward transport of cytokinins, water, nutrients in the outer parts of the xylem

*Core of woody xylem*

c

Downward flow of auxins from apex, and sugars and rooting co-factors from leaves in the phloem

Transport of water, mineral salts and cytokinins

Root hairs arising from epidermis

Xylem

New vascular tissue developing

*A*

Root cap

d

Auxins have many functions, including stimulating the development of the woody tubular transport system called xylem. The xylem tubes extend as a continuous system from just below the apical bud, through the stem, to the roots. They are the pathway for water, mineral salts and hormones to be transported from the roots. As the shoot tip grows, the auxin it produces causes extensions to be made to the top of the xylem, so that the flow from the roots is preferentially directed to the tip [Fig. 1.1]. In this way the tip never grows away from its water and nutrient supply.

The liquid in the xylem contains dissolved mineral salts absorbed from the soil and recirculated from storage organs. In addition, it contains hormones made in the root tips called cytokinins (or kinins). Kinetin is one of the best known of these hormones. One of the functions of cytokinins is to promote cell division. The xylem tubes are dead so cytokinin cannot stimulate them, but when it reaches the young cells in the apical bud it promotes cell division and further growth. The dividing cells produce auxin, and thus the cycle is repeated. The vigour of the roots, and their production of cytokinin, controls the growth of shoots.

If the shoot tip is removed, cytokinins, water and mineral salts continue to pass up from the roots but there are no young cells to metabolize the cytokinin. The hormone accumulates in the upper part of the severed shoot where it stimulates any young cells which are capable of cell division. Those most likely to respond are in the youngest bud, that which is nearest the tip. Here the cells begin to divide, produce auxin and establish their xylem connection to the main system. In due course they develop as the replacement leading shoot.

In addition to their role in apical dominance the auxins and cytokinins also play a major part in the control of shoot and root development. If a shoot is cut off, auxin will still continue to pass back from the tip towards the cut surface, where it accumulates. Here it stimulates root development. This has been exploited for years, and for those species which do not readily root, a little auxin (hormone rooting powder) applied to the base of the cutting, can bring success.

In much the same way, when a piece of root is severed from the parent plant it continues to produce cytokinin, which passes up to the cut surface and accumulates. Here it stimulates adventitious buds to form. This may be seen in portions of root of most weeds, with perennial roots, such as *Rumex* spp. (the docks), or *Taraxacum officinale* (dandelion), and in the roots of plants with a suckering habit, for example *Rubus idaeus* (raspberry), *Rhus typhina* (sumach tree), *Amelanchier* spp. (snowy mespilus) and *Prunus domestica* (plum). However, cytokinins are not readily available for routine use to promote buds on root cuttings. The alteration of the ratio of root:shoot by pruning will alter the balance of cytokinin:auxin within the plant and may lead to the formation of surplus roots or buds. This may be seen when large numbers of branches are cut from a tree, such as when a neglected tree is being brought back under control. The amount of cytokinin made by the roots will be the same, but the removal of branches means that the root:shoot ratio is increased. Therefore, the amount of cytokinin reaching the remaining branches is increased. This stimulates dormant buds to develop and new buds to form on the trunk and around the cut surfaces. These then grow out as masses of soft whippy shoots. They may be called epicormic sprouts or water shoots.

Whilst different plants have different sensitivity to auxins and cytokinins, and different natural levels of production of these hormones, none the less these principles are generally applicable to all plants.

The supply of auxin and cytokinin can be controlled by varying the severity of pruning, by timing (root activity is low in winter) and by the use of artificial hormones. This enables us to control plant growth and anticipate how a plant will respond to particular pruning practices. However, there are many practical considerations which require us to prune plants for reasons unrelated to the hormone balance.

## The reasons for pruning

### To ensure healthy vigorous growth in new plants

When a plant is to be moved from one site to another, it is almost inevitable that it will suffer some root damage. The severity of the damage will depend upon the growing system which has been used, and will be minimal in shrubs grown in containers and bedding plants in modules. Field-grown trees and shrubs are usually undercut with a tractor blade or winched, which severs tap roots and enables the plants to be dug from the ground by hand. These bare-rooted plants may be sold directly, or rootballed in a net of compost. Prior to planting, any broken, decayed or dried roots should be cut cleanly across, to reduce the risk of disease-causing organisms entering, and the roots should be spread out over a gentle mound of soil in the base of the planting hole. Roots which are too long to be accommodated should be cut cleanly to fit the planting hole, rather than being bent round and crammed in.

The pruning of roots will promote the development of fibrous roots for water and mineral salt absorption. The planting hole should be prepared thoroughly, taking particular care on clay soils and reclamation sites to ensure that it can drain freely, so that the new plant does not stand in a hole full of water after the first rainstorm.

Waterlogging of a damaged root system is likely to encourage diseases like 'root death', caused by *Phytophthora cinnamomi* and *P. cambivora*.

To prevent damage to the new roots as they develop, it is essential to minimize movement of the root system in the planting hole. This is achieved by firming the soil around the roots and by staking, but it is also important to prune back the top of the plant to reduce wind rock. This also reduces the amount of leaf which will be carried, and thus reduces water loss in the first season of growth.

Gardeners are often reluctant to prune newly planted shrubs, fruit bushes and roses, but for bare-rooted plants it is really essential, so as to avoid excessive water stress when the leaves form. The reason for this is again due to a hormone. When a plant is under water stress, for example when the young leaves lose water rapidly in spring sunshine, but the roots cannot replace all that is lost, the plant produces abscisic acid (ABA), in its leaves. This has two functions. Firstly it causes closure of the stomata on the leaf surfaces resulting in a reduction in water loss. Secondly, and more importantly, it induces strong dormancy in

lateral buds. As a result, these buds will not grow and a stalky plant without basal branches will result.

In contrast, if after planting the top is pruned back to stems bearing four or five buds, these will not produce enough leaf to cause severe water stress, the hormone will not be produced, and the buds will be able to grow with vigour and develop at a rate appropriate for the root system. The result is a shapely plant with strong basal branches.

Incidentally, this dormancy effect on buds can be used to produce straight-stemmed trees without any low side branches, by deliberately exposing grafted rootstocks to water stress. This is achieved by undercutting the root systems and allowing any rootstock suckers to grow. The resultant abscisic acid suppresses all the lower buds on the graft [Fig. 1.2]. Only the apical bud grows, giving a straight stem with dormant buds along its length. The suckers are later removed.

If a large tree is to be moved to a new site, it is not sufficient to rely on pruning and staking to ensure successful establishment. In the three years prior to removal, the root system must be progressively pruned to promote formation of a fibrous root ball. This is most easily achieved by digging a narrow trench part of the way around the perimeter of the root ball to sever the main roots gradually. As a general rule, the root ball should be about ten times the diameter of the lower trunk. The fibrous roots which develop are not only highly efficient at water absorption, but they also help to bond the root ball together when it is finally lifted. Despite these preparations, the successful transplantation of a large tree requires considerable skill and aftercare.

**Maintenance of health and vigour**
Plants which are not maintained often become a dense or tangled mass of branches. The inner shoots are deprived of light and die back, and in wind many twigs rub on each other and may become injured or broken. These conditions lead to a greatly increased risk of disease. Prevention is largely a matter of commonsense, involving removal of shoots to create an open framework of branches through which air can circulate freely. Cut out any branches which are broken, or are rubbing on others and

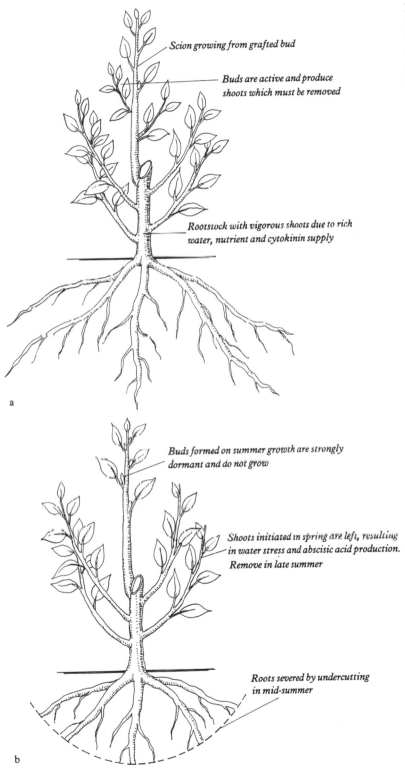

Scion growing from grafted bud

Buds are active and produce
shoots which must be removed

Rootstock with vigorous shoots due to rich
water, nutrient and cytokinin supply

a

Buds formed on summer growth are strongly
dormant and do not grow

Shoots initiated in spring are left, resulting
in water stress and abscisic acid production.
Remove in late summer

Roots severed by undercutting
in mid-summer

b

**Fig. 1.2
Producing a
straight-
stemmed,
grafted tree.**
(*a*) The traditional
way. Regularly cut
off side growths to
channel nutrients
to the apex. (This
also cuts off most
of the leaves and
reduces growth).

(*b*) The improved
method. Induce
water stress to
promote dormancy
in stem buds. This
reduces pruning
and gives improved
growth.

may cause injury. Remove feeble stems, and those which grow across the centre of the plant, and remove any branches showing signs of pests, disease or die back, taking care to cut right down to clean healthy wood.

### Pests and diseases

*Stem-boring caterpillars.* These usually produce a hole in a branch from which brown pellets of chewed wood may fall, and may be seen on the ground below. The affected branch is weakened and may break in stormy weather, or when laden with fruit, or may simply die back. Examples include the wood leopard moth (*Zeuzera pyrina*) and goat moth (*Cossus cossus*) on many tree species, the currant clearwing (*Synanthedon tipuliformis* syn. *Aegeria tipuliformis*) on red and blackcurrants, the raspberry shoot moth (*Lampronia rubiella*) on blackcurrants and raspberries and the pine shoot moth (*Rhyacionia buoliana*).

*Cankers.* These are shallow depressions in the bark, often rounded or oval in shape with flaking or scaly edges. They are due to death of the underlying tissues and gradually spread around the stem until it is girdled and dies. Cutting out is the remedy usually recommended, followed by painting with a fungicidal paint. This may be grossly disfiguring, and it may be more acceptable to leave the cankers and accept that the plant will suffer a gradual decline.

*Fructifications.* Small or large bracket fungi or creamy spots or jelly-like growths, are all signs of substantial infection, likely to require major surgery. However, pruning may be helpful in some cases, such as in the control of coral spot (*Nectria cinnabarina*), which is only a moderately invasive parasite on most plants. If a cut branch reveals staining, it should be further cut right back to healthy wood. For diseases which do not show staining it is prudent to cut back at least 15 cm (6 in) below the first sign of disease.

*Abnormal Foliage.* Plum trees and occasionally cherries or apple may be affected by the fungal disease silverleaf (*Chondrostereum purpureum*). They develop a whitish sheen on the leaves of isolated branches. This gradually spreads to the whole tree and dieback occurs. Later, small purple bracket fungi appear on the dead wood. At an early stage the disease may be arrested by removal of affected branches. These should be cut back to healthy wood in which there is none of the characteristic dark brown staining.

Wilting of foliage may be indicative of stem disease such as dutch elm disease (*Ceratocystis ulmi*). Removal of affected branches may not help the tree to survive but it will minimize the risk of falling timber, and reduce the invasion of secondary diseases.

*Gums and slime flux.* Infestation by wood-boring beetles, minor injury, or even a spell of hot dry weather can stimulate the exudation of sticky gum from *Prunus* spp., but a more serious cause of exudates is bacterial infection.

### Common bacterial problems

*Fire blight* (*Erwinia amylovora*). Affects many in the family *Rosaceae*. This is characterized by reddish dead leaves clinging to dead branches, as if scorched by fire. Affected parts may exude whitish sticky drops of slime.

*Bacterial canker of plum and cherry* (*Pseudomonas syringae* pv. *mors-prunorum*). The plant suffers a generalized dieback with shallow cankers exuding amber gum; in summer brown spots on the leaves drop out to leave a 'shothole effect'.

*Poplar bacterial canker* (*Xanthomonas populi* syn. *Aplanobacter populi*). Branches become girdled and die and in spring a creamy bacterial ooze emanates from cracks in the wood.

*Slime flux.* A general term for bacterial infection of broad-leaved trees in which the wood becomes water soaked and watery fluid oozes through wounds or cracks. It is usually associated with dieback. Trees may survive with this condition for many years but they will become progressively more dangerous and liable to shed limbs or to fall.

The exudation of resin by conifers is not usually indicative of disease, but is a normal response to minor injury, for instance by pine shoot moth (*Rhyacionia buoliana*) and pine resin gall moth (*Petrova resinella*).

### Control of plant size

Heavy pruning of stems is usually accompanied by a flush of growth around the cut surfaces. This gives the impression that the pruning has stimulated an increased growth rate. However, the reduction in leaf area for photosynthesis and the removal of a reservoir of stored foods, is really a retarding process and is more likely to alter the type of growth than to increase the overall growth. Roots for example are likely to cease growing or even die back and this will affect top growth in subsequent years.

The use of pruning to prevent trees and shrubs from outgrowing their position is very common practice. It is a form of frustration of the natural growth rate and it is always less satisfactory than selecting a more modestly sized or less vigorous plant at the outset.

One of the most drastic techniques for reducing crown size of trees, most often seen in urban areas, is the practice of pollarding. In this case, a trunk with a few main branches is allowed to develop but all other top growth is removed. The plant responds by producing a flush of sappy growths at the site of the principal cuts, which are thinned to three or four main shoots. These are allowed to grow for several years before being removed, and the cycle repeated. Alternatively, the shoots may be cut off every year.

Reduction in vigour may be achieved in some plants by use of dwarfing rootstocks, and is most successful for top fruit. Even in this case there are some vigorous varieties such as the cooking apple, 'Bramley's Seedling,' which do not make suitable plants for the smaller garden. Among cherries, the rootstock 'Colt' confers a semi-dwarfing habit on the top growth.

Root pruning has the same effect as the use of dwarfing rootstocks. The loss of root tips results in a reduced supply of cytokinins, and a reduced capacity for water and mineral salt absorption. As a result, the top growth is curtailed. Root pruning is not easily performed on large specimens, though it may occur incidentally when roots are severed during ground works. This is especially common in urban roadside trees when trenches are dug for laying or maintenance of mains services like gas, electricity and water.

The removal of shallow roots to level paving slabs, or in grassland to reduce interference with mowing machinery, are further examples.

However, it is in the art of Bonsai that regular root pruning plays a major part in preventing coarse growth, and ensuring short internodes and small leaves in keeping with the miniature habit. The plants should be grown in a small root-restricting container such as a rigid plastic net, which is plunged into a larger ornamental container. At regular intervals, say once a year, it is removed and the roots which have grown out of the root ball container are trimmed off. The plant is then replunged in its original container which is refilled with fresh soil. This ensures healthy growth, but maintains the tight dwarf habit.

## Plant form (formative pruning)

Selective removal of buds on the young plant, so as to control plant form, is perhaps the most obvious reason for pruning. It is essential for the training of fruit trees and bushes, to achieve a shape which will permit efficient interception of light for photosynthesis, and a robust branch habit to support the weight of fruit. At the same time the plant must be economical in the ground area it occupies, and should support its fruit in a manner that allows swift and easy harvesting. For garden plants an additional consideration is to produce a pleasing appearance, both during the growing season and also in winter when the leaves have fallen. The common shapes of free-standing trees are the traditional open-centred type, pruned to provide a straight stem with three or four main (scaffold) branches forming a goblet shape branch framework, and the centre-leader types which retain a central stem bearing tiers of branches to give an overall spindle or pyramid shape. Shapes suitable for use against walls include the espalier, cordon and fan.

One of the simplest pruning techniques is the removal of all lateral branches from plants to produce a straight central stem. This is normal practice in glasshouse tomato growing, resulting in stems of 10 m (30 ft) or more, trained along horizontal support wires, and bearing very accessible fruit trusses. In forestry plantations the removal of all lateral branches produces straight trunks of timber with a minimum of knots.

Straight stems can also be encouraged in plants with a naturally contorted habit, e.g., (*Salix babylonica* 'Tortuosa' (syn *S. matsudana* 'Tortuosa')), by coppicing. This involves cutting off the parent plant at or about ground level. The dramatic alteration of the root:shoot ratio promotes bud development on the stump and on the roots. These buds grow very fast and straight, under the influence of the generous nutrient, water and hormone supply from the rootstock. The resultant shoots may be harvested for use as giant cuttings to produce instant trees of easily rooted species such as willow. If thinned out, the remaining few shoots perform even more spectacularly and the effect is further enhanced by the large leaves that such shoots bear. A paulownia treated this way may grow 8 m (25 ft) in a season, with huge leaves.

Some trees and shrubs grow with a narrow erect habit without requiring pruning. They include *Populus nigra* 'Italica' (Lombardy poplar) a range of conifers and junipers including *Juniperus communis* 'Hibernica', and the branchless or columnar apple trees derived from the natural mutation 'Wijcik'. These include the ornamental crab apple *Malus* 'Maypole' and both dessert and culinary cultivars.

All the above may provide a useful option for those who lack the courage to control plant form by pruning.

The hard pruning of shrubs to stimulate vigorous shoots is used for several ornamentals which have attractively coloured stems, since the brightness of colour is greatest in the young wood, e.g. *Cornus alba* 'Sibirica' (red-barked dogwood), *Salix alba* 'Britzensis' (syn. 'Chermesina') (orange-stemmed willow).

The vigour of coppice shoots has led to the suggestion that old shrubs can be rejuvenated by hard pruning. One should always remember though, that some plants seem to lack functional buds on the old stem bases and their roots may be incapable of forming new buds. Conifers in particular are unlikely to survive severe pruning. Furthermore, a plant which does respond is likely to produce a great mass of shoots which require subsequent thinning, and several years' growth and training if a shapely plant is to be achieved ultimately. It is worth considering whether a more realistic alternative might be to start afresh with a new plant, giving the opportunity to undertake some soil improvement in the rooting zone and to redesign the landscape.

**Pruning for fruitfulness**

Through a process of trial and error over many years, systems of pruning have been developed to maximize the flowering and cropping potential of different trees and shrubs. These are discussed at length in later chapters. They vary according to whether the flowers are usually borne on wood which has grown in the current year or on wood which was produced in the previous year.

Thus, the canes of autumn-fruiting raspberry may be cut down completely in winter, and fruit will be borne on the new canes produced in spring. Whereas the spring-fruiting forms will only bear fruit on canes grown the previous year, so pruning is confined to those older canes which have previously fruited. Likewise in ornamentals, where for example *Sambucus nigra* (elderberry) and *Buddleja davidii* (butterfly bush) flower on current season wood but *Amelanchier* spp. (snowy mespilus) and *Ligustrum* spp. (privet) flower on the previous season's growth.

In addition, the position of flower buds on a branch is of great importance. Some trees produce short stubby twigs called spurs which carry the flower buds, whilst others tend to bear their flowers at the tips of the branches. Use of an inappropriate method of pruning can be disastrous and this underlines the need to know one's plants. In general, hard pruning produces non-flowering vigorous shoots, so bringing a neglected tree back into full bearing should be carried out over a few years if some fruiting is required in the meantime.

Conversely, pruning of roots or interference with the downward transport of sugars by girdling the stem, or bending them downwards, tends to promote flower bud formation. Treatment with some growth retardants has the same effect and if a plant is suffering root disease, it may respond by producing unusually heavy flushes of flower. Although the physiology of flower bud initiation is complex, the common feature in each of these cases seems to be a retention of sugar in the aerial parts of the plant.

Fruit thinning is the selective removal of fruitlets so as to prevent an excessive crop of small fruit in favour of a more modest crop of larger fruits. In grapes, this allows each grape to grow to its full potential without the bunches becoming too congested.

For herbaceous plants like melons and

pumpkins grown in temperate areas, it is necessary to reduce the number of fruits to a realistic number that the plant might bring to maturity. Commercially, apple fruitlets may be thinned by spraying with the growth regulator and insecticide carbaryl.

The removal of lateral flower buds so as to promote growth of single specimen blooms is called disbudding, and is routinely practised on chrysanthemums, carnations and dahlias. It is important to rub out unwanted buds, or fruitlets, when they are tiny, to minimize injury.

## When to prune

The timing of pruning for any particular plant is partly dependent upon the reason for the pruning, but is substantially determined by unrelated practical considerations. These vary from one species to another so it is unsatisfactory to make generalizations and this once again stresses the need to know one's plants. As the old adage says:

*Prune when the knife is sharp*

Special considerations which demand that pruning is carried out at a particular time of year are as follows.

### Excessive bleeding

In spring, as food reserves in the root system begin to be mobilized and root respiration increases, there is an increase in the concentration of dissolved salts in the water-conducting system of the wood (the xylem). This leads to a very vigorous water uptake from the soil, by osmosis. At this time of year there will be few leaves and therefore the plant will be losing only a small amount of water by evaporation (transpiration). The consequence of the strong water intake and low rate of water loss from leaves is a substantial build up of pressure in the xylem, which may extend for the first 10 m (30 ft) or so of the stem. This gradually diminishes with increasing distance from the roots, due to the resistance to flow within the narrow xylem vessels. It a plant is cut whilst in this condition, water will exude from the wound as a steady stream of drips, and continue for days or even weeks, resulting in a serious loss of mineral salts. Such plants include grapevines and *Betula* spp. (birches).

To avoid this problem, either prune such plants while they are fully dormant, in winter, or wait until the leaves are fully opened in summer and prune during the day when the evaporation of water from the leaves will not only reduce the pressure in the xylem but will in fact generate a strong tension in the system, and hence prevent any bleeding.

Other plants have a different pressurized system of tubes which bleed profusely when cut. These are the laticifers or latex canals from which an opaque white or yellow 'milk' may leak. In time, this usually seals itself but it may stain foliage and stems, and also paving. Latex is sticky and catches dirt, to add to the shabby appearance. It is unlikely to threaten the life of the plant but does represent a loss of complex metabolites which could reduce vigour. Plants of this type include *Juglans regia* (walnut), *Ficus elastica* (rubber plant), and many *Euphorbia* spp. (spurges).

To avoid the problem, pruning should be carried out when the plants are fully dormant.

### Practical convenience

An advantage of winter pruning of deciduous trees is that the lack of leaves allows a better appreciation of plant shape and recognition of disease problems. As a general rule the work should be done in the latter half of the winter. This reduces the likelihood of frost damage to the newly pruned shoots and provides less opportunity for entry of pathogens, since healing will be rapid during spring. On the other hand, pruning in autumn or early winter reduces the risk of severe physical damage such as wind rock and wind throw during winter storms. In commercial orchards the scale of the pruning operation is such that it may have to be started early so as to ensure that it is completed by spring. The use of pruned branches strewn on the orchard floor may also provide a decoy for rodent pests, luring them away from young trees and minimizing winter losses, especially when there is a heavy snow ground cover, denying access to other food sources.

### Spread of disease

There are several special cases of plant disease transmission which strongly influence the timing of pruning. The fungal parasite *Chondrostereum purpureum* which causes silver leaf disease of *Prunus* spp. is readily spread by airborne spores, which invade wounds and cuts. These spores are released from the small, purplish fruiting bodies on the trunks of severely infected trees. Since these are produced in autumn and early winter the airborne inoculum is highest at these times. It is therefore recommended that where possible, pruning of these species should be undertaken in summer. The genus *Prunus* also suffers from a disease called bacterial canker caused by *Pseudomonas syringae pv. mors-prunorum*. This disease is characterized by large shallow areas of dead bark (cankers) on the branches and stems, and also leaf-spotting symptoms called 'shotholing'. Curiously trees do not initiate new cankers during the spring or summer, so summer pruning is unlikely to cause

any worsening of the condition. The wounds should have healed by autumn when the plant is vulnerable to attack once again.

When a plant is being severely pruned or in the formative pruning of a young plant, it is desirable to avoid mid to late summer work since the resultant vigorous shoots (water shoots) are unlikely to harden sufficiently to withstand the winter frosts. If killed, these could provide an opportunity for entry of pathogens such as *Nectria cinnabarina* (coral spot).

As a general rule, where there is a risk of disease spreading from older to younger wood, it is prudent to remove as much of the older wood as soon as possible, after it has borne its flowers or fruit, provided this will not unduly affect the future productivity of the plant.

# CHAPTER 2
# *How to Prune*

When you have decided that the time is right for pruning and you have identified which parts to remove, your next consideration must be to perform the job in such a way that the plant heals rapidly with minimal risk of infection. In addition growth should be stimulated in the right buds. To achieve these objectives all cuts should be made cleanly, with no crushing or fraying of twigs. This requires that suitable tools are selected. Do not attempt to use lightweight secateurs for stout shoots. The result will be bruised stems, ruined tools and an aching wrist.

## Pruning to a bud

Identify a bud which is pointing in a suitable direction on the stem which you intend to shorten. Make an upwardly sloping cut, starting on the opposite side of the shoot to the bud, and level with the bud, so that the top of the cut finishes just above the bud.

Cutting the stem obliquely helps rainwater to run off, but avoid cutting so obliquely as to expose an excessive surface area for entry of disease or frost.

If the cut is made above this level, the length of stem above the bud, called a stub or snag, will die back and provide an ideal site for invasion by coral spot, canker etc. If the cut is made a little below the level of the bud, there is a high risk of physically damaging the bud with the secateurs, or of failure of the bud, due to dieback [Fig. 2.1]. This may even occur in a well placed cut if the air is very hot and dry, or if the cut surface becomes wet or frozen.

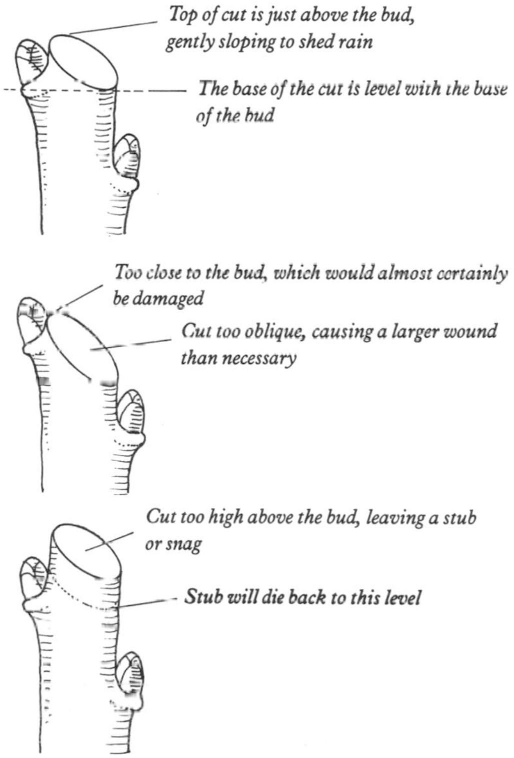

## Removal of a branch

This operation involves making a wound of considerable size and there is a significant risk of introducing disease. If this were to lead to major decay the consequence may ultimately be loss of the entire specimen. This concern

has led many workers to examine trees in which decay has occurred, to try to identify the route the infection has taken through the plant. An understanding of the path the disease has followed can help to pinpoint the vulnerable part of the plant's system.

In the past, trees were considered to be passive victims of attack by fungi. Recently however, the idea has been put forward that trees may confine fungi into zones or compartments. Doctor Alex Shigo and his colleagues at the US forest service are credited with recognizing and appreciating this compartmentalization of disease.

**Fig. 2.1 Pruning to a bud.**

*Top of cut is just above the bud, gently sloping to shed rain*

*The base of the cut is level with the base of the bud*

(*a*) A correctly placed cut.

*Too close to the bud, which would almost certainly be damaged*

*Cut too oblique, causing a larger wound than necessary*

(*b*) Pruning too close to the bud.

*Cut too high above the bud, leaving a stub or snag*

*Stub will die back to this level*

(*c*) Pruning too far from the bud.

**Fig. 2.2** Natural barriers to decay in a woody stem.

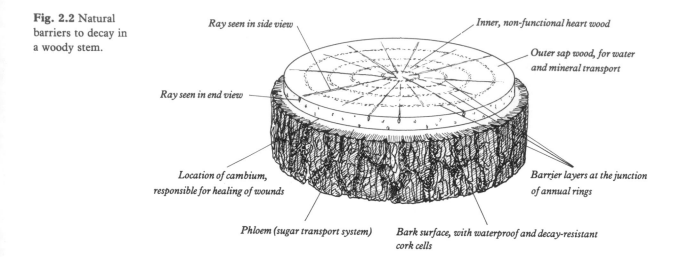

*Ray seen in side view*

*Inner, non-functional heart wood*

*Outer sap wood, for water and mineral transport*

*Ray seen in end view*

*Location of cambium, responsible for healing of wounds*

*Barrier layers at the junction of annual rings*

*Phloem (sugar transport system)*

*Bark surface, with waterproof and decay-resistant cork cells*

In wood there are several natural barriers which may obstruct the progress of a fungal pathogen. The most effective of these are the strips of living cells called rays, which radiate outwards from the centre, across the wood. These help to prevent lateral spread of infection. The cells are not physically robust, but they are alive and this enables them to manufacture phenolic compounds which are antimicrobial [Fig. 2.2]. The barrier they present is not a continuous one composed of large vertical sheets of cells, but rather a very large number of separate strips, which vary from one to about five cells' thick. They may be seen quite easily in the cross section of a tree trunk, and they usually provide the site along which timber splits when it dries.

The penetration of a fungus inwards from a superficial wound towards the centre of the tree, is obstructed by another prominent feature of wood, namely the annual rings. These are both a mechanical barrier of densely packed thick-walled cells, and also a layer of living cells which, like the rays, can react to attack by producing protective chemicals. Each annual ring is a complete vertical cylinder which has great potential for limiting the spread of decay.

The outer surface of the wood or xylem is coated in another layer of living cells, called cambium. This produces fresh xylem each year on the outer surface of existing xylem, and

is thus responsible for creating the annual rings. If decay occurs in the outer xylem the cambium will lay down a protective layer of living cells and then continue to produce new layers of fresh xylem. In this way the new functional xylem is protected and even a thoroughly rotten or hollow tree can continue to survive.

Although decay of the older xylem does not jeopardize the survival of the tree immediately, it does increase the risk of branch shedding and tree stability in storm conditions, so it does have significance.

These various barrier layers limit the spread of disease across the stem, but they do not give any control over organisms moving vertically up and down the trunk through the tubular xylem cells. The mechanisms available to the plant to seal this system are rather poor, and rely on blockage of the system by deposits of gums and crystals or by the ingrowth of living cells. No organized defensive layer develops, so clearly this represents the most likely route for the entry of pathogens. All branch removal should therefore be undertaken in such a way as to minimize exposure of this open tubular xylem.

Where a branch emerges from a stem the vertical xylem tubes on the surface of the stem separate around the branch and rejoin below it, like water flowing around an island in a river. This xylem tends to build up to form a more or less prominent branch collar. It is most noticeable when a branch has died some years before, or if the bark is stripped off to reveal the xylem. Clearly if the branch is cut flush with the trunk as older books suggest, the xylem of the collar will be damaged and this will invite invasion by fungi both upwards and downwards into the outer part of the xylem of the stem. The modern recommendation in the light of these anatomical investigations is to cut the branch just beyond the branch collar. This is often difficult to identify, but its position may be located by reference to a further feature, namely the branch bark ridge. This is a ridge of rough bark above the branch. If the saw is placed on the branch just in front of the bark ridge and the cut is made, not vertically, but a little forwards away from the trunk, the cut is likely to be in the best location, missing the branch collar but removing the branch without leaving a protruding stub.

Having identified the best position in which to make the final cut, it is important to take preliminary action to remove the weight of the bough. It would be most unfortunate if, after carefully considering where to make the cut so as to minimize the injury, the bough was to fall and break lower branches. If the limb broke when only partially severed, it would probably split the stem and tear down a long strip of bark.

Provided there is a clear space below the bough to allow the main part to fall safely to the ground, it can be removed in two stages [Fig. 2.3]. Firstly make a cut in the underside of the branch about 30 cm (12 in) from the trunk. Cut upwards at least a quarter of the way through the branch, or until the saw is pinched and cannot be easily moved due to the bough flexing under its own weight. Now make a second cut on the top side of the branch about 35 cm (14 in) from the trunk. Continue cutting until the bough falls. It should fall to the ground, more or less level, leaving a short stump. Cut this stump off, in accordance with the guidelines already given, using a single downward cut (no cut on the underside). Even a short stump may have a significant weight, so support it firmly as the cut progresses, to ensure that it does not twist and tear the bark. The end result is a smooth surface cut just beyond the bark ridge and branch collar, giving the best opportunity for repair with minimum risk of decay [Fig. 2.4].

Some people may feel that this recommendation leaves a rather prominent wound, which is aesthetically less pleasing than the traditional flush cut. However the growth of the tree in the next few years will gradually disguise any initial projection, and the improved healing of the wound is more than adequate compensation.

As a matter of interest, this position for branch removal is more or less the same as was recommended in some texts in the 1930s and was called 'branch ring pruning'. In this case, the branch collar below the branch was identified as a swollen area called the branch ring and the branch was severed at this point, perpendicularly to its axis. This would have produced a wound of minimum surface area, especially in branches growing nearly vertically, whereas a flush cut would produce a large oval wound. At the time, claims were made that this method gave improved healing but it never became popular and there was no scientific study to evaluate the practice critically.

The development of the chainsaw, which enables vertical sections of the wood to be cut and examined with relative ease, has provided the opportunity for the recent studies of the progress of infection of trees. This in turn has led to an appreciation of the compartmentalization of disease and the recommendations for the position of pruning cuts.

### Treatment of cut surfaces

Most people, if asked, would probably say that a pruning cut should be painted to promote healing and resist infection. This view is reinforced by the knowledge that several proprietary paints are sold for the purpose. However, the efficacy of pruning paints and sealants are not proven and the current view among professionals in this field is that they are of doubtful value.

Ideally a treatment should provide a complete barrier for micro-organisms which lasts for several years. It should keep the underlying tissues in a moist condition to encourage the formation of a natural wound callus, and it should exclude oxygen to

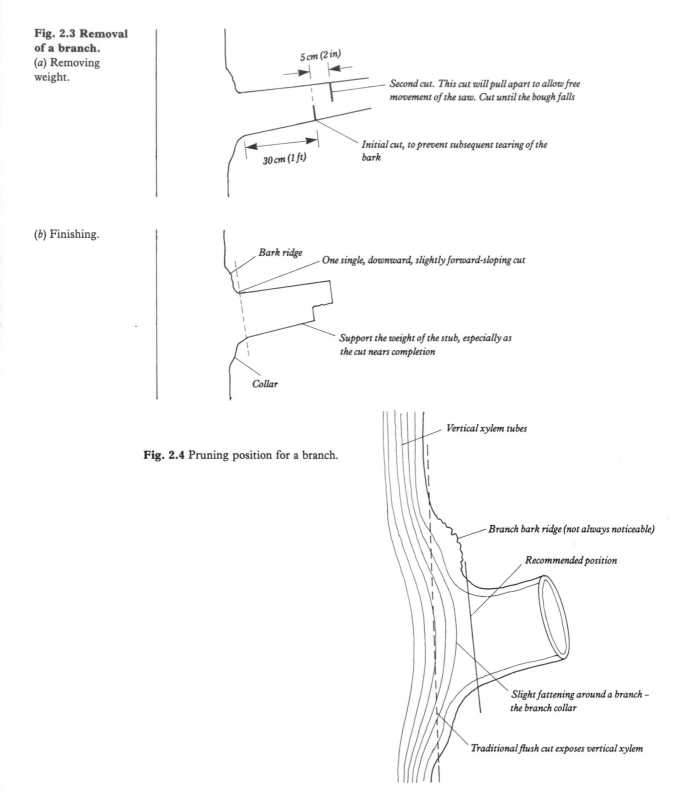

**Fig. 2.3 Removal of a branch.**
(*a*) Removing weight.

5 cm (2 in)

*Second cut. This cut will pull apart to allow free movement of the saw. Cut until the bough falls*

*Initial cut, to prevent subsequent tearing of the bark*

30 cm (1 ft)

(*b*) Finishing.

Bark ridge

*One single, downward, slightly forward-sloping cut*

*Support the weight of the stub, especially as the cut nears completion*

Collar

**Fig. 2.4** Pruning position for a branch.

*Vertical xylem tubes*

*Branch bark ridge (not always noticeable)*

*Recommended position*

*Slight fattening around a branch – the branch collar*

*Traditional flush cut exposes vertical xylem*

produce an unfavourable environment for fungi. However no product meets these specifications and in practice fungi are often found within or beneath the paint. To overcome this objection one might think that incorporation of a fungicide would be the answer. Unfortunately most of these are phytotoxic and impede callus formation, and they may even break down the compartmental barriers by killing some of the living cells within the wood.

Furthermore the protection must persist for a long time, ideally several years, until the wound is completely healed, and in that time some products may break down, others become leached out by rain or they may creep through the tissues and become ineffective as a protective barrier.

Few chemicals meet these requirements for a persistent immobile and non-phytotoxic wound dressing. However bitumen paint and cresylic acid are available to amateurs, and octhilinone is also available professionally. A quite different approach has been exploited in recent years and seems to be very successful. If a fresh wound is inoculated with the fungus *Trichoderma viride*, it becomes established in the wound, does no harm itself and acts as an antagonist to other fungi, preventing them from establishing. This has been very successful in protecting *Prunus* spp. from silver leaf disease (*Chondrostereum purpureum*) and is approved for use on English elm to protect against Dutch elm disease (*Ceratocystis ulmi*). It is likely that other fungi will be discovered with similar beneficial activity.

The question remains: to paint or not to paint? Personally I like the appearance of a bitumen-treated wound. The dark colour blends in with the trunk and if the pruning has been carried out sensitively, the casual observer cannot tell that the tree has been worked upon at all. On the other hand, if one is pruning to contract, it may be in one's interest to leave cuts untreated (or even to paint them bright colours) to show clearly just how much work has been done.

As far as the tree is concerned, it is probably best to treat the outer edges of the wound with bitumen or latex paint to retain moisture in the cut bark and promote callus growth, whilst treating the centre of the wound with a fungicide or beneficial fungus.

## Removal and control of water shoots

Water shoots or epicormic sprouts are the vigorous growths which arise from the stem around the site of major pruning wounds, or in some trees, such as *Tilia* sp. (lime), from around the lower trunk. They may be removed with a stout knife or secateurs but more are likely to grow unless the plant's vigour is curbed in some way. They arise in response to an altered hormone balance in the plant, which stimulates bud development in the bark. The superficial nature of this growth renders them liable to control by application of a mildly herbicidal auxin hormone as a spray or a paint. Current recommendations suggest spraying the shoots when they are about 10 cm (4 in) long or applying hormone paint to pruning wounds. Napthylacetic acid is the hormone recommended. The growth retardant maleic hydrazide also gives control, if sprayed on to the trunk of trees after the shoots have been cut off.

Many variegated ornamentals have leaves in which the edge is of one colour e.g. white and the core is of a contrasting colour e.g. green. This is due to the layering of the two colour types throughout the whole plant, like a hand in a glove, and is called a periclinal chimaera. In these plants, water shoots being superficial in origin, may possess cells of the outer layer only and would be of uniform colour such as all white. The control of water shoots is therefore necessary in these plants to maintain the attractive variegation.

## The removal and control of suckers

Suckers are shoots arising from buds which form spontaneously on the roots of some plants. The term is sometimes used erroneously to describe water shoots. However true suckers can be seen to be growing from the soil at some distance from the stem. They are often stimulated by root injury and in some plants this habit is exploited as a means of propaga-

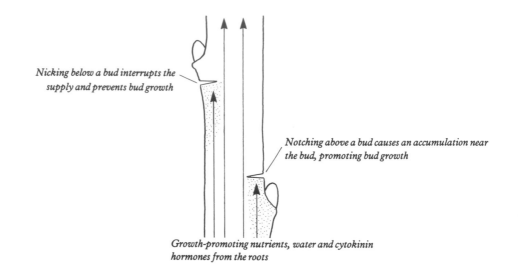

*Nicking below a bud interrupts the supply and prevents bud growth*

*Notching above a bud causes an accumulation near the bud, promoting bud growth*

**Fig. 2.5** Nicking and notching.

*Growth-promoting nutrients, water and cytokinin hormones from the roots*

tion, including *Rhus typhina* (sumach tree), *Rubus idaeus* (raspberry). If a plant is grafted onto a rootstock, as most roses and fruit trees, and many ornamentals are, then the suckers will be characteristic of the stock and not the scion, and must be removed.

If the plant is a periclinal chimaera on its own roots (see Water Shoots, above) then the suckers arising from the roots will be mainly derived from the core tissues, and will lack the outer layers. Thus a variegated shrub with leaves having white edges and green centres would have suckers bearing all green leaves. However chimaeras need not only relate to leaf colour. In the thornless forms of *Rubus fruticosus* (blackberries) the outer tissues are genetically thornless but the core is genetically prickly. Suckers arising from these plants will therefore be prickly, giving rise to the mistaken idea that the plant is grafted onto a prickly rootstock.

Removal of suckers is usually by pulling them firmly so that they snap off at the root. In many cases this is ineffective and a portion of root has to be dug out and removed. This is not satisfactory as it leads to fresh crops of suckers. The choice of rootstock is a major factor in determining the scale of this problem on fruit trees, but it is a natural trait of some species, which cannot be prevented. Sprays of the

auxin hormones will effectively control suckers, or they may be scorched off with contact herbicides.

## Other methods of controlling growth

### Nicking and notching

The removal of shoots as a means of controlling plant form and size is not the only method available to the plantsman. Long before the discovery of plant hormones, gardeners learned that a bud could be either prevented from growing or induced to grow by making a cut either below or above it. Such cutting was called nicking or notching [Fig. 2.5], respectively, but nowadays these terms are often used imprecisely.

The method involves removing a small wedge of bark, cutting down into the wood, just below or above a bud as required. This cuts through the phloem transport system in which auxins are carried and also disrupts the flow in the xylem which carries cytokinins from the roots. A cut below a bud allows auxins to reach the bud from the apex, but the cytokinin level is very low due to the severed vascular system below. This reinforces the dominance of the apex and keeps the bud dormant. A cut above a bud, however, allows cytokinins to stimulate the bud in the absence of auxin, resulting in growth.

This notching to promote growth of a bud is usually practised in spring, before the buds have broken and as the sap flow is beginning to rise. It remains a useful technique.

### Bark ringing or ring barking

Various techniques have been developed for disrupting or impeding transport in the phloem. They are usually carried out in the early summer and the consequence is that sugars and other products of metabolism are retained in the aerial part of the tree, resulting in promotion of flower buds. The reduction in the flow to the roots leads to reduced root activity in the following season and a resultant curbing of vegetative growth. If flowering and fruiting is heavy, in the season following treatment, this will also drain some of the plant's reserves and prevent a resumption of the vigorous vegetative conditions. These tech-

niques are widely used in fruit production to induce early flowering in newly established orchards, and to reduce the cost of manual pruning, to control size. Home gardeners faced with an over vigorous but barren tree, say a plum, would be well advised to try one of the following methods. The risk of killing the tree is minimal provided these dimensions are not exceeded. Make the cuts on the lower trunk but well clear of the soil.

### Complete girdling or ringing

Remove a complete ring of bark about 1 cm ($\frac{3}{8}$ in) wide [Fig. 2.6]. After a season's growth the wound will be covered in a rough growth of callus and within this tissue, new phloem will develop.

### Partial ringing

Remove an incomplete ring of bark up to 2 cm ($\frac{1}{2}$ in) wide, but leave an undamaged bridge about 2 cm ($\frac{1}{2}$ in) wide.

Alternatively, cut a strip in a spiral so that

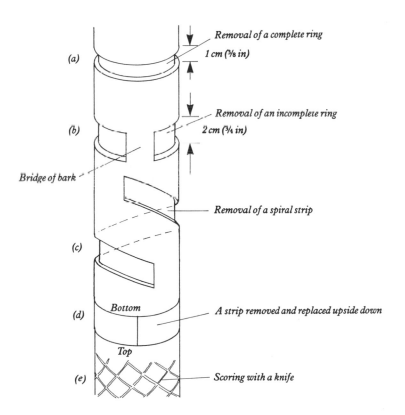

(a) Removal of a complete ring — 1 cm (³/₈ in)

(b) Removal of an incomplete ring — 2 cm (³/₄ in)

Bridge of bark

Removal of a spiral strip

(c)

(d) Bottom / Top — A strip removed and replaced upside down

(e) Scoring with a knife

**Fig. 2.6** Bark ringing to curb vigour.

the movement up and down the phloem requires some lateral transport, which is less efficient.

### Ring inversion

Remove a complete ring of bark up to 2 cm ($\frac{1}{2}$ in) wide, but replace it immediately in an inverted position. Tie it down with some bio-degradeable elastic or rubber material so that subsequent growth is not impeded, or use raffia or garden twine, but in this case remember to cut it after about ten weeks, to prevent constriction.

Phloem functions very poorly when inverted but gradually new cells will be produced with the normal orientation.

### Bruising and scoring

Since phloem lies just beneath the surface it may be damaged by bruising the bark with a baton. This may be the origin of the old saying:

*A woman, a dog and a walnut tree, the better you beat them, the better they be!!*

It would seem to be a rather indiscriminate practice which is no longer fashionable.

The phloem can also be wounded by scoring the bark with a sharp knife. A series of zig-zag cuts around the trunk would probably be the easiest option for the beginner wishing to minimize risk whilst obtaining some benefit from the treatment.

### Branch angle

If branches are bent down to the horizontal or even lower, they behave as if they have been girdled. Their growth is slow and their flowering and fruiting is enhanced. This has been recognized for many years and exploited by training fruit trees into espaliers or by plant-ing at a shallow angle to the ground as in the growth of cordons. The same effect can be achieved on a bush or pyramid tree by tying down individual branches with strings, or bending them down using weighted pegs. This practice is known as festooning.

### Chemical pruning

Mention has already been made of the use of auxins, maleic hydrazide and contact herbi-cides for the removal of water shoots and suckers. However chemicals have also been in-vestigated as alternatives to the physical re-moval of shoots.

Perhaps the most successful group are the growth retardants including daminozide (Alar, B9, Dazide) chlormequat and paclobutrazol (Bonzi, Cultar) which promote branching and reduce extension growth, leading to bushy plants with earlier and heavier flowering. They are used on many plants, from summer bedding to ornamental and fruit trees.

The selective removal of shoot tips by mildly toxic chemicals, has also been explored. Such products are called chemical pinching agents, or feathering agents, since they replace the job of pinching out the shoot tips and they promote growth of the side shoots or feathers. So far, results have been mixed, and none can be said to be entirely satisfactory. They include methyl esters of fatty acids and long chain alcohols like nonanol, as well as mild contact herbicides like diquat. After application they may need to be rinsed off. They cannot be used on evergreens due to severe leaf scorching and before sale plants still require a hand pruning to restore them to perfect form. These disad-vantages virtually outweigh the advantages and these products have not become popular in commercial practice.

# CHAPTER 3

# *Tools and Equipment*

The choice of the exact model of each type of tool is very much a matter of personal preference. It depends upon the amount of work which you intend it to undertake, and the price, as well as the comfort with which it fits the hand, its weight and balance. As a general rule, especially with hand tools, buy the best you can afford, keep them sharp and well adjusted, and they will repay you with years of service.

Power tools are slightly different, since the range gradually extends from models suitable for the keen amateur, through to those appropriate for large commercial contractors. Clearly it is necessary to identify the likely usage the tools will have, and buy a good model of that type. For occasional or infrequent use it is sensible to consider hiring power tools rather than buying.

## Hand tools for pruning trees and ornamental shrubs

### Knives

A sharp, stout folding knife with a slightly forward curving blade 7.5–10 cm (3–4 in) long is invaluable for swift removal of water shoots and smaller twigs, as well as for nicking and notching (see previous chapter). Make sure the blade is well sprung and the handle is comfortable [Fig 3.1]. They were traditionally stags' horn or wooden handled, though nowadays many are plastic.

### Saws

Several sizes and designs are available, each with its own particular uses. However, they all have some features in common. Since they are intended for cutting living wood, they have teeth set quite widely in two rows to cut a wide slot, so as to minimize sticking. The blades are designed to resist bending. They are generally narrow, but of thick metal, and short, about 35 cm (14 in). Long blades are supported and tensioned along one side of a triangular or rectangular bow.

Double-sided saws tend to catch when used in confined spaces, and can cause accidental injury to nearby boughs. They are tempting to buy, as they provide two saws for the price of one tool, but are a false economy and should be avoided.

A very popular design is the gently forward curving Grecian saw. These may have a handle or may be mounted on an extension pole (pole saws) for cutting branches at height. A hook for pulling down branches is a useful addition to the pole (see Tree Pruners below).

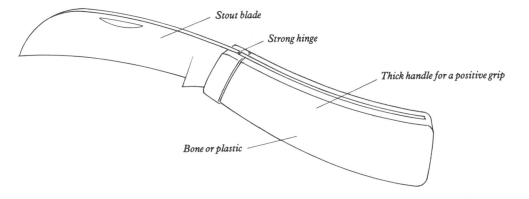

Stout blade

Strong hinge

Thick handle for a positive grip

Bone or plastic

**Fig. 3.1** A strong pruning knife.

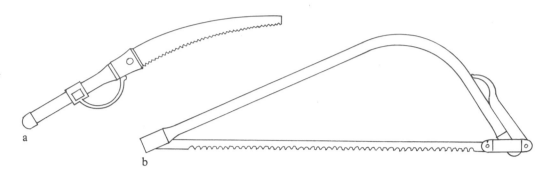

**Fig. 3.2 Saws.**
(*a*) The Grecian saw. Excellent general purpose pruning saw. May also be mounted on a long pole. Miniature folding versions are available for the pocket or belt.
(*b*) Triangular bow saw. Useful for awkward corners, where a large rectangular bow would not fit, but not as good for large branches.

A 17 cm (6–7 in) folding saw for the pocket, or to clip on the belt, is a very handy tool.

When they become blunt through use, most of these saws can be sharpened with a file, and the teeth reset to restore the cutting edge [Fig 3.2].

Bow saws, however, are usually fitted with a blade that has been hardened. This may be described as a 'hardpoint blade' and may have a blue edge due to heat treatment. These blades are very durable but when they are eventually blunted, cannot be easily sharpened and should be replaced.

The triangular bow saw allows access into awkward places, but for large boughs the rectangular pattern is to be preferred.

### Shears

Clipping hedges is tiring at the best of times, but it is made almost impossible by blunt or poorly adjusted shears. Check that the tensioning screw between the blades can be easily adjusted to give freedom of movement whilst ensuring a close movement of the blades. A wavy edge to the blades tends to prevent twigs from slipping out and so is a useful feature, as is a notch at the base of the blades for cutting through large twigs.

Apart from this, the comfort of the handles, and the weight, are probably the most important features. From time to time, run a file across the blades to keep the edge sharp, but do not file the mating surfaces of the blades. A rubber pad between the handles, on some models, acts as a shock absorber and prevents jarring of the wrists, when the blades are closed forcibly.

Occasionally, clean the blades with a stiff brush and soapy water to remove gummy deposits. Dry them, and then oil with a light mineral oil.

### Tree pruners

These are poles up to 3 m (10 ft) long, bearing on top a hooked device which can be placed over a shoot. A levered blade severs the shoot when operated by a handle at the base of the pole.

These tools are most suitable for cutting off branches of fruit and other minor cutting tasks, but they are often sold with a Grecian pruning saw attachment and may provide a useful dual purpose [Fig. 3.3].

**Fig. 3.3** Tree pruners. Useful for pruning small branches at height and for thinning thorny subjects.

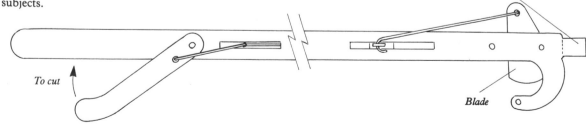

*Process for a saw attachment*

To cut

*Blade*

## Secateurs and long-arm pruners, loppers or parrot beaks

These are grouped together because they all share the same kinds of action and differ only in the size of material that they are intended to cut. The secateur is designed for one-handed use and should be able to cut in a single, controlled movement. Never wriggle the tool from side to side or use multiple cuts to sever a branch. If it cannot be cut cleanly, then it is too large for that tool and a long-handled, heavy duty tool should be used instead.

There are two styles of blade action, each of which have their devotees.

'Bypass action' allows the cutting blade to slide slightly alongside a second blade or rest. This means that there is no bruising on the side of the stem adjacent to the cutting blade. This type of secateur should therefore be used with the cutting blade towards the centre of the plant. If poorly adjusted or cheaply made, it is possible for this design to twist in the hand and trap twigs between the blades.

'Anvil action' involves the movement of the cutting blade against a flat anvil. These inevitably cause some crushing to the stems. In addition, if the blade is not sharp the cut may be incomplete, resulting in some tearing of the bark. The anvil may in time become scored but in most models is replaceable.

Some secateur models have blades coated in non-stick materials. This is unlikely to make any significant difference to their operation.

There are some commercial operations where powered secateurs would be useful, for example in pruning vines, or in orchards. A range of pneumatic tools is available for this purpose, which operate from a portable air compressor.

## Hand tools for rustic hedgelaying

This job has its own distinctive tools in addition to the saws already mentioned. At all times, the cutting tools must be kept razor sharp, which is best achieved by running a cylindrical stone over them at regular intervals. If there is wire or litter in the hedge the tools may become nicked, so a flat file is also handy to make on-the-spot repairs.

A sledge hammer will be required, to knock in posts, and an axe is useful for pleaching heavy stems and for fashioning stakes from hedgerow timber.

The job involves grappling with tangled, overgrown and thorny plants and carries a very great risk of injury to hands and head. It is highly desirable to have had a recent anti-tetanus injection and to wear strong, old clothing. The feet and ankles should be protected from accidental blows by the use of

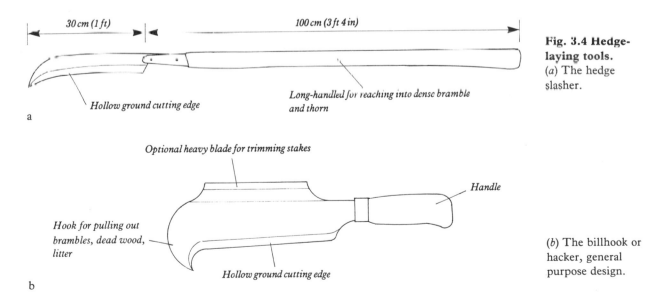

*30 cm (1 ft)*　　*100 cm (3 ft 4 in)*

*Hollow ground cutting edge*

*Long-handled for reaching into dense bramble and thorn*

a

*Optional heavy blade for trimming stakes*

*Handle*

*Hook for pulling out brambles, dead wood, litter*

*Hollow ground cutting edge*

b

**Fig. 3.4 Hedge-laying tools.**
(*a*) The hedge slasher.

(*b*) The billhook or hacker, general purpose design.

strong leather boots. A close-fitting hat or cap prevents scalp injuries, and the hands should be protected by hedging gauntlets. These are made from extremely thick leather and are long enough to protect the wrists. They are usually mitten-style, and the one for the hand wielding the billhook is usually slightly softer, to permit an easier grip. Ordinary gardening gloves give no protection against thorns in this situation.

### The Billhook or hacker

This is the principle hedging tool, used for the cutting of stems (pleachers or plashers) as well as for topping the supporting stakes and general trimming. It consists of a blade about 30 cm (1 ft) long, usually curved or beaked at the top, and a short handle. The back of the hacker may bear another straight blade.

A wide range of variations exist, many being distinctive to local districts such as the counties of Wales and the English Midlands. The blade should be thick to give solidity and weight. The cutting edge should be hollow ground to avoid bouncing off a stem if the blow is slightly ill-aimed. For the beginner, it is wise to avoid double-sided blades, or those with a hook on the back facing the operator.

### Hedge slashers [Fig. 3.4]

These are long-handled tools with a curved or straight blade which are wielded with both hands. They are used in the initial clearing of brambles, dead wood and debris from hedge bottoms, clearing ditches and for general trimming. The handle is usually about 1 m (3 ft) long, with a blade 30 cm (1 ft) long.

Bill hooks serve the same general purpose.

## Power tools

Recently there has been good progress in the development of reliable and lightweight petrol engines. The resultant power tools are both easy to handle and comparatively inexpensive, so not surprisingly they have found a ready market amongst amateur gardeners as well as professionals. Electric motors are even more lightweight and much less expensive, but they have the disadvantage of a flex and the requirement for a nearby power source.

All power tools are potentially very dangerous and should only be used in accordance with manufacturers' instructions, by adults wearing the appropriate safety clothing. They are also rather noisy, so if you will be using them for any length of time, wear ear protectors, and consider the neighbours.

### Chainsaws

These superb tools, which take the hard work out of cutting logs, cannot be unreservedly recommended because of the horrific injuries which they can inflict. It is tempting to use them for any stout trunk but some situations are too dangerous. Only trained tree surgeons should use them whilst tree climbing. In hedgelaying, be very careful if using them to cut the stem bases, lest they kick back or catch twigs which whip into your face or hands.

Wonderful tools but for safety's sake reserve them for logging at ground level.

### Hedge trimmers

As the name suggests, these are only for trimming and are likely to keep jamming if used on hard woody twigs. Having accepted this limitation, they are excellent tools for taking the drudgery out of manually shearing hedges. Choose one with a long cutter bar for quicker coverage of the hedge, and also to achieve a smooth contour. The flex of electric models is rather a nuisance and is inclined to get in the way. A few models can be powered from a car battery, enabling them to be used in remote locations, and I have found these thoroughly satisfactory despite the expectation that they might exhaust the battery. On the other hand, the cordless models with built-in rechargeable batteries, are said to be suitable only for light domestic use.

### Shredders

For many people, disposal of prunings is as much of a headache as the job itself. If burning is not permitted, a shredder may be the answer. Many models are available, most of them taking branches up to 4 cm ($1\frac{1}{2}$ in) diameter. The resultant chippings may be composted and used as mulches on flower beds and borders.

# PART I

## ORNAMENTAL PLANTS OUTDOORS

# CHAPTER 4
# Nursery Training of Trees

Few amateurs can be bothered about growing trees to a specification, in the same way that nurserymen are, but the principals of training and pruning young plants, if not the actual measurements, will certainly be of interest to anyone who likes to raise their own plants. This chapter and the next, therefore, should be read by home gardeners with a view to adapting the techniques described to suit their own needs.

The smaller size of gardens today has meant that amateur gardeners are less inclined to plant large ornamental trees than they once were. Their demand is now more for small trees, while the larger ones are being bought or raised by local authorities and estates (both private and public).

Forestry and timber trees, of course, are a completely different subject.

## What is a tree?
By definition a tree is 'a woody perennial with a distinct stem'. A shrub, on the other hand, is 'a woody perennial, usually smaller than a tree, with several or many persistent stems arising from or near the ground'.

A point these days is that the clearly defined line that used to exist between trees and shrubs has become somewhat blurred. This is because our smaller gardens need smaller plants and it has led to certain traditional trees being grown rather differently, for example with more than one stem – the so-called multi-stemmed trees. A good example of this is the *Betula pendula* 'Golden Cloud' (golden birch), which is probably grown more as a multi-stemmed plant than as a single-stemmed tree.

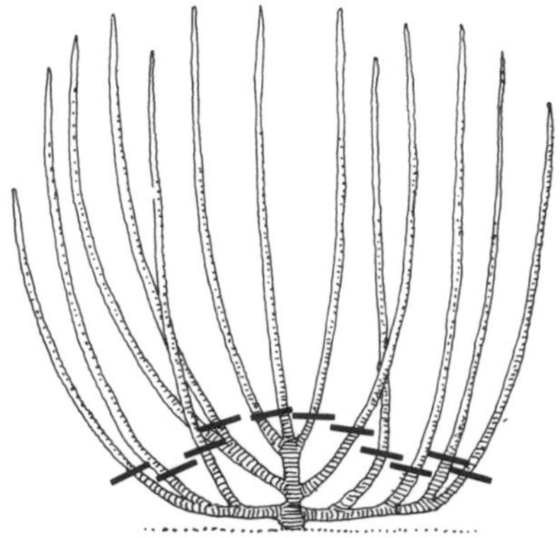

Many *Cornus* (dogwood) and *Salix* (willow) species are also far more attractive when grown as stools [Fig. 4.1] rather than as conventional trees; it shows up their colourful winter bark to far better effect. This, though, is always open to influence by personal preference so that something which has normally been grown as a tree (e.g. some of the birches and maples) may well be preferred by some gardeners as stools. And who is to say that they are wrong?

However, not all trees with ornamental bark are stooled, *Acer griseum* and *A. davidii* 'George Forrest', for example, should still be grown traditionally because it is not only their young bark that is pretty and they make first-rate specimen trees.

There are, of course, recognized tree forms and sizes, and it is essential for nurserymen to be guided by these, if not actually ruled. Many countries have their own specifications or 'standards' for tree sizes.

## What shape is a tree?
Along with the different sizes, trees also vary in their shape. The fundamental shape is a 'standard'; that is, a traditional tree with a well defined, single trunk of reasonable height. Examples include the 'central leader standard' and the 'branched head standard', both self explanatory.

A central leader tree [Fig. 4.2] has a single leader that is allowed to continue growing throughout the life of the tree. It will not continue to grow taller for ever, of course; after

**Fig. 4.1** Certain *Cornus* and *Salix* are best grown as stools for winter bark effect.

**Fig. 4.2** A central leader tree.

a number of years, the leader will become less distinct and the tree will form a more or less rounded head. Ornamental examples include species of *Parrotia*, *Sorbus* and *Liquidambar*.

Some other trees perform better and look more attractive when grown as 'branched head standards'. These are formed by taking out the top of the central leader, which encourages more and stronger side shoots to form.

Not all trees, of course, have to be grown specifically as a central leader or branched head type. Magnolias, for example, will naturally form a bushy tree [Fig. 4.3]. All we have to do is make sure that it is well balanced and upright.

**Fig. 4.3** A branching head tree.

## National standards

To help buyers and sellers of trees, many countries, including the United Kingdom and the United States, have 'standards' for nursery trees (and many other plants). The primary purpose of these is to enable a buyer and seller

to discuss an order, both knowing exactly what the other one is talking about.

For example, if customer A wants to order a batch of betulas or acers from nurseryman B, he might well specify that they should be of such-and-such an age and comply with a given standard. Nurseryman B would then know exactly what is wanted and customer A will know what he is getting.

There is, however, nothing compulsory about ordering to a standard, nor growing to one. It is merely a convenience, albeit a very important one. It is certainly worth using if you are buying or supplying nursery stock in large quantities and dealing with local authorities etc. It operates in both directions and eliminates any uncertainty about what is wanted. It avoids the need for having to spell out an order in the minutest detail; and all too often omitting something vital.

It sets a useful standard with which any nurseryman would do well to comply, this leading to good quality and uniformity. Whilst not the law of the land, national standards do, nonetheless, represent an excellent target at which to aim. They set a high standard that every good nursery will want to achieve and usually does.

Where the amateur gardener is concerned, the individual specification for any particular plant has no significance, but he or she would be wise to buy always from a reliable source.

## The effect of propagation

Tree raising is often undertaken on a small scale by enthusiastic amateurs but it is important to realize that it requires more knowledge and expertise than, say, growing shrubs does. This is chiefly because it is harder to produce a plant with a trunk than one which, in the main, grows as a bush. Then again, shrubs are usually propagated by cuttings. Trees are more often grown by budding or grafting onto a rootstock.

Although some ornamental trees are grown from seed, the list gets shorter every year because the most popular ones are now usually modern hybrids which fail to come true. Any plant in a commercial nursery that varies noticeably from its parent is unfit for sale under its parent's label and must be either discarded or set aside. These differences are not necessarily concerned with a plant's colour or shape; less tangible characteristics, such as vigour, may also be involved. These are the things that have to be watched out for.

There is no need to go into the propagation of trees in detail; this is covered admirably in other books. However, an outline knowledge of the different methods by which trees are propagated is needed if they are to be grown well.

Trees, for the most part, are propagated by seed, grafting, budding and, to a lesser extent, cuttings.

One might think that the most widely used method is seed. After all, it is cheap, easy and gives an enormous return for comparatively little outlay. However, not all trees come true from seed. Most hybrids will exhibit characteristics from previous generations. Seed is, though, used for some naturally occurring species as well as for hybrids that have been in existence for a long time and for which a true breeding line has become established.

On the whole, seed is used for producing rootstocks for budding or grafting other subjects. Sycamore, hawthorn, beech, laburnum, cherry, rhododendron, robinia and mountain ash (rowan) are all in common use as rootstocks. Indeed all genera, with the exception of *Malus*, *Prunus* and the edible fruiting *Pyrus*, are almost invariably raised on seedling rootstocks. The exceptions are worked onto cloned and vegetatively produced rootstocks which possess a known and stable habit.

An important benefit of using rootstocks for tree production is that they have been chosen for their lack of suckers. Lilac used to be terrible for this when it was raised on common lilac rootstocks. Now, privet is used instead and there are no suckers at all.

For fruit trees, rootstocks have been of greater importance than in ornamental work for nearly 80 years. Not only is uniformity in tree size vital in an orchard, but the rootstocks influence the vigour and the ultimate size of the tree that is being grown on them. For this reason, clones of each individual rootstock have been established and these are propagated vegetatively from cuttings, stooling or layering as appropriate. Recently, these hitherto fruit tree rootstocks have become widely used for raising ornamental varieties of suitable trees, including, crab, pear and quince, flowering cherry and plum etc.

Just as with any other budding and grafting, it is most important to make sure beforehand that the rootstock and scion are compatible. Many years ago it was found that the pear variety 'Williams' was incompatible with quince rootstocks, but not before an enormous number of trees had broken at the union during gales. Now, when budding, slivers of another scion variety are introduced under the 'Williams' bud, or an interstock is used when grafting.

Although there are different systems used for grafting and budding, depending on the genus and species of tree being propagated, the after-care and training of the resulting trees are largely the same. However there is one important exception to the ways in which grafting and budding are normally done.

As a rule, the union is made a few centimetres from the ground. Thus, it is the scion variety that forms the stem of the tree. This is called 'low working' and, generally speaking, it produces a better tree [Fig. 4.4a]. Sometimes, though, the rootstock is allowed to grow up and form the main stem. Two or more buds or a single graft are then worked onto the top. The usual occasions when this is done is for weeping trees and for dwarf standards [Fig. 4.4b].

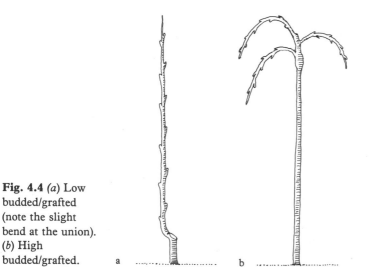

**Fig. 4.4** (*a*) Low budded/grafted (note the slight bend at the union). (*b*) High budded/grafted.

a        b

*Previous page:*
Masses of vigorous
'water shoots'
growing from the
stubs of branches,
after heavy
pruning.

Very sensitive use
of pollarding in an
Oxfordshire, UK,
village.

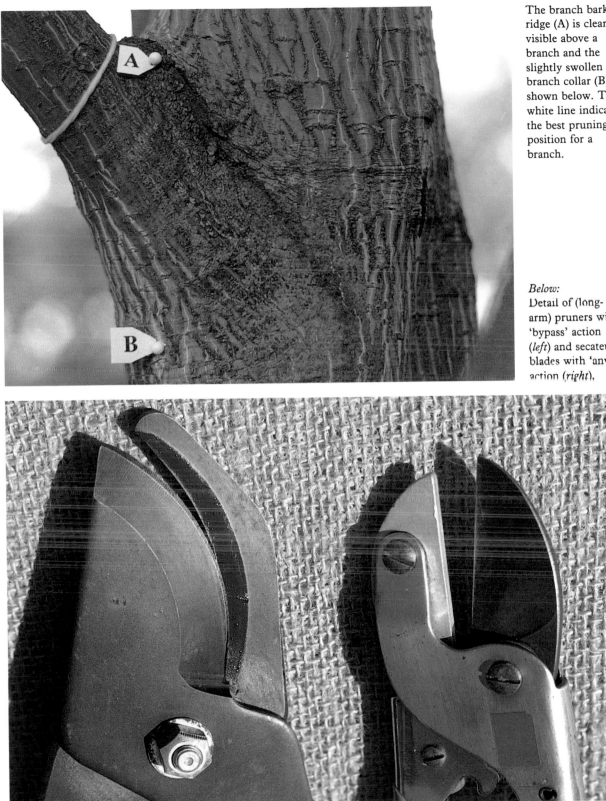

The branch bark ridge (A) is clearly visible above a branch and the slightly swollen branch collar (B) is shown below. The white line indicates the best pruning position for a branch.

*Below:*
Detail of (long-arm) pruners with 'bypass' action (*left*) and secateur blades with 'anvil' action (*right*),

A young budded sorbus making strong growth after being headed back the previous winter. Growth is kept straight by repeated tying to a cane.

A young tree of *Sorbus aria* 'Lutescens' having been recently pruned to promote well-branched and balanced growth.

*Cornus alba* 'Spaethii' on the nursery just after tip pruning for a second time to further encourage a well-branched, bushy habit.

A fine crop of *Hedera colchica* 'Dentata Variegata'.
If not sold immediately further tying and
trimming will be required.

If left to grow unpruned *Paulownia tomentosa* will grow to a medium-sized tree flowering in early summer.

*Below:*
Hard pruned every winter *Paulownia tomentosa* produces dramatically large leaves, but no flowers.

For normal low-worked trees, budding, particularly 'chip budding', is to be preferred to grafting because the resulting stem is straighter than from a graft. This is further aided by placing an aluminium bud guide over the bud before it grows out.

## Raising trees by budding

Although budding is not strictly pruning, it is a vital stage of tree formation and training and, as such, is relevant.

Right at the start, the rootstocks must be planted evenly spaced and upright. Only in this way will a straight stem be produced. Budding takes place during the latter half of the summer. Most buds will stay dormant throughout the winter and break into growth in the following spring. Those that grow out in the autumn were normally budded early on in the summer. The stock is headed back to just above the bud during the late winter; if it is done any sooner, it may in a mild season result in the bud growing out. If this happens and the weather turns very cold, the young shoot may be killed.

It is worth remembering that 'Colt' rootstock is not particularly hardy so is best left until last. The aluminium bud guide is put in place during the early spring, soon after heading back.

## Forming the young tree

In late spring, the worked bud will have grown out into a shoot. At the same time there will also be a varying number of shoots and possibly suckers on the rootstock below the bud; these must be rubbed or pinched out while they are still small.

From then until late summer, a good nurseryman will look at his developing trees at least once a fortnight. Any further suckers must be nipped out and any side shoots developing on the main stem should be stopped when 10–12 cm (4–5 in) long. These shoots will help to thicken the stem and therefore play an important part in building up and strengthening it. However, they must never be allowed to grow too large or the stem and the future branched head of the tree will suffer.

### Stem building

Something that must be remembered is that a tree which is growing without competition for light and space will only develop a very short trunk before branches start to grow out. In the nursery, we have to encourage the stem to grow to the height we require and at the same time to develop width; the tree must not be allowed to grow at will. Elsewhere in Europe, stem building in the nursery is carried a stage further by thickening the stem at the expense of the head of the tree. This technique gives rise to 'light headed' or 'light crown' trees (see page 35).

To produce a sturdy tree, we have to strike a balance between the upward progress of the main stem and its thickening. A tall but thin stem is useless.

During the first year's growth, most trees will need the support of a cane, with extension growth being tied to it on a regular basis. The exceptions are horse chestnut, ash and sorbus which are normally self-supporting. They are also exceptions to the general rule that maiden trees will need 'topping' at the end of their first year; unless growth is poor, in which case it is delayed for a year.

### Topping

Topping affects a tree in three important ways. It greatly lessens apical dominance which, as a result, encourages side shoots to form and the stem to thicken.

The ideal height at which to top a vigorously growing tree is 2.1 m (7 ft). *Acer platanoides* (Norway maple), *Laburnum* spp. (golden rain tree) and *Prunus* 'Kanzan' (Japanese cherry) are good examples of this. Less vigorous subjects, such as species of *Malus* (crab apple), *Pyrus* and *Prunus subhirtella* (ornamental cherry) are better topped at 1.9 m (6 ft).

*Tilia* spp. (limes) are even slower growing, so 80–90 cm (2 ft 8 in–3 ft) is more appropriate. To avoid an open-centred tree and maintain a dominant and straight central stem, the topping cut is made just below the leaf joint above the desired bud. This will leave a snag to which the growth in the following growing season can be tied. The new growth should preferably be tied in with masking tape when it is some 3 cm (1¼ in) long, usually in late spring. The snag and the tape are normally removed towards the end of the summer.

Because of their slow growth, tilia do not

normally need topping. However, if vigorous trees like sycamore, *Malus* 'Profusion', *M. floribunda*, *Crataegus* spp. (ornamental thorn) and *Ulmus glabra* (Scots elm) are left untopped, they will soon become top heavy with few, if any, side shoots. As is so often the case, not all trees fit neatly into one category or the other. *Prunus avium* 'Plena', for instance, produces an amply strong stem without topping and seldom becomes top heavy. However, when not topped, the central leader often grows vigorously in the early part of the growing season without side shoots forming. Towards the end of growth, the apical dominance lessens and side shoots appear near the growing point. When this happens in consecutive years, we end up with the undesirable characteristic known as 'tiered' branching, that is two or more tiers of branches with clear stem between them. If growth receives a check early in the growing season, the vigour of the leader will be reduced with a consequent prevention of tiering. Topping will do this; so will transplanting at the end of the first growing year. *Prunus avium* 'Plena' is usually topped rather

than transplanted as transplanting would also slow down the increase in stem circumference.

*Pinching back side shoots*

The other factor involved in forming the new tree stem is the treatment of the side shoots. These help to thicken the stem so the complete removal of side shoots on trees other than vigorous growers (ash, horse chestnut etc.) should be resisted. They should normally be kept pinched back to 10–12 cm (4–5 in) long. This will allow them to build up the stem without causing a reduction in growth.

Certain trees, such as *Prunus subhirtella* (ornamental cherry) and *Malus* spp. (crab apple), are inclined by nature to become bushy in their first year rather than grow upwards. Pinching back the side shoots periodically during the growing season will lead to a much better tree.

Trees grown from cuttings and microropagation are also inclined to throw up a large number of side shoots so pinching is also important with these. Any suckers or water shoots arising from the rootstocks must be removed as well.

At the end of the first growing season, any thick side shoots are best cut out completely to prevent scarring of the stem. Those of moderate size are shortened to about two leaf buds and weak ones can be left whole.

Do the job properly and cleanly with a sharp knife or secateurs and use a wound paint on *Prunus* and *Laburnum* spp. to stop any silver leaf (*Chondrostereum purpureum*) infection.

## Forming the crown

By the end of the year following topping (usually the first year of growth), the tree should have a well formed head with a number of weaker side shoots lower down. This is the time at which to decide what type of crown the tree should have. Generally speaking, gardeners in the UK seem to prefer a well developed crown, but the Continental light-headed shape is becoming more popular.

The exception is in the genus *Sorbus*. None of its species will make a good light-headed tree and in fact the removal of unwanted lower shoots and branches at the end of each growing season does much to improve its shape.

The weaker-growing Japanese cherries are

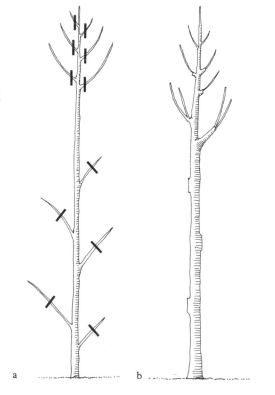

**Fig. 4.5 Pruning for a 'light' crown'.**

(*a*) The head is spur pruned each winter. The laterals are retained and only lightly pruned.
(*b*) Light crown tree after a few years' growth. The shoots are pruned back hard each winter.

a     b

also a special case. If they are pruned hard, as they would be to form light-headed trees, they seldom make satisfactory growth so they should be only lightly pruned to help shaping.

### The light-crown system

The light-headed, Continental system of pruning is only carried out at the nursery. Once the tree is in its final position, normal pruning takes over. To form a light-crown tree, all new shoots that form part of the crown of the tree are pruned hard back in the nursery each winter [Fig. 4.5a]. This should leave a stump 1–3 cm long, depending on the species. Always cut back to a bud.

After two or three years, a spur system will have formed with all new shoots still arising close to the main stem [Fig. 4.5b].

If a spur fails to produce a shoot, it is cut hard back, in the hope that another will develop. Lower down the stem, laterals will still be growing out and several of these should be left each winter. They will act as sap drawers to avoid too severe a check on growth and, as always, will help to build the lower stem. *Acer platanoides* (Norway maple), *A. campestre* (hedge maple), *Carpinus* (hornbeam), *Crataegus* (ornamental thorn), *Laburnum*, (golden rain tree), *Platanus* (plane), ornamental *Pyrus*, *Salix* (willow), *Tilia* (lime) and most *Malus* (crab apple) species respond well to light-headed pruning.

Neither *Aesculus* (horse chestnut) or *Fraxinus* (ash) spp. break readily after hard pruning so are best treated like *Sorbus* (see above) and pruned lightly. The lower shoots must be retained on species of *Fraxinus* longer than on *Aesculus* but are removed no later than the early summer preceding sale.

The main limiting factor of the light-crown system in the UK is its uncertain acceptability with buyers. Before embarking on it, therefore, nurserymen should make sure that it meets with their customers' approval. The alternative is to grow trees of a more conventional shape, for which the 'developed-crown' system should be adopted.

### The developed-crown system

With this, the crown shoots are not spurred back each winter; instead some 25 cm (10 in) of new growth is allowed to remain each year. A

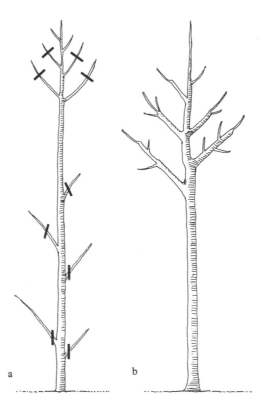

**Fig. 4.6 Pruning for a 'developed crown'.**
(a) Each winter, the head shoots, and subsequently the new growth on the head shoots, are pruned back to leave about 25 cm (10 in). Lower down, vigorous laterals are removed completely; weaker ones are shortened.
(b) Developed crown tree after a few years' growth. All shoots below the crown are removed before sale.

little more is left on the lower branches and a little less on the upper to maintain a good shape [Fig. 4.6] Below the crown, all vigorous shoots are cut hard back but weaker ones are allowed to attain 10–12 cm (4–5 in), and are then stopped in order to build up the stem. They are cut off during the winter before sale.

*Claimed benefits of the developed-crown system*
1. A better appearance straight after planting.
2. Fewer unhealed scars caused by late removal of heavy lower laterals.

*Claimed benefits of the light-crown system*
1. Fewer leaves in first season after planting out leads to less water loss and, hence, quicker establishment.
2. Less susceptible to vandals tearing off branches and breaking the stem.
3. Less bulky; therefore easier to transport.

## Supporting young trees

The most important thing to realize is that budded and grafted trees, especially top worked, will need more attention in their first two or three years than others will. This is because the unions are their weakest point and, as such, the shoots that grow out from the scion must be supported against breakages of any sort. Damage is not always obvious, but may even be caused by birds settling on them as perches!

During the initial growth and training of the stem, most trees are tied individually to 2.4 m (8 ft) canes. These are pushed in alongside each tree and the new growth is tied to the cane regularly to give support and to ensure that the stem grows straight. Exceptions to this include most species of *Sorbus*, *Fraxinus* (ash) and *Aesculus* (horse chestnut), which are strong enough to grow straight and without support.

Once the stem has formed, wires can be stretched between stakes at each end of the rows, at suitable heights for the tree's requirements. Normally the lower wire would be some 60 cm (2 ft) off the ground with the upper one about 30 cm (1 ft) below the height of the lowest branch. The trees are either tied directly to the wires or to canes, which are themselves tied to the wires.

## Forming young weeping standards

Weeping trees are very popular in small gardens. Their height is restricted and, to a large extent, pre-determined in the nursery.

The stem of a weeping tree is supported and kept straight and vertical until it reaches 1.2–1.5 m (4–5 ft) tall. At that point, it is either topped or simply allowed to form a weeping habit naturally by not supporting it above that height. Depending on the ability of the variety in question to produce side shoots, the original shoots coming from the buds or graft can be tipped to encourage branching or left intact. It must be remembered that all but the lightest

tipping will cause the tipped shoot to stiffen, and this may not always be desirable. In this way, any height of tree can be grown in the most appropriate and attractive way.

An important part of pruning branched-head trees is to remove shoots and branches that are crossing from one side of the head to the other. This ultimately leads to overcrowding and trees with a poor appearance.

Trees that have been top worked, either by budding or grafting, are a rather special case because the main stem and the branches are not of the same kind. The obvious point here is that no shoots must be allowed to develop below the union. The important part of the tree is the head; the stem is simply there to support it and plays no other part. In most cases, if shoots are allowed to develop from the stem section (or below the union on low-worked trees) they will be stronger than the scion variety and can, if allowed to, dominate it.

Building the head is done in just the same way that it is for low-worked or seedling trees. Some trees, especially upright conifers, naturally form feathers and side shoots right down to near the ground. Where this is so, they should be retained to form part of the tree. Only the lowest ones, that are likely to interfere with cultivations or which spoil the line and appearance of the tree, are removed.

The stem must be kept reasonably straight, well defined and upright. There are no rules regarding the desirable height of the lowest feathers/branches, this varies with the species.

Weeping trees will usually need the support of a cane for the first few years to establish a good basic and upright shape. After that, they normally grow perfectly well on their own.

# CHAPTER 5

# Nursery Pruning and Training of Shrubs, Roses, Climbing and Herbaceous Plants

In this chapter details are given of pruning carried out during plant propagation and subsequent growing on. The general principles apply to both the professional and hobby gardener.

## Pruning the young plant

This is nearly always formative and done to produce a high quality plant for later use in either the garden or landscape.

The pruning of young trees is usually aimed at retaining the dominant apical bud and encouraging this to develop into a strong, single leading shoot. With shrubs the reverse is most often the aim; what is required is a plant with as many basal shoots as possible. To this end, apical dominance is discouraged by repeated removal of the apex, so as to stimulate lateral growths.

## Aspects of quality relating to pruning

It is difficult to be succinct when defining shrub quality, but criteria that should be included are: trueness to type; freedom from pest and disease; an adequate root system; of a usable size; bushy, not drawn and uniform. Some of these criteria relate to pruning and are further defined and discussed below.

### Height

In commerce height is usually stated in the contract between the nurseryman and the purchaser. It is important to the specifier as it largely determines the initial impact and often the spacing appropriate for the plants. British Standard 3936 Part I quotes a minimum height for many shrubs and states that pruning should have been done when appropriate to give a bushy habit.

### Habit and bushiness

These criteria are as important as height when trying to specify a good quality plant. British Container Growers, a group of leading nurserymen, have produced a *Specification of Standards for British Container Grown Stock*. In this publication, amongst other criteria, the plant habit and number of breaks present on each plant are specified in an attempt to define further what is a good plant. The difference in what represents good quality in different markets is accepted and two grades specified. Premium quality plants are called 'Garden Grade' and intended for the domestic market. Good quality, although perhaps smaller and younger plants, are called 'Amenity and Ground Cover Grade' and intended for the amenity and landscaping markets. Within both grades acceptable plant habit is defined. In 'Garden Grade' plants, the number of breaks in the lower third of the plant is specified. In 'Amenity and Ground Cover Grade' plants, the total number of breaks is used as the criterion rather than just those coming from the lower third and in some cases a slightly lower figure is acceptable.

### Uniformity

This is extremely important in commercial production. The shrub is seen as a product that must be available in large uniform batches to facilitate high volume sales. The drive towards uniformity starts with cutting selection and

**Fig. 5.1** Four young plants of *Helichrysum serotinum* (curry plant) showing what degree of uniformity can be achieved and is highly desirable in commercial production. The plants have been trimmed at least twice to stimulate the bushy, well-rounded shape seen.

**Fig. 5.2** A good batch of *Lavandula angustifolia* 'Hidcote'. Note the uniformity in shape and size between all the plants.

preparation, this then continuing through the life of the crop [Figs. 5.1 and 5.2].

Clearly, the hobby gardener may view his plants somewhat differently. If growing only for himself, small batches in which there is some variability in size may be an advantage, allowing placement of suitably shaped individual plants into specific situations.

Uniformity is usually an advantage to both groups of horticulturalists. Take the amateur gardener giving away a batch of plants to his friends. Who gets the good, bushy specimen and which unfortunate its tall, leggy companion? Much easier if they are all the same!

## Nursery pruning and training of shrubs

### Stock plants

It is essential that the stock plants from which it is intended to take cuttings are kept in a vegetative (that is, non-flowering), free-growing condition. Such a plant will yield the maximum number of easy-to-root cuttings. A good stock plant is a young one. Once a plant's vigour begins to decline, it is better replaced with a new one.

The hobby gardener should interpret this advice as selecting cutting material from fairly vigorous non-flowering shoots [Fig. 5.3].

To keep a stock plant in the condition described above, hard annual pruning will be needed. This must still be done whether or not cutting material is required. In some seasons, hard pruning; in other years when cuttings are not required, but it is intended to retain the stock plant, pruning must still be done and resultant prunings disposed of.

### Taking and preparing the cuttings

The operations of cutting removal and preparation are forms of pruning. This is not a book on propagation, so details will not be given; only suffice to say that the prepared cuttings must be uniform at the time of insertion if a uniform crop of plants is to be produced [Figs. 5.4 and 5.5]

**Fig. 5.3** Nursery stock plant of *Senecio* 'Sunshine'. The plant has been maintained in the correct vegetative condition and has numerous shoots available for cuttings.

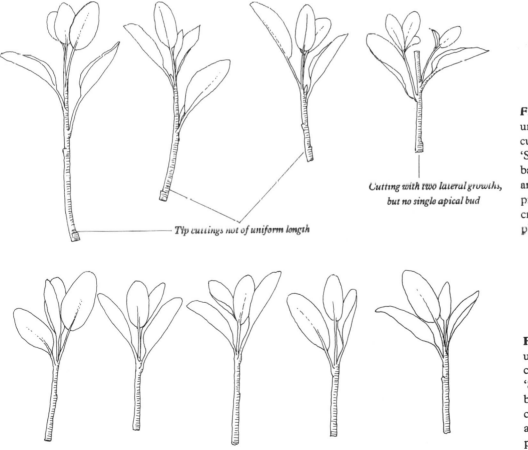

*Cutting with two lateral growths, but no single apical bud*

*Tip cuttings not of uniform length*

**Fig. 5.4** A non-uniform batch of cuttings of *Senecio* 'Sunshine'. Such a batch will not root and grow on to produce a uniform crop of young plants.

*Tip cuttings all of very nearly the same length and stage of development*

**Fig. 5.5** A uniform batch of cuttings of *Senecio* 'Sunshine'. Such a batch has every chance of rooting and growing on to produce a uniform crop of young plants.

**Fig. 5.6** A newly potted young rooted cutting of *Forsythia* 'Lynwood'. The apical bud has just been pinched out in order to stimulate the production of lateral growths.

*Buds that will be stimulated to grow out*

*Growing tip removed*

**Fig. 5.7** A young plant of *Forsythia* 'Lynwood' at a slightly more advanced stage of development than in Fig. 5.6. The plant has responded to being 'pinched' by producing two lateral growths. This is the start of a well-furnished plant. Subsequent pinching of these growths will promote the development of more laterals.

### Potting the rooted cuttings

At this stage the rooted cuttings are given a routine pruning, often referred to as 'pinching', to remove the apical bud and encourage basal branching. This should lead to the development of a bushy, well-balanced plant. To ensure uniformity, it is important that this pinching is done with equal severity to all plants [Figs. 5.6 and 5.7].

A few plants, such as most members of the genus *Daphne*, resent any form of pruning and are not pruned at this stage.

Just prior to potting, the roots of the rooted cuttings may be trimmed. This is done mainly to aid getting the roots into the pot and any extra fibrous root that may be produced is really a bonus.

Once potted, it is very important to ensure that each plant is given adequate space in which to develop. At first it may appear that

space is being wasted, but the effect of 'pinching' back is to encourage the development of laterals. The plant's habit, which ideally should be compact and bushy, will be spoilt if they are drawn upwards to become leggy by being grown too close together.

### Subsequent potting

When ready, the potted 'liners' are put into larger 'finishing' pots. At this stage, most should be tip pruned again to encourage further a bushy habit [Figs. 5.8 and 5.9]. After further growth, the plants should reach their saleable size as good quality, bushy, uniform plants.

Fairly recently, there has been a trend to offer for sale larger 'specimen' plants, this being in response to the call for instant effect by many customers. These are grown on for longer and often potted on into larger pots a number of times. During this growing on period, attention should be paid to the growth of the plant and, if necessary to maintain a good, well-furnished plant, further tip pruning should be done.

### Field-grown plants

The same general principles apply as for container-grown plants. Pinching of the growing shoots is done at stages corresponding with the container-grown plants to encourage a bushy habit. Not only pruning, but adequate spacing is necessary if the desired bushy habit is to be developed.

### Herbaceous plants

These do require pruning at the end of the growing season. They die down to ground level and at the beginning of the dormant season the dead growth should be cut away. At the same time all fallen leaves and general detritus should be removed. This is important, as such material can harbour pests or diseases from one season to the next.

## Production of roses

The production of roses is a fairly complex process involving different operations for the various forms of plant that are grown. Here it is intended to detail where some form of pruning or training is important.

## Shrub roses

The vast majority of shrub roses are produced by budding the cultivar onto a briar rootstock. The rootstock most widely used is *Rosa corymbifera* 'Laxa'. The first pruning occurs when the rootstocks are planted. The stems are reduced to 15 cm (6 in) and the roots shortened to the same length using a guillotine. This pruning of the roots makes planting easier and is said to encourage the production of a more fibrous root system.

The rootstocks are next pruned the following late winter. This operation is known as 'heading back' and involves cutting down the briar to just above the cultivar bud that was inserted by 'T' or 'shield' budding the previous summer. Any buds that have broken dormancy and grown out during the summer following budding, known as 'shot buds', should be pruned hard back at the time of heading back.

This severe pruning forces the cultivar bud to grow out. The bud produces a shoot that rapidly elongates. This shoot is very vulnerable to wind damage until the union between the briar and cultivar shoot has hardened and become lignified. To prevent the wind causing damage, graphically described as 'blow outs', the new shoots are shortened back to 5–8 cm (2–3 in) once they have made approximately 15 cm (6 in) of growth. This operation is usually done in early summer.

At the same time a check is made for sucker growth and any found should be removed as close to the briar root system as possible. *Rosa corymbifera* 'Laxa' is good in this respect as it produces only a few suckers.

## Standard roses

Standard roses are produced on a single upright stem.

Hardwood cuttings of selections from *Rosa rugosa*, for example *Rosa rugosa* 'Hollandica', are taken 20 cm (8 in) long, stored in damp sand until late winter, and then inserted into cultivated ground. One year is then allowed for these cuttings to root, establish and make top growth. The following late winter, all growth is removed to just above ground level.

Of the resulting strong growth, one shoot is selected and tied up a cane. This shoot is repeatedly tied in at approximately 15 cm (6 in)

intervals. It is very important that this shoot, which will form the main stem of the standard rose, is kept straight. All other basal growths are removed as soon as they appear.

The following autumn a stem almost 2 m (6 ft) tall will have been produced. This is then trimmed to 1.5 m (5 ft), and is then ready to be lifted and replanted at a wider spacing to allow for head development, or sold.

As far as the briar is concerned, at this point the cycle is repeated since it is the trimmings from the tallest stems that are used as hardwood cuttings. It is claimed that by continually choosing only the tallest stem for propagation, the more vigorous plants have been selected for over the years, any weak plants possibly infected with virus, being avoided.

At this stage the hobby gardener can buy in these standard briar stems and complete the process to raise a standard rose.

The standard stems are replanted some time between late autumn and late winter and tied

**Fig. 5.8** A young plant of *Cornus alba* 'Spaethii' which has been recently potted up. At the same time each growing point was pinched to encourage further what is already a fairly bushy habit.

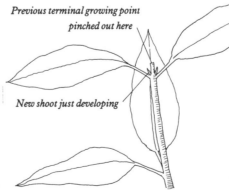

*Previous terminal growing point pinched out here*

*New shoot just developing*

**Fig. 5.9** Detail of the plant of *Cornus alba* shown in Fig. 5.8. The point at which a young growth was pinched can be clearly seen and two new shoots are just beginning to develop.

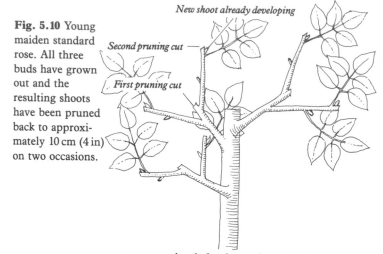

**Fig. 5.10** Young maiden standard rose. All three buds have grown out and the resulting shoots have been pruned back to approximately 10 cm (4 in) on two occasions.

New shoot already developing

Second pruning cut

First pruning cut

to a strained horizontal wire for support. Budding is done a little before the normal shrub roses. Three buds should be applied per stem in an upward spiral, each 5–8 cm (2–3 in) apart. The total length of stem over which the buds are budded should not exceed 18 cm (7 in).

The following summer briar growth above the inserted buds is allowed; indeed, it is necessary to keep the briar alive. Any shoots from below the buds are treated as suckers and removed as soon as seen. The next late winter, head back the briar to just above the top inserted bud. In the spring, all three buds should break dormancy and grow out strongly. At this stage young standard roses are very susceptible to wind damage. If allowed to get too long, the new shoots are prone to break out at the point of union with the briar. Extension growth proceeds too rapidly with respect to the strengthening of the union.

Once each new shoot is about 20 cm (8 in) long, it should be pruned back to about 10 cm (4 in). This pruning may need to be repeated several times until extension growth ceases in late summer. By such pruning, wind damage is reduced and a well-branched head is produced [Fig. 5.10]

**Climbing and rambling roses**

These are planted and budded in the same manner as shrub roses. The subsequent growth in the maiden year should at first be caned and then trimmed to keep it manageable.

**Grading and pruning**

Roses are lifted, graded and pruned after the maiden year's growth from early autumn onwards.

To be up to B.S.3936, Part 2 Roses, a shrub

**Conventional stem heights**

| Description | Stem height* |
|---|---|
| Standard | 100–110 cm (3 ft–3 ft 4 in) |
| Half standard | 75–85 cm (2 ft–2 ft 4 in) |
| Weeping standard | 125–180 cm (3 ft 10 in–6 ft) |

*Stem height is measured from ground level or 'nursery mark' to the base of the lowest cultivar bud.

**Fig. 5.11** First- and second-grade roses. The plants are shown as they appeared in late summer. They were in their first season of growth following budding and are referred to as 'maidens'. There is no chance for the second-grade rose to become first grade, since even if a third basal growth was produced there would be insufficient time for the growth to ripen sufficiently before lifting for sale in the autumn.

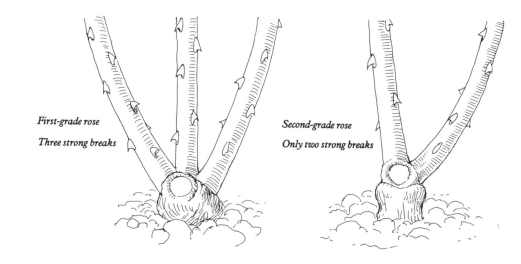

First-grade rose

Three strong breaks

Second-grade rose

Only two strong breaks

rose should have a minimum of two strong, well-ripened shoots, each at least 20 cm (8 in) long. There should also be, as a minimum, three strong roots at least 20 cm (8 in) long, plus plenty of fibrous root. In practice the industry grades to a higher standard with three strong shoots required on a first grade rose and two for a second grade rose [Fig. 5.11]. The hobby gardener and professional would do well to note that once planted, first or second grade roses, if correctly pruned, are both capable of giving excellent results. Plants below grade two are not recommended.

How hard the shrub is pruned prior to despatch depends on its intended method of sale. Shrubs intended for pre-packing are generally left with 23–30 cm (9–12 in) of shoots. Those intended for bare-root, root-wrapped or containerized sale are pruned back harder to 8–10 cm (3–4 in). Once received by the gardener, these roses, whatever their method of sale, should be treated as newly planted roses as detailed in Chapter 11.

## Nursery training and pruning of climbing plants

Cuttings are most often taken in late spring and, following about two months under rooting conditions, are potted individually into

**Fig. 5.12** A young, well-grown and tied plant of the climber *Hedera colchica* 'Dentata Variegata'.

*Plant has been tied to cane at four places*

**Fig. 5.13** A young plant of *Lonicera japonica* 'Halliana' in dire need of tying up. A batch of such plants, if left untied for much longer, would soon become a tangled, inseparable crop failure.

9 cm (3 in) pots. At this stage the plants are not caned and no attempt is made to control growth.

The following spring each plant is potted up into a three- or four-litre pot. The previous season's growth is trimmed back to 10–15 cm (4–6 in). Each pot has a 1 m (3 ft) cane inserted into it. The pots are lined out and the canes tied to strained horizontal wires. Subsequent vigorous new growth must be kept tied onto the canes and several ties will be required during the growing season [Fig. 5.12]. Once growth has reached the top of the cane, frequent trimming will be required to keep growth under control and prevent the plants becoming hopelessly tangled together [Fig. 5.13].

Ideally, a plant just reaching the top of its cane should be offered for sale. Older plants that have had to be frequently trimmed are not a good purchase as the roots will be found to be badly pot-bound.

For details on pruning at planting time, and subsequent pruning and training, please see the appropriate entry in Chapter 10.

## Nursery training and pruning of conifers

### Propagation

When grown from cuttings, training and pruning of conifers starts with cutting selection. A uniform batch of cuttings should be prepared. Where the young tree should have a central leader, such as × *Cupressocyparis*

*43*

**Fig. 5.14** A non-uniform batch of *Chamaecyparis lawsoniana* 'Stardust' cuttings. Such a batch would not produce the desired uniform crop of young plants.

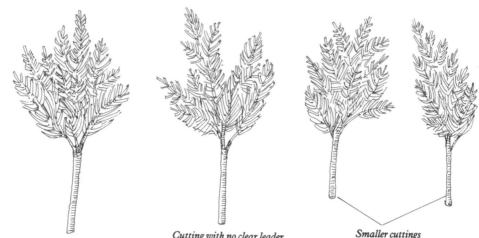

*Cutting with no clear leader*          *Smaller cuttings*

*leylandii*, it is important that each cutting selected has a clear single growing point that will develop into a central leader. Poor cutting selection, some with several growing points, will not produce a well-shaped uniform batch of plants [Figs. 5.14 and 5.15].

### Growing on

Selected forms of the genera *Chamaecyparis* (cypress), *Thuja, Cupressus* and × *Cupressocyparis* (Leyland cypress) used for specimen plants or for hedging should have dense foliage from top to bottom and have a clear central leader.

Whether grown in containers or in the open ground, it is essential that there is sufficient space around each plant to maintain and encourage growth down the sides. Plants grown too close together lack foliage on the sides and look poor when planted out. Light trimming may be done in the summer to encourage thickening of the growth on the sides of the trees. Competing double or multiple leaders should be removed as soon as seen.

Conifers that do not produce a clear central leader should be clipped to ensure a good bushy habit. The degree to which this is done varies according to the market being supplied. In the United States of America, a dense

**Fig. 5.15** A uniform batch of *Chamaecyparis lawsoniana* 'Stardust'. The cuttings are all of approximately the same size, each with a clear leader. Such a batch of cuttings has the potential to produce a good uniform crop of young plants.

compact plant is preferred and frequent clipping is therefore required. In the United Kingdom, a more open plant showing more of the growth characteristics of each plant would appear to be desired, and less clipping is done. The hobby gardener can, of course, clip his bushy shaped conifers to his own taste.

## The use of plant growth regulators

Pruning is done to regulate the growth of plants. For many years research workers have looked for chemicals, natural or synthetic, that when applied would favourably modify the growth of plants.

A synthetic plant growth regulator, known chemically as paclobutrazol and sold as 'Bonzi' to professional growers by Imperial Chemical Industries plc, is used extensively in the UK on ornamental pot and bedding plants to improve plant sturdiness and flowering. In the United States, paclobutrazol is sold under the trade name 'Bonzi' for ornamentals and 'Clipper' for tree trunk and soil application.

This chemical is now being evaluated for use on hardy ornamental nursery stock. Amongst the range of benefits that have been found are reduced vegetative growth and probably reduction in the need for pruning, greater uniformity, more compact plants, improved leaf colour, increased flowering and advanced flowering. Very promising results have been achieved with a range of hardy container grown shrubs. It is stressed, however, that this chemical is still under evaluation and no label recommendation for use is yet given. The outlook for the future, however is very favourable.

# CHAPTER 6

# *Trees*

## Inspection and pruning of trees prior to planting

The tree, or trees, should be supplied to the form requested. Trees may be personally selected and this is excellent practice, especially when large trees are being purchased. Smaller trees, often required in larger numbers, may be ordered quoting the appropriate specification as in British Standard 3936.

**Fig. 6.1**
*Agrobacterium radiobacter* var. *tumefaciens* (crown gall) on *Prunus* (cherry). A plant with such an infection should be refused.

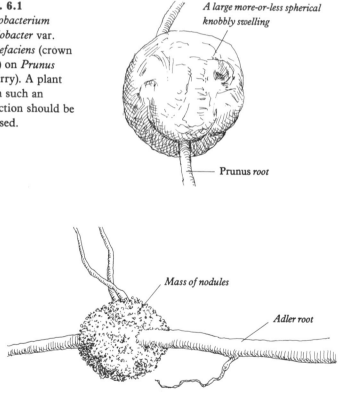

*A large more-or-less spherical knobbly swelling*

— Prunus *root*

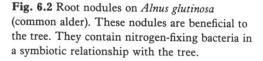

*Mass of nodules*

*Adler root*

**Fig. 6.2** Root nodules on *Alnus glutinosa* (common alder). These nodules are beneficial to the tree. They contain nitrogen-fixing bacteria in a symbiotic relationship with the tree.

The following should be checked upon delivery, prior to planting.

### The root system

If the trees are bare-rooted, they should have been covered during transport and remain covered or heeled-in until final planting. It is most important that the root system has not dried out and is not allowed to do so. Check for dryness and refuse trees whose roots are dry, especially if the whole tree feels light in weight. Such trees are dead, or nearly so.

An inspection should be made for *Agrobacterium radiobacter* var. *tumefaciens* (crown gall) which is most common on apples, cherries, elms, hawthorn, peaches and pears. Symptoms are spherical-like knobbly swellings at the junction of the stem and root [Fig. 6.1]. Such infected plants should be refused. However, do not confuse this with root nodules sometimes found on the roots of some species, including *Alnus* (alder) [Fig. 6.2]. These contain nitrogen-fixing bacteria and form a symbiotic relationship between the tree and bacteria which is beneficial to the tree.

The root system should also be checked for damage. See that its extent is in proportion to the head of the tree. If excessive damage has been done, with many main roots broken or torn and fine fibrous roots stripped away, again the tree should be refused. If only limited damage has occurred, then broken roots may be cut cleanly back to sound root.

With seedlings, whips and transplants, it is the root system that requires the closest inspection. Subsequent training and pruning of such trees should be the same as described under nursery production in Chapter 4.

### The stem

The stem should always be closely inspected. The length of clear stem and its circumference 1 m (3 ft) above ground level, this being visible

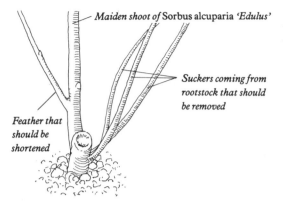

*— Maiden shoot of* Sorbus alcuparia *'Edulus'*

*Suckers coming from rootstock that should be removed*

*Feather that should be shortened*

**Fig. 6.3** *Sorbus aucuparia* 'Edulus' budded onto *Sorbus aucuparia* rootstock. In this example heading back has been done correctly and no snag has been left.

as the 'nursery mark' on the stem, can be measured and checked against that ordered.

If the tree has been budded or grafted, check the condition of the union. Refuse those where the union is obviously poor or fungal attack – often *Nectria cinnabarina* (coral spot) – is visible. The union of trees of about light standard size can be checked by bracing the stem between the hands and the knee. Apply only adequate pressure to bend the stem gently. Silence is golden – if the union makes a noise, this may indicate a poor union beneath the bark.

The stem should be reasonably straight. Bud guides or 'bud ups' should have been used with budded trees, or good initial training employed with grafted trees, to ensure that a straight stem without a conspicuous dog-leg is produced. Trees with badly bent stems should be rejected.

Occasionally, trees where 'snagging' has been omitted by the nurseryman may be offered [Fig. 6.3]. If the snag has not died back into the rootstock, it may be pruned away prior to planting. If die-back into the union or stock has occurred, then the tree should be rejected.

Standard trees should have a length of clear stem. This should be free of defect and have no large scars. During their production, lateral shoots are left on what will be the clear stem, to function as 'stem builders' and help in the thickening of the stem. Trees intended to be

sold as 'feathered' have laterals which have been allowed to develop normally. If stem builders are left on the stem too long, a temptation as it leads to the tree more rapidly gaining in girth, when they are removed excessively large scars will be left. Likewise, feathered trees may be 'converted' to standard trees by unscrupulous nurserymen, by removing the feathers just prior to dispatch. Again, tell-tale large scars will be left up the stem. In both cases such trees should be rejected; no gardener wants an ugly stem that is prone to infection until, and if, the scars callus over.

The operation of lifting field-grown trees requires skill and care by the nurseryman. The stem is very vulnerable to damage, especially to the poorly-aimed blade of a spade. For this reason, skinning of the bark towards the base of the stem should be carefully looked for and any badly damaged tree rejected. An old, deceitful trick is the application of a smear of mud to such wounds. If spotted, do not hesitate to complain.

**The head**

The purchaser should be clear as to what type of head he requires, be it standard with a central leader, standard with a bush head, or any other shape.

In the type of tree that normally has a central leader when young, it is essential that this is present. The nurseryman should supply trees with a good, clear, strong central leader. Forked or double leaders should not be present [Fig. 6.4]. If allowed to develop, they will form the main branches of a tree that is structurally flawed and weak [Fig. 6.5]. The narrow angle

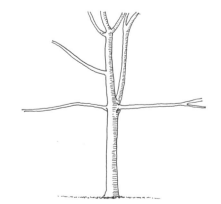

**Fig. 6.4** Young lime tree (*Tilia* sp.) that has unfortunately been allowed to develop a double leader.

**Fig. 6.5** Closer view of young lime tree in Fig. 6.4. This tree is structurally flawed, being weak at the point where the two main branches meet at a narrow angle. Later in life the tree will be liable to splitting at this point.

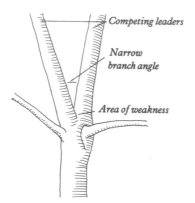

Competing leaders

Narrow branch angle

Area of weakness

between the two or more branches, and the huge forces acting on the point of union, make the tree very liable to splitting. This is a disaster which ruins the shape of the tree, greatly damages the trunk and in all probability leaves the tree in an unbalanced and dangerous state.

When a tree is supplied with a double leader, the seriousness of the fault depends on the extent to which the double leader has developed and the species of the tree. Where a double leader has only appeared recently, appropriate formative pruning to remove it may be all that is necessary [Figs. 6.6 and 6.7]. Where leaders have been allowed to become established over several seasons and, in effect, a multi-stemmed tree allowed to develop, this should be rejected unless a tree of this form is

**Fig. 6.6** Young ash (*Fraxinus* sp.) with a conspicuous double leader. Removal of the competing leader will allow a well-shaped tree to develop.

**Fig. 6.7** Young ash (*Fraxinus* sp.) after the double leader had been removed. Freed from competition, the single leader should grow on to develop into a well-shaped head.

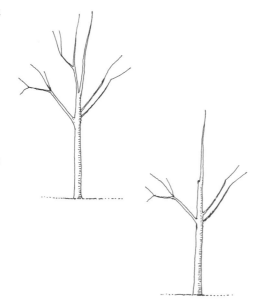

desired as with, for example, *Prunus* 'Amanogawa' or a multi-stemmed birch.

The head of the tree should be fairly symmetrical with respect to its development around the main stem. Growth should not be all one-sided. Poorly placed and crossing branches should be removed at the time of planting. The size of the head should also be in approximate proportion to the roots.

During lifting and transport the head of the tree is liable to damage, so the branches should be tied in and sheeted over. Unfortunately some species such as *Robinia pseudoacacia* (false acacia) produce wood that is inflexible, brittle, and very liable to damage. Such damage should be looked for at the time of acceptance. Limited damage can be rectified by pruning off the damaged section to a sound bud. Provided excessive damage has not been done, and the head remains balanced after pruning, this may be acceptable.

## Pruning at or just after planting

Some experts advocate moderate or severe pruning of the head at the time of planting. Where lifting and replanting is done with care, and correct maintenance can be carried out after planting, such pruning should not be necessary. Every tree has its own characteristic branching pattern. It is this that enables us to identify many trees from a distance in the winter. Pruning the head disrupts this pattern and can be seen for many years after planting.

Where severe root damage has occurred during lifting, reducing the head by pruning helps restore balance. Water loss by transpiration should be reduced during the first growing season, as this gives the roots a chance to recover and establish before a heavy demand is placed upon them.

If pruning is considered necessary, it should be done carefully, making every effort to retain the natural habit of the tree. Cuts should be made back to a bud and the opportunity taken to remove dead, diseased and misplaced shoots. Branches are generally reduced by approximately one third of their length.

An example of where this pruning is unfortunately often necessary is a specimen tree or shrub, previously intended to be permanently planted, falls foul of a new building development. The gardener wishes to save an established valuable plant, but root preparation by digging around and placing a compost around the severed roots to encourage the formation of a new fibrous root system is often not possible because of lack of notice. Upon lifting such an unprepared plant, considerable root damage is unavoidable and head reduction will help in its re-establishment.

## Staking at planting

### Young trees

Transplants and whips below 1.5 m (5 ft) do not need staking. Recent research has clearly shown that young trees establish better and are less likely to be blown over if left unstaked.

### Trees above 1.5 m (5 ft) tall

Such trees, whether bare-rooted or container grown, have inadequate root spread to resist being blown over by wind or damaged by vandals. Initial support is therefore necessary, but only until the root system is capable of carrying out its own normal supportive role.

The aim should be to stake in a way that the stem is allowed to flex in response to wind, as it would naturally. This has the following advantages. The stem, already an unnatural shape if trained as a standard by the nurseryman, is encouraged to develop its natural conical shape, becoming thickest at ground level and tapering towards the head. Such a shape is mechanically sound. Flexing exerts pressure on the roots and may stimulate their anchoring function.

Using a short stake, extending a quarter to one third up the stem, with a single tie, allows such development [Fig. 6.8]. A tree planted in the dormant season with care, into good soil conditions, should be capable of self-support at the end of the first growing season. Stake removal should, however, be delayed until the start of the second growing season. The tree then has a favourable period in which to establish further and gain the correct balance between head and roots before the first winter gales.

Unfortunately, many standard trees are still staked with a long stake extending to the base of the crown or, in some cases, reaching right into the head of the tree [Fig. 6.9]. Such a tree is protected to some degree from vandals, but

**Fig 6.8** Birch (*Betula* sp.) tree staked with a short-stake, not extending more than one third the height of the tree. A tree staked in this manner can usually have its stake safely removed at the start of the second growing season following planting.

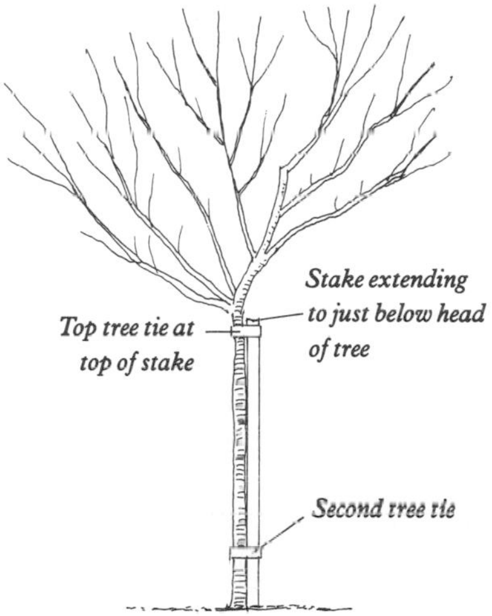

Top tree tie at top of stake

Stake extending to just below head of tree

Second tree tie

**Fig. 6.9** Tall staked *Prunus* (cherry) tree. A tree of this age and stature is well established and should now be able to stand without a stake. It will, however, need careful and gradual 'weaning' off such a tall stake.

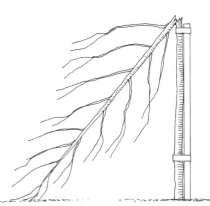

**Fig. 6.10** Young tree with stem snapped by vandals at the vulnerable point just above the upper tie.

**Fig. 6.11** Young *Betula* cv. with *Betula pendula* suckers arising from the base. Such suckers should be pulled or cut away as close to the main stem as possible. This should ideally be done as soon as the suckers are seen and not when they are as large as on this tree.

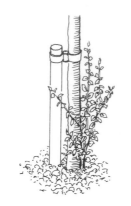

unfortunately examples of trees with the head snapped off just above the upper tie are all too common [Fig. 6.10]. Using a tall stake to support a feathered tree has the further disadvantage that feathers may foul against the stake. These may have to be pruned away and this will spoil the balanced head so carefully nurtured by the nurseryman!

A tree supported with a tall stake may also never be capable of fully supporting itself. Sudden removal is not recommended since this would leave the tree open to stem breakage in strong wind or into developing a permanent leaning stem. Instead, the tree may be 'weaned' off the stake. First, the old pair of ties should be removed. Find a point at which the tree just remains erect if tied and re-tie. The length of the stake above the tie may now damage the stem in wind and should be sawn off just above the tie. At the start of the next growing season, reassess the situation. Release the tie and find the point where the tree will just remain upright if supported. Repeating this process over a number of years will finally enable the stake to be removed.

## Growing on and formative pruning

### Tending young trees

Trees planted out as whips and transplants will need formative pruning into the required shape as detailed in Chapter 4. Trees should not just be planted out and forgotten; continued attention over the important first few years will be required in order that a well-shaped specimen will be the result at maturity.

*Feather removal*
Young trees bought in as feathered trees and intended to be grown on as standards, should have their feathers removed flush with the stem at the appropriate time. Such pruning should not be left until removal results in large wounds up the stem.

*Double leaders*
Despite attention at planting time, double or twin leaders may develop and will need reducing to one.

*Reversion*
Some trees with variegated foliage, for example *Acer platanoides* 'Drummondii', are prone to revert and produce shoots with all-green foliage. Such growth should be pruned out as soon as seen; if left, this stronger growth will soon dominate the tree.

*Suckers* [Fig. 6.11]
Grafted or budded trees may produce shoots from the stock. If spotted early enough, these may be simply rubbed out; later they should be pulled out or cut away as close as possible to the point of origin on the stem or roots. This will then also remove any buds at the base of the sucker and re-growth should not recur.

### Advanced nursery stock and semi-mature trees

The establishment of these trees can be difficult and requires extra care, as a certain amount of die-back may occur. This should be removed in late summer whilst it is obvious. This pruning should not be done in spring when bleeding from the pruning cuts may further stress the tree.

Sometimes, if growth has been slow and restricted in the nursery, subsequent growth – once the tree is planted out – may be excessively slow despite every care and attention. A condition can arise whereby the bark has hardened, thereby preventing expansion. A technique used to relieve this condition is to slit the bark with the point of a sharp knife, deep enough to penetrate the tissues beneath the bark. One long cut should run from the head to the base of the trunk. This cut is made after the main flush of growth, allowing time for the cut to callus over before the winter. The restriction to growth should be relieved by this operation.

## The maintenance of mature trees

Here it is the author's intention to introduce the reader to some of the basic concepts involved in tree surgery. This will be of use when discussing and deciding what work is to be done by specialist arboriculturalists. Such work needs practical training, involves skilled and sometimes potentially dangerous work, and under no circumstances should be undertaken without professional assistance.

Any major pruning of large trees should be done by a competent tree surgeon approved by the Association of British Tree Surgeons and according to British Standard 3998:1966 'Recommendations for Tree Work'.

### Crown lifting

This entails the removal of the lower branches so as to lift the crown of the tree where clearance for tall vehicles must be maintained [Fig. 6.12]. It may also be necessary for trees close to buildings, to allow light to the windows.

Crown lifting is a costly and difficult operation, especially given a busy roadside situation. In an attempt to reduce the need for this pruning, several different approaches may be adopted. At the outset, trees with a

**Fig. 6.12** *Tilia* (lime) street tree whose head has been raised to allow clearance for double-decker buses and tall lorries.

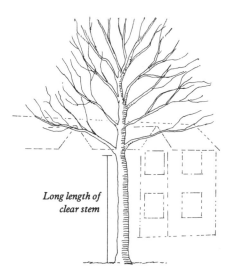

Long length of clear stem

particularly long length of clear stem may be purchased from nurseries. Species and clonal selection is very important and species such as *Malus tschonoskii* have become very popular largely because of their narrow, columnar habit. Other selected clones of trees with a more upright habit of growth have appeared first in the USA, where they are known as 'tailored trees', and more recently in Europe. Examples are *Acer platanoides* 'Columnare' and *Sorbus aucuparia* 'Sheerwater Seedling'.

### Crown thinning

There are several reasons for crown thinning. It may be carried out to allow extra light to penetrate through the crown to adjacent windows or space below the tree. Wind resistance is also reduced and this may be important with a weak branch system, which could be dangerous either to the tree as a whole or to those below.

This is an operation which requires careful consideration and is best approached in the following order. Firstly, remove all dead and diseased growth. Next, remove any badly placed limbs, for example those that are crossing or rubbing and those with a narrow crotch angle. Finally, thin to the required degree.

### Crown reduction

In contrast to crown thinning, crown reduction results in an overall reduction in the size of the head. All major branches are shortened to a point just above a major limb. The amount of cutting back can be severe and it is important to try to retain the habit and balance of the tree. It is frequently done to 'stag-headed' trees, where the upper and outer limits may have died back considerably, and in this instance it should be coupled with other methods of improving the health of the tree, for example placement of fertilizer into the root zone.

### Lopping

Lopping is the indiscriminate cutting back of the branches of a tree. It may be done to render a tree safe, which it will only do in the short-term; more often it is done out of ignorance of the correct technique.

Lopping can only be condoned on a tree if its

**Fig. 6.13** An unfortunate *Aesculus hippocastanum* (horse chestnut) that has been lopped twice during its life. This had lead to the tree's natural habit being ruined. In such a restricted space, tree removal would have been a better course of action.

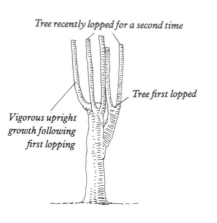

*Tree recently lopped for a second time*

*Tree first lopped*

*Vigorous upright growth following first lopping*

sole purpose is to act as a screen for a short time. In all other circumstances it is incorrect [Fig. 6.13].

### Epicormic shoots

These are vigorous shoots that spring out directly from the trunk or main branches, often as a result of hard pruning, or the death of a limb higher up. They can be a severe nuisance, especially in trees prone to their production, such as *Tilia × europaea* (common lime). Remove them as necessary, as close back to the main branch as possible.

In fruit trees, epicormic shoots may take the form of 'water-shoots'. These should be removed at the same time as normal dormant-season pruning. The pruning cuts can be treated with a wound paint containing plant hormone, which should suppress future shoots [Fig. 6.14].

**Fig. 6.14** Epicormic shoots erupting through the bark of *Tilia × europaea* (common lime).

## A-Z list of trees and their pruning needs

### ABIES (fir)

The young tree must have a dominant leader at planting. Very little pruning is required and all side branches should be retained.

### ACER (maple)

Here only the larger tree-like species are considered. For shrubby species see Chapter 7.

Prune only when fully dormant as some species bleed badly if cut when the sap is rising. Where possible, train to have a central leader.

Variegated forms, such as *Acer platanoides* 'Drummondii' and *Acer negundo* 'Variegatum', tend to produce reverted green shoots that should be removed as soon as seen. Do not hard prune the coloured leaf forms of *Acer negundo* (box elder) as this increases their propensity to produce green-reverted shoots.

As mentioned with the shrubby species, they are very susceptible to coral spot and this must be cut out and burnt as soon as seen.

### AESCULUS (horse chestnut)

Young trees should have a leader when planted. If this is subsequently lost it will be necessary to select one, as two will be produced because of the opposite buds.

Prune in the winter. When mature the main branches hang down to touch the ground, so do not let laterals develop below 3.6 m (12 ft) from the ground. *Aesculus parviflora* is a suckering shrub producing a clump of vertical stems. Pruning is only necessary if you wish to limit its growth.

### AILANTHUS (tree of heaven)

*A. altissima* is very strong growing when young, and can extend as much as 2.7 m (9 ft) in one year. Such vigorous growth is pithy and may be subject to winter damage. Keep as a centre-leader tree, re-selecting a leader if the original is lost.

To give a tropical effect with large compound leaves, a young tree can be cut down to ground level just as the buds begin to break. The vigorous growth that results is further encouraged by feeding and irrigation.

**ALNUS** (alder)
Very little pruning is required by most species as they naturally produce a central leader and grow on to develop into a well-shaped tree.

**ARAUCARIA**
*Araucaria araucana* (monkey puzzle) is the only hardy species. Plant with a central leader and retain. Much later in the tree's life, remove laterals back to the trunk as they die.

**ARBUTUS**
Evergreen shrubs or trees which are best left to grow naturally. As the tree or shrub matures, old lower branches will be shaded out and die. Remove these to expose the handsome bark.

If damaged by storms or very severe cold, these evergreens regenerate quite well. Do not prune until you can see where the new growth is coming from.

The above serves for all species except the larger-growing *Arbutus menziesii* which should, if possible, be trained to have a definite clear trunk.

**BETULA** (birch)
In general, little pruning is required. Retain a central leader and re-select a leader if the original is lost. Lower laterals may be trimmed up over two or three years to eventually leave a clear stem of 1.2–2.1 m (4–7 ft), if desired, to give a more natural effect. Prune in late summer – never in spring, when a lot of bleeding will occur.

Multi-stemmed birch look attractive and natural. They can be produced by hard pruning a sapling to 60–90 cm (2–3 ft) at planting, and selecting several resultant leaders; or a convincing effect can be produced by planting several small trees with their stems almost touching in a common hole.

*B. nana* (the dwarf birch) is a shrub and requires no pruning.

*B. pendula* 'Youngii' (Young's weeping birch) requires its leaders to be trained upright until the required height is reached. The leader is then released, arches over and the height of the tree is determined.

**CARPINUS**
*Carpinus betulus* (hornbeam) requires little pruning. Train as a single-leader tree, as a standard with a clear stem of 1.8–2.4 m (6–8 ft). *C. betulus* 'Fastigiata' has a pyramidal habit when young and has been widely used as a street tree. Unfortunately, the head broadens in later life. Crown reduction can be done successfully to reduce this width, whilst still retaining the overall habit of the tree. Pruning must be done when the tree is fully dormant, or else excessive bleeding will occur in the spring.

**CASTANEA**
*Castanea sativa* (sweet chestnut) forms a beautiful large tree with deeply fissured bark. As a young tree, retain a central leader and remove feathers to form a standard.

Much later, as a mature tree, it may become dangerous and liable to drop its large limbs suddenly. By careful selective crown reduction, the life of such a tree can be greatly extended without such risk.

**CATALPA**
*Catalpa bignonioides* (Indian bean tree) can be grown as a large shrub or as a standard tree. If grown as the latter, the central leader should be retained and laterals removed up to 1.8–2.4 m (6–8 ft).

A young tree may be hard pruned nearly to ground level. If well fed and watered during the following growing season, very vigorous growth with massive leaves will result, giving an exciting tropical effect.

*C. bignonioides* 'Aurea' (golden Indian bean tree) and *C. bignonioides* 'Variegata' are much less vigorous cultivars, usually grown as shrubs, although the former will occasionally make small tree-like proportions in a sheltered site. *C. bignonioides* 'Aurea' may be periodically pruned to keep within bounds and stimulate large-leaved new growth. Pruning should be done in early spring.

**CEDRUS** (cedar)
Maintain a central leader as long as possible with all species.

*Cedrus atlantica* and *Cedrus deodara* (deodar) require the same formative pruning as *C. libani* and fortunately are less prone to wind or snow damage.

The Complete Book of Pruning

*Cedrus libani* (cedar of Lebanon) with its tabulate, or tiered arrangement of branches, is unfortunately prone to wind and snow damage. To help alleviate this, remove branches that lie upon another, being very careful to retain the habit of the tree. Survey mature trees and remove any dead wood as soon as it is noticed.

## CHAMAECYPARIS (false cypress)

There are several species and cultivars. For their pruning as hedging, please see the page 94.

When young chamaecyparis require very little, if any, formative pruning. Several leaders will develop, but this will not detract from the overall shape.

As the tree ages, erect or fastigiate forms such as *C. lawsoniana* 'Erecta' may have leaders that fall away and spoil the outline. These leaders are often weighed down by snow or blown out by gales. Such shoots should be wired back in as inconspicuously as possible.

Dwarf or slow-growing forms will need no pruning.

## × CUPRESSOCYPARIS

× *Cupressocyparis leylandii* (Leyland cypress) is available as several clones. × *C. leylandii* 'Leighton Green' and 'Naylor's Blue' are reliable; avoid 'Stapehill', which has a poor drought tolerance.

To ensure good stability when grown either as a specimen or a hedge, plant when young, ideally 60 cm (2 ft) or less tall. The plant should be either field-grown or definitely not root-bound if grown in a container.

Select and retain a single leader from planting.

For pruning as a hedge, see page 95.

## CUPRESSUS (cypress)

A dominant leader is usually present. When damage occurs, the tree normally produces another leader, although some pruning to shape and reduction of new leaders to one, may be necessary.

*C. macrocarpa* (Monterey cypress) has been used as a hedging plant in the past, but it does not tolerate clipping as well as × *Cupressocyparis leylandii* and is not reliably hardy.

## DAVIDIA

*Davidia involucrata* (pocket-handkerchief tree) requires little pruning. A central leader will form naturally in the young tree. As the head develops, gradually remove a few lower branches so that a length of clear stem is produced. This allows the conspicuous white bracts, for which the tree is famous, to be viewed from beneath.

## FAGUS

*Fagus sylvatica* (beech) requires attention in the early years after planting to ensure that a single leader is maintained and feathering is done to produce a clear-stemmed standard.

If planted wide apart, with little competition between the trees, it is prone to develop a double leader. The same condition may be caused by the vulnerable apical bud being damaged by a late spring frost.

A tree with double or several leaders may eventually develop into a large, dangerous tree. The head of the tree will be very weak because of the narrow angles between the base of the branches. Such a tree is likely to drop a large, heavy bough suddenly – a problem for which beech is unfortunately renowned.

*Fagus sylvatica* 'Dawyck' (Dawyck beech) naturally maintains a leader and forms a tall, columnar tree. No attempt should be made to remove the lower branches to produce a standard.

## FRAXINUS (ash)

*Fraxinus excelsior* (common ash), and other species, all require the same treatment. Retain the central leading growth for as long as possible. Attention will be required if the apical bud is damaged because the opposite bud arrangement on the stem will mean double leaders will be produced. The early development of a head due to the loss of a single leader is undesirable. If this is allowed to occur, a large head with long branches that are liable to break out under stormy conditions will be produced.

## GINKGO

*Ginkgo biloba* (maidenhair tree) has its own very distinctive growth habit consisting of 'short shoots' or spurs and 'long shoots' where extension growth occurs. From seed, growth habit is very variable.

Very little pruning is desirable except to maintain a single leader in the young tree.

## GLEDITSIA

*Gleditsia tricanthos* (honey locust) is the most commonly grown species. Train as a standard with a central leader. *G. tricanthos* 'Sunburst' is thornless and produces bright yellow young leaves. Although less vigorous, training is as for the species. *G. tricanthos* 'Elegantissima' is a compact shrub-like form and cannot be trained as a standard tree.

Prune in late summer to avoid bleeding, which is a danger with spring pruning.

## JUGLANS (walnut)

Train as a central-leader standard. Young trees are susceptible to late spring frosts that may kill the leading shoot. If this should occur, re-select another leader. They bleed badly if pruned in the spring and should only be pruned in late summer.

## JUNIPERUS (juniper)

For tree-like forms, retain a central leader and leave feathers unpruned.

Shrub-like forms often have several leaders. Dead growth may accumulate and look unsightly within the centre. This should be cut out and cleared away in mid-spring; neighbouring plants which are allowed to crown out or overhang the juniper will aggravate this problem. Full exposure to the sun and good air circulation around the plant are essential.

Dwarf and prostrate forms are not normally pruned. The spread of prostate plants can be reduced by cutting out entire shoots so as to reduce the spread, but retain the characteristic shape. Indiscriminate clipping spoils the appearance of the plant.

## + LABURNOCYTISUS

+*Laburnocytisus adamii* is a graft hybrid (chimera) consisting of the tissues of both *Laburnum anagyroides* and *Cytisus purpureus*. When young, it can be trained as a central leader or bush-headed standard tree. The tree's fascination is that it produces both normal laburnum flowers and purple broom flowers, plus intermediate flowers of a coppery pink.

Normally no pruning is necessary to the mature tree, but occasionally the laburnum tissue will grow out of the chimera and, being more vigorous, begins to take over. Any such growth should be removed.

## LABURNUM (golden rain)

A genus of small fast-growing, comparatively short-lived trees. Young plants can be trained as central-leader or bush-head standards.

A problem is that all parts of the plant are poisonous, in particular the seeds which are a hazard to children. This danger can be reduced by planting *Laburnum × watereri* 'Vossii', which sets much less seed and is more floriferous than *Laburnum anagyroides* (common laburnum).

The same cultivar can be trained to form a laburnum archway. The trees in this situation are spur pruned, the annual extension growth being pruned back to two buds in early winter. A classic plant association is to allow *Wisteria sinensis* to grow up the laburnum archway. A beautiful colour combination is produced as the flowering times of both plants coincide. As detailed in Chapter 10, vigorous growth of wisteria is controlled by twice-yearly pruning.

## LARIX (larch)

The larches all have a very distinctive habit with a single straight stem. If the apical leader is lost, select another, and prune in winter.

*Larix decidua* (common or European larch), *L. kaempferi* (Japanese larch), and their hybrid *L. × eurolepis* (hybrid or dunkeld larch), all make fine specimens. Larch are all very demanding of light. Where grown in close stands, the lower branches will be shed as they become shaded. When grown in the open, the lower branches will persist and a fine specimen feathered down to the ground will develop.

## LIQUIDAMBAR

*Liquidambar styraciflua* (sweet gum) makes a beautiful tree, the acer-like foliage giving very good autumn colour.

When young, train to retain a strong central leader. As the tree matures, feathers may be left on or removed to form a central leader standard.

## LIRIODENDRON (tulip tree)

*Liriodendron tulipifera* can eventually make a very large tree and careful early formative pruning is necessary.

Select a young feathered tree with a good central leader. Maintain the central leader and remove the feathers as the head develops.

Occasionally, mature branches will develop strong vertical shoots. If left these will throw the head of the tree out of balance and should be removed.

## MALUS (crab apples)

A genus of small to medium-sized trees. The normal form for an ornamental crab apple is a branched-head standard tree. Weak-growing pendulous cultivars, such as *Malus* 'Red Jade', are often grown as small feathered trees.

Very little pruning is required. The thick, crowded head that develops in many trees is considered a desirable and distinctive characteristic. Any attempt to thin or open up the head of such a tree may have the very undesirable effect of stimulating the production of vigorous epicormic 'water shoots' that look very unsightly. These will then have to be repeatedly removed.

Most trees are budded or grafted. The type of stock employed will, to a very large extent, determine the vigour and overall size of the mature tree. Trees of cultivars such as *M.* 'Golden Hornet' are available on the very dwarfing rootstock M27. These will remain very small and are suitable for growing in a large pot or container on a patio.

As with any worked tree, remove all suckers coming from, at, or below the graft union.

## MESPILUS

*Mespilus germanica* (medlar), although producing edible fruit, is today mostly grown as a small ornamental tree. When young, it is usually trained as a standard or half-standard branch-head tree.

The main branches spread out in a wide, spreading, attractive and characteristic way. No pruning is recommended except the removal of any dead wood in late summer.

## MORUS

*Morus alba* (white mulberry) is the traditional food plant for silk worms, forming a small to medium-sized tree. Train initially as a central-leader tree, although eventually it will develop into a branch-head tree.

*Morus nigra* (black mulberry) requires the same initial training as the white mulberry. It is frequently found as a venerable specimen in an old garden. Such old trees are often very heavily branched and skilful bracing may be necessary. This is done to prevent these branches breaking under their own weight. Unfortunately this is likely during a summer storm when the branches are laden with fruit and in full leaf.

## PAULOWNIA

*P. tomentosa* is the best known species, but *P. fargesii* and *P. lilacina* are also grown. All grow in the same manner and have the same pruning requirements.

They are very fast growing when young, but the growth is soft, pithy and liable to winter damage. If possible, select a sheltered, sunny position. The sun will help ripen the wood and shelter will assist both winter flower-bud survival and enable the large foliage to remain in good condition during the summer.

As a young tree, grow with a central leader. If this is killed in the winter, prune back to a strong bud on the main stem. Allow side branches to develop after a clear stem of 1.8 m (6 ft) has been produced.

Conspicuous flower-buds are formed in the autumn, carried through the winter to open the following late spring. These are liable to winter damage, often mainly mechanical damage and late spring frost. Good regular flowering should only be expected in a mild area with a sheltered site.

A young tree can be pruned to give a rich, tropical effect useful in summer displays. The plant is cut down to within 5–8 cm (2–3 in) of the ground in spring before growth commences. The shoots that rapidly develop are thinned to one. Heavy feeding and irrigation results in very strong growth with large heart-shaped leaves.

## PICEA (spruce)

These evergreen conifers start as seedlings with a strong apical leader. This must be retained as the central leader throughout the development of the tree. To obtain the best specimen, well furnished with branches down to ground level, give plenty of light, removing any competition as soon as seen, and ensure good fast-growing conditions.

## PINUS (pines)

Most pines grow with a strong central leader. This should be retained. If lost through insect or weather damage, several competing shoots will be produced. Thin these down in spring when about 5–8 cm (2–3 in) long, to one shoot that is best in line with the rest of the trunk. Good growing conditions are also required if the central leader is to be retained.

As the tree ages, older branches may die off. This depends partly on the species concerned and the growing conditions. For example, it usually occurs with *Pinus sylvestris* (Scots pine), especially if grown close together, whereas *Pinus pinea* (umbrella pine or stone pine) may often produce permanent branches low down on the trunk.

Other species differ again: *Pinus pumila* (dwarf Siberian pine), being a dwarf shrub or medium-sized bush, and *Pinus mugo* (mountain pine), a large shrub or bushy tree. In both cases this is their normal habit and no formative pruning should be done.

## PLATANUS (plane)

Both *Platanus × hispanica* (London plane) and *Platanus orientalis* (oriental plane) are fast-growing large trees.

Select and retain a central leader. Aim to produce a tree with 4.5–6 m (15–20 ft) of clear stem.

*P. × hispanica* is very tolerant of pollution and pruning, and widely used as a street tree. Where space is available, it is admirable for this purpose. Where necessary, for example to give clearance for tall vehicles, crown lifting may be done on younger trees to give a greater length of clear stem. In a mature tree, complete lower limbs may be removed again to give increased clearance, but care must be taken to retain a balanced head. The practice of lopping to reduce the size of the head destroys the habit of the tree and cannot be advocated.

## POPULUS (poplar)

Most trees within this genus are strong growing when young and a central leader should be selected. For fastigiate cultivars such as *Populus nigra* 'Italica' (Lombardy poplar), very little pruning is necessary and laterals should be left as they occur naturally. Most others are best grown with a length of clear trunk. Pruning, if necessary, should be done in mid-winter to avoid excessive bleeding.

Many are surface rooting and damage to this system must be avoided or else troublesome suckering will result.

*P. × candicans* 'Aurora' is unusual in having young leaves variegated creamy-white and pink. Normally a medium to large-sized tree, it can be kept smaller and the variegated effect much increased by pruning extension shoots hard back in winter.

## PRUNUS

The pruning of *Prunus triloba*, *P. tenella*, *P. glandulosa* and evergreen species, is detailed in Chapter 7.

All species and cultivars are susceptible to varying extents to *Chrondrostereum purpureum* (silver leaf). Attack is through open wounds. To limit pruning, care should be taken initially to select a tree that will grow naturally to the required shape and size. If severe pruning is necessary, large cuts should only be made in the growing season before late summer. Such wounds will seal and heal over relatively quickly, in contrast to large cuts made in winter that remain open to infection for a long time.

*Prunus avium* (gean) and the bird cherries (including *P. padus*) are best trained as central-leader standards, a central leader being selected and retained during nursery formative pruning.

Japanese cherries show a remarkable diversity of habit. The almost fastigiate *P.* 'Amanogawa' requires no pruning, being naturally multi-stemmed from near ground level.

Those that produce a branched-head standard, whether top or bottom-worked, should have early formative pruning so that a balanced head with main branches regularly spaced around the main stem is formed. Such early corrective pruning will avoid massive tree surgery later in life.

*P. serrula* (Tibetan cherry), grown for its glorious bark, is trained as a standard with feathers being removed whilst still young, to give a clear wound-free stem for display.

Weeping forms may be top or bottom-worked. Top-worked trees need early formative pruning to ensure that a balanced head is produced. Bottom-worked trees should have a leader taken up a cane whilst in the nursery. Once tall enough, the leader is allowed to fall over and the head to develop. If a young tree of a weeping cultivar – such as *P.* 'Hilling's Weeping' – can be purchased, an attractive idea is to run the leader up a tall cane or pole for a height of several metres, allowing laterals to develop as a leader is trained upwards. Over several years a tall tree is formed with a central stem and tiers of pendulous branches along its length. Such a tree, in flower from top to bottom, is a beautiful sight.

## PSEUDOLARIX

*P. amabilis* (golden larch) requires an acid soil. Care should be taken to retain a clear leader and encourage its development by giving good cultural conditions. Plenty of space and light should also be ensured to stimulate the development and retention of horizontal lateral branches.

## PSEUDOTSUGA (Douglas fir)

Strong-growing on moist, but well-drained soils, no pruning is usually necessary. A strong terminal leader, plus tiers of laterals, will develop naturally.

## PTEROCARYA (wing nut)

Fast-growing, deciduous trees. When young, train as a central-leader standard. The new growth is liable to damage from late spring frosts. If the leader is damaged, train in another.

When young, formative pruning should only be done when fully dormant in mid-winter to prevent bleeding; and for the same reason, if major cuts need to be made to a mature tree, this should be done in late summer.

## PYRUS (pear)

Ornamental pears may be grown as either feathered or central-leader standard trees. The upright or columnar shape of some cultivars, for example *Pyrus calleryana* 'Chanticleer', makes them an admirable choice for use as street trees where space is often limited. Here, they can develop their natural habit without any need for pruning.

*Pyrus salicifolia* 'Pendula' makes a very attractive small weeping tree. In common with most weeping trees, the leader must be trained up vertically to the height required before the head is allowed to develop.

Unfortunately, many species are susceptible to *Erwinia amylovora* (fire blight). For details, see entry under **Cotoneaster** in Chapter 7.

## QUERCUS (oak)

Deciduous species such as *Quercus petraea* (sessile oak) and *Q. robur* (Common oak) should be pruned to form central-leader standards, but *Q. robur* 'Fastigiata' should be left unpruned to grow naturally.

Evergreen species, for example *Q. ilex* (holm oak) are best grown as feathered central-leader trees.

Mature *Q. robur* may become 'stag-headed' when the upper and outer branches die back. This is often due to a lowering of the water table. Removal of this dead wood will often arrest this decline for a considerable period.

## ROBINIA

Deciduous trees that should be trained as central-leader standards. Pruning is best done in late summer so as to avoid excessive bleeding.

The wood of trees of all ages is brittle. Old trees which are considered dangerous should have their limbs shortened.

*R. pseudoacacia* (false acacia) is the most commonly grown species and should be treated as above. *R. pseudoacacia* 'Frisia' is a widely planted yellow-leaved form. It is much better in a sheltered position away from the strongest winds.

*R. hispida* (rose acacia) is best treated as a wall shrub and is dealt with in Chapter 10.

## SALIX

Those forming shrubs or species when grown as pollards for winter stem effect are discussed in Chapter 7.

Tree-like species can be divided into those with an upright habit and weeping trees. The upright trees, of which *S. alba* (white willow) is typical, should be grown on the nursery to have a central leader. *S. fragilis* (crack willow) has a wide, branching habit and it is difficult to retain the leader for long. Once planted out, and as the head develops, space out the main branches, avoid narrow branch angles and prevent over-long extension.

The weeping willows are usually grown to have a length of clear stem, but once branching is allowed to start, comparatively few rapidly-extending branches are produced. The branches eventually become very large and heavy. An attempt must be made to keep the head of the tree balanced, early formative pruning will hopefully prevent serious leaning and the need for bracing or branch removal as the tree matures.

## SEQUOIA

*S. sempervirens* (Californian redwood) is capable of growing into a very large tree. It prefers a sheltered site, not growing well where it is exposed to strong winds. When young, ensure leader and all laterals are retained.

Very little pruning is necessary. If suckers develop around the base of the tree, prune away annually in the winter.

*S. sempervirens* 'Adpressa' is an attractive dwarf form whose new growth is cream-coloured. A watchful eye must be kept for reverted strong vertical shoots. If these are not rapidly removed, they soon take over and the plant assumes tree-like proportions.

## SEQUOIADENDRON

*S. giganteum* (wellingtonia or mammoth tree) is potentially a very large tree capable of exceeding 30 m (100 ft). Young trees should be given a sheltered position. The leader and all side branches must be retained. The size to which the tree grows depends on the depth of the soil and if there is any shelter for the leading shoot. Often growth ceases once the leader, because of its height, becomes very exposed. Old trees often lose their leader due to being struck by lightning.

Very little pruning is required, but old, dead branches should be cut back to the trunk.

## SORBUS

Within this genus a wide range of tree and shrub types is found.

Strong-growing trees, typified by *S. aucuparia* (rowan) are usually trained as central-leader standards. Once the standard form is produced, the subsequent development of the head varies greatly. Several cultivars have been selected for upright growth and are suitable for use where space is restricted, examples being *S.* 'Joseph Rock' and *S. commixta* 'Embley'.

Less strong-growing species, such as *S. cashmiriana* and *S. vilmorinii*, form bush-head standards.

The genus contains several shrubby members and these are best left to grow naturally. *S. reducta* is very unusual in being a dwarf suckering shrub.

Recently, the practice of growing species from seed, not budding them onto *S. aucuparia* stock, and allowing them to develop into multi-stemmed shrubs or trees has been advocated. This has several advantages. The tree assumes the habit it would in the wild, which is very attractive. No suckers are produced as they often are on budded trees. The adoption of this production method, plus the recent introduction of several new species that appear to be small trees or shrubs, should result in what amounts to a new range of plants for use by the landscaper and gardener.

## TAXUS (yew)

For pruning as a hedge or in topiary, please see Chapters 8 and 9 respectively.

Yew also makes a fine specimen plant and may be left to grow naturally, as should the cultivars, many of which have very distinctive habits. If pruning has to be done to reduce size, this should be done carefully in mid-summer and over several seasons. To retain an informal outline it is better to remove whole branches at their base rather than trim back any other laterals. Such trimming will result in many new shoots and present a clipped appearance.

The branches of fastigiate forms may tend to fall out of place due to age or snow damage. Plastic-coated wire can be tied around the entire tree to pull the growth back into position. New growth will rapidly hide the wires. If necessary, a length of steel tubing may be used as a stake, being placed in the centre of the tree so that the growth hides it. If a formal fastigiate shape is required, the tree may be clipped in mid-summer.

## THUJA

For pruning as a hedge, see Chapter 8.

*T. plicata* (western red cedar), when grown as a specimen, should have a central leader selected and all laterals retained. Eventually a fine tree, well furnished down to the ground, will be produced.

## TILIA (linden or lime)

When young, limes are best trained as central-leader standards, formative pruning being continued to retain a single leader for as long as possible.

*Tilia × europaea* (common lime) has been very widely planted in the past as a street, avenue and park tree. Unfortunately, it is the worst

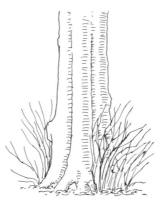

**Fig. 6.15** Typical suckers surrounding the base of *Tilia × europaea* (common lime). These shoots are a nuisance and require frequent removal by pruning back as close to the main stem as possible.

lime for producing epicormic shoots, both around the base and from burrs up the stem. Ideally, these should be rubbed off when young, but usually require removal by annual hard pruning when young [Fig. 6.15]. This hybrid has the potential to grow into a large tree and in many urban areas there are numerous examples of where topping or pollarding has been resorted to control its size. Today a far better choice would be a cultivar such as *T. cordata* 'Greenspire', with a more regular and compact head.

## ULMUS (elms)

A genus of trees that have been decimated by *Ceratocystis ulmi* (syn. *Ophiostoma ulmi*) (Dutch elm disease), spread by *Scolytus scolytus* (large elm bark beetle) and *Scolytus multistriatus* (small elm bark beetle). *Ulmus minor vulgaris* (syn. *U. procera*) (English elm) was, until the 1970s, a familiar and much-loved feature of the British countryside, being frequently allowed to develop into a hedgerow tree. Today, only small trees exist, these being suckers produced by now dead trees. Unfortunately, these only persist for a few years until they, too, are killed by the disease.

## ZELKOVA

*Zelkova carpinifolia* is the most commonly grown species. As a young tree, train to have a central leader plus a length of clear stem. Once allowed, several ascending branches will develop from one level, eventually producing a tree with a very distinctive silhouette.

# CHAPTER 7

# *Shrubs*

## General principles

### Eventual size

Many shrubs will grow and flower satisfactorily if just left to their own devices, but at the stage of deciding what shrub to plant in a particular position, thought must be given to its eventual overall size. Sadly, this basic point is often overlooked, and results in the annual 'haircut' treatment with consequent loss of the characteristic habit of the shrub and often loss of flowers. This loss of habit is important as the branch structure of shrubs can be distinctive and very attractive, especially with deciduous shrubs in the winter.

### Feeding and watering

Pruning must be done in conjunction with the correct feeding and watering regime. For example, *Cornus alba* 'Sibirica', when cut down hard in early spring, is expected to produce vigorous growth which bears the vivid red stem the following winter. The plant must then be fed with a top dressing of fertilizer to provide nutrients, and mulched to retain an adequate moisture supply to enable the required rapid extension growth.

### Removal of dead, damaged and diseased wood

Regardless of the pattern of growth exhibited by particular shrubs, certain basic precepts apply to all. Dead, damaged and diseased wood should be removed. This is usually done on an annual basis at the same time as other pruning is done. If a shrub is damaged, pruning and repair is best done as soon as possible to prevent ingress of disease.

Diseased wood should be removed and burnt as soon as possible. This is especially important with *Nectria cinnabarina* (coral spot) which used to be considered only saprophytic – that is, able to live off dead material – but now appears to have altered in its aggressiveness and become parasitic. This fungus is certainly capable of moving from dead to live wood which it then proceeds to kill. This increased pathogenicity has been noted particularly with elaeagnus, acer, ulmus, cercis, fagus and magnolia.

### Garden hygiene

Good garden hygiene should be practised. Woody debris should not be left lying around. Plant supports must be checked and any showing fungal fructifications removed and burnt. An area of weed-free bare or mulched ground should be left around each shrub and any over-dense growth cleared to encourage good air circulation.

### Control of suckers

Suckering can occur when a shrub is produced by budding or grafting. Suckers are unwanted growth occurring from the rootstock and they should be removed as soon as seen.

Suckers may appear from the stem of the stock. Removal of such suckers whilst they are small is easy, by simply rubbing out the shoot between thumb and stem of stock. When larger, the sucker should be pulled from the stock so as to remove the shoot, plus all dormant buds at its base.

Suckers may also appear from the stock root system, often as a result of previous damage, for example the over-zealous use of the gardener's fork. Such suckers should be traced back to their origin on the stock and carefully cut or pulled off. Cutting suckers off at ground level will not cure the problem as they will simply grow again.

### Control of reversion

Reversion is said to occur when a variegated shrub suddenly produces a normal green-leaved shoot. Such reverted shoots should be removed as soon as they are seen, since having the normal amount of green pigment (chlorophyll) in their leaves, they will be more vigorous and rapidly dominate the shrub.

Technically, variegated shrubs are known as chimeras; the plant consists of two tissues – one normal and the other deficient in chlorophyll. In cross-section of a stem we can distinguish periclinal chimeras, where the deficient tissue is in a ring around the inner normal tissue, and sectoral chimeras, where a section of the stem is composed of abnormal tissue [Figs. 7.1 and 7.2].

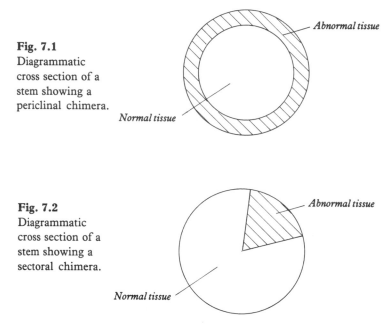

**Fig. 7.1**
Diagrammatic cross section of a stem showing a periclinal chimera.

*Abnormal tissue*

*Normal tissue*

**Fig. 7.2**
Diagrammatic cross section of a stem showing a sectoral chimera.

*Abnormal tissue*

*Normal tissue*

This is of direct interest to the horticulturist since periclinal chimeras produce leaves with variegated margins, for example *Ilex × altaclerensis* 'Golden King' with green leaves and a bright yellow margin. Sectoral chimeras produce plants with variegation tending to be in the centre of the leaf, for example *Ilex aquifolium* 'Golden Milkboy' with green leaves splashed with gold in the centre.

Some variegated shrubs are inherently more unstable than others and hence more prone to produce reverted shoots. Such shrubs require frequent attention, but they may be beautiful and well worth the extra labour. Excessively hard pruning can aggravate the problem, causing shoots to be produced deep within the plant stem from so-called epicormic buds.

These are formed from normal central tissue and may burst through the abnormal tissue and produce a shoot of normal green growth. A cultivar liable to revert in this manner if hard-pruned is *Ilex × altaclerensis* 'Lawsoniana'.

## Formative pruning
Upon planting out, young shrubs will produce a number of vigorous shoots from the base. Early formative pruning is necessary to ensure that these shoots are well spaced and will lead to the shrub later having an attractive well-balanced shape. Overcrowded, crossing or unbalancing shoots should be removed. This is particularly important with shrubs that produce a basic framework and then as they mature put on growth around the periphery, not normally producing more vigorous shoots from the base. Shrubs of this type include plants from the genera *Magnolia*, *Acer* and *Hamamelis*. They are frequently grown to form specimens where their shape and habit is very important.

## Pruning deciduous shrubs
These fall naturally into a number of groups depending on their pattern of growth and particular method of training.

### Those growing from around their periphery
This group consists of shrubs that, once mature, do not produce vigorous new growth from their base, but gradually enlarge by putting on limited annual extension growth around their periphery. Flowering occurs on shoots developing into spurs.

Early formative pruning is essential. Later in the life of the shrub little pruning will be required, the shrub naturally producing a pleasing form.

### Those flowering on one-year-old wood
A second group are those shrubs that flower on one-year-old wood. The flowers may be produced directly on this wood as with forsythia, or on short laterals produced on this wood as with deutzia, philadelphus and *Ribes sanguineum*.

As a group they tend to be spring or early-summer flowering and require pruning immediately after flowering.

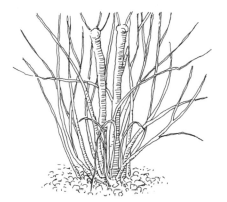

**Fig. 7.3** A mature weigela bush badly in need of pruning immediately after flowering. Old and dead wood has been allowed to accumulate.

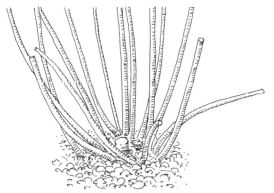

**Fig. 7.4** The same weigela after summer pruning. Very old and dead wood has been removed at ground level. Stems that have flowered have been pruned back to where new strong growth is arising.

*Renewal pruning*

Renewal pruning is practised, the idea being to keep the bush young with an adequate supply of one-year-old wood to ensure a good display. If left to themselves, the shrub will develop a preponderance of old non-flowering wood. Pruning should consist of pruning main stems down to strong new shoots coming from the lower part of the shrub. As the bush ages, one third to a quarter of the oldest stems should be removed at ground level to encourage strong new growth [Figs. 7.3 and 7.4].

Pruning should be followed by application of a general purpose fertilizer at 30–60 g per m² (1–2 oz per sq yd) annually plus mulching.

**Those flowering on the current season's growth**

The third group are those flowering on the current season's growth. If left to themselves these shrubs become an unattractive mass of twigs.

*Hard pruning down to ground level or to a basic framework*

Hard pruning down to ground level with subjects such as hardy fuchsias, or to within a few buds of a basic framework, as with cultivars of *Buddleja davidii*, is done in the early spring. Pruning just as the buds begin to swell allows a sufficiently long growing season for growth to be made prior to flowering [Figs. 7.5 and 7.6]. Pruning should be followed by a top dressing of a general purpose fertilizer at 60–120 g per m² (2–4 oz per sq yd).

**Those pruned for foliage or special stem effect**

A fourth group comprises shrubs pruned hard for special effect. This effect may be from their

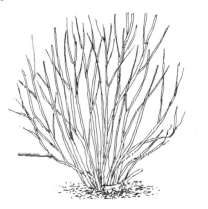

**Fig. 7.5** *Buddleja davidii* cultivar before pruning in early spring.

**Fig. 7.6** *Buddleja davidii* cultivar after pruning in early spring. Prune back the previous year's growth to within two or three pairs of buds of the permanent framework.

**Fig. 7.7** *Corylus maxima* 'Purpurea' (purple-leaf filbert) cut down very hard in late winter.

**Fig. 7.8** *Corylus maxima* 'Purpurea' (purple leaf filbert) showing the vigorous growth and large leaves produced as a result of hard pruning followed by feeding.

foliage or winter stem colour. Most of these shrubs would flower on one-year-old wood, but when pruned in the manner to be described, they do not flower at all.

### Foliage effect

Where a special effect from foliage is required, the shrub is allowed to develop a basic framework, the height of which can be varied to suit the position of the shrub, and then cut down to this each spring. If this is followed by copious feeding and watering, very rapid vigorous growth with foliage much larger than normal is produced [Figs. 7.7 and 7.8].

This technique is very effective with *Corylus maxima* 'Purpurea' (the purple-leaved filbert), *Sambucus racemosa* 'Plumosa Aurea', and *Cotinus coggygria* 'Foliis Purpureis' (the purple-leaved smoke bush).

### Special effect

A modification of this pruning back to a framework can be applied to large-leaved trees such as *Ailanthus altissima* (tree of heaven) and *Paulownia tomentosa*. Young trees are cut down to ground level in early spring and then heavily fed. Extremely rapid growth, the foliage several times normal size is produced, to give a very dramatic sub-tropical effect.

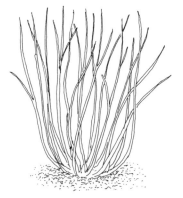

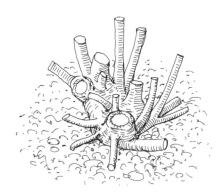

**Fig. 7.9** *Cornus alba* cultivar, showing red winter stem effect before pruning in early spring.

**Fig. 7.10** *Cornus alba* cultivar after pruning in early spring. The growth is cut down to almost ground level.

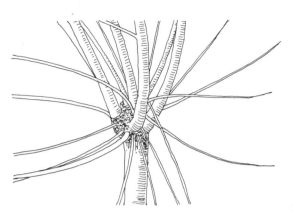

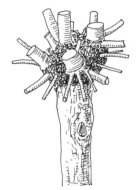

**Fig. 7.11** *Salix alba* 'Chermesina'. A young pollarded plant, as it would appear in late winter before pruning.

**Fig. 7.12** *Salix alba* 'Chermesina'. A young plant just after pruning in early spring. Rapid new extension growth will be made in the following summer. This new growth will bear the richly coloured bark for winter display.

*Winter stem colour*

The winter stem colour, for which some *Cornus* species (dogwoods) and *Salix* species (willows) are justly famous, is most vividly developed on one-year-old wood.

*Cornus alba* cultivars, *Cornus stolonifera* 'Flaviramea' and some *Salix* species are cut down to almost ground level in early spring [Figs. 7.9 and 7.10].

*Salix alba* cultivars and dogwoods can be allowed to form a single woody stem to a required height and then cut back to the top of this stem every year, a technique known as pollarding [Figs. 7.11 and 7.12]. After the shrubs have been cut down to ground level or

pollarded, they certainly do not look attractive, but top dressing with general purpose fertilizer at 60–120 g m² (2–4 oz per sq yd) and mulching will stimulate very rapid growth. Soon the ugly pruning cuts will be covered by foliage.

## Evergreen shrubs

Provided adequate space has been allowed, evergreen shrubs need little pruning. Winter damage may be a problem, especially a cold winter causing prolonged periods of frozen soil and desiccating winds from the east. Such damage is best cut away in mid spring, just as the buds are beginning to swell and the true extent of the damage can be clearly seen.

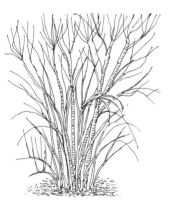

**Fig. 7.13** Old weigela bush before renovative pruning.

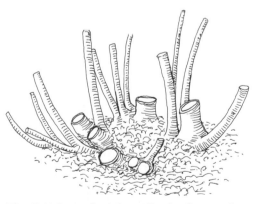

**Fig. 7.14** Same shrub immediately after pruning. All very old shoots have been cut down to ground level. Other shoots have been pruned to approximately 30 cm (12 in) off the ground.

**Fig. 7.15** Vigorous new shoots coming from the weigela shrub that was hard pruned the previous winter.

Timing is critical: too early, and the shrub may suffer further damage; too late and soft growth will be encouraged that is liable to damage the following winter.

A few evergreen shrubs such as *Hypericum calycinum* (rose of Sharon) and *Santolina chamaecyparissus* (cotton lavender) benefit from hard pruning in spring.

## Renovation

Despite the gardener's good intentions vigorous shrubs such as French hybrid lilacs, hardy hybrid rhododendrons, common laurels and philadelphus can become overgrown. The unfortunate may also find they are presented with this situation upon moving house.

Faced with such shrubs, the gardener has two options. The shrub may be grubbed out and replaced or it may be decided to attempt to renovate it. Clear advantages of renovation are that the cost of new plants is avoided and mature-sized, well-shaped plants can be obtained in a short time. An initial disadvantage is that just after pruning the shrubs do not look attractive, but growth in the year following pruning should be rapid.

The pruning is simple. All weak shoots are cut down to ground level and other main shoots cut down to approximately 30 cm (1 ft) above the ground. This is done in the winter with deciduous shrubs, but in spring, just as growth commences, for evergreen subjects such as rhododendrons. Feeding, mulching and irrigation must also be carefully attended to, especially in the first growing season following pruning [Figs. 7.13 and 7.14].

The shrub's response will be to produce several shoots from each of the shortened shoots. Formative pruning with the aim of restoring the shrub's characteristic habit should now begin. In some cases the vigorous shoots produced may be very soft and vulnerable to winter damage. If this is the case, wait until the following late winter or early spring before pruning, when any winter damage can also be taken into account. From each stump several shoots will have been produced. Remove all the weakest shoots, leaving only two or three of the strongest per stump. The shoots will now produce the framework for the renovated shrub [Figs. 7.15, 7.16 and 7.17].

Complete removal of the shrub's branch

**Fig. 7.16** Old stem showing many new shoots breaking out along its length.

**Fig. 7.17** The first stage in formative pruning. Remove the weakest shoots, leaving only two or three. If this is done to all the other old stems of the bush, then these remaining strong ones, plus new growth from the base, will form the basic framework of the renovated shrub.

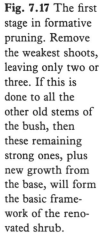

system, as described above, is best for all evergreens; however, deutzia and philadelphus can be renovated over two years, half the branches being cut down in year one, the other in year two. This has the advantage that the shrubs continue to look moderately attractive during the process of renovation.

Shrubs suffering badly from winter injury can have a modified form of renovation applied to them, pruning back to where growth is still alive in spring, plus cultural care as described. If damage is very severe, this amounts to complete shrub renovation.

## A–Z list of major shrubs and their pruning

### ACER (maples)

Here only the shrub-like members of this genus are considered. Early formative pruning is all that is necessary to ensure that branches are well positioned. All species are susceptible to coral spot and this must be pruned out and removed as soon as seen.

*Acer negundo* 'Flamingo' is an exception. It can be grown either as a shrub or a tree. As a shrub it can be lightly trimmed occasionally in the summer, taking care to cut back to just above a node or just to remove the growing point. This will maintain a compact branching system and give a brighter colour, the young leaves being coloured pink and those just behind brightly variegated. This cultivar is prone to reversion and any such shoots should be removed as soon as possible.

### AMELANCHIER (snowy mespilus)

A genus of large shrubs or small trees. When grown as a shrub, remove the oldest shoots in winter. If desired as a small tree, select a central leader but retain side shoots to function as stem builders for as long as possible.

### ARALIA

Deciduous shrubs mainly grown for the beauty of their large compound leaves. Pruning should generally be avoided as this spoils the characteristic, curiously crooked habit which is attractive in winter and gives the plant great architectural value.

Ideally, these shrubs should be grown on well drained soil in a sunny situation. On poorly drained soil or in shade, soft pithy growth may be produced which will be liable to winter damage. Such damaged growth must be pruned away the following spring since it is very liable to be attacked by coral spot which can then progress to kill the whole shrub.

They tend to have a suckering habit, especially if the root system is damaged by injudicious forking. With normal green-leaved plants only allow a few such shoots to develop if you want to increase the area occupied by the shrub. Those removed can be used as propagational material.

The magnificent variegated cultivars of *Aralia elata* should not be allowed to sucker. They are grafted and suckers from the rootstock will be green-leaved, stronger in growth and soon dominate the plant.

### ARBUTUS (strawberry trees)

Evergreen shrubs with beautiful bark, requiring little pruning. All except *Arbutus menziesii* should be left to grow naturally. *A. menziesii* grows larger than the rest and is normally grown as a tree, a central leader being selected in the young plant.

Fortunately, they will respond well to hard pruning, should this be necessary after storm damage or cold damage after a very severe winter.

### ARCTOSTAPHYLOS

Evergreen ericaceous shrubs or trees. Prostrate shrubby species need their branches thinned, otherwise the overlaid branches will lose their leaves.

### ARONIA (chokeberry)

Pruning is done in winter to remove at ground level a proportion of old shoots and to encourage the production of new vigorous wood.

### ARTEMISIA

Aromatic herbs, sub-shrubs and shrubs with green or grey foliage.

The object of pruning is to keep the plant young and producing lots of dense foliage. Old, leggy plants are unattractive. Fairly hard pruning, into old wood where new shoots can usually be seen developing, should be carried out in spring as growth commences.

Further pruning to remove the flowers may be necessary in the summer as the yellow flowers tend to distract from the foliage. Good clones such as *Artemisia* 'Powis Castle' seldom flower.

## ATRIPLEX

Two species *A. canescens* and *A. halimus* (tree purslane) are grown for their silvery-grey foliage. As they age they tend to become lax and open out, but this can be corrected by annual shortening of growth in spring, at the same time removing any winter-damaged shoot tips.

## AUCUBA

Evergreen shrubs tolerant of shade and poor soil. No pruning is necessary although they will respond to renovative pruning if needed.

## AZALEA

See under **Rhododendron** (page 79).

## BALLOTA

*Ballota pseudodictamnus* is a small shrub entirely covered with white hairs and grown for its grey-leaf effect. Winter damage may be severe and every spring hard pruning is necessary, both to remove winter damage and to correct its straggling habit.

## BAMBOOS

All members of the different genera can be covered under this one heading.

Old clumps may benefit from the removal of flowered canes, dead canes and some old canes. This should be coupled with feeding and mulching around their base to encourage new growth. This treatment should be carried out in the spring.

Contrary to popular opinion, the flowering of a bamboo does not always herald its death. The flowering of bamboos is a complex subject. Some species, such as *Arundinaria humilis* and *A. chino* have flowered several times in cultivation without ill effect, whilst *Thamnocalamus falconeri* appears to die after flowering.

*Arundinaria auricoma* (syn. *Arundinaria viridistriata*) produces green leaves, striped yellow, or canes about 1 m (3 ft) high. It is unusual in that it may be cut down to ground level every year in autumn to encourage the production of new canes the following year.

## BERBERIS

Grown as a free-standing shrub no pruning is essential. Deciduous species such as *Berberis thunbergii*, if they become overcrowded, can have dead and the oldest branches removed completely at ground level during the growing season. Evergreen species such as *Berberis darwinii* are best pruned soon after flowering. Whether grown as an informal hedge or as specimen shrubs, complete branch removal as detailed above is better than clipping so that the characteristic habit of the shrub is maintained.

## BUDDLEJA

Shrubs within this genus fall into three groups regarding pruning.

To consider first those that flower on the current season's wood, for example *Buddleja davidii* cultivars. Hard pruning to within a few buds of a basic framework is done in early spring [Figs. 7.5 and 7.6].

*Buddleja alternifolia* flowers on the previous season's wood. Flowered shoots, plus all dead wood, should be cut out to promising new shoots as soon as flowering has finished. This species is often trained as a standard and allowed to form a small tree. The strongest shoot of a young plant is selected and tied to a stake. This is taken up to a height of at least 1.2 m (4 ft), side shoots being removed. Once the required height is reached, normal growth is allowed – perhaps pinching the shoots once or twice to develop a round-headed small tree with a semi-pendulous habit. Pruning is then the same as for the normal shrub.

*B. globosa* flowers from large buds made the previous growing season. Little pruning is required, but it can be trimmed into shape after flowering. If the bush should become too large or open, hard pruning can be done during the dormant season, but at least one year's flowering will be lost.

*B. fallowiana.* See page 111.

## BUPLEURUM

*Bupleurum fruticosum* is an evergreen shrub

suitable for growing in windswept maritime situations or sheltered positions inland. As the shrub ages, it becomes untidy with over-thick growth trailing down to the ground. Once this stage is reached it is best cut down to ground level in the late spring, whereupon it will regrow strongly. If grown as a hedge it should be clipped in spring.

## BUXUS (box)
For treatment in topiary and hedging, please see page 94. When grown as an informal shrub, little pruning is required. Over-vigorous shoots can be removed from a base within the bush in late spring, so as to make pruning invisible and retain the informal shape. Overgrown leggy specimens can also be cut down to ground level in late spring. Generous feeding, watering and mulching will result in vigorous new growth.

## CALLICARPA
Pruning, if necessary, is best done in spring as growth commences. Young shoots, killed by a severe winter, and very old wood should be removed.

## CALLUNA (heather or ling)
The comparatively fertile garden conditions compared to the poor natural habitat of this plant encourage rapid, open, lax growth; pruning is intended to prevent this and produce compact bushy plants.

Remove half the previous season's growth as growth recommences in mid spring. Do not cut into old wood as this does not break freely. Spring pruning allows those cultivars grown for winter foliage colour to look their best and encourage new growth upon which flowers will be borne in summer. Hand shears are usually the best tool for this task; if using electric trimmers take care not to cut back too severely.

Despite this pruning, eventually the plants will become woody and straggly. At this stage they are best replaced by new young plants.

## CAMELLIA
For Camellia grown as a wall shrub, see page 112.

In common with most evergreens, little pruning is usually necessary. Young plants may have excessive flower buds removed to encourage negative growth and dead-heading is desirable on those that do not shed spent flowers freely.

Careful formative pruning in the early years may be necessary to ensure a good well-balanced overall shape. Late spring frosts sometimes damage new growth; wait until it is clear where regrowth is to occur and then prune back accordingly.

## CARYOPTERIS
A genus of mid to late summer-flowering shrubs. Some dieback is to be expected, particularly after a hard winter. Prune back to new growth as this becomes apparent in mid spring.

## CEANOTHUS (Californian lilac)
Evergreen species are tender, and best treated as wall shrubs (see page 113). Deciduous species flower on the current season's wood and are pruned in mid spring. The previous year's growth is cut back to within 8 cm (3 in) of a permanent framework of branches.

## CERATOSTIGMA (hardy plumbago)
Both *Ceratostigma plumbaginoides* and *C. willmottianum* are somewhat tender, aerial growth being killed back, often to ground level in a cold winter, but the roots surviving.

*C. plumbaginoides*, only growing to approximately 20 cm (8 in) tall, is best cut down to 1–2 cm ($\frac{1}{2}$–1 in) above ground level in mid spring. *C. willmottianum*, a larger shrub, may produce shoots that remain alive to some height after a mild winter. In mid spring, once growth has started, cut back to where the first shoots are evident.

## CERCIS (Judas tree)
Other than formative pruning when young, no pruning is required.

## CHAENOMELES (Japanese quince)
Grown as a free-standing shrub, no pruning is required. For pruning as a wall shrub, see page 113.

## CHOISYA TERNATA (Mexican orange)
This evergreen may suffer damage in a cold

winter, so plant with the aim of providing protection from cold desiccating winds. The removal of winter-killed growth may be necessary and should be done in spring. Old flowers should be removed by tip pruning. This will encourage both a more compact habit and reflowering later in the summer.

This shrub will respond to hard rejuvenative pruning in spring if it has become too large or developed a gappy habit.

The newer cultivars *Choisya ternata* 'Sundance' and *Choisya* 'Aztec Pearl' are marginally less hardy, requiring more shelter, but the same pruning.

## CISTUS (sun roses)

All need full sun and a well-drained, not rich, soil to produce well-ripened wood. None are fully reliably hardy, but *C. laurifolius*, *C. × cobariensis* and *C.* 'Silver Pink' are among the hardiest.

Any pruning should be done in late spring when the extent of winter injury will be obvious. Avoid pruning into old wood as this does not break freely.

## CLEMATIS

Only sub-shrubs and herbaceous non-climbing species are dealt with here. For other species and cultivars see entry in Chapter 10 (pages 114–15).

The species *C. heracleifolia* and *C. integrifolia* should be hard pruned in winter. *C. recta* is completely herbaceous and should be cut down to ground level in the winter.

## CLERODENDRUM

*C. bungei* is technically a sub-shrub and hardy, but its growth is usually at least killed part way down to the ground in winter. In spring, cut back to where new growth is coming from, which may be ground level.

*C. trichotomum* and its form *C. trichotomum fargesii* are both large deciduous shrubs that require no regular pruning.

## CLETHRA

*C. alnifolia* (sweet pepper bush) and *C. tomentosa* spread by suckers, eventually forming dense thickets. Older branches in a clump may be cut out at ground level in the winter.

The more tender *C. arborea* and *C. monostachya* form large shrubs or small trees given very favourable conditions. They may be trained to a single leader, but side shoots are retained.

## COLLETIA

A genus of very spiny late summer/autumn-flowering shrubs of which *C. armata* is the hardiest and most common. No pruning is required, although if an awkwardly-placed branch is produced it does respond well to pruning.

## COLUTEA (bladder senna)

These plants may be grown as a tree or as a shrub. If they are to be grown as a tree, take a single leader to form the stem. Prune back to within two buds of the head every year. As a shrub, cut back the previous annual extension growth to two buds above a permanent framework, or simply cut out oldest and weakest wood. All pruning is done in late winter.

## CONVOLVULUS

*C. cneorum* is a slightly tender, small, evergreen shrub. No pruning is usually required save trimming to remove winter damage and to shape in spring.

## CORNUS

This genus, for the purposes of pruning, falls into three groups. *Cornus alba*, plus its cultivars, and *C. stolonifera* 'Flaviramea', when grown for winter coloured stem effect, are coppiced annually [Fig. 7.9]. They may, however, be left to form large shrubs, in which case only the periphery of new growth will have brightly coloured stems.

Other species, including *C. mas* (Cornelian cherry), *C. nuttallii* and *C. kousa* require no pruning.

*C. controversa* and its variegated cultivars should be trained to have a definite leader which will eventually form a trunk. Ample space should be left around the plant to allow the characteristic tiered branches to develop. *C. alternifolia* has a less well-defined tabulate habit and may be trained as *C. controversa* or left to grow naturally.

## CORONILLA
*C. glauca* is a tender small shrub. It may suffer severe winter damage which should be removed in late spring once growth has re-started.

## CORYLOPSIS
Pruning is not advised since this may spoil the attractive arching habit of some species.

## CORYLUS (hazel)
*C. colurna* (Turkish hazel) forms an erect tree. Select a central leader at an early stage.

*C. avellana* is a suckering shrub and has traditionally been coppiced on an approximately seven-year cycle for the production of brushwood [Fig. 7.9]. *C. avellana* 'Tortuosa' (the corkscrew hazel) is a cultivar grown for its characteristic contorted growth, which is especially noticeable in winter. No pruning is required.

*C. avellana* 'Purpurea', *C. avellana* 'Aurea', and the stronger growing *C. maxima* 'Purpurea' can be coppiced annually, plus fed, irrigated and mulched to produce vigorous growth coupled with striking large, coloured leaves [Figs. 7.7 and 7.8].

## COTONEASTER
For pruning when grown as hedges, see page 95, and as wall shrubs pages 115–16.

When grown as free-standing shrubs no pruning is necessary unless it is required to restrict their spread. Care should be taken to maintain their natural habit which is often an important feature, as with *C. × watereri*, its clones, and *C. horizontalis* (the herring-bone cotoneaster). It is usually preferable to remove a branch to ground level from where new growth will appear, rather than give an overall trim.

If prostrate forms such as *C. dammeri* outgrow their space, again removal of entire branches is preferable to maintain an irregular outline rather than to clip back to a defined straight edge.

*Erwinia amylovora* (fire blight), characterized by dead twigs with blackened, as though burnt, dead leaves and flowers still remaining on infected branches in early to mid summer can

be a problem. The wood of infected branches is stained dark red. Prune out to where wood is no longer stained and burn prunings [Fig. 7.18].

A wide range of genera within the *Roseacae* are attacked, including *Crataegus, Pyracantha, Pyrus, Stransvaesia* and *Sorbus*.

## CRATEAGUS (thorns)
For pruning as a hedge, see Chapter 8 (page 95). Nearly all species may be grown as a small tree, when a central leader is run up to the desired height, before the characteristic bushy head is allowed to develop. When grown as a shrub, no pruning is required.

## CYTISUS (brooms)
Prune after flowering. Remove about two-thirds of the previous year's growth, cutting just above where new growth is beginning. Avoid pruning into old wood that does not respond well [Fig. 7.19 and Fig. 7.20].

By pruning in this manner the shrub is

**Fig. 7.18** The appearance in mid-summer of a branch of *Cotoneaster × watereri* attacked by *Erwinia amylovora* (fire blight). Note the dead, but still retained leaves and flower clusters.

**Fig. 7.19** *Cytisus* cultivar just after flowering. Many unwanted seed pods are developing, plus new growth.

**Fig. 7.20** Old flowered shoots of *Cytisus* pruned back to where new growth is beginning. This is done over the entire bush, removing about two thirds of the previous year's growth. Avoid pruning into old wood that does not respond well to pruning.

encouraged to produce new growth for flowering next year, rather than a mass of unwanted seed pods. Habit is also much improved. Left to themselves, brooms rapidly become open and very leggy, often splitting at the base. They are best regarded as shrubs with a short useful life, but this can be extended by the pruning advised.

*Cytisus battandieri* is most often grown as a wall shrub and is dealt with in that chapter (see page 116).

## DABOECIA (St. Dabeoc's heath)
In order to maintain bushy, compact plants shear off old flower stems plus most of the previous year's growth in spring just as new growth commences.

## DAPHNE
No pruning is necessary. *D. blagayana* and *D. cneorum* are dwarf spreading species. Growth will be denser and more attractive if trailing growths are pegged down to layer and top-dressed with soil rich in organic matter.

## DECAINSNEA
*D. fargesii* does not need regular pruning. Late frosts will sometimes kill new top growth which should be later pruned back to where sound and new growth is apparent.

## DEUTZIA
This flowers on short laterals from one-year-old wood and a system of renewal pruning is required [Fig. 7.3 and 7.4].

## DIERVILLA
This genus flowers on the current season's wood. They have a dense suckering habit. Prune approximately one-third of growth

down to ground level each spring. Once overcrowded, dig up, split and replant young sections in enriched soil.

## DIPELTA
Large strong-growing shrubs, not requiring annual pruning. If too large or vigour failing, cut about one-fifth of oldest shoots down to ground level or to where strong new growth is emerging. This should be done after flowering in early summer.

## ELAEAGNUS
A genus consisting of evergreen and deciduous species, none of which requires regular pruning.

Reverted shoots on variegated evergreen cultivars should be removed, as should suckers on grafted plants. In contrast to general recommendations, take time to be sure that a shoot has reverted. New growth may initially appear all green, only to become variegated as the shoot matures.

*Elaeagnus × ebbingei* is liable to winter damage which may then become infected by *Nectria cinnabarina* (coral spot). This, left untreated, is capable of spreading and killing the whole shrub. Winter-killed branches should be removed as soon as recognized in the spring.

## EMBOTHRIUM
*Embothrium coccineum* (Chilean fire-bush) requires little or no pruning. Misshapen branches may be corrected after flowering. Somewhat tender and only suitable for milder climates, winter-damaged growth can be removed in mid to late spring.

## ENKIANTHUS
*Enkianthus campanulatus* is the species most widely grown. This, and the more uncommon species, require no pruning except for deadheading after flowering as for rhododendrons (see page 80).

## ERICA (heaths)
The heaths exhibit a range of habits and any pruning done should endeavour to preserve this. Annual pruning, where recommended, may in itself seem unnatural, but one should remember that their natural habitat is often

windswept with poor soil, the comparative shelter and rich garden soil leading to a rather loose, open habit.

Annual pruning is done after flowering, just as new growth is about to start. Do not prune in late autumn or winter.

Where overall clipping is recommended, this should be done with care, cutting just below the base of the flower-spike so as not to cut into old wood.

The angle at which the clippers are used should be varied to avoid a too formal, just-clipped appearance. Clippings should be removed immediately, or else browning will occur beneath them. Avoid excessive trampling on the plants.

Winter-flowering species such as *E. carnea*, *E. ciliaris* and *E.* ×*darleyensis* should be clipped in mid spring, just as new growth commences.

*E. arborea* and the hardier *E. arborea* 'Alpina' do not require annual pruning. Specimens that have been damaged by frost or snow, or become lanky through age, may have offending limbs cut hard back in mid spring.

The spring-flowering *E. mediterranea* should be pruned in late spring as the flowers fade. This allows time for new growth and flower bud development before winter.

*E. cinerea* (bell heather) and *E. tetralix* (cross-leaved heath) are summer and autumn flowering. Pruning is done in early spring as growth begins. The new shoots subsequently developed will then have time to develop and flower a few months later.

## ESCALLONIA

When grown as a free-standing shrub, an effort should be made to maintain the arching habit that most plants within this genus have.

Pruning is not necessary every year, but is done when required to invigorate the shrub or to control its size. This may be done immediately after flowering, cutting old branches back to well-placed new shoots.

Escallonia are liable to winter damage, but are seldom killed outright in mild areas. Dead and winter-damaged growth should only be removed once it is clear where new growth is coming from in late spring or early summer. For escallonia grown as hedging, see page 95.

## EUCALYPTUS

The hardier species such as *Eucalyptus dalrympleana* and *Eucalyptus gunnii* may be successfully grown as evergreen trees or foliage shrubs, especially if grown from seed of high altitude provenance.

Small young plants that have not become pot-bound, should be planted in a site sheltered from northerly or easterly winds in spring.

Attractive perfoliate, glaucous, juvenile foliage will be first produced. If needed for cut foliage or as a foliage shrub, regular hard pruning by coppicing or pollarding [Figs. 7.9 and 7.10, plus Figs. 7.11 and 7.12] in late spring will keep the plant in the juvenile condition. Foliage may be cut at any time, but excess removal should be avoided in winter.

If the tree is allowed to develop, the foliage will change to the adult sickle-shaped form and tree-like dimensions rapidly assumed.

Trees may be badly frosted or killed down to almost ground level in a severe winter. Regeneration growth will usually occur from the lignotuber at the base of the stem. Once it is clear where re-growth is coming from, pruning back to this point can be done in spring. The plant may then be left to develop as a natural looking, multi-stemmed tree or shoot numbers reduced once it is clear which are the strongest growths.

## EUCRYPHIA

A genus of ornamental trees or shrubs flowering in mid to late summer. They are best left unpruned.

## EUONYMUS

The deciduous species such as *E. alatus* (spindle bush) and *E. europaeus* (spindle tree) require very little pruning.

*E. japonicus* is a densely branching evergreen. No pruning is necessary unless it is used as an informal hedge when individual shoots may be pruned in spring. Variegated forms such as *E. japonicus* 'Latifolius Albomarginatus' are prone to revert and this should be pruned out as soon as seen.

*E. fortunei* is a trailing and self-clinging evergreen. This species and its variegated cultivars, e.g. *E. fortunei* 'Silver Queen', can be used as ground cover or against a wall where a minimum of support will be necessary.

## EUPHORBIA

Most plants in this genus are herbaceous, but *Euphorbia characias* and the form *E. c. wulfenii* are shrubby evergreens. Both produce numerous upright stems which give the plant a strong architectural effect. Flowered stems are best cut down to either a new strong growth or ground level immediately after flowering. At the same time, stems badly damaged by winter weather can also be removed.

## EXOCHORDA

These shrubs have a potential for a suckering habit but are best grown on a leg before laterals are allowed. Epicormic growths may develop on the branches. Both suckers and epicormic shoots may be removed in winter unless required as replacement branches. Alternatively, epicormic shoots may be rubbed out between finger and thumb whilst still small in spring.

After flowering, old and overcrowded growth may be removed.

## × FATSHEDERA

×*Fatshedera lizei* is a bi-generic hybrid between *Fatsia japonica* and *Hedera hibernica*. It forms an evergreen shrub with a rather untidy habit. Shoots start growing vertically and then collapse under their own weight.

It is a little tender and removal of winter damaged growth after a severe winter may be necessary in mid-spring.

## FATSIA

*Fatsia japonica* is an evergreen shrub flowering in late autumn. Main branches start at or near ground level and, being very little branched, give the shrub a very architectural habit.

Old leaves may be removed in spring to improve overall appearance. As the shrub ages, it can get rather gaunt in appearance. Old branches should be cut down to ground level in spring. Following pruning, several new shoots will appear around the base of the old stem.

## FORSYTHIA

Shrubs within this genus flower on one-year-old wood. A young plant requires little or no pruning.

As the shrub ages, renewal pruning is necessary to ensure an adequate supply of wood for flowering. The oldest wood is removed down to a strong shoot or ground level. This is done after flowering just as new growth commences [Figs. 7.3 and 7.4].

Such pruning is not required every year, but should be done when it is apparent that the vigour and amount of one-year-old wood is declining.

## FOTHERGILLA

No regular pruning required.

## FUCHSIA

*Fuchsia magellanica*, *F.* 'Riccartonii' and 'Hardy Fuchsias' may be grown permanently outside. In cold inland gardens, planting approximately 2.5 cm (1 in) deeper than normal and placing a layer of ashes, bracken or peat around the base of the stems for the winter will give some protection.

Rake away this top dressing in spring and cut back branches to where new growth is apparent: Normally this will be around ground level. *F. magellanica*, in a normal winter, will retain some of the old wood and gradually build up a framework.

In very mild areas little dieback will occur and fuchsias may be used as hedging. Pruning back to a formal outline is done in spring.

## GAULTHERIA

Evergreen, low-growing or prostrate shrubs, spreading by underground stems. Very little, if any, pruning is required.

*G. shallon* is used for game coverts and ground cover. If it becomes untidy, it can be cut hard back in spring.

## GENISTA

*G. hispanica* normally forms a compact rounded shrub. A light clipping after flowering helps to keep the plant both compact and vigorous.

## GRISELINIA

See page 96.

## HALIMIUM

A genus of rather tender, low-growing, evergreen shrubs. They do not respond well to pruning and this should be restricted to the removal of winter-killed growth in the spring.

## HAMAMELIS (witch hazel)

Pruning is not normally necessary. Their natural habit of growth is a major attraction and they should be allowed to develop naturally.

Hamamelis are commonly propagated by grafting onto *H. virginiana*. Suckers may appear and, if seen, should be removed as soon as possible. Regard any shoot coming from below ground level as a sucker.

## HEBE

A genus of evergreen shrubs of variable hardiness. In general, the larger the leaves and more showy the flowers, the less hardy the plant.

Pruning is most often needed in late spring with the less hardy kinds. This is to prune away dead growth to where new shoots are apparent. Fortunately, hebes have the ability to shoot from old wood.

Snow and wind may also damage the branch system, and pruning away broken shoots and re-shaping should also be done in spring.

Some, such as *H. dieffenbachii* have rather open and straggly growth and shortening of the branch system in spring may be done to correct this fault. Unfortunately, some of the more compact tidy growers, for example *H. rakaiensis*, may sometimes have a branch killed in the winter. This will have to be removed in the spring, pruning being done well within the canopy to try to hide the branch removal.

*Hebe hulkeana* frequently sets a heavy crop of seed. This should be removed in summer to relieve the plant of the strain and help extend the life of the plant.

## HIBISCUS

*Hibiscus syriacus* requires no regular pruning. *Nectria cinnabarina* (coral spot) may be a problem and infected wood should be cut out as soon as seen.

## HIPPOPHAE

*Hippophae rhamnoides* (a buckthorn) is most often grown as a shrub and no pruning is required. It can be trained into a small tree when a leader should be selected and laterals reduced.

## HYDRANGEA

*H. macrophylla* and *H. serrata* flower on one-year-old wood. Old flower heads should be left over winter to provide some winter interest and protect flower buds. In early spring (mid spring in cold districts) the old flowered stems are cut back to fat flower buds. As winter or early spring frost damage can occur, care should be taken to select undamaged buds. At the same time, old or thin shoots can be cut down to ground level. This will rejuvenate the bush and allow the remaining wood better summer ripening.

*H. paniculata* and its cultivars flower on current season's wood. These are cut back annually to ground level or to a framework leaving only two to four buds on each shoot in early spring. This should be accompanied with feeding and mulching to encourage vigorous growth.

## HYPERICUM (St. John's wort)

*H. calycinum* is stoloniferous and seldom more than 30 cm (1 ft) in height. Cutting back hard in spring to 2.5 cm (1 in) above ground level will tidy the plant and may help control *Melampsora hypericorum* (hypericum rust).

The shrubby species are tender to varying extents. The degree to which dieback will occur depends on the severity of the winter. In the spring, the point at which regrowth occurs should be clearly visible. Remove all dead and thin growth, pruning back to where these new shoots are apparent.

## ILEX

If grown as a free-standing shrub, little pruning is necessary. Disfigurement by leaf miner can be removed by light pruning in mid spring or late summer.

*Ilex aquifolium* (common holly) makes a good formal hedge. Pruning should be done in late summer with secateurs. Overgrown hedges can be cut hard back at the same time, but the operation is best spread over three years.

The different cultivars of *I. aquifolium* and *Ilex × altaclerensis* (Highclere holly) vary considerably in the natural shape. Strong growers with a dominant leader may be allowed to form pyramidal trees or must be pruned early in their life if a dense bush is required.

Some variegated cultivars such as *I. ×altaclerensis* 'Lawsoniana' tend to revert frequently and such green shoots must be removed as soon as seen.

## KALMIA (Calico bush)
Very little pruning is required except dead-heading after flowering.

Old straggly bushes may be rejuvenated by hard pruning back into old wood in spring from which new shoots will appear, but this must be accompanied by good growing conditions if good regrowth is to be produced.

## KERRIA
Flowering occurs on one-year-old canes that also have the brightest green stems, valued for winter colour. Prune out old canes to strong new shoots or ground level as flowers fade.

## KOLKWITZIA
*K. amabilis* (beauty bush) has an attractive arching habit that should be retained. It flowers on one-year-old wood and annual pruning consists of removing old flowered shoots and weak wood immediately after flowering, as shown in Figs. 7.3 and 7.4.

## LAURUS
*Laurus nobilis* (bay laurel) is slightly tender and may suffer winter cold damage. Leads should be left to grow naturally. If killed down to ground level by a severe winter, re-growth from the base will frequently occur.

Bay is often grown in a tub and clipped to shape. This clipping is done several times during the summer. In winter, such plants are best housed in a glasshouse or conservatory to avoid unsightly damage.

## LAVANDULA (lavender)
*L. angustifolia* (old English lavender) and its many cultivars, left unpruned become open, straggly unattractive plants. Annual pruning should be done in mid-spring. Clip to remove old flower stems, plus most of the previous year's wood, leaving a few shoots for new growth. Do not cut back into old wood.

Do not prune after flowering as this renders the plant liable to winter injury, but just the spent flower heads may be removed if thought necessary by the tidy gardener.

Old plants will slowly respond to hard pruning, but it is better to start again with new plants.

## LAVATERA
The popular cultivars and hybrids of *L. thuringiaca* (tree mallow) are not fully hardy and may suffer winter damage. Left unpruned, they become very open and untidy. Prune back to a basic framework in spring after the danger of frost is past.

## LEDUM
Very little pruning is necessary. Dead-head after flowering

## LEIOPHYLLUM
Treat as for a winter-flowering heath. Trim over in spring.

## LEPTOSPERMUM
All species are tender, including the most widely grown, *L. scoparium* and its cultivars. All require the shelter of a south-facing wall. Very little pruning is necessary. Remove winter-killed growth, plus a little of the flowered growth to encourage bushiness after flowering in late sping.

## LEUCOTHOE
Very little pruning is required. If necessary, old unsightly stems may be removed at ground level after flowering in spring.

## LEYCESTERIA
*L. formosa* has a stool-like habit, breaking freely from the base. Pruning consists of cutting out at ground level old and weak growth before growth commences in spring.

## LIGUSTRUM
*L. ovalifolium* (oval-leafed privet) is widely used for hedging. For pruning as a hedge, please see entry under **Ligustrum** in Chapter 8.

Other species may be grown for foliage, flowers or fruit. Pruning in early spring to remove old or over-congested growth should respect the characteristic habits which some of these species have.

## LONICERA

Only shrubby species are considered here. For climbers, see pages 117–18.

Old wood which is weak should be cut back either to a promising new shoot or ground level, after flowering, as shown in Figs. 7.3 and 7.4.

The evergreen *L. nitida* may be used in topiary (see page 101) or as a hedge (see page 97).

## LUPINUS

*Lupinus aboreus* (tree lupin) is the only common shrubby member. Pruning consists of removing spent flower-heads to prevent seed development. In spring, young growth may be shortened and old growth cut out completely. This shrub is normally short-lived.

## MAGNOLIA

Sharp, well-set tools are essential since the wood is pithy and the bark easily damaged. Pruning should be done in mid summer once extension growth has finished. Pruning in winter is not advised since wounds are slow to heal and dieback may occur.

For *M. delavayi* and *M. grandiflora*, frequently grown as wall shrubs, see Chapter 10 (page 118).

Young tree magnolias, such as *M. campbellii*, should be trained to have a central leader. Growth may be damaged by frost and if the leader is lost another should be trained in.

Bush magnolias need very little pruning. Occasionally dead-heading may be required to prevent the development of a prodigious amount of fruit which will weaken the bush. Flowers should be cut off at their base, rather than broken out as with *Rhododendron*, because the growth buds are just below the flowers.

Cultivars of *M. × soulangeana* may produce a mass of epicormic shoots along their main stems. Unless some are required to furnish the bush, they should be rubbed off, using finger and thumb, as soon as they appear.

## MAHONIA

*M. aquifolium* (Oregon grape) is a low-growing, suckering shrub widely used for ground cover. Under good conditions it requires no pruning. Under poor conditions, such as heavy shade, it may become thin, straggly and full of fallen leaves. Here it may be rejuvenated by pruning down to 10–20 cm (4–8 in) in mid-spring.

Other species, such as *M. pinnata* and *M. japonica*, require no pruning.

The various clones within the grex *M. × media*, for example 'Charity', 'Buckland' and 'Lionel Fortescue', have a very erect habit. Whilst this can produce a shrub with a desirable architectural habit, too often gaunt, leggy plants are seen. Removal of the growing point from a young plant in late spring will result in more lateral growths and more flowers. Old plants that have become bare at their base can be renovated by cutting approximately one-third of the shoots down hard in late spring, this stimulating new basal growth. The following year more shoots can be cut down until the desired effect is produced.

## MYRICA

Members of this genus require very little pruning.

## NANDINA

*Nandina domestica* (sacred bamboo) requires a sheltered position in full sun. Old, gaunt stems are removed at ground level in spring, this stimulating the production of new basal shoots.

## NEILLIA

These shrubs have a stool-like habit. Pruning after flowering consists of removing some of the oldest wood down to ground level and reducing the height of the tallest stems.

## OEMLERIA

*Oemleria cerasiformis* (syn. *Osmaronia cerasiformis*) (Oso berry) should be pruned after flowering in early spring. The oldest and weakest stems should be removed.

## OLEARIA

A genus of evergreen shrubs, some of which are tender. Winter damage should be removed, pruning back to where re-growth is apparent in spring.

Those flowering early are pruned after flowering to remove the old flower shoots. Those flowering in late summer are left until the following spring when they are pruned in the same manner.

## OSMANTHUS

Evergreen shrubs requiring little pruning. Pruning just to shape after flowering in spring is suitable treatment for *O. delavayi*. The autumn-flowering *O. heterophyllus* is better pruned, in similar manner, in late spring just before growth starts.

## PACHYSANDRA

*Pachysandra terminalis* is widely grown as low-growing ground cover. Shearing over to approximately 8 cm (3 in) above ground level in spring is only necessary when growth becomes thin.

## PAEONIA (tree peony)

The shrubby peonies require no regular pruning. Old flower-heads die back to a terminal bud, but many look tidier if removed after the flower has faded.

Remove any dead growth which will be easier to see in the summer rather than the winter.

## PARROTIA

*P. persica* forms either a large shrub or small tree. The wide-spreading, largely horizontal branches are a beautiful feature and no pruning should be done.

## PERNETTYA

A genus of evergreen, dense-growing, suckering shrubs renowned for their winter display of marble-like berries. No regular pruning is required, except for the removal of the oldest shoots in spring. If they become too invasive, offending shoots should be removed at ground level, taking care also to remove any remaining roots or suckers.

## PEROVSKIA

*P. atriplicifolia* and the selection 'Blue Spire' are those most commonly grown. Flowering occurs in late summer; growth is left during winter, the grey stems providing winter interest, and pruning is done in spring just as the buds break. The annual growth normally dies back to near its base during winter and pruning consists of pruning hard back to where new shoots will be seen at ground level, or on a small permanent framework.

## PHILADELPHUS (mock orange)

Shrubs producing their sweetly scented flowers on short laterals from wood produced the previous year. Renewal pruning is practised [Figs. 7.3 and 7.4]. Immediately after flowering, old wood should be pruned out either to a promising new shoot or ground level. Aim to remove about one-fifth of the major branches per year. Feed and mulch generously after pruning to encourage new growth.

## PHILLYREA

A genus of evergreen shrubs. Overgrown plants respond well to hard pruning within the canopy after flowering in late spring. Overall reduction in size should be done gradually over a number of years, a few shoots being pruned each year.

## PHLOMIS

Evergreen, somewhat tender shrubs needing a well-drained sunny position. *P. fruticosa* (Jerusalem sage) is the most widely grown species. Remove winter-damaged growth and old flower stems in spring, back to new shoots which by then will be apparent. Try to keep the proportion of new growth high in the shrub, removing weak and woody growth at the same time.

## PHOTINIA

*P. villosa* is a deciduous species, mainly grown for its autumn leaf colour. No regular pruning is required.

The evergreen *P. ×fraseri* is a variable hybrid proving hardy in a sheltered position. The clone 'Birmingham' has coppery-red, and 'Red Robin' red young foliage. Any winter damage should be cut away to older wood that will re-shoot in mid spring.

## PHYSOCARPUS

This group of shrubs produces many shoots at ground level. Pruning should consist of removing at ground level the oldest shoots, plus any thin or weak shoots after flowering.

## PIERIS

Dense-growing, evergreen shrubs. No regular pruning is necessary.

The young, colourful shoots of *P. formosa*, its forms, cultivars and hybrids, are susceptible to late spring frost and should ideally be grown under dappled shade, plus sheltered from the north and east. Slight damage to this young growth may require no pruning as the shoots may continue to grow, or new shoots appear from immediately below. If severe winter damage should occur, prune back to undamaged older wood in late spring.

## PIPTANTHUS

*P. nepalensis* (syn. *P. laburnifolius*) (evergreen laburnum) is a slightly tender evergreen late spring-flowering shrub, requiring shelter from cold winds. After the danger from frost has passed, cut down to ground level old worn-out branches and prune back any winter damage to sound growth.

## PITTOSPORUM

A genus of tender evergreen shrubs requiring a sheltered position. *P. tenuifolium* is amongst the hardiest – like its many cultivars, it is grown for its attractive foliage which is often cut and used in floristry. Pruning consists of cutting out winter damage in spring.

## POTENTILLA

Left to themselves, shrubby potentillas develop a thick mass of growth that collects old leaves and looks very untidy. In early spring, take out weaker wood to the base, this opening up the centre of the bush, and shorten the previous year's growth by half.

The smaller lower-growing forms require similar treatment, involving removing weaker wood and shortening the strongest shoots.

## PRUNUS

A genus of widely varying plants. Ornamental trees are covered in Chapter 6; fruit trees are dealt with in Chapter 15; those used in hedging are mentioned in Chapter 8; and those suitable for topiary are included in Chapter 9.

*P. tenella* (dwarf Russian almond) requires no pruning. *P. triloba* and *P. glandulosa* (Chinese bush cherry) should all have stems cut back to almost ground level in mid spring immediately after flowering. *P. triloba* is sometimes grown as a half-standard and in similar manner all growth should be cut back to a couple of buds around the head of the tree.

The evergreen *P. laurocerasus* and *P. lusitanica* can be left to grow naturally and make fine screening plants. When grown in this manner, if it is necessary to regulate or reduce the size, this should be done by hard pruning individual branches in such a manner as to retain the informal shape of the shrub.

## PYRACANTHA (firethorn)

Training and pruning as a wall shrub is covered in Chapter 10 (see page 119). When grown as free-standing shrubs they require no regular pruning.

## RHAMNUS

A genus of deciduous and evergreen shrubs, best allowed to develop naturally. *R. alaternus* 'Argenteovariegata', being a little tender, requires a sheltered position and may, after a hard winter, need pruning in spring to remove winter damage.

## RHODODENDRON

Azaleas, which form a series within the genus *Rhododendron*, are included here. This is a massive group of plants, including evergreen and deciduous shrubs, many species and numerous cultivars.

In general, they require no regular pruning. Some species and hybrids may be propagated by grafting. Any suckers which arise from the rootstock should be removed as soon as seen.

As the flowers fade, the flower-heads should be removed by bending the base of the main stalk between finger and thumb [Fig. 7.21]. This prevents waste of energy in seed production and stimulates new growth. This is especially important with small, young plants, but hardly practical with very large mature plants.

Bud blast caused by the fungus *Pycnostyanus azaleae* kills flower buds [Fig. 7.22]. Infected buds should be removed and burnt.

Many rhododendrons will respond well to renovative pruning, this being carried out immediately after flowering [Figs. 7.13, 7.14, 7.15 and 7.16]. When successful, new shoots

**Fig. 7.21**
*Rhododendron*
'Doc' being dead-
headed immed-
iately after
flowering in early
summer. New
growth will rapidly
appear from where
faded flowerhead
was removed.

**Fig. 7.22** A bud of
*Rhododendron*
'Cunningham's
White' infected
with *Pycnostysanus
azaleae* (bud blast).
Flower bud be-
comes brown, then
silvery, but does
not drop off. Tiny,
black pinhead-like
structures appear
from infected buds
in spring. Any
such infected buds
should be removed
and burnt as soon
as seen.

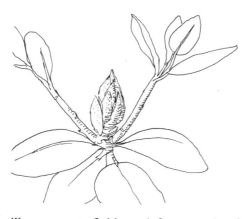

will appear out of old wood. Some species, for
example *R. ponticum*, *R. augustinii* and those
collectively known as 'Hardy Hybrids', will
respond well. With large specimens of choice
species it may be a risky procedure.

*R. ponticum* is widely used for screening and
informal hedging. Where necessary, regular
annual pruning can be done after flowering,
concealed cuts being made well into the
bushes.

## RHODOTYPOS

*Rhodotypos scandens* should be pruned after
flowering, removing old flowered shoots to
ground level or to strong new shoots.

## RHUS

The pruner is warned: some species, in
particular *R. vernix*, *R. toxicodendron* and
*R. succedanea*, can cause a skin rash on contact.
People vary in their sensitivity to different
species. Put on thick gloves and overalls to
cover all bare parts of the body before starting
to prune members of this genus.

Tree species such as *R. verniciflua* should be
trained to have a single leader when young,
pruning being done just before leaf fall to
minimize bleeding.

Several species, including *R. typhina* (stag's
horn sumach) and *R. glabra* (smooth sumach)
may form either trees or shrubs.

*R. typhina* 'Laciniata' and *R. glabra* 'Laciniata' may receive special pruning for foliage
effect. The shrub is allowed to form a woody
group of stems and then regularly pollarded in
early spring. This is combined with heavy

feeding and mulching to produce vigorous large-leaved growth.

### RIBES (currants)
Members of this genus flower on the previous season's growth. After flowering, remove old flowered branches down to a bud as close to ground level as possible. In the case of *R. san-guineum* and its cultivars, up to one third of the old branches should be removed each year [Fig. 7.3 and 7.4]. *R. sanguineum* 'Brockle-bankii', a yellow-leaved cultivar, and *R. odora-tum* are less strong-growing and although the same pruning pattern should be followed, less wood should be removed each year.

*R. speciosum* is often grown as a wall shrub, and pruning details are given in Chapter 10 (see page 120).

### ROMNEYA (tree poppy)
These plants do best in a sunny, well-drained position. The extent to which top growth is killed depends on the severity of the winter, dying down to ground level after a cold winter. Pruning should be left until spring when growth should be cut down to that still alive or, failing this, down to ground level.

### ROSMARINUS
*R. officinalis* (common rosemary) and its culti-vars are not fully hardy and may suffer damage, even in a fairly mild winter. Pruning back to undamaged growth should be done after flowering in late spring. Pruning at the same time to shorten excessively long, straggly growth is good practice, but account should be taken of the characteristic habits of cultivars such as *R. officinalis* 'Miss Jessopp's Upright' (syn. 'Fastigiatus').

### RUBUS (brambles)
Species grown for their display of white stems in winter, for example *R. cockburnianus*, *R. biflorus* and *R. thibetanus* should have their canes pruned down to ground level annually in early spring. If left, old canes lose their attractive white covering [Figs. 7.23 and 7.24].

Other species grown for their flowers require different treatment. They produce flowers on laterals from the previous season's wood. *R. odoratus* should have old flowered canes removed in early autumn. *R. delicious* does not

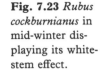

**Fig. 7.23** *Rubus cockburnianus* in mid-winter displaying its white-stem effect.

**Fig. 7.24** *Rubus cockburnianus* cut down to ground level in early spring. New shoots will already be developing below ground level to grow up rapidly during the summer and provide the next winter's display.

produce enough new wood from the base to allow all old wood to be removed after flowering. Only a proportion should be cut away, leaving a framework of older branches. *R.* 'Benenden' should be pruned in the same manner as *Philadelphus* [Figs. 7.3 and 7.4].

### RUSCUS
*R. aculeatus* (butcher's broom), *R. hypoglossum* and *R. ×microglōssus* should have old discolou-red stems removed at ground level in mid spring.

### RUTA
These shrubs are likely to be damaged in winter and require hard cutting back to un-damaged growth, plus removal of weak growth in spring.

Grown mainly for their foliage effect, the yellow flowers may be removed in summer if thought to detract from the pronounced glau-cous-blue foliage of cultivars such as *R. graveolens* 'Jackman's Blue'.

**SALIX** (willow)

Only those that are naturally shrubs or those grown for winter stem effect are considered here. For trees, see pages 58–9.

Shrubby willows need no pruning. *S. aegyptiaca* and *S. gracilistyla* 'Melanostachys' (syn. *S. melanostachys*), when grown for catkins, have the previous year's growth reduced to a few centimetres just before shoot growth commences.

Small willows, for example *S. × boydii* and *S.* 'Stuartii' frequently planted in the rock garden, require no pruning.

Strong to medium growing willows such as *S. alba* cultivars, *S. daphnoides* and *S. irrorata* may be grown for the colour of their young stems which give a colourful winter stem effect. When grown this way, plants are pollarded or coppiced annually in early spring [Figs. 7.9, 7.10, 7.11 and 7.12].

**SALVIA**

This genus contains many herbaceous species and sub-shrubs. Of the sub-shrubs, only *S. officinalis* (common sage) is reliably hardy. Prune to remove winter damage and old growth in spring.

Some of the tender species such as *S. microphylla* and *S. elegans* (syn. *S. rutilans*) may be planted at the base of a south or west-facing wall. Pruning consists of cutting back to growth still alive and undamaged, or just above ground level, when growth is just beginning in spring.

**SAMBUCUS** (elder)

When grown for foliage and fruit, a few old branches should be cut out at their base during the dormant season to maintain the vigour of the bush.

Coloured and cut-leaved cultivars such as *Sambucus racemosa* 'Plumosa Aurea' may be grown and pruned for special foliage effect as described for *Rhus typhina* 'Laciniata' and shown in Figs 7.7 and 7.8.

**SANTOLINA**

*S. chamaecyparissus* (lavender cotton) and the other species require frequent pruning. If left unpruned, the plants sprawl and are short-lived. Prune after flowering to remove old

flower stems and stalks. Eventually, despite this pruning, the shrub will become overgrown. When this occurs, cut back very hard in spring. Re-growth will be very rapid.

If grown just for foliage, or as a hedge, trim in mid spring and again as flower buds appear.

**SARCOCOCCA** (Christmas box)

These evergreen shrubs require very little pruning. Dead or worn out growth should be pruned to ground level in spring.

**SENECIO**

The evergreen species *S. greyi*, *S. laxifolius*, *S. monroi* and the hybrid *S.* 'Sunshine' all require the same pruning. In mid spring old flower stalks, leggy growth and any winter damage is removed. The weight of snow may cause branch breakage or permanent displacement; such branches should also be pruned away.

When grown in association with other grey-leaved plants in a grey border, the yellow daisy flowers of these shrubs may be inappropriate and they can be removed as the flower buds appear in summer.

**SKIMMIA**

Pruning is seldom necessary for these evergreen shrubs. If required, pruning should be done in spring.

**SORBARIA**

Strong-growing shrubs flowering on the current season's growth. Pruning is as for *Buddleja davidii* and carried out in mid winter [Figs. 7.5 and 7.6]. A larger framework should, however, be allowed to develop, strong basal growths being used to replace old parts of the framework.

**SPARTIUM**

*Spartium junceum* (Spanish broom) is a large shrub. Left unpruned it develops a top-heavy straggly habit. Trim shoots back to within 25 cm (10 in) of a framework in mid spring.

**SPIRAEA**

Shrubs in this genus fall into two groups. *S. × vanhouttei* and *S.* 'Arguta' are members of the group that flower on one-year-old wood.

Pruning consists of removing older flowered wood just after flowering in early summer to encourage new growth on which next year's flowers will be borne. Old shoots may be either cut down to ground level or just above a suitable new growth.

Others, such as *S. japonica* and *S. douglasii*, flower on the current season's growth. This group is hard pruned to within 10–13 cm (4–5 in) above ground in late winter.

## STACHYURUS
*S. praecox* and *S. chinensis* have graceful arching habits that should be preserved. Annual pruning is not required, but occasionally old wood may be removed at ground level, in the spring after flowering, to encourage the production of new growth.

## STAPHYLEA (bladder nut)
These generally have a suckering habit. Pruning is done in the winter, removing some of the oldest wood.

## STEPHANANDRA
*S. incisa* is grown for its very graceful habit and *S. tanakae* for its habit plus the rich brown of its stems, most noticeable in the winter. In early spring cut out at ground level some of the oldest branches, being careful to retain the overall shape.

## STEWARTIA
This genus requires no regular pruning.

## STRANVAESIA
See **Photinia** on page 78.

## STYRAX
Stronger-growing members of this genus, for example *S. japonica*, can be trained with a single leader to form small trees. Other shrubby species need no formative pruning.

Late frost may damage new growth which will then need trimming back.

## SYCOPSIS
Evergreen winter-flowering shrub of which only *S. sinensis* is in general cultivation. No regular pruning is required.

## SYMPHORICARPOS
Dense-growing, suckering shrubs. There is little need for regular pruning, but occasionally the oldest shoots may be cut out at ground level in early spring.

## SYRINGA (lilac)
Cultivars of *S. vulgaris* require little pruning except the removal of old flower heads to prevent waste of energy in seed production. After several years, renovative pruning may be required [Figs. 7.13, 7.14, 7.15 and 7.16]. Plants are often grafted onto common lilac or privet. Common lilac suckers are not easy to distinguish from those of the flowering cultivar and any shoot coming from below ground level should be removed as soon as seen.

*S. ×prestoniae*, *S. reflexa*, *S. meyeri* and *S. microphylla* require light renewal pruning immediately after flowering. Small branches that have borne flowers are cut back to vigorous new growth and a few of the oldest stems removed at ground level.

## TAMARIX (tamarisk)
*T. tetandra* and *T. parviflora* are spring flowering on the previous year's growth. Long, untidy growth may be removed after flowering.

*T. ramosissima* (syn. *T. pentandra*) and *T. gallica* flower on the current season's growth in summer. Pruning consists of shortening flowered shoots to within 5–8 cm (2–3 in) of an established framework.

## TEUCRIUM
*Teucrium fruticans* (shrubby germander) is not fully hardy and is usually given a sheltered site. An untidy grower, unwanted growth can be cut back in spring, but not until new growth indicates the extent of winter injury.

## ULEX
Dense, spiny shrubs which over time accumulate a lot of dead growth. Every two or three years after spring flowering, prune back growth that has flowered, opening up the centre and removing dead growth.

Very straggly, over-grown plants can be hard pruned to almost ground level in spring.

## VACCINIUM

Members of this genus grown as ground cover in the ornamental garden require no regular pruning. For blueberries grown as fruiting plants, see Chapter 16 (see page 198).

## VIBURNUM

Overall, little pruning is required. Those deciduous species that produce vigorous growth from the base may have worn out old branches removed in early spring. Care must be taken, however, since others grow from the periphery of a permanent framework and do not produce strong basal shoots. In the case of *V. plicatum* 'Mariesii', the very characteristic horizontally tiered nature of the branching is a very important characteristic and must be retained. Winter-flowering species such as *V. farreri* are pruned after flowering in mid spring.

Evergreen species require little pruning, but any winter damage may be removed in spring. Overgrown plants of *V. tinus* respond well to hard rejuvenative pruning in late spring.

## WEIGELA

Members of this genus flower on short laterals produced on the previous year's wood. Pruning should aim to keep a good balance between older and young wood, renewal pruning being carried out just after flowering [Figs. 7.3 and 7.5].

The yellow-leafed *W.* 'Looymansii Aurea' needs slightly harder pruning than green-leafed cultivars grown for their flowers. This is because the best large-leafed foliage is produced on young vigorous wood.

*W. florida* 'Variegata' needs the same pruning as the rest of the genus, but it is very inclined to throw reverted shoots and these should be removed as soon as seen.

## ZENOBIA

Shrubs with a suckering habit. Prune after flowering. Dead-head and shorten weak growth to where new growth is apparent. Occasionally some of the oldest wood may be removed at ground level.

# CHAPTER 8

# *Hedges*

## Origins and purpose

The traditional image of the English country-side is of a gently undulating landscape, divided into a patchwork of small fields of various shades of green, by a criss-cross pattern of hedgerows with hedgerow trees. This view was typical of much of lowland Britain from the eighteenth century till the mid twentieth century, where the principal land use was agricultural pasture. The hedges performed a dual role. They were barriers to prevent the straying of livestock, and they were boundary markers to identify land ownership. This pattern may still be seen along the Welsh borders, and also in northern France, but elsewhere changes in agricultural practice have completely altered the rural scene. The increased mechanization of agriculture from the 1940s onwards led to a drop in the farming population, so that manpower was not available for the traditional hedgerow mainten-ance. The increased profitability of arable farming led to a demand for larger fields, so that many thousands of miles of hedge were re-moved in the drive to achieve higher yields of cereals, and to facilitate the use of machinery on a grand scale.

Even where livestock were kept, they were continuously housed and machines were used to harvest the pasture for feeding (zero grazing) or for making hay or silage. In these cases the role of hedgerows as barriers was obsolete. Some farmers grubbed them out by the mile. Others retained them and used the flail mower to trim their top and sides. The result of this practice is to produce a narrow strip of muti-lated shrubs, hollow at the base and providing neither barrier to livestock nor cover for wild-life. The top is cut annually so that it produces little or no flower bud and no winter food for birds, and this token relic serves little purpose agriculturally, environmentally or aesthetic-ally.

The rate of hedgerow removal has declined since the 1970s, when it had been estimated at 5000 miles per year in England alone. How-ever, even with schemes to curtail the over production of cereals such as the 'Set aside' scheme, it is unlikely that there will be any significant replacement of lost hedgerows in the countryside.

In the domestic landscape too, hedges have had mixed fortunes. In the fifteenth and sixteenth centuries, they were very popular. They were clipped to produce a close surface texture with dense foliage, and were used in formal designs such as the dwarf box hedges of English knot gardens, and French parterres. Yew was planted and clipped to form mazes, and hedges were sculpted into shapes resembling walls with colonnades, arches and castellations, taking them into the realms of topiary.

From the seventeenth to the eighteenth centuries the formality of these gardens was replaced by the new fashion of the grand vista, with its uninterrupted views of distant park-land, often with a lake in the foreground. This was the hallmark of designers like Capability Brown, and in their schemes hedges had no part to play, not even for the distant boundar-ies at the edge of the estate. These had to be stock proof and to achieve this the sunken ditch or 'ha-ha' was developed.

From the mid nineteenth to twentieth century the hedge again became an important feature of the domestic landscape. In the new suburban housing developments of Victorian Britain the hedges provided a boundary between gardens, and was used to divert the eye, to form screens and to create areas of privacy, as well as providing seasonal effects such as flowers, and fruits. The cumulative mileage of such hedging must run into thousands of miles, giving food and shelter to a host of wild animals.

The manicured tightly knit 'formal hedge' still has a place as a living structure making an unequivocal statement, such as the clear definition of a boundary fence, or as a structural element in a geometrical garden design.

In the 1960s many suburban housing estates were built to an 'open plan' design, which prohibited householders from growing boundary hedges. Their use of rows of shrubs which have a more relaxed appearance and are not regularly clipped has led to the now widely used 'informal hedge'.

A more recent interest reflects the concern over the loss of traditional rural hedgerows. In the urban fringe, some of the larger gardens are using native plants and traditional hedgerow management, such as hedge laying, in an attempt to recreate the countryside, in their garden. This is a small movement still in its infancy which is generally associated with wild corners, wild flower meadows and a desire to keep alive traditional skills.

Hedgerows today are in competition with many other instant forms of fencing, available through garden centres. These include wood-en panels of various designs, wire netting, pre-cast walling blocks as well as ranch style post and rail fencing, available in wood or in snap-together plastic.

These promise an immediate effect, no maintenance and a very narrow profile occupying a minimum of space. In contrast a hedge requires regular maintenance and takes several years to reach its intended size. A further problem is the availability of hedging plants. They are required in quantity, and used to be available in bundles of 50 or so, field grown, freshly dug, and sold bare-rooted at modest cost. Nowadays such plants are rarely found. Most are retailed in containers, in which they have been grown, and sell at a price which is acceptable for a specimen tree or shrub, but outrageous for hedging quantities. Fashion also plays a part in shaping people's preferences. *Ligustrum* spp. (privet hedge), so extensively planted in the 1930s and 1940s, has hardly been planted since. *Lonicera nitida*, often erroneously called a 'box' hedge, was popular in the 1950s but many were killed in the bitterly cold winter of 1963, and when replaced, the ×*Cupressocyparis leylandii* (Ley-

**Fig. 8.1** Formal hedge profiles to reduce self shading, and to shed snow.
(*a*) Rounded.
(*b*) Chamfered.

*Formal hedge profiles to reduce self-shading and to shed snow*

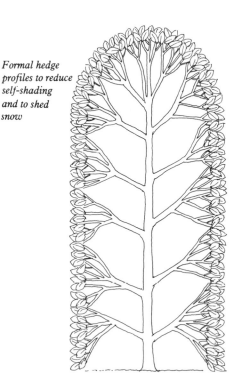

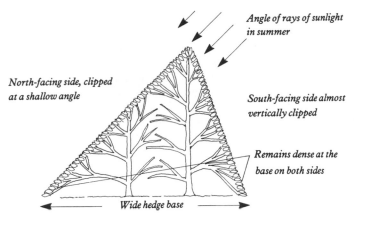

**Fig. 8.2**
Asymmetric hedge
profile to minimize
self shading of the
base of the hedge.

Angle of rays of sunlight
in summer

North-facing side, clipped
at a shallow angle

South-facing side almost
vertically clipped

Remains dense at the
base on both sides

Wide hedge base

land cypress) had come into vogue. This has made a very powerful impact on the suburban scene, but its popularity is now declining in favour of a wide variety of alternatives. *Fagus* spp. (beech) and *Carpinus* spp. (hornbeam) will probably emerge as the new favourites.

## Formal hedges

The production of a hedge with a formal close-knit surface, right down to soil level, is the result of advance preparation and good after-care. The plant should be well branched at the outset and planted into well prepared ground at a suitable density. Care should be taken to place plants precisely on the planting line to avoid kinks in the line. If it is intended that the hedge should be flat-topped or wide, it is desirable to plant in a double row either side of a length of sheep netting. This will define the boundary line while the plants are small and may later be used to tie in any straggling branches. The growth of the plants through the fence, to interlock with each other, helps to create a stable hedge which will resist splitting when laden with snow or in stormy weather.

To create a dense branch framework at the base of the hedge it is necessary to encourage short stocky growth with frequent lateral branching. This is achieved by lateral tipping of the sides of the young hedge, to overcome apical dominance and promote laterals. In addition the hedge should be shaped to ensure that the lower branches receive adequate light. As young plants this is likely to present no difficulty, as the top is naturally narrower than the base [Fig. 8.1], but as the hedge thickens

above, there is increasing risk of the basal branches being shaded and ultimately dying to produce a bare base. Little can be done to retrieve the situation if this occurs. It is advisable therefore to avoid allowing the hedge to grow too long before clipping and, if possible, adopt a hedge profile with gently sloping sides so as to minimize self shading. If circumstances permit, the hedge sides can be cut fairly erect on the south-facing side.

This asymmetric profile increases light interception on the north side, but this advantage must be weighed against the greater area that such a hedge occupies [Fig. 8.2]. Once the hedge has reached the desired height and shape, it requires regular light clipping to maintain its quality.

In recent years various chemical growth retardents have been marketed specifically for use on hedges. Two products have current approvals for use in the UK. They are maleic hydrazide and dikegulac sodium. In addition, paclobutrazol has recommendations for use on trees and shrubs, so could have potential. The precise recommendations for use depend upon the plant species, but in general they are applied during an active phase of growth. They may be sprayed onto uncut foliage and allowed time to be absorbed, before cutting, or applied to the freshly trimmed hedge. In either case growth is stopped and the plant remains in the newly cut condition for several months. Hawthorn and privet hedges respond particularly well.

One drawback with privet is that it is semi-evergreen, and when sprayed and cut, the younger foliage is removed leaving only older leaves. These have to provide the foliar cover right through to the next spring, and in my experience most of them are lost in autumn, leaving a very bare hedge for several months. This is something of a loss of amenity value and shelter for wildlife during the winter.

The regular close clipping of a formal hedge, so as to maintain the surface texture, will almost certainly remove most of the flower buds, and therefore there will be no winter berries. All-year-round amenity value in these plants is usually provided by the retention of leaves. The choice of species should therefore take the leaf size and shape into consideration. If the hedge is to be of modest size the plants must have small leaves, for example *Buxus* spp. (box tree), but large-leaved plants are suitable, if a little coarse, when the hedge is large, for example *Prunus laurocerasus* (cherry laurel).

## Renovating a neglected hedge

If a hedge is allowed to become overgrown with long leggy shoots, or if it develops bare patches at the base, some drastic action will be required to restore it to good condition. Some species cannot tolerate this treatment and will have to be replaced. Others grow so slowly that it may be better to start afresh with new plants. Alternatively it may be possible to disguise the problem by some careful planting.

If severe pruning is chosen, then it is sensible to do it all at the same time, both sides and top, cutting back about 15 cm (6 in) more than the desired final size.

On the cut stems new buds will be stimulated, and they will give bushy growth which can be clipped lightly for two to three years to form a dense surface, gradually thickening the hedge until it reaches the required size. Winter is the best time for this treatment, giving a minimum delay before new growth appears and minimizing the duration of the ugly cut condition. See the species list at the end of this chapter for notes on the tolerance of each species to hard pruning.

See also the section on the laying of rustic hedges as a method of revitalizing a bare and gappy hedge.

If the species is unsuitable for hard pruning it may be desirable to dig it out and replant.

This may be a very difficult task, and the decision should not be undertaken lightly, especially when the hedge is old, access is difficult or the hedge is long. The possibility of filling in the bare base or covering it up with new plants should not be overlooked. Gaps may be filled with plants of the same species, or the opportunity may be taken to introduce some new variety, such as roses, yew or privet. Alternatively a low hedge or row of ornamentals could be grown at the hedge base to screen the bare areas. Suitable shade-tolerant subjects would be *Buxus* spp. (box tree), *Lonicera* spp. (shrubby honeysuckle) or *Euonymus* spp. for growing as a low hedge; or *Hypericum calycinum* (rose of sharon), *Vinca* spp. (periwinkle), *Alchemilla mollis* (lady's mantle), or *Hedera* spp. (ivy), as an ornamental foreground.

## Informal, flowering and mixed hedges

The ornamental value of a hedge may be greatly increased by choosing plants which will produce flowers in summer and fruits in winter. These will require pruning in such a way that flower buds are retained, and in general this means that arching shoots are allowed to grow from the main hedge body. The control of size is achieved by selective removal of shoots using secateurs – shears would leave cut twigs which look quite out of place on an otherwise natural plant shape.

Some plants form their flower buds on woody twigs which grew the previous year. Since the buds are fully formed during the winter they are able to break open and flower early in spring, as soon as the weather is suitable. This may even be before the foliage so that the flowers are seen throughout the dense framework of leafless twigs (for example *Forsythia* spp., *Chaenomeles* spp. (Japanese quince), *Prunus spinosa* (sloe), some of the loveliest harbingers of spring. Usually, however, leaves obscure any flowers produced within the hedge, so that growth produced one year should be thinned but substantially left, so that it will bear flowers the next spring. After flowering, if fruits are not an ornamental feature, these growths are cut back and there is sufficient time for new growths to mature, for flowering the following year.

Those plants which flower on wood produced in the current year, may be pruned in winter by cutting back quite severely. In spring vigorous growth occurs and bears flowers in mid to late summer. The dead flowers may be removed, unless ornamental fruit is produced, but other growth may be left to enable the plant to produce food stores. In winter pruning restores the plant to the desired size.

The use of several species together in a hedge can be highly decorative. Splashes of evergreen, autumn colours, flowers and fruits combine to give year-round interest. However, the different rates of growth of different species, their differing tolerance to shade, and various plant habits all combine to make a very untidy appearance. The shrubs are inclined to be torn apart in stormy weather and it is generally not satisfactory as an informal hedge. When clipped, however, the mixed hedge works rather better and perhaps merits the more glamorous description 'Tapestry hedge'.

An old hedge may be used to provide support for a wide variety of climbers. This is not strictly a mixed hedge and the plants should be treated separately from the point of view of pruning. If the climber is an annual, the hedge may be clipped in spring or autumn

without damaging the climber. Perennial climbers will however obscure the hedge, so that selective shoot removal with secateurs is all that can be done. This results in an informal hedge base, with the informality exaggerated by the overgrowth of climber (see Table 8.1).

## Environmental hedges

The importance of hedges to birds is self-evident to anyone who has watched birds feeding their young on the nest. The hedge provides shelter from the weather, cover from predators, a food supply in the form of insects and berries, sites for nest building and vantage points for territorial and mating displays.

Though less obvious, many other animals also rely on either the hedge or its associated banks or ditches. In particular, small mammals, reptiles and amphibia use hedges as corridors for movement between habitats and may nest in, and find food in, hedge bottoms.

The invertebrates too are found in abundance on hedges and on the characteristic herbaceous plants found alongside them.

The wildlife value of hedges can be maximized by care in the choice of species, and subsequent aftercare [Fig. 8.3]. Hawthorn is host to a very wide range of invertebrates providing food for many other animals. Elm, hazel and beech are also good but hornbeam, holly, conifers, and most ornamentals are poor. A hedge with a wide base of 1 m (3 ft) provides most cover for small animals, and a minimum height of 1.2 m (4 ft) is recommended to encourage birds. Pruning should allow flowering and fruiting to occur so as to provide nectar for insects and winter bird food. Clipping the hedge will produce the close surface texture which gives a dense leafy shelter. These four requirements – a wide base, reasonable height, flowering and close texture – may all be combined as follows.

Plant the hedge on as wide a base as space permits and for the first few years clip the outer plants so as to develop sloping hedge sides. The ultimate shape should be a wedge, usually referred to as an 'A' profile.

Do not clip the top twigs, so that they remain as wispy shoots. These provide vantage points for displaying birds and will bear flowers and fruit. They may be allowed to grow on to form hedgerow trees if desired. Clip the sides of the

---

**Table 8.1 Climbers suitable for planting into or growing over hedges**

*Aristolochia macrophylla* (Dutchman's pipe)
*Aristolochia sempervirens* (evergreen birthwort)
*Calystegia sepium* (bellbine, large bindweed)
*Clematis montana* (small-flowered clematis)
*Eccremocarpus scaber* (not fully hardy so treat as an annual)
*Fallopia baldschuanica* (syn. *Polygonum baldschuanicum*) (Russian vine)
*Hedera helix* (English ivy)
*Humulus lupulus* (hop) (variegated forms are available)
*Lonicera periclymenum* (woodbine or honeysuckle)
*Passiflora caerulea* (passion flower) (top gets frosted but base survives)
*Rosa wichuraiana*, *Rosa canina* (scrambling roses)
*Tropaeolum speciosum* (climbing nasturtium)

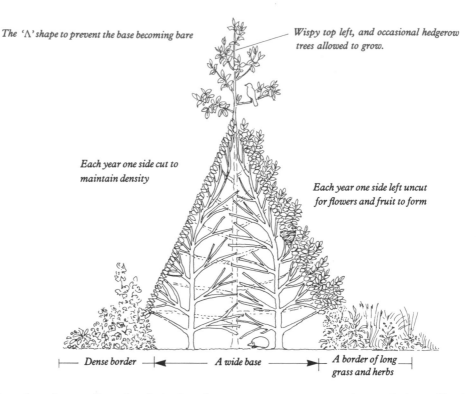

The '∧' shape to prevent the base becoming bare

Wispy top left, and occasional hedgerow trees allowed to grow.

Each year one side cut to maintain density

Each year one side left uncut for flowers and fruit to form

Dense border | A wide base | A border of long grass and herbs

**Fig. 8.3** The ideal environmental hedge.

hedge, in winter after the fruit has been stripped. This will cause minimum disturbance to birds. If possible do not clip both sides each year, but rather, clip one side one year and the other side the next year. The heavier growth will be more difficult to trim than if it was cut annually, but in compensation, only one side has to be cut. This allows abundant flowering and fruiting whilst maintaining the impression of a hedge under control.

On a large scale, hedges may be maintained in this way by cutting with a flail trimmer. Use a light flail and make two passes along the side to be cut, one low one and the other covering the upper half of the side. These hedges are very suitable for use as agricultural boundaries and have been widely adopted by conservation-minded farmers as a contribution to wildlife, which can be implemented at little or no commercial cost.

The use of growth-retardant chemicals is very successful on *Craetagus* (hawthorn) and is not known to present any hazards to birds and insects. However, some products specify that livestock should not have access to treated foliage for six weeks and it is important that the products should not be allowed to contaminate

water courses, such as ditches. Check the limitations of use on these products before use.

## Traditional laid hedges

The laying of a hedge creates a stockproof barrier out of a gappy overgrown hedge or one which has become bare at the base. It is a technique which is still widely practised in the English Midlands and Welsh borders and

---

**Table 8.2 Plants suitable for hedge laying**

*Acer campestre* (field maple)
*Alnus glutinosa* (alder)
*Carpinus betulus* (hornbeam)
*Corylus avellana* (hazel)
*Crataegus monogyna* (hawthorn)
*C. laevigata* (Midland thorn)
*Fagus sylvatica* (beech)
*Ilex aquifolium* (holly)
*Malus sylvestris* (crab apple)
*Prunus cerasifera* (cherry plum or myrobalan)
*Prunus domestica institia* (bullace)
*Prunus spinosa* (blackthorn or sloe)
*Quercus robur* (oak)
*Ulmus* spp. (elm)

would be more commonly seen in domestic gardens if the technique of laying was more widely understood. There are many regional variations in style but the general purpose Midlands hedge provides a suitable model which could be used in most situations.

Plants which are suitable for laying are listed in Table 8.2. These have the ability to regrow following severe cutting, and their bark is pliable enough to allow the laying of stems without breaking off. Poisonous species should not be used where livestock have access. Any size of tree may be laid, but old wood tends to be dry and brittle and with the weight of the branches a large tree may be difficult to handle when its base has been cut. Stems are best for laying when they are up to 15 cm (6 in) diameter. They must also have enough height to bridge any gaps between plants, and to be held by at least two stakes. These are placed about 75 cm (2 ft 6 in) apart so the stems should

ideally be at least 2 cm (6 ft) tall before laying. It does not matter whether this tall growth is branched and twiggy or consists of straight shoots, as it will eventually form an almost horizontal framework. To achieve the desired height it may be necessary to leave the hedge untrimmed for three years or even more, before laying can begin.

If the site is sloping, the hedge should be laid uphill. This looks more pleasing and helps to maintain an upward slope on each stem. If laid flat or with a downward slope, branches tend to die back.

Using a slasher, cut out any bramble (*Rubus*) or briar (*Rosa*) and other hedgerow weed which is obscuring the stem bases. Clean out any stones, litter or wire that may blunt tools, cause them to slip or cause injury. Remove any elderberry (*Sambucus*) by sawing or cutting it out at soil level. The stump can be treated with herbicide to kill it off. This is because elder is so

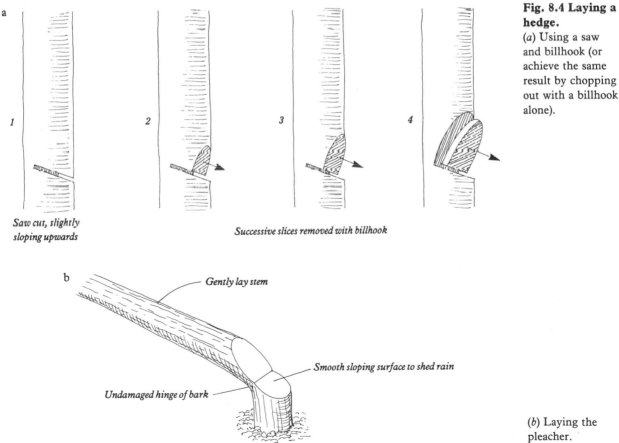

a

1

*Saw cut, slightly sloping upwards*

2

3

4

*Successive slices removed with billhook*

b

*Gently lay stem*

*Smooth sloping surface to shed rain*

*Undamaged hinge of bark*

**Fig. 8.4 Laying a hedge.**
(*a*) Using a saw and billhook (or achieve the same result by chopping out with a billhook alone).

(*b*) Laying the pleacher.

**Fig. 8.5** Trimming a split stem. If the wood is brittle or the distance *a* is too short, splits can occur as shown. Cut off the stump with a saw and trim up rough surfaces.

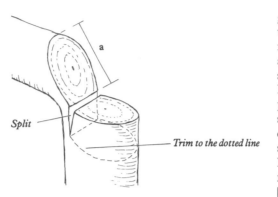

Split

a

Trim to the dotted line

vigorous that it will shade the hedge causing a bare patch.

Start at the top of the slope, or alongside a gap and work backwards down the slope or away from the gap. With upward strokes of the slasher, cut the branches between stems so that they no longer interlock. Using a billhook or saw, remove any low horizontal branches which would prevent the stem being laid down away from you (uphill or into the gap). Remove any other branches which give the hedge excessive width, front or back, or which are inextricably tangled with other stems.

Using the billhook, cut and lay each stem in turn. The procedure is quite straightfoward, but requires stamina and some courage. At about 10 cm (4 in) from the ground, make a cut into the near side of the stem. This should be

gently sloping upwards and should go about three-quarters of the way through the stem. It may be cut with a small hand saw, chain saw or a billhook [Fig. 8.4*a*]. Now chop away the near side of the stem, down onto the cut, so that a long wedge is removed. This chopping may be performed with one hand whilst holding the stem with the other. When the wedge has been cut deeply enough into the stem, it will suddenly feel more pliant and may be gently laid down away from you with the stem forming an angle of about 30° to the ground [Fig. 8.4*b*]. A long tapering wedge gives greatest flexibility and good control over the depth of the cuts. Any protruding stub can be trimmed off to minimize frost injury and entry of disease [Fig. 8.5].

Each stem, called a pleacher (or plasher) is cut and laid (pleached) in turn, forming a series of parallel stems at a 30° angle to the ground. They are very vulnerable at this stage and may be easily broken off by wind and storms. They are stabilized, and pinned into place, by inserting cheap untreated timber stakes, placed either upright or at an angle, sloping in the opposite direction to the pleachers. These are spaced according to the height of the hedge but commonly about 75 cm (2 ft 6 in) apart.

At the end of the hedge when the last stems are laid there will be a gap. This is filled by weaving pieces of brushwood back into the hedge in the opposite direction.

At this stage the hedge looks very untidy, but

**Fig. 8.6** The main components of a laid hedge.

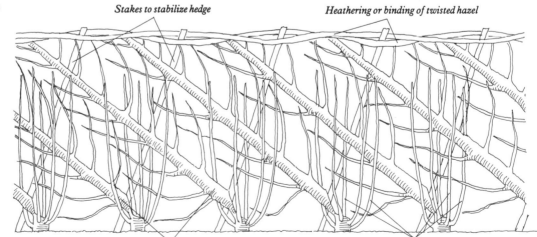

Stakes to stabilize hedge

Heathering or binding of twisted hazel

Pleachers cut and laid

'Coppice shoots' arising from cut stumps

do not despair. Weave long lengths of hazel called wands, heathering or bindings in and out of the stakes, to create a finished top to the hedge. Knock all stakes in to a level height [Fig. 8.6]. Trim the tops of the stakes to leave attractive clean cut surfaces. Pull pieces of brushwood into any thin areas, and insert new plants into larger gaps. Trim off the brushwood to create a neat finish. The result is a substantial living hedge of angled stems. In time vigorous coppice shoots will grow from the stem bases and grow through the brush to form a living stockade of vertical shoots. This results in great stability after one or two years, by which time the stakes and heatherings will have begun to decay.

Light trimming with shears over the next few years will create a dense hedge with an impenetrable core of branches. Even after 20 years of trimming, if the hedge bottoms become thin and bare, the core will remain as a barrier to stock and against trespassers.

The hedge may eventually need relaying. This is more difficult and requires removal of dead wood so that the best stems can be selected for pleaching. Those vertical shoots arising from angled stems are cut and laid forming pleachers on pleachers. An alternative approach is to cut the entire hedge off, therefore coppicing about 7.5 cm (3 in) from the ground, and then manage the new growth as if it were a new hedge.

When newly cut and laid, the hedge is neat and tidy but rather thin and it gives little shelter to wildlife. However, as the years pass, it becomes an increasingly valuable habitat.

## Hedgerow plants for every need

In the following alphabetical list of plants, most of the subjects used in temperate areas are described, together with an account of their suitability for different kinds of hedging. It is possible to grow virtually any shrub in rows and call them an informal hedge, but the list here is confined to those which have been known to perform well in practice. For plants which are not listed, the general pruning requirements may be summarized as follows.

For non-flowering deciduous hedges and evergreens, trim soon after the spring flush of growth. This allows sufficient time for any stimulated growth to harden before winter, and ensures that the hedge looks its best for most of the year. If growth is vigorous a second clipping in early autumn may be required. For flowering hedges, observe carefully to determine whether flowers are borne on wood formed the previous year or on new shoots of the current year. In the former case (flowering on old wood), delay clipping until after flowering. If this is very early in the year flowering may be followed by a growth flush. Opinions vary as to whether one should prune immediately after flowering but before the growth (i.e. in spring), or whether to wait until the growth has occurred (i.e. in summer). If pruned in spring there will be growth after pruning, leaving a very informal or in some people's view, an unkempt appearance, for most of the year and abundant flowering. Summer pruning will give a 'tidy', but for some people an overgroomed appearance for most of the year, but flowering will be confined to the older branch framework within the hedge.

If flowers are borne on shoots produced in the same year, then pruning must be undertaken in winter before bud break so that the plants have all spring to make the necessary growth to bear the flowers. These plants will inevitably have an informal appearance for most of the year since they will probably not flower until midsummer, when the shoots have grown sufficiently.

## ACER CAMPESTRE (field maple)

Also sometimes called hedge maple, due to its frequent occurrence in agricultural hedges. It makes an attractive hedgerow tree to about 7 m (25 ft) and forms attractive tree screens, the foliage turning golden yellow in autumn. It is rather a dry and brittle wood, but can be laid successfully. It is best used as an ingredient in mixed hedges, rather than on its own.

## ALNUS INCANA (grey alder)

This is a very hardy tree, capable of growing on exposed coastal sites and also on very wet soils. It makes a tree to 7 m (25 ft) and has been widely planted in recent years as tree screens, for shelter, in orchards of top fruit. It may be cut and laid successfully. It is a useful ingredient in mixed hedges.

## BERBERIS DARWINII, B. GAGNEPAINII, B. SANGUINEA (syn. B. PANLANENSIS) B. × STENOPHYLLA

These evergreen barberries are suitable for informal flowering hedges. They do not recover well if cut back hard, so care should be taken to prevent them becoming bare at the base. Ensure that the lower branches are not shaded, by thinning out the upper arching branches after flowering in spring. The spiny leaves and stipules add to their value as impenetrable hedges. *Berberis gagnepainii* and *B. sanguinea* are small and dense in habit to about 1.5 m (5 ft). *B. darwinii* and *B. × stenophylla* will grow to 2.5 m (8 ft), have longer sprays of foliage and have the freer form of a wholly informal hedge.

## BERBERIS THUNBERGII

This deciduous shrub also produces yellow flowers in spring and is well known for its red autumn leaf colour. It makes an attractive informal hedge to about 1 m (3 ft). For added effect it may be mixed with the slightly faster growing red-leaved form 'Atropurpurea', which may also be used alone for an informal red hedge.

The form 'Atropurpurea Nana' is a dwarf subject growing to about 50 cm (1 ft 6 in). Like all barberries it flowers on shoots which grew the previous year, so it is suited to an informal habit. However, this looks untidy in a dwarf hedge so it should be clipped, after flowering. These forms are all capable of recovering from severe pruning.

## BUXUS SEMPERVIRENS (common box)

An evergreen shrub growing to about 3 m (10 ft) which responds well to clipping throughout the summer to produce a close textured formal hedge or for topiary. It is poisonous and should not be used where livestock have access. The form 'Handsworthensis' is recommended for tall hedges and screens, while the form 'Suffruticosa' is the dwarf form or 'edging' box which may be used for the miniature formal hedges in parterres, knot gardens, and as a decorative edging to paths.

Frequent clipping with generous feeding should prevent it becoming bare at the base,

but if an old hedge requires renovation, it may be cut back hard and should recover, although regrowth will be slow.

## CARPINUS BETULUS (hornbeam)

A versatile plant which deserves wider appreciation. As a specimen plant it makes an attractive deciduous tree particularly suited to urban planting, while as a clipped hedge it develops a close texture and the dead leaves remain attached to the twigs until well into the winter. This is due to the maintenance of its juvenile habit by clipping. A habit it shares with *Fagus* sp. (beech). Clipping should be performed in mid to late summer, to produce a formal hedge. Its fairly rigid stems enable it to be grown tall but narrow. Hornbeam also responds well to hard pruning and can be cut and laid. It is a useful addition to a mixed hedgerow where its dry leaves give variety to its winter appearance.

## CHAENOMELES SPECIOSA (Japanese quince or japonica)

A rather thorny deciduous shrub which bears red, pink or white flowers very early in spring before the foliage. The flowers are the main attribute of this plant as a hedge, though its rather stiff habit and thorns do make it impenetrable. It should be pruned in early summer after flowering, but it will not make a very close textured surface so is best used as a semi-formal hedge.

## CHAMAECYPARIS LAWSONIANA (Lawson's cypress)

This evergreen conifer is available in a bewildering range of forms, each with its own characteristic habit and colour. Many of these are suitable for producing an informal screen of trees. However, for hedging purposes choose the 'type' species if it is available, or the named form 'Green Hedger'. These have a dense texture when pruned. Trim lightly in early summer, following the annual flush of spring growth. Clipping tends to disfigure the attractive sprays of foliage, so tidy up afterwards with some careful secateur work. Avoid hard pruning back to older wood as this plant may not recover.

## CHAMAECYPARIS PISIFERA (Sarawa cypress)

An evergreen conifer not widely used as a hedge but which has potential in a semi-formal setting. There are several named forms which feature the delightfully soft and fluffy juvenile foliage. Among the best are 'Plumosa', 'Squarrosa' and 'Boulevard'. Treat as for *Chamaecyparis lawsoniana*.

## CORYLUS AVELLANA (hazelnut)

The erect unbranched stems of hazel do not readily produce side branches when pruned so it is a most unlikely hedging subject. However, it is a very valuable addition to a laid hedge since its stems are very pliant and regenerate well after cutting back hard.

## COTONEASTER SIMONSII

A semi-evergreen with small inconspicuous flowers much visited by bees, and large red berries which birds enjoy. It is best grown as an informal hedge and may reach 2 m (6 ft). Light pruning is all that is required to keep it tidy. Do this in late summer or in early winter after the berries have been taken. If it becomes overgrown it may be cut back very hard in winter.

## CRATAEGUS MONOGYNA (hawthorn, quick, or May blossom)

An extremely hardy and versatile plant which grows well in most districts including coastal sites. It becomes tightly matted when regularly clipped as a formal hedge. It also bears white flowers much visited by insects, and red berries or haws which are eaten by birds in winter. It withstands hard pruning and is probably the best plant for hedge laying. It should form the main ingredient of environmental hedges in the UK since it is a native plant with very high wildlife value. Although it is the principal hedgerow plant in rural areas it is not favoured in apple-growing areas since it may act as a reservoir for the bacterial disease fire blight.

## CRATAEGUS LAEVIGATA
(Midlands thorn)

As for *C. monogyna* above.

## × CUPRESSOCYPARIS LEYLANDII (Leyland cypress)

This evergreen conifer has been extensively planted in the UK over the past 20 years, to form instant screens in suburban areas, and windbreaks in agriculture. Unfortunately its rapidity of growth requires that it should be clipped twice a year in spring and autumn. It does not produce a very tight foliage surface, giving a semi-formal appearance. Unclipped it may grow to 15 m (50 ft) in 16 years. Before planting this subject, give serious consideration to its suitability. Once it has grown out of reach it may require expensive maintenance or lopping. It is only moderately tolerant of hard pruning.

Alternate planting of green and golden forms gives an interesting tapestry effect (for example 'Leighton Green' and 'Castlewellan Gold').

## ELAEAGNUS × EBBINGEI and E. PUNGENS

Evergreens, with oval leathery leaves, suitable for large informal shelter hedges on coastal sites. They may be lightly pruned in spring to control size. They can grow to 2.5 m (8 ft).

## ESCALLONIA RUBRA var. MACRANTHA

This fast-growing evergreen has glossy dark green leaves bearing clusters of red flowers, much visited by bees. It is suitable for coastal sites but will not tolerate extreme cold. However it can regenerate if cut down by frosts. It is good as a wide informal hedge to 2 m (6 ft). Trim off winter-damaged shoots in spring and shorten new growth after flowering in mid summer.

## EUONYMUS JAPONICUS

This is a rather unfashionable glossy evergreen shrub, which was widely planted in suburban London for its ability to withstand pollution. It may be clipped into formal hedges 1–2 m (3–6 ft) high. It develops a close texture when clipped frequently (spring and autumn) and may be used as a dwarf hedge. For added interest, the yellow-splashed foliage of the form 'Aureus' (syn. 'Aureopictus') is recommended.

**FAGUS SYLVATICA** (common beech)

This is one of the finest hedging plants for formal work. It is deciduous but retains its brown dry leaves throughout the winter. In spring they fall and are replaced with new soft pale green foliage. Clip annually in mid summer, to promote a flush of growth giving a close knit mesh of twigs. The wood is very tough and hard, enabling the hedge to be grown very tall, but on a narrow base. This is seen at its best in the magnificent hedge at Meikleour in Perthshire, Scotland which is clipped to a height of 26 m (85 ft) and is 550 m (600 yds) long.

For added interest some plants of the purple-leaved forms may be included. These are variously described as 'Purpurea', 'Riversii' and 'Cuprea', the so-called 'Copper Beech'.

**FUCHSIA 'Riccartonii'.**

In mild districts this makes a delightful informal flowering hedge. It should be clipped in spring to remove any winter damage, cutting back to within one or two buds of the woody framework. It is usually kept at about 1–2 m (3–6 ft) but has the potential for twice this height.

**GRISELINIA LITTORALIS**

A plant for coastal sites. It can withstand constant wind. Its oval evergreen leaves are thick and almost fleshy, but become blackened by hard frosts. It clips to a good formal hedge and may reach 2 m (6 ft) or more.

Clip in spring to remove winter damage. It is not usually so vigorous as to require further treatment, but where there is little risk of frost damage a further trim in mid summer will keep a tidy appearance.

**ILEX AQUIFOLIUM**

Holly is an excellent evergreen plant for formal, impenetrable hedges and for use as ornamental trees within a hedge. It responds to clipping very well, producing a very strong branch framework which may be grown to considerable height 7 m (25 ft) or more with little risk of damage by storms, snow, etc. However, it is slow growing and the dead leaves rot very slowly so that they may drift into adjacent areas of garden and cause a nuisance. Clipping

in spring is recommended since the unsightly cut leaves are soon hidden by the new shoot growth.

In an environmental hedge, holly trees provide winter shelter and may produce berries. Holly in a rustic hedge may be laid successfully, but is rather brittle.

**LAURUS NOBILIS** (bay laurel)

A good evergreen for use in mild districts, including coastal sites. It clips very well to make a formal hedge. Its glossy, wavy edged leaves have the added value as flavouring for savoury dishes. It is damaged by hard frosts so may need spring pruning. Do not trim it late in the year as the resultant fresh growth will be vulnerable to winter damage.

**LAVANDULA ANGUSTIFOLIA**

The lavender is a greyish white dwarf shrub with aromatic foliage, bearing purplish flowers on erect stalks in summer. These stalks may be removed by clipping in autumn, and straggly growth tidied by a spring treatment. Lavender does not tolerate severe pruning. It is useful as a dwarf hedge, tolerant of dry soils and coastal sites, but should be considered to be rather short lived.

**LIGUSTRUM OVALIFOLIUM** (oval-leaved privet) and **L. VULGARE** (common privet)

These semi-evergreens are so common that they are generally regarded as boring, or even worse. However, as hedging plants they are extremely effective. They clip well to give a close texture for formal hedges; they are fully hardy and they retain leaves for most of the year, providing year-round shelter. The new growth is soft and easily clipped and the plants are readily propagated and should be inexpensive. Golden forms are available to provide added interest. They should be clipped in spring to remove the flower buds, since the creamy white flowers smell unpleasant and the subsequent black fruits are poisonous. They will require a second trim in autumn. Chemical growth retardants are extremely effective on privet.

Reversion in
*Elaeagnus × ebbingei*
'Limelight'. The
all green shoot
should be removed
as soon as possible.

Vivid red barked
shoots of *Salix alba*
'Britzensis'
produced on new
growth following
annual pollarding
in early spring.

*Opposite:*
The beautiful
natural vase shape
of *Hamamelis
mollis* 'Pallida'.
Only formative
pruning whilst the
shrub is young
may be required.

Rhododendron: strong new growth coming from where a faded flower head has been removed before seed was set.

*Opposite above:*
The traditional image of rural England. Note the maintained hedgerows in the foreground and the neglected one behind, which has become a gappy line of trees.

*Opposite below:*
History in the hedgerow. The low sloping stems are evidence of hedge laying in former times. The dense twiggy layer at 1 m ($3\frac{1}{4}$ ft) represents the height at which it was maintained for a time, before growing to 2 m ($6\frac{1}{2}$ ft), where a second twiggy layer marks a more recent period of maintenance. Now gappy and neglected, its function is performed by a wire fence (*behind*).

Excellent surface texture and strong form in a well-maintained holly hedge.

*Opposite above:*
An unusual form of mixed hedge with evergreen conifer (× *Cupressocyparis leylandii*) planted behind deciduous hawthorn (*Crataegus monogyna*). This provides considerable year-round interest and density in winter. However, the hedge does occupy a wide strip.

*Opposite below:*
A section of hedge immediately after laying, in the general purpose 'Midlands' style. In a few years the hedge will become thickened with twiggy growths, while the core of laid stems will provide a stockproof barrier for many years.

With patience and
frequent attention
to clipping,
fascinating shapes
may be created in
privet.

*Below:*
Old skills still
survive. A
beautiful knot
garden in Barnsley
House, the garden
of Mrs Rosemary
Verey.

## LONICERA NITIDA

This small-leaved evergreen plant is often erroneously called a box hedge, which is not surprising as it bears absolutely no similarity to its honeysuckle relatives. It has brittle arching stems and whilst it can be clipped to a tight formal habit I prefer it in a more relaxed style allowing the stems to spread a little. Its flowers are insignificant, so trim in spring and autumn or just in autumn according to your preference. This seems to be a very popular nesting subject for robins and wrens.

Do not let it grow much more than 1 m (3 ft) tall as it is inclined to suffer storm damage. It may be killed by very severe weather, but is generally considered hardy for the UK.

## OLEARIA AVICENNIIFOLIA and O. MACRODONTA (New Zealand holly)

These evergreen shrubs which bear white daisy-like flowers are extremely wind resistant and suitable for coastal sites. They are best grown informally to about 2 m (6 ft) but may be clipped. If overgrown they can be brought back under control by hard pruning which should be carried out in spring. They are generally trouble free and merit wider use.

## PHOTINIA DAVIDIANA (syn. STRANVAESIA DAVIDIANA)

This is an evergreen shrub with leaves and habits very much like *Prunus lusitanica*, but with the added value of bunches of red berries which persist well into the winter. Suitable for large informal screens.

## PITTOSPORUM CRASSIFOLIUM and P. TENUIFOLIUM

These small-leaved evergreen shrubs are excellent for mild districts and coastal sites, and may grow to a considerable size, up to 3 m (10 ft). They are usually clipped as formal hedges to about 1.5 m (5 ft). If allowed to grow without clipping they produce sprays of foliage which lasts a long time when cut and is much used commercially as a florist's greenery. They may require spring pruning if damaged by winter frost. They recover well from hard pruning.

## POTENTILLA FRUTICOSA

These shrubs should not be overlooked for an informal flowering hedge, since their flowering period extends for several months. They do not produce very strong branches so should be maintained as small hedges to about 1 m (3 ft). In spring cut out some of the older shoots at their base, to promote new growth. Several are available including yellow, white and red-flowering forms.

## PRUNUS CERASIFERA (cherry plum, myrobalan), P. DOMESTICA INSTITIA (bullace) and P. SPINOSA (sloe or blackthorn)

All three species have a place in rustic hedges, whether maintained by clipping or by laying. They all flower early in the season before the foliage, and have a close thorny habit. When hard pruned they produce suckers from the roots, which help to maintain density at the base.

## PRUNUS LAUROCERASUS (cherry laurel)

This very large-leaved evergreen is unfashionable at present, perhaps because of its coarse foliage, which looks unattractive when clipped. However, it is very suitable for large hedging screens of 5 m (15 ft) or more. It should be clipped in spring so that the new growth covers the cut foliage. If it becomes too large it may be pruned hard back to old wood. If allowed to grow informally it becomes very wide.

## PRUNUS LUSITANICA (Portuguese laurel)

Similar to *P. laurocerasus* but with a narrower leaf, and even more hardy. An excellent plant for a large evergreen hedge.

## QUERCUS ILEX (evergreen or holm oak)

This is a small-leaved dark green plant which clips well to form a rigid formal hedge. It is highly recommended for coastal districts. In severe weather the foliage may go brown but it is likely to sprout again from the older wood.

## RHODODENDRON PONTICUM

This familiar large-leaved evergreen with its pinkish-mauve flowers makes a grand informal hedge for the larger estate. Trim after flowering to remove faded flowers. If it becomes bare at the base or overgrown, it may be cut back hard and will regrow. It is hardy throughout the UK but suffers leaf scorch when exposed to wind. It is very tolerant of shade. This is a large subject, up to 5 m (15 ft).

## ROSA RUGOSA

Several species of rose may be used to add variety to mixed hedges or to increase the wild-life value of an environmental hedge. However, *Rosa rugosa* may be used alone to form a dense prickly thicket, due to its vigorous and suckering habit. It produces large fragrant flowers which produce large fleshy hips giving an extended season of interest. The plant withstands clipping but is best used as a semi-formal hedge, to 1.5 m (4 ft). Prune in autumn to remove the tattered remains of hips.

## ROSMARINUS OFFICINALIS

Common rosemary makes a fragrant informal hedge with evergreen foliage and bluish flowers. It tolerates dry conditions. Prune lightly by shortening branches after flowering. It is capable of growing to 1.5 m (5 ft) but may split over 1 m (3 ft). A form with an upright habit suitable for hedging is 'Miss Jessopp's Upright' (syn. 'Fastigiatus').

## SANTOLINA CHAMAECYPARISSUS
(cotton lavender)

This subject is unrelated to lavender but its growth, use and pruning are exactly as suggested for lavender. This plant is greyish with yellow flowers. It is useful as a dwarf informal hedge but is inclined to become straggly.

## SYMPHORICARPOS DOORENBOS HYBRIDS

This snowberry tends to produce a thicket of slender erect stems which do not mat together even after clipping. It is used quite commonly as an informal hedge tolerant of shade, but it is not an ideal plant. It suckers freely and spreads into adjacent ground. Forms with white or pink berries are available for hedging: 'White Hedge' and 'Erect' respectively.

## TAMARIX RAMOSISSIMA 'ROSEA' (syn. T. PENTANDRA)

The tamarisk has curious feathery branches with tiny leaflets and a rather loose open habit. It is not really suitable for hedging, but its tolerance of sandy soils and windy conditions enable it to grow very well in exposed coastal sites. The plumose branches bearing pink flowers, swaying in the sea breeze, is a truly delightful sight in late summer. This species flowers on wood of the current season so it may be pruned quite hard, in early spring. It will grow to 3 m (10 ft).

## TAXUS BACCATA (yew)

This is the traditional evergreen material for topiary and formal hedging where a very close texture is required. Its dark foliage adds to the effect of density and solidity. It is very hardy and tolerates most conditions including heavy shade. To obtain a close texture clip twice a year in spring and again in mid summer. For an established hedge a clipping in summer will suffice. Formal yew hedges of considerable size may be seen in the great gardens of England, the result of many years' work. Yew is generally a slow-growing plant and may require 20 years to reach 2 m (6 ft). It is poisonous and should not be planted where livestock have access.

## THUJA PLICATA (western red cedar)

This dark-leaved evergreen is similar to *Chamaecyparis lawsoniana* in its appearance. However its leaves are glossy and have a sweet scent when crushed. Clip in summer after the flush of spring growth. It makes an excellent formal hedge with a potential to reach considerable height. It should be maintained as a small hedge by regular clipping since it does not recover well from severe pruning.

## ULMUS MINOR var. VULGARIS (syn. U. PROCERA)

The elms are frequently encountered in agricultural hedges due to the suckering habit of the roots of old trees. These suckers are not usually attacked by the beetle which carries Dutch elm disease until they reach the size of small trees. Elm lays very well and provides a useful ingredient in mixed hedges. A form recommended for garden hedges is *Ulmus minor* 'Jacqueline Hillier' (syn. *Ulmus × elegantissima* 'Jacqueline Hillier').

# CHAPTER 9

# *Topiary*

Topiary is the ornamental training and clipping of trees and shrubs into clearly defined shapes. Where topiary ends and hedging, knots and parterres begin is difficult to define. Hedges may be of comparatively simple formal shape or highly ornamental with elaborate patterning; in the latter, topiary is definitely involved. Knots consist essentially of low hedges laid out in a pattern to form a regular framework. In essence, a parterre is a more complicated form of knot garden. In both knots and parterres, the skill of shaping shrubs is involved just as in topiary.

## The history of topiary

Topiary is one of the oldest gardening art forms, its history going back to at least Roman times, the Latin *toparius* meaning garden designer.

During the Dark Ages, topiary was no longer important, but gardening skills, including those of clipping and shaping shrubs, were kept alive in the monasteries.

Topiary re-emerged in Renaissance Italy. The French became obsessed with this art during the seventeenth century, as it expressed in their eyes the dominance of man over nature. Topiary reached its zenith with the completion of Versailles, designed by André le Nôtre.

In England clipped shrubs began to be popular in Tudor times; indeed, Henry VIII's accounts for Hampton Court Palace reveal the purchase of topiary. The Dutch acted as suppliers of these plants and the influence of William and Mary favoured this trading connection. The use of topiary peaked during the seventeenth and early eighteenth centuries.

The Landscape Movement, whose main advocates were William Robinson, his protégé Lancelot 'Capability' Brown and Humphry Repton, successor to Brown, in the second half of the eighteenth century swept away formality

and with it topiary. Levens Hall, the oldest topiary garden in England, having been started in 1689, was one of the very few escapees. Westbury Court, of a similar age and now a very rare example of a garden in the Dutch style, also contained topiary. Very fortunately the art of topiary also continued to be practised in cottage gardens.

The middle of the nineteenth century saw a tremendous revival of interest and practice of topiary, despite the 'natural' garden so strongly advocated by William Robinson. Few of the gardens we know today for their topiary date from before the nineteenth century, the Edwardians and Victorians loving to include clipped specimens in their gardens to add what they considered was old-fashioned charm.

The Arts and Crafts movement was topiary's saviour. This is typified by Rodmarton Manor, designed by Ernest Barnsley, who trained with the architect J. D. Sedding and knew Reginald Blomfield, both of whom wrote idealizing rural skills and prompting a return to a more formal style of gardening including the use of topiary.

Hidcote, started by Laurence Johnson in 1907 in the best of arts and crafts tradition, incorporated much formal hedging and topiary. This, in turn, influenced the design of Sissinghurst.

Today topiary is still a very popular art form, being widely seen in both large and small gardens.

## The shrubs used for topiary

To be suitable for use as a topiary specimen, a shrub should have the following qualities. It must be capable of withstanding frequent clipping, have dense small-leaved foliage and not grow too fast. Other desirable characteristics are hardiness, freedom from pests and insects, and long life. With such a long list of essential, or at least desirable characteristics, it is not surprising that comparatively few plants are really suitable.

## BUXUS SEMPERVIRENS (common box)

An evergreen shrub or small tree, tolerant of most soils, including chalk and growing well in sun or part shade. Masses of small dark green leaves are produced on a slow-growing plant.

Box is the mainstay of the Dutch topiary exporting industry. Large numbers of plants are grown and trained to largely traditional shapes such as peacocks, or formal shapes such as cones, pyramids, spirals and balls. Employing seedling box plants, and a combination of training wires and frequent clipping, small topiary plants are produced in about six years.

The plant lends itself particularly well to topiary. It naturally has a dense habit and very good covering of small leaves. Providing it is done at the correct time, it responds well to clipping, producing ever denser growth, the small leaves allowing shears to be used without visual detrimental effect. It is capable of producing new growth from old wood and this means that it is possible to renew old, gappy plants by careful hard pruning.

Clipping should be done in late spring when all danger of frost is past. This is an important point to watch as frost after clipping can cause severe damage.

The species has given rise to many forms and variations. *Buxus sempervirens* 'Suffruticosa', a dwarf cultivar known as 'Edging Box' is frequently used to edge paths and borders, and for knot gardens and parterres.

## CRATAEGUS MONOGYNA (common hawthorn)

Left to itself, this is naturally a deciduous small tree or large shrub. It is very widely planted as a stock-proof field boundary hedge and tolerant of the most vicious pruning, as indeed is annually seen when tractor-mounted flail mowers set about long-neglected hawthorn hedges. It is rapid growing and thorny; when pruned annually it produces a good impenetrable hedge.

As a subject for topiary it is not very popular; however, sometimes a plant is left above the hedge line and trained most often as a simple spherical shape. Frequent clipping, that may be done at any time of the year, is necessary to keep a neat outline. Clipping often also tends to help with leaf retention in winter, which gives a better appearance.

## FAGUS SYLVATICA (common beech)

Although most commonly clipped as a simple formal hedge, topiary may be practised on beech so that arches and features such as moon gates may be cut into it. The fact that, when clipped, beech retains its leaves in winter, improves not only the appearance of the hedge, but also the definition of such features.

## ILEX AQUIFOLIUM (holly)

An evergreen shrub more commonly planted for hedging than for topiary. Holly does, however, stand hard clipping well and will make very effective simply-shaped topiary specimens.

Clipping is best done in mid spring when new growth will quickly hide cut leaves and stems. Secateurs, rather than shears, should be used as less ugly half-cut leaves will be produced and more attention given to shaping and pruning individual shoots.

Some cultivars are better than others for this specialized application. *Ilex × altaclerensis* 'Lawsoniana' in particular is not recommended as it tends to revert very readily when subjected to hard pruning as in topiary.

## LAURUS NOBILIS (culinary bay)

Being a Mediterranean native, this shrub is not reliably hardy except in the most favoured districts. Elsewhere, when shaped as a topiary specimen, it is best grown in a pot or container and taken into a frost-free environment for the winter.

When grown as a 'Berlin Stem' with a bare stem surmounted by a ball, it is suitable for inclusion in a small garden, patio, courtyard or, of course, in the herb garden to add an element of formality.

Trimming with secateurs will be required several times during the summer.

## LIGUSTRUM OVALIFOLIUM (common privet)

Common privet is very widely used for hedging, but less widely employed for topiary. It is rather unfairly despised by some because of its rapid growth and ability to compete with other plants very successfully for water and nutrients. A failing is that it may lose its leaves during severe winter weather and is best regarded as semi-evergreen.

Clipping with shears will be needed several times during the growing season if a neat appearance is to be maintained. Finely detailed topiaries have been produced using privet, but a high degree of maintenance is required.

## LONICERA NITIDA

This shrubby honeysuckle is a small-leaved evergreen producing dense growth that responds well to clipping.

For topiary it has limitations. In size nothing above 1.2 m (4 ft) should be attempted. It is subject to winter injury during severe winter weather and has the annoying habit of sections dropping out of place, especially if snow is allowed to lie on it for any length of time.

Frequent clipping during the growing season is required – about once per month is necessary for a clear outline.

## PHILLYREA ANGUSTIFOLIA

This shrub has been valued as a small-leaved evergreen capable of withstanding clipping for hundreds of years, old authors frequently referring to the planting of phillyreas.

It can be clipped to form balls and regular domes. Being of comparatively small size and easily constrained, it associates well and is in proportion with the dwarf box hedges of knot gardens and parterres.

## PRUNUS LUSITANICA (Portugal laurel)

A handsome evergreen shrub. It can be clipped to form simple conical shapes. In cold areas it makes a good substitute for the bay. At Hidcote, high up in the Cotswolds, this substitution has been successfully employed, bay not proving hardy, and *Prunus lusitanica* making a satisfactory alternative. *Prunus lusitanica* 'Myrtifolia', with leaves smaller and neater than the type, is perhaps even more suitable for topiary work.

## TAXUS BACCATA (common yew)

The aristocrat of the topiary world, this plant contains all the qualities wanted to the fullest degree found. Evergreen, it produces dense fine foliage that tolerates clipping very well.

Yew has a moderate growth rate and will respond favourably should growth get out of hand and hard pruning be required.

Being normally a tree, topiary of any size can be produced and the plant is very long-lived. The fact that the young growth is pliable, yet strong and permanent, plus its ability to stand very severe clipping, means that a very wide range of shapes can be produced.

## The practice of topiary

Topiary shapes may be formed by using three different methods: free-shaping, use of metal frames, and pre-forming.

### Free-shaping

This is the classical method of practising topiary.

To start with, the initial shape of a shrub or small tree may suggest a topiary design or the gardener may know the shape he desires. By clipping and only allowing extension growth where wanted, the shape is gradually produced.

In general it is better not to fight nature too hard. Aim to produce a fairly simple, not over-elaborate shape that is ideally broader at its base than top. This helps confer stability and avoids the problem of shaded growth dying out.

If only one specimen is to be produced, the plan for the finished piece can rest in the practitioner's head, the shape developing as his fancy takes him. The ultimate shape of the topiary should be apparent after three to four years. The formation of a topiary garden with several specimens often within a confined space does, however, require prior thought and a plan to be produced at the beginning. Birds, animals and informal shapes are cut by using pruning shears. Initial work should be careful and slow. Cut a piece, and then step back and look at the result. Then proceed again. It may be useful to have a helper standing some distance away, who can see the overall effect and give advice.

Regular and geometric shapes can be cut with the aid of string as a cutting guide. These shapes also have the distinct advantage that they may be added to at a later date and the overall piece may evolve with time. For example, a regular cone may be produced first, and then a vertical shoot allowed to grow out of the top with which to form another shape on top.

Little wiring or supporting system should be necessary with simple shapes. As a design becomes more complicated, a system of support using wires or bamboo stakes may be necessary. Watch the tightness of ties and make certain that growth is not constricted at any time.

Remember the topiary is a living plant. Frequent clipping, as necessary for a young plant being trained, puts a strain on the plant. Regular feeding and irrigation as the plant establishes will encourage healthy growth and enable the final shape to be achieved more rapidly. Try to keep the centre of the topiary as open as possible and remove any dead growth. Clipping at short intervals whilst the topiary is young will result in much branched dense

growth that will give the smooth dense outline that is to be desired. Allowing growth to become excessively long and then only clipping lightly, will result in an open, gappy shape, a specimen of poor quality.

When starting, it is best to begin to try to produce simple shapes such as cones, pyramids, domes, spheres or cubes. These are relatively easy to produce and excellent shapes in themselves. They also have the advantage, as mentioned earlier, that a more complex shape may be allowed to develop out of them.

More complicated shapes can be attempted as the gardener's skill increases. Here wires and support may be needed. For the most intricate shapes, yew and, to a lesser extent, box, are the best species to work with.

Shoots must be carefully selected and trained into position using wires which are themselves firmly secured to the rest of the plant [Figs. 9.1 and 9.2].

A spiral may be produced in one or two different ways. The first involves starting with a pre-formed cone shape. A string is tied to the top of the cone and then taken around the cone in a spiral shape. The dense growth of the plant will ensure that the string stays in place. Using the string as a guide, cut into the cone. Gradually form the spiral and cut back right into the cone until the main stem is reached.

Initially, the effect may be poor, with much old wood exposed, but with yew re-growth will occur and gradually the shape and overall appearance will improve.

The second method involves taking a young pyramid-shaped plant whose stem is still pliable. Insert a cane as near to the main stem of the plant as possible. Bend and tie the main stem around the cane to form a spiral.

**Metal-framed topiary**
This is a fundamentally different technique from free-shaping.

The first stage is the production of a metal frame, this being of the overall shape of the topiary to be formed. In the USA, a ready-made frame from a specialist supplier may be available; elsewhere the services of a blacksmith will be required. An advantage of this method is that the overall size and shape of the topiary can be seen before starting. Produce a plan of the frame to be made. The overall outline is

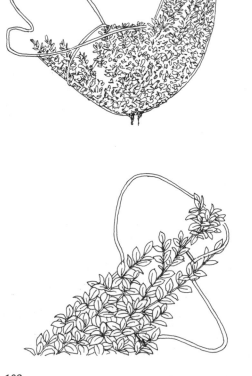

**Fig. 9.1** A cockerel in the process of development from a young box plant. The outline of the wire frame employed can be seen.

**Fig. 9.2** Detail of the head of the cockerel. It can be seen that both tying in and close clipping of growth is used to produce the shape required.

produced by the blacksmith and then given a three-dimensional shape by using circular hoops. The frame can be designed to be attached to an existing plant or to rest on the ground and be placed over a young plant.

Once the frame is in position, producing the topiary involves tying new growth onto the frame. Care should be taken to keep the inside of the topiary as open as possible to allow good air circulation. Shoots arising within the framework should be first pulled outside the framework and then tied to it.

Frequent clipping will be required to mould the tied-in shoots to the overall shape of the frame. As time goes by, the growth gradually thickens and the frame is obscured.

## Maintenance of established topiary specimens

This is time-consuming and requires a skilled and sensitive approach to the plant. Clipping is done to maintain the desired shape. It should be remembered that this operation removes the young leaves of the plant, whose function is to photosynthesize and gain energy for the plant. Clipping is, therefore, a drain on the plant. The just-clipped, smooth, perfect outline is much to be admired, but there is always the danger of over-clipping.

Clipping in late summer or early autumn reduces the associated stress and the plant is able to recover before winter. Unfortunately, treatment once per year does not keep the plant to the degree of perfection wanted by most gardeners.

Clipping in spring will encourage growth and is to be encouraged on damaged or neglected plants. For details of when to clip individual species, see the section on the shrubs used for topiary.

Frost can be damaging after clipping, this being particularly the case with box and care should be taken not to clip when there is any danger of frost.

If one encounters old, neglected or damaged plants, rejuvenation and repair should be attempted. Yew in particular is capable of withstanding very hard pruning and will break again from old wood.

For finely detailed topiary, secateurs or sharp hand shears are the best tools for the job. For large specimens or comparatively simple shapes, electric or petrol driven reciprocating cutters may be used and save considerable time.

## Pre-formed topiary

An additional type of topiary that has its origins almost entirely in the USA. The Borough of Torbay in Devon, England, has, however, also exhibited this form of plant sculpture both at the Chelsea Flower Show and in Torbay. The Torbay series had its origin with the traditional carpet-bedding schemes, this two-dimensional display being developed into this three-dimensional topiary. These plant sculptures may not be considered topiary in the traditional sense, but the fact that they are made of plants that are trained and clipped link these two art forms.

There are three basic types of pre-formed topiary:

### A frame filled with soil and moss into which the plants are plugged

This is the type used to create large pre-formed topiary both in the USA and England. Metal frames are constructed and put into position. To reduce weight, much of the inside of the structure is filled with expanded polystyrene. A compost, usually peat based, is used to hold moisture and nutrients and plants packed into the surface of the structure at very high density. Plants used for the Torbay exhibit included *Echeveria* and *Alternanthera*, all of which exhibit bright leaf colourings. Those which extend in growth during the summer are trimmed and may even be shaped to give a textured finish.

### A plant grown in a container which forms the frame for the topiary

The second type uses a trailing plant, often *Ficus pumila*. The plant is placed in a container which forms part of the frame for the topiary. As the plant grows it is pegged out over the surface of the framework. Eventually, the whole surface is covered and the shape of the topiary completed.

### A potted plant with a frame attached to it

The final type involves what is usually a single potted plant. A wire frame, forming the outline of the desired eventual shape is anchored to the

**Fig. 9.3** Ivy spiral being formed using a galvanized wire spiral and cane for support and training.

**Fig. 9.4** Young box plants with metal framework. Eventually a small pyramid will be formed.

pot. As the plant grows, it is carefully tied to the frame. Growth in inappropriate directions is trimmed off.

Using this system, and a plant such as a cultivar of *Hedera helix*, a very diverse range of shapes can be produced; for example, it provides another method to produce a perfect living spiral [Fig. 9.3].

### Maintenance of pre-formed topiary

Pre-formed topiary requires much attention both whilst they are being trained and once they are fully formed.

With those having a foam-filled frame plus peat-based compost, watering and feeding must be attended to carefully. The compost must not be allowed to dry out and plants such as *Alternanthera* must be regularly trimmed to maintain the desired effect.

Plants growing over a framework [Fig. 9.4] must have new growth frequently pegged down or trimmed off if excessive. As with any other potted plant, watering and feeding must be attended to regularly.

# CHAPTER 10

# Climbing and Wall Shrubs

Climbers are basically weak-stemmed plants that have devised ways to climb up towards the light. Wall shrubs have no special modifications to help them climb, but for display or reasons of hardiness we choose to grow them against walls.

## The use of climbers and wall shrubs

The gardens of today's modern houses are typically rather small, but they all have walls and often lengths of fencing. These surfaces offer an extra vertical dimension upon which to grow a very wide range of interesting plants.

Climbers and wall shrubs have the very important quality of being able to soften the stark, angular lines of new buildings and may be used to conceal unsightly buildings and structures. Contrary to some modern opinions, architects do not set out to create ugly buildings and the function of such plants should be to complement buildings, helping them to blend into the landscape, but not to completely hide them. The same is true of older buildings; nobody would want to conceal an old wall of weathered Cotswold stone, but the patterned growth of *Parthenocissus henryana* forming a light tracery over part of its surface adds to and does not detract from this feature.

Selecting a climber or wall shrub with the correct degree of vigour is very important. Choosing a wildly over-vigorous plant and then attempting control by pruning is not a recipe for success. A south or west-facing wall is a favoured growing position, being warm and sheltered. The opportunity may be taken to grow some marginally hardy climber or wall shrubs in these positions, thus increasing the diversity of plants that can be grown. Good examples of marginally hardy wall shrubs requiring such a favoured situation are *Clianthus puniceus* (lobster's claw), *Fremontodendron* 'California Glory' and *Caesalpina japonica*.

Fig. 10.1 *Wisteria* sp. A clear demonstration of the twisting method of climbing employed by this genus.

### How climbers climb

Before considering the pruning of such plants it is wise to consider how they climb and what method of support they will require.

*Twining stems*

Climbing plants have evolved with a range of modifications to help them climb. Twining stems that twist around their support are frequently met and well known examples are *Lonicera periclymenum* (common honeysuckle) and *Wisteria sinensis* (Chinese wisteria) [Fig. 10.1].

*Twisting leaf stalks*

Others, including many members of the genus *Clematis*, have twisting leaf stalks or petioles [Fig. 10.2]. The vines (*Vitis*) climb using

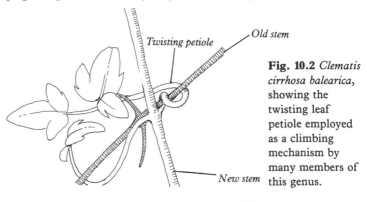

*Twisting petiole*

*Old stem*

*New stem*

Fig. 10.2 *Clematis cirrhosa balearica*, showing the twisting leaf petiole employed as a climbing mechanism by many members of this genus.

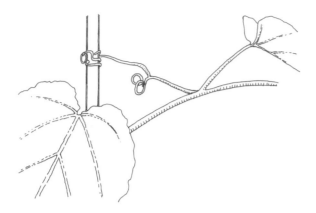

**Fig. 10.3** Tendril of *Vitis coignetiae* twisting around a lightning conductor attached to a building.

twining tendrils [Fig. 10.3].

In some genera the tendrils are further modified so that their tips, on contact with a hard surface, flatten out to produce adhesive pads that cling tightly to the surface. This is well developed in *Parthenocissus tricuspidata* (Boston ivy).

*Adventitious roots*

Plants such as *Hedera helix* (common ivy) and *Hydrangea petiolaris* (climbing hydrangea) produce adventitious roots from their aerial stems. These roots attach strongly to walls or tree trunks. These plants require no additional supporting system, but first shoots may need guidance to 'find' the wall [Fig. 10.4].

*Thorns*

Roses and *Rubus* spp. (brambles) have thorns which are not only for defence. The thorns are hook-shaped, catching on the branches of

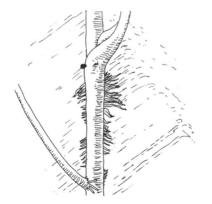

**Fig. 10.4** *Hedera* sp. producing adventitious roots, these adhering strongly to the brickwork.

shrubs, helping the rose or bramble grow over the plants below.

*The scandent habit*

Finally, we come to plants with a lax or scandent habit. These are typified by plants such as *Jasminum nudiflorum* (winter jasmine) and *Forsythia suspensa* whose long flexuous shoots tend to fall upon and over other plants.

**Support systems on walls and fences**

Turning from how plants climb to support systems, the would-be cultivator can begin to appreciate that certain systems are best suited to plants with specific methods of climbing.

*Trellis*

Trellis gives good support for a wide range of climbers. It is particularly suitable for plants with twisting stems or petioles. In either case, the plant can twist around the trellis and gain support. The fact that support is offered in both horizontal and vertical planes is important, allowing the plant to travel over the support and not to be confined as it may be on horizontal wires [Fig. 10.5 and 10.6].

The trellis should be secured about 8 cm (3 in) away from the wall. If the trellis is hard against the wall, the climber cannot twine around it and its function is largely lost. As the twining stems age they thicken; if space is restricted between the trellis and the wall, the trellis may be broken or pushed off the wall. Having an air circulation between the trellis and the wall has also been found advantageous in helping to reduce the incidence of red spider mite and mildew.

*Horizontal strained wires*

These are excellent for many wall shrubs. For reasons discussed under trellis, the wires should be 5–8 cm (2–3 in) away from the wall and spaced about 23 cm (9 in) apart vertically. The wires are threaded through vine eyes or closed eyes. Vine eyes are hammered directly into the mortar of old walls. Newer walls will have hard mortar and closed eyes, with an adequate stem length, should be inserted by drilling and plugging holes. The wire on long runs should be stretched tight by use of strainers.

Such a system is excellent for climbing and

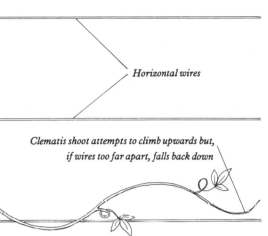

**Fig. 10.5**
Clematis growing
on horizontal
wires. Shoot
effectively confined
to horizontal plane
if widely spaced
horizontal wires
alone used as
support system.

*Horizontal wires*

*Clematis shoot attempts to climb upwards but,
if wires too far apart, falls back down*

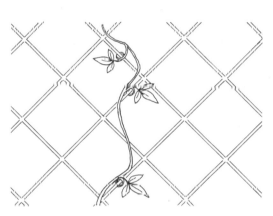

fencing are all very effective in providing support for climbers. They are better for plants that will not put a considerable weight on the support system, and will be cut down at the end of the year, for example the herbaceous *Lathyrus latifolius* (perennial pea) and *Ipomoea* (morning glory) treated as an annual.

**Fig. 10.6** Clematis on trellis or netting. The fact that support is provided in two dimensions allows the plant to climb at will.

rambling roses and nearly all wall shrubs, including those with a scandent habit. As noted earlier, climbers may tend to grow only horizontally along with wires, but vertical wires can be positioned to overlay the horizontal so that a system of squares or rectangles is produced that is ideal for climbers.

### Free-standing support

*Living trees and shrubs*
This system can be very effective, especially as it is entirely natural. Careful consideration must be given to the relative size and vigour of supporting plant and climber; an excessively vigorous climber will seriously weaken the growth of the supporting plant and its weight may bring it to the ground. A stable, long-lasting plant association will not be formed. *Rosa* 'Paul's Himalayan musk' growing into a tree is a beautiful sight in summer. Clematis such as *Clematis viticella* 'Purpurea Plena Elegans' can be grown over early summer flowering shrubs such as *Buddleja alternifolia*. The buddleja is followed by the flowers of the clematis in later summer. The clematis is not excessively vigorous as it is cut down hard in late winter, this having the effect of tidying the plant and preventing the shrub from carrying an excessive haulm of clematis.

Careful choice of supporting plant and climber can greatly extend the time for which flowers can be seen in one area of the garden. A good association having, overall, a very long

#### Lead-headed nails
Can be used on brick and mortar walls, being driven into the mortar or the interstices of stone walls. Their use is best limited to where only a few ties are required – for example, with some loosely retained wall shrubs.

#### Netting
Plastic mesh, plastic-coated steel, galvanized wire netting (pig netting) and chain-link

season of flower is the summer-flowering *Clematis* 'Etoile Rose' with its bell-shaped, cerise pink flowers well displayed when grown on the winter-flowering *Chimonanthus praecox* (winter sweet). The waxen yellow flower of the winter sweet can also be clearly seen since the clematis is semi-herbaceous and should be cut down to the ground in mid winter, the old haulm being cleared away.

If the supporting plant and climber are chosen to flower at the same time, clearly thought must be given to the flower-colour combinations then produced. A widely praised combination is using the yellow flowered *Laburnum × watereri* 'Vossii' to form both an archway and a support for *Wisteria sinensis* with its mauve racemes of flowers. In this plant association the wisteria is much the stronger growing and pruning several times a year will be required (please see alphabetical listing for details).

### Larch poles with stub branches

Poles with stub branches left approximately 30 cm (1 ft) long can be used as serviceable supports for a range of climbers, including clematis and rambling roses.

### Pergola and archway features

These are good systems for vigorous growing subjects that will clothe both the sides and top horizontal bars of such systems. Suitable plants include vines, rambling and climbing roses, wisteria and the stronger-growing lonicera (honeysuckles).

Choose subjects that are either adapted to a hard annual pruning system or a replacement system so that a manageable and tidy effect is possible.

## Preparation for and planting of climbers

The soil at the base of a wall is often very dry and may have a high pH (lime content) because of the mortar dropped during the process of construction. To help counteract the problem of dryness, planting should be carried out at

**Fig. 10.7** Planting a climber.

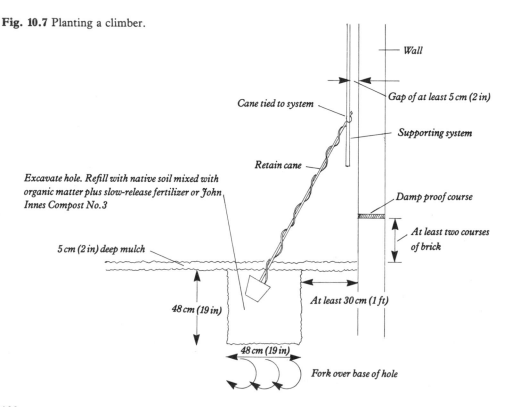

Wall

Cane tied to system

Gap of at least 5 cm (2 in)

Supporting system

Retain cane

Damp proof course

Excavate hole. Refill with native soil mixed with organic matter plus slow-release fertilizer or John Innes Compost No.3

At least two courses of brick

5 cm (2 in) deep mulch

48 cm (19 in)

At least 30 cm (1 ft)

48 cm (19 in)

Fork over base of hole

least 30 cm (12 in) away from the wall. Take out a hole approximately 45 cm (18 in) square by 45 cm (18 in) deep. Fork over the base of the hole. This is done to alleviate any soil compaction and facilitate good drainage.

If the excavated soil is of good quality, it may be made into a planting compost by adding organic material such as garden compost, peat, tree planting compost, or peat substitute materials, plus a slow-release fertilizer such as bone meal. In the place of organic matter, granules of water-retaining polyacrylamide gel (such as 'Broadleaf P4') or seaweed extract with similar water-retaining and soil structuring properties (for instance 'Alginure') may be added to the soil. This may be of special benefit where a dry situation cannot be avoided. Poor soil, which is often found at the base of a wall, sometimes consisting mainly of broken bricks, mortar etc., is best removed and replaced with John Innes Compost No. 3 if just planting one or a few climbers. Where several are to be planted, a plant compost based on bought-in good loam should be made up.

The container-grown plant, whose roots should be moist at the time of planting, is removed from its container. If the plant shows early signs of being pot-bound, gently tease some of the roots apart from the mass.

In the case of the majority of climbers and wall shrubs, plant the root ball so that once planted it is at the same level as when it is in its pot. Clematis should be planted so that the crown of the plant is 5–7.5 cm (2–3 in) below soil level.

The final soil level should be at least two courses of bricks below the damp-proof course (DPC) in the wall to prevent any possibility of rising damp.

The cane that the container-grown climber was trained onto should be retained and, if long enough, used to 'show' the climber where the supporting system is and tied to it [Fig. 10.7].

Finally, the newly-planted plant should be well watered in and a mulch at least 5 cm (2 in) deep applied.

## Initial training and general pruning principles

Early training and pruning to produce a sound basic framework is very important. Consider-

able directing of growth, removal of misplaced shoots, even if very vigorous, and tying-in will be required. New growth must be attended to frequently as once growth has become twisted together the job of training is very difficult and new growth of wall shrubs left free is very liable to wind damage. Outward-facing (breastwood) should be removed in order to keep the plant tight up against the supporting system.

Just as with ordinary shrubs dead, diseased or damaged growth should be removed. Pruning should be done to obtain maximum coverage and maximum effect. With many climbers, this means maintaining balanced growth and pruning away excessive vigour.

### Timing of pruning

In general the precepts of pruning shrubs can be followed. Those that flower early in the season on the previous season's wood, for example *Forsythia suspensa*, *Abeliophyllum distichum* and *Clematis montana* are pruned immediately after flowering.

Those plants that flower on the current season's growth after mid summer are pruned when dormant, for example *Clematis × jackmanii*.

## Damage to buildings by climbers

### Damage to pointing

Climbers such as *Hedera* (ivy) and *Hydrangea petiolaris* that produce adventitious roots should not be allowed to grow up walls where the pointing and mortar is soft. Soft mortar will be penetrated by these roots and when an attempt is made to remove or reduce the climber, soft particles of mortar will come away with the roots. It should be remembered that where such a plant is allowed to climb over a wall and it is later removed, the tips of the adventitious roots will adhere to and remain obvious on the wall for a long time afterwards.

### Bridging of damp proof course

Where climbers, especially those adhering to the wall, are not planted initially well away from the wall as recommended earlier, there is a chance that the damp proof course will be

**Fig. 10.8** Climber 'bridging' the damp proof course of a wall.

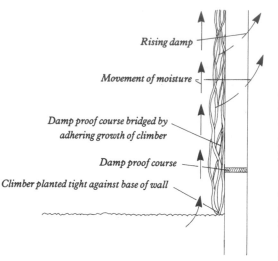

Rising damp

Movement of moisture

Damp proof course bridged by adhering growth of climber

Damp proof course

Climber planted tight against base of wall

bridged – this leading to problems of rising damp [Fig. 10.8]. If this problem should occur the only cure is complete removal of the offending plant.

### Blockage of gutters and down pipes
If climbers are allowed over gutters of a house, falling leaves in the autumn may well collect in the gutter and be washed along to block both gutter and down pipes. To prevent this problem, vigorous climbers should be kept pruned away from the gutters, and as a further precaution netting may be placed over the gutter.

### Lifting of roof tiles
Pruning must be carried out to prevent over-vigorous climbers getting up onto tiled roofs. If allowed, shoots will grow beneath the tiles, upsetting their placement and, if the roof is un-lined, grow into the roof void.

Displacement of tiles can render them more liable to being blown off during high winds. Driving rain or snow can also penetrate between the tiles.

## A–Z of major climbers and wall shrubs and their pruning

### ABELIA
Beautiful late summer and autumn-flowering deciduous shrubs, revelling in full sun and often grown against a south-facing wall. They

are somewhat tender; winter damage should be removed mid-spring and at the same time over-crowded and some old wood should be re-moved.

### ABELIOPHYLLUM
*Abeliophyllum distichum* is the only species. It flowers very early in the year and is usually grown on a south-facing wall to help prevent frost damage to the flowers, the shrub itself being hardy.

As a young shrub, train to form a framework on wires. After flowering cut back a proportion of the laterals arising from their framework to maintain vigorous growth which is required as this plant flowers on the previous season's growth.

### ABUTILON
A genus of shrubs, all of which are tender to some degree, and generally given the protec-tion of a wall.

*Abutilon megapotamicum* is tender and grown against a south-facing wall, all growth being tied in before winter to obtain maximum wall protection and straw or other insulating material placed around the base. The follow-ing early summer all winter-killed or damaged growth should be removed.

*Abutilon vitifolium* is the hardiest species and is best grown by a wall with only a few ties from the main stem to the wall to prevent the plant being blown over in strong winds. Winter damage should be assessed in early summer and dead growth pruned away. The slightly hardier *Abutilon × suntense* requires the same treatment.

### ACACIA (wattle)
Evergreen trees or shrubs. Only the hardiest species will grow outside and then the protection of a south-facing wall is required. *Acacia dealbata* (silver wattle) is the 'Mimosa' of florists.

Pruning after flowering in spring or early summer consists of dead-heading, thinning where necessary and the removal of winter-killed growth. If too large for their position or badly damaged in winter, they will respond to hard pruning in late spring.

## ACTINIDIA

*Actinidia chinensis* (Chinese gooseberry) produces edible fruits called 'Kiwi' fruit. Its pruning is described in Chapter 16 under soft fruit (see page 208).

*A. kolomikta* is grown for the unusual coloured variegation of its leaves, many of which have the terminal half coloured creamy-white flushed pink. It is best grown on a south or west-facing wall to encourage leaf colour development. Train the main growth to cover the space available. In mid to late summer, when much of the leaf has faded, cut back excess growth to 15–23 cm (6–9 in) of the established framework. Spur back these same growths to one or two buds in early to mid winter. Do not leave until late winter as excessive bleeding may occur.

## AKEBIA

Strong growing climbers which, if space permits, can be left to grow unrestricted, for example over a tree stump in a wilder part of the garden.

Where necessary, or when grown on a wall or pergola, pruning can be done after flowering in early summer. All flowered shoots are removed and the rest is thinned.

If pruning has been neglected, cut down completely to about 90 cm (3 ft), clear away the dense mass of growth and start again.

## AMPELOPSIS

This genus climbs with coiling tendrils and includes strong growers. They may be used to grow up into trees where no pruning is necessary.

If grown on walls a number of mature shoots (rods) are trained to form a permanent framework which is tied to supporting wires.

After leaf fall in early winter (not later so as to avoid excessive bleeding) the previous year's growth is cut back to within a bud of the permanent rods. Over the years twisted, knotted spurs build up at these pruning points and these in themselves have great character.

*Ampelopsis brevipedunculata* is the most commonly seen species, being vigorous and unusual in producing blue fruits. *A. brevipedunculata* 'Elegans', with foliage mottled and tinged pink, is less vigorous and suitable for small gardens.

## ARISTOLOCHIA

A genus of very vigorous twining climbers, including *Aristolochia macrophylla* (Dutchman's pipe). They are difficult to grow in a tidy manner; prune in summer after flowering, thinning out shoots and removing unwanted growth.

## BERBERIDOPSIS

*Berberidopsis corallina* (coral plant) is an evergreen twining climber best grown up vertical wires on a cool, shady wall. Only moderately hardy. Very light cosmetic pruning may be required in the spring.

## BUDDLEJA

*B. colvilei* is upright growing, almost self-supporting, and only requires ties to keep it close to the wall. It flowers on short shoots from the previous year's growth and only thin weak growth should be removed in the spring. *Buddleja crispa*, *B. fallowiana* and *B. forrestii* are best allowed to form a framework that is trained fan-wise on a south-facing wall. They all flower on the current season's growth in summer. Flowered growth should be pruned back to two or three buds in early spring.

## CAESALPINA

*Caesalpina japonica* and *C. gilliesii* may be grown against a sunny wall. Training is difficult and they are best left as free-standing bushes, although some ties may be required to keep them reasonably close to the wall.

Restrictive pruning to limit their spread and, in the case of *C. gilliesii* removal of winter damaged growth, should be done in the spring.

## CALLISTEMON (bottle brush)

Evergreen, sun-loving shrubs that must have the protection of a south-facing wall. Little pruning is necessary, the arching growth with terminal flowers being the characteristic habit.

As the shrub matures, renewal pruning should be practised, cutting out the oldest shoots to ground level after flowering to encourage new basal growths. If this is neglected, the persistent seed capsules weigh down the excessively long shoots of old branches, and an untidy gaunt-looking bush develops.

## CAMELLIA

Hybrids of *Camellia reticulata* and *C. saluensis* need the protection of a wall, and even then should only be attempted in very favoured areas, being better conservatory plants for the rest.

The race of hybrids known collectively as *C* × *williamsii* are hardy in the south, but in the colder north will benefit from the protection of a wall.

All the cultivars of *C. japonica* are hardy, but like all camellias their flowers are frost-sensitive so wall culture may save the flowers in a difficult spring.

For all species and cultivars, fan-train a well-spaced framework and allow side shoots to fill the spaces. Remove surplus shoots, plus shoots growing away from the wall after flowering in mid-spring.

Unfortunately, the cultivars of *C. japonica* usually fail to drop their finished blooms. To keep the display attractive, the plants should be dead-headed during flowering so that finished browned blooms do not spoil the display of newly opened flowers.

## CAMPSIS

Slightly tender vigorous deciduous climbers requiring a south-facing wall if growth is to be ripened and flowers produced.

*Campsis radicans* (trumpet vine) climbs using adventitious aerial roots, but needs a little support until established.

*Campsis* × *tagliabuana* 'Madame Galen' is a selected clone from the cross *C. grandiflora* × *C. radicans*. It is hardier than its parents, but definitely needs a support on which to be trained.

A well-shaped framework should be formed that covers all the allotted area, including the base. Pruning then consists of cutting back all annual extension growth to within two or three buds of the permanent framework in early spring.

## CARPENTERIA

*Carpenteria californica* is an evergreen summer-flowering shrub. It is somewhat tender, requiring the shelter afforded by a south or west-facing wall and is best planted well in front of the wall to form a free-standing bush.

**Fig. 10.9**
Evergreen ceanothus. Pruning and training in the first season following planting.

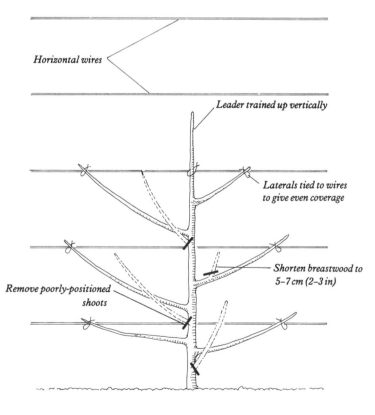

Horizontal wires

Leader trained up vertically

Laterals tied to wires to give even coverage

Shorten breastwood to 5–7 cm (2–3 in)

Remove poorly-positioned shoots

Wall-training is not recommended.

Little pruning is required. Spent flowers should be removed and winter-damaged growth pruned back to live wood in mid to late spring.

As the shrub matures, some older branches will become exhausted by flowering and thin at their tops due to frost damage. Periodic removal in spring to ground level of one or a few such branches will stimulate strong renewal growth.

## CEANOTHUS (Californian lilac)

Deciduous ceanothus are hardy, more frequently grown as free-standing shrubs and their pruning is explained in Chapter 7.

Evergreen ceanothus are tender, requiring the protection of a wall which they clothe all the year round with their foliage and in the late spring or early summer further decorate with flowers in shades of blue.

Plant out container-grown plants in the spring. Ensure the plant is not pot-bound as ceanothus in particular are prone to developing this condition. Once pot-bound, the root system of this genus seems singularly unable to escape.

Training is best onto wires. In the first year, a leader is taken up vertically and laterals spaced out over the wires. Growth is rapid and tying-in will need to be done at frequent intervals or else the shoots will tend to grow away from the wall and be difficult to bend back into position [Fig. 10.9].

Much breastwood, that is shoots coming out from the plane of the wall, will be produced. Shorten these shoots to 5–7.5 cm (2–3 in) early in the season, but leave them a little longer – 7.5–10 cm (3–4 in) – towards the end of the season.

Most evergreen ceanothus, for example *C. × veitchianus*, *C. dentatus*, and *C. thrysiflorus* flower on the previous season's wood. In the second and subsequent years, pruning is done immediately after flowering in early summer. Flowered shoots are cut back to 7.5–10 cm (3–4 in), breastwood is shortened to the same length and laterals tied in as required [Fig. 10.10].

A few evergreen ceanothus such as 'Gloire de Versailles' and 'Autumnal Blue' flower in summer on the current season's extension

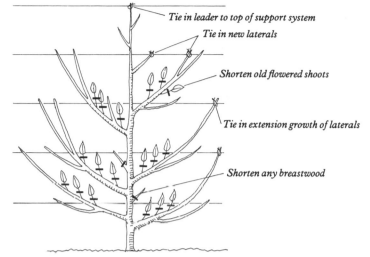

Tie in leader to top of support system

Tie in new laterals

Shorten old flowered shoots

Tie in extension growth of laterals

Shorten any breastwood

**Fig. 10.10**
Evergreen ceanothus. Pruning and training in subsequent years. Pruning done immediately after flowering (for exceptions please see text). Tying in of laterals must be done several times during the growing season.

growth. Here pruning must be done before flowering in early spring, shortening strong shoots to two or three buds.

## CELASTRUS

Very vigorous climbers. Grown up into trees they require no pruning, but are too vigorous for training on a fence or wall. If necessary, pruning out dead wood should be done in early summer when live wood can be distinguished from dead.

## CHAENOMELES
(flowering quince or japonica)

Although perfectly hardy, these early flowering shrubs are valuable wall shrubs for north or east-facing situations.

Starting with a young plant, and tying onto wires, an informal espalier framework is first established. This may consist of one leader taken up vertically, but if the young plant has more than one shoot, several may be taken up and spaced evenly on the wall to form an informal espalier.

Laterals are freely produced and these are spaced out and tied in to cover the space allocated [Fig. 10.11].

Breastwood, coming out from the plane of the wall or fence, and unwanted laterals, are shortened to four to six leaves in early summer. Further growth will usually occur from these pruning cuts and these shoots are reduced to two or three leaves in late summer. This

**Fig. 10.11**
*Chaenomeles* sp.
Initial training.

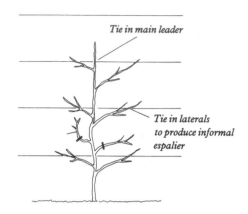

Tie in main leader

Tie in laterals
to produce informal
espalier

pruning results in the formation of spurs.

In the second and subsequent years, pruning is done after flowering in early to mid summer. Growth needed to complete the framework is tied in. All remaining shoots are shortened to four to six leaves. Secondary shoots may develop as a result of this pruning and these should be shortened to two or three leaves in the late summer. This summer pruning contains the shrub neatly against the wall or fence and builds up spur on which flower-buds are formed. After a number of years the spurs may become congested and some may be

**Fig. 10.12**
Planting and
pruning a young
clematis plant.

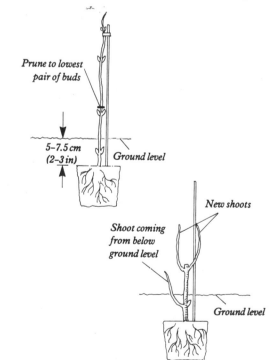

Prune to lowest
pair of buds

5–7.5 cm
(2–3 in)

Ground level

New shoots

Shoot coming
from below
ground level

Ground level

**Fig. 10.13** The
result of correctly
pruning a young
clematis plant.

removed in winter.

## CHIMONANTHUS

*Chimonanthus praecox* (winter sweet) is a hardy, deciduous, winter-flowering shrub. It is best grown against a sunny wall to ripen the wood which should ensure good flowering.

A permanent framework is tied to wires. The shrub is spur pruned, the previous season's growth being shortened to one or two buds after flowering in late winter.

Vigorous extension growth from the buds remaining will appear in spring. This growth will then have the summer and autumn to ripen and produce buds that will open the following winter.

## CLEMATIS

Pruning for all climbing clematis should start at planting, except if planting is done in summer or autumn when this pruning should be deferred to the following spring. Cut back the young plant to the lowest paid of buds. This pruning must be associated with the correct preparation, planting, feeding and mulching.

Such pruning will encourage the young plant to produce new shoots from the base and, hopefully, from below ground level [Figs. 10.12 and 10.13]. This hard initial pruning conveys the following advantages: the plant should be better furnished at its base; the plant is less at risk if damaged at its base, since it is unlikely all the shoots will be damaged; the plant should be better able to cope with an attack of clematis wilt caused by *Aschochyta* spp. and other causes. When this occurs a stem, or the complete plant, usually in active vigorous growth, suddenly collapses and wilts. If a single stem is affected it should be cut down to ground level. The same applies if the complete plant is affected. By having several stems there is a chance that only one or a few will be attacked. If the whole plant has to be cut down, dormant buds may still grow out from below ground level.

With regard to subsequent pruning after initial pruning, clematis fall into four groups:

### Group 1

These are non-climbing and comprise only a few species such as *C. heracleifolia* and *C. recta*.

Their pruning is described under **Clematis** in Chapter 7 (see page 70).

## Group 2

Clematis that flower on one-year-old wood. The group includes the very vigorous species *C. montana* and *C. chrysocoma* plus the much less vigorous *C. alpina* and *C. macropetala*. The plant is allowed to form a framework over its allotted area. Pruning is then done immediately after flowering, cutting back the previous year's wood that has just flowered to a few centimetres of the main framework.

*C. alpina* and *C. macropetala* may be pruned in the manner above, but they are unlikely to need much pruning since they are not strong growing.

*C. armandii*, an evergreen early-flowering species, is also in Group 1. It should be pruned after flowering. Excessive trailing growth can be cut back to suitably placed new shoots that will be beginning to grow at this stage.

*C. montana* is very vigorous, and is best grown up into a tree where no pruning is done. If growth should become excessive after a number of years, hard renovate pruning down to 60–90 cm (2–3 ft) can be carried out in late winter or early spring. Alternatively, *C. montana* can be allocated a fairly large area of wall and pruned as detailed above. The long lengths of annual growth will then hang down and give a cascade of flowers

## Group 3

This contains clematis that flower in summer or autumn entirely on the current season's growth. Contained within Group 3 are:

The species *C. campaniflora*, *C. orientalis*, and *C. ×jackmanii*, 'Comtesse de Bouchard', 'Hagley Hybrid' and 'Perle d'Azur'.

The Texensis group of hybrids, including 'Duchess of Albany', 'Etoile Rose', and 'Gravetye Beauty'.

The Viticella group that includes *C. viticella*, its cultivars such as *C. viticella* 'Minuet' and *C. viticella* 'Royal Velours', plus *C. viticella* hybrids including 'Ernest Markham', 'Huldine' and 'Lady Betty Balfour'.

If left to themselves, clematis in this group begin to grow and then flower from where they finished last year. One year's growth becomes piled upon another and the plant becomes very bare at its base.

The entire previous season's growth is removed down to about 30 cm (1 ft) above ground level in late winter or early spring.

## Group 4

This contains clematis that flower from late spring to mid summer on the previous season's wood, and again on the current season's wood in late summer and early autumn. Contained within Group 4 are:

The Florida groups of hybrids, including 'Duchess of Edinburgh' and 'Belle of Woking'.

The Lanuginosa group of hybrids, including 'Beauty of Worcester', 'Henryi' and 'Nelly Moser'.

The Patens group of hybrids, including 'The President' and 'Vyvyan Pennell'.

The pruning of clematis in Group 4 is not easy to do satisfactorily. Normal practice is to trim only lightly to tidy the plant after the final flowers in the autumn. After a number of years growth becomes collected and congested at the top of its allotted area. The plant should then be hard-pruned as for Group 1 in late winter or early spring. This means a fresh start is made; the early crop of flowers is lost, but the plant once again evenly covers its allotted space and flowers later in the season on current season's growth.

## CLIANTHUS

*Clianthus puniceus* (parrot's bill or lobster's claw) is an evergreen, scandent shrub requiring the protection of a south or west-facing wall in a favoured area.

Train as an informal fan when young. In spring, remove any growth that has been killed by the winter and occasionally remove old branches.

Remove faded flowers, not allowing them to set seed as this can be heavy and will weaken the shrub.

## COTONEASTER

*Cotoneaster horizontalis* is a deciduous free-fruiting species that produces branches with a characteristic 'herring-bone' pattern. It is very useful for planting against a north or east-facing wall where the branches will naturally adhere themselves to the wall. If extra height is required, only the main branches require tying in.

Other evergreen species can be grown as wall shrubs, their initial training being the same as for chaenomeles [see Fig. 10.11]. Off-white flowers are produced, to be followed by berries. After flowering, extension growth is produced in early to mid-summer; this is pruned to four to six buds. Re-growth may occur, and this is shortened in early autumn if necessary to two or three leaves. The summer pruning exposes the berries for autumn display, forms the spur on which next year's flowers will be produced, and keeps the shrub constrained fairly tightly against the wall.

## CYTISUS

*Cytisus battandieri* (Moroccan broom or pineapple broom) is an evergreen shrub. It may be grown as a free-standing shrub in fairly favoured localities, but elsewhere it is better growing against a south or west-facing wall. The plant may be grown either free-standing against the wall, or trained and tied to it. Winter killed shoots should be pruned back to live wood in mid-spring, when shoots that are unwanted and lean out too far can also be removed.

## ECCREMOCARPUS

*Eccremocarpus scaber* (Chilean glory flower) is a short-lived perennial using tendrils to climb. Growth may be untouched in a mild winter, but after a moderate winter the stems may be killed down to almost ground level. Prune down to new shoots and clear away dead growth in spring. A severe winter may kill this plant.

Early removal of the prodigious amount of seed produced in the summer may help extend the flowering season.

## EUCALYPTUS

See page 73.

## FALLOPIA

*Fallopia baldschuanica* (syn. *Polygonum baldschuanicum*) (Russian vine) flowers pink-tinged, and *F. aubertii* flowers white, only becoming pinkish in fruit. The latter is a more common plant and is often confused with the true Russian vine. Both are very vigorous, fast-growing deciduous plants that climb by twining. They are widely used for screening or growing up into old trees. Where space is available, no pruning is necessary.

These plants are difficult to restrict in a confined space because of the considerable amount of growth made each year. Severe annual pruning can be done in early spring to remove all previous excess growth. Because of the amount of pruning that will be required, where space is limited another less-vigorous climber is probably a better choice.

## × FATSHEDERA

× *Fatshedera lizei* is a bigeneric hybrid between *Fatsia japonica* and *Hedera hibernica*. It has a sprawling habit and may be used as a ground cover or trained up north and east walls. Pruning is seldom necessary, although it may suffer winter damage and top growths may need pruning back to undamaged growth in spring.

## FORSYTHIA

*Forsythia suspensa* is best grown as a wall shrub, where its pendant habit can be used with advantage. A framework is developed and tied to the wall. From this, long weeping stems develop that bear the flowers in spring. Following flowering these weeping stems are cut off close to the permanent framework. During the summer, a new crop of pendant stems grow out, which flower the following spring.

## GARRYA

*Garrya elliptica* (tassel bush) is an evergreen winter flowering shrub. There are separate male and female plants, but it is the male that is commonly grown as it produces attractive long catkins. The clone 'James Roof' is a vigorous male plant with extra long catkins.

In sheltered areas, the plant may be grown with success as a free-standing shrub, but more often it is seen grown as a wall shrub being suitable for north and east-facing walls.

Only the major branches of the framework

need to be tied to the wall. Size and spread may be contained by pruning in mid spring as the catkins fade, but before new growth commences. Cut back to within the bush so that the pruning cuts are hidden and the informal outline retained.

Old overgrown specimens can be cut hard back to the original framework in spring. The response at each site of pruning will be the production of numerous new shoots.

## HEDERA (ivy)

*Hedera helix* (common ivy) is a native plant that can be used to clothe walls of any orientation. It should only be planted after some thought as it grows very fast and can be difficult to remove (see page 109). Better choices might be a less vigorous variegated cultivar such as *H. helix* 'Goldheart', *H. colchica* (Persian ivy) with large dark green leaves, or the variegated *H. colchica* 'Dentata Variegata'. *H. algeriensis* 'Gloire de Marengo' (syn. *H. canariensis* 'Gloire de Marengo'), may also be used but is liable to winter damage.

Once the top of a wall or other support is reached, and more light is received, ivy will change from its juvenile form, with aerial roots and deeply lobed leaves, to the adult form without roots and rounder leaves; flowering will commence. Such adult growth, although slower, tends to grow out and away from the wall. Annual pruning will be necessary to prevent its weight pulling the plant off the wall. An annual clipping, plus removal of large outgrowing sections, can be done in late spring to early summer.

## HYDRANGEA

*Hydrangea petiolaris* is a deciduous self-clinging climber. The adventitious aerial roots hold the plant firmly to the wall, but even greater security is achieved if the plant is allowed to anchor itself onto the top of the wall.

Flowering shoots grow out from the wall. After several years the climber may grow out too far from the wall. These horizontal shoots may be cut carefully back to a bud nearer the wall in the spring. In order not to lose too many flowers and not to lose the natural growth habit, this cutting back should be done over a number of years.

## JASMINUM

*Jasminum nudiflorum* (winter jasmine) is a deciduous winter-flowering shrub with a scandent habit of growth. It may be grown as a wall shrub or as a free-standing shrub when it forms a low-growing ground-covering plant.

When grown as a wall plant a permanent framework is trained in. The annual extension growth on which the flowers are produced should be cut back to a bud near the permanent framework immediately after flowering. Framework branches will need to be replaced or they will become excessively congested.

*J. officinale* is a vigorous climber and difficult to train; indeed, it is best to let it grow naturally and accept its free-growing habit. If necessary, some of the oldest wood may be cut out after flowering. *J. beesianum* is similar to *J. officinale*, being less vigorous and requiring the same pruning, as does *J. × stephanense*, a hybrid between *J. officinale* and *J. beesianum*.

## LONICERA (honeysuckle)

The pruning of shrubby non-climbing honeysuckles is dealt with under **Lonicera** in Chapter 7 (see page 77).

For the purposes of pruning, the climbing honeysuckles can be placed into two groups. The first flower on the current season's growth and of these *L. japonica* is by far the most common. A difficult plant to restrain, pruning is best done by clipping back growth in early to mid spring [Fig. 10.14].

*Flowers can also be produced from auxiliary buds*

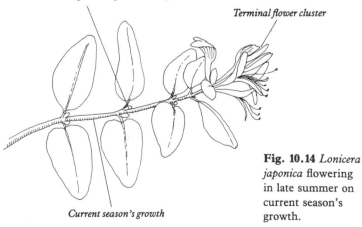
*Terminal flower cluster*

*Current season's growth*

**Fig. 10.14** *Lonicera japonica* flowering in late summer on current season's growth.

**Fig. 10.15** *Lonicera periclymenum* flowering in early summer on short laterals produced from the previous season's growth.

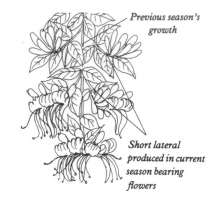

*Previous season's growth*

*Short lateral produced in current season bearing flowers*

The second group contains those honeysuckles that flower on short laterals produced from the previous season's growth [Fig. 10.15]. The group includes *L. periclymenum*, *L. × americana*, *L. tellmanniana* and *L. tragophylla*. Pruning should be done immediately after flowering. Old weak growth should be removed. Some of the branches that have flowered should be pruned back to where new strong shoots are developing. These new shoots can be tied in to attempt formal training, but if space permits are better left to fall to give a graceful cascade of flowers the following season.

## MAGNOLIA

The evergreen species *Magnolia delavayi* and *M. grandiflora* are often grown as wall shrubs.

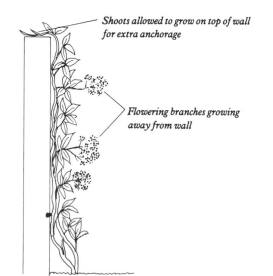

*Shoots allowed to grow on top of wall for extra anchorage*

*Flowering branches growing away from wall*

**Fig. 10.16** *Pileostegia viburnoides* growing on a wall.

*M. delavayi*, with its very large leaves, is only rarely seen as a large multi-stemmed shrub or small tree in favoured areas. It is usually best regarded as somewhat tender and grown as a wall shrub. A tall wall is required as initially a strong leader is trained up vertically.

*M. grandiflora* is hardier and much more frequently seen as a free-standing shrub. As such it is very successful, although some shelter is still advisable. When grown as a wall shrub on a south-facing wall, flowering may be more profuse. It should be trained for two-thirds its height against the wall, but only the main stem and major laterals need to be secured. The plant is strong growing and once the intended area is covered, excessive growth may be pruned away in mid summer.

## PARTHENOCISSUS

A genus consisting of climbers attaching themselves by tendrils that may twist around a support or adhere by pads produced at the end of the tendrils.

*Parthenocissus henryana* is a moderately vigorous self-clinging species, best grown on a wall and suitable for a fairly small area.

*P. quinquefolia* (Virginia creeper) is a vigorous climber, more or less self-clinging, and better for the aid of wires when grown up walls.

*P. tricuspidata* (Boston ivy) is a very vigorous climber, suitable for growing up into trees, onto towers and high walls.

Pruning is best done in early winter as later pruning will cause bleeding. Remove excessive growth. This is especially necessary with *P. tricuspidata*; unchecked it can cause the forms of damage explained earlier in this chapter (see page 109).

## PHYGELIUS

*Phygelius aequalis* is tender, requiring the protection of a south-facing wall. Although technically a shrub, it usually dies down to ground level during the winter. Prune down to ground level in spring.

*P. capensis* (cape figwort) and newer hybrids related to this species are hardier. They may be grown as herbaceous plants in the border,

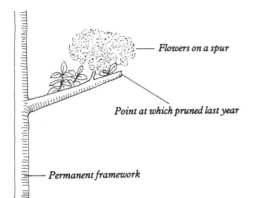

**Fig. 10.17** Wall-trained pyracantha. Flowering in spring.

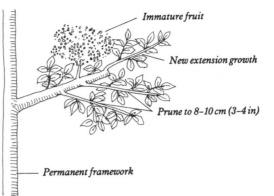

**Fig. 10.18** Wall-trained pyracantha. Production and pruning of primary extension growth in mid-summer.

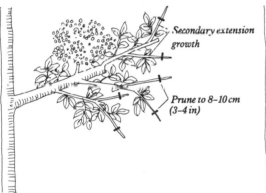

**Fig. 10.19** Wall-trained pyracantha. Production and pruning of secondary extension growth in early autumn.

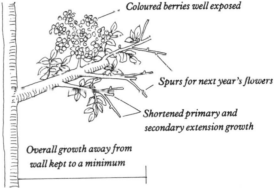

**Fig. 10.20** Wall-trained pyracantha. Result of growth and pruning over one growing season from Fig. 10.17.

being pruned down to ground level in the spring. They will spread by rhizomes. This species may also be grown as a wall shrub against a south-facing wall. Main stems are tied against wires to a maximum height of about 2 m (6 ft). Pruning consists of cutting back to these main stems, that usually survive the winter, in spring.

## PILEOSTEGIA

*Pileostegia viburnoides* is an evergreen self-clinging climber producing aerial adventitious roots.

Pruning usually only consists of stopping or shortening surplus extension growth in the summer once the plant's allotted space is filled. Flowering shoots grow away from the wall and may become quite heavy. For this reason it is

advantageous, if possible, to allow the plant to grow over and adhere to the top of the wall for extra anchorage [Fig. 10.16]. If these flowering branches become too long they may be shortened in the spring.

## PYRACANTHA

Pyracantha is a genus of evergreen hardy shrubs. They can be grown as either free-standing or wall shrubs.

As wall shrubs they can be trained to almost any shape, formal or informal. The first stage is to train and tie in the framework, shortening any breastwood that may be produced.

On the mature plant flowers are produced in spring on short spurs from the previous year's shoots [Fig. 10.17]. After flowering, new shoots appear. These shoots should be cut back to

8–10 cm (3–4 in) in mid summer to expose the berries [Fig. 10.18]. Subsequent secondary growth may occur and this should be pruned to 8–10 cm (3–4 in) in early autumn [Fig. 10.19].

Using this method of pruning the plant is contained against the wall, spurs to produce flowers annually are formed, and a good display of the fruits is achieved [Fig. 10.20].

## RIBES

*Ribes speciosum* is a little tender and is best grown against a sunny wall where its fuchsia-like flowers can be clearly seen and appreciated.

Growth should be trained fan-wise against the wall. New shoots from the base should be tied in and used to replace the oldest shoots which will have lost vigour and should be removed at ground level. Replacement pruning and tying in is done in late summer.

## ROBINIA

Most of the plants in this genus are trees and their pruning is dealt with in Chapter 6.

*Robinia hispida* (rose acacia) is a medium-sized suckering shrub producing racemes of deep rose flowers. Unfortunately its wood is very brittle and liable to wind damage. It is best grafted onto *Robinia pseudoacacia*, treated as a wall shrub, and grown on a sheltered sunny wall.

Tying in of new extension growth must be regularly attended to during the summer. Very little pruning is necessary except removal of any suckers from the stock and any wind damaged shoots.

## SCHIZANDRA

A genus of deciduous and evergreen twining shrubs, usually grown on a shady wall. When young, space out several shoots fan-wise to cover the wall. Once the top of the wall is reached, pendular growth is then allowed to develop. Flower spurs will form on this pendular growth.

Pruning consists of thinning out the older and weaker pendular growth in winter before the buds break out.

## SCHIZOPHRAGMA

*Schizophragma integrifolium* and *S. hydrange-*

*oides* are deciduous self-clinging climbers producing adventitious aerial roots. Despite being self-clinging, additional support in the form of ties to wires will also be needed.

Two types of growth are produced – extension growth that grows adpressed to the wall and produces adventitious roots, plus flowering growth that grows out from the wall and is semi-pendulous. Pruning consists of the removal of excessive extension growth in the dormant season.

Both plants can also be grown up into trees or over low stumps and mounds. When grown in this manner no pruning is required.

## SOLANUM

*Solanum crispum* and *S. crispum* 'Glasnevin', its longer flowering form, are vigorous semi-evergreen scramblers. They can be grown on a wall or allowed to scramble over a low support such as a tree stump. Growth as a free-standing, but rather untidy plant is also possible in a sheltered spot.

Growing as a wall plant involves tying in growth fan-wise to cover the allotted space. Further young growth is then tied in loosely during summer and autumn, but final pruning and tidying up left until the spring.

In spring, however, whatever method of growing is employed, all growth damaged by the winter is cut back to promising new shoots. Old and weak growth is also removed.

*S. jasminoides* is a semi-evergreen fast growing twining climber. It is best suited to warm walls and is more tender than *S. crispum*. Pruning is the same as for *S. crispum*, but winter damage and hence spring pruning is likely to be more severe.

## SOPHORA

The evergreen *Sophora microphylla* and *S. tetraptera* (the New Zealand 'Kowhai') are only really successful in favoured areas where they may be grown as wall shrubs.

Very little pruning is required, but wayward shoots may be removed after flowering in spring.

## TRACHELOSPERMUM

A genus of evergreen, tender, self-clinging, twisting climbers requiring the warmth of a sunny sheltered wall. No regular pruning is required.

## VITEX

*Vitex agnus-castus* (chaste tree) and *V. negundo* are deciduous members of this genus and best grown as wall shrubs.

A well-shaped framework that evenly covers the area allocated should be developed first. Pruning then consists of removing the old flowering shoots to within two or three buds of the permanent framework in early spring.

## VITIS

The ornamental vines should be pruned in exactly the same manner as described for **Ampelopsis** (see page 111).

## WISTERIA

Deciduous twining climbers, *Wisteria floribunda* (Japanese wisteria) is a fairly vigorous species twining in a clockwise direction. *Wisteria sinensis* (Chinese wisteria) is a very vigorous species that twines in an anti-clockwise direction.

Despite their vigour, using a system involving pruning twice a year, they can be constrained to a pre-determined and limited size.

In the garden or landscape they can be used in a wide variety of ways, including up into trees, on walls and pergolas, as free-standing shrubs, and may be trained to make standard plants.

*Importance of correct initial purchase*
Wisterias can be propagated by seed or by grafting. Plants produced from seed are unreliable in their flowering characteristics and grafted plants, where the scion comes from a known good plant, should always be purchased. Be certain to check that the plant you select has been produced by grafting at the same time of purchase. A wisteria can take several years to flower, and discovering that you have obtained a poor plant is very disappointing after several years of waiting.

*Training and pruning as a young wall plant*
Wisteria can be trained formally as an espalier with a single main stem and horizontal laterals, or less formally, but with most of the laterals

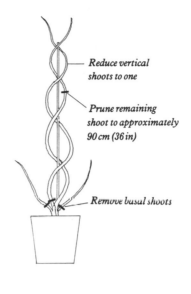

**Fig. 10.21**
Wisteria. Pruning after purchase, but before planting.

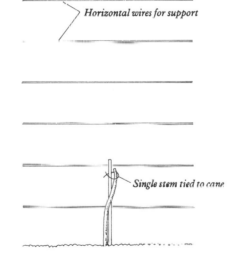

**Fig. 10.22**
Wisteria. Newly planted plant.

spread out horizontally over the wall. Whatever system is adopted, aim to have the horizontal shoots 38–45 cm (15–18 in) apart to allow the flowering racemes to hang down freely for best display without fouling the branch below.

To produce an espalier-trained wisteria, start training and pruning in the first season [Figs. 10.21 and 10.22].

During the first season's growth, the topmost lateral is taken up to form the vertical shoot. Laterals are tied in at approximately 45°. They are not initially tied in horizontally as this might check the growth of the young

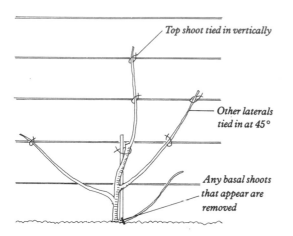

**Fig. 10.23** Wisteria. Training in the first growing season.

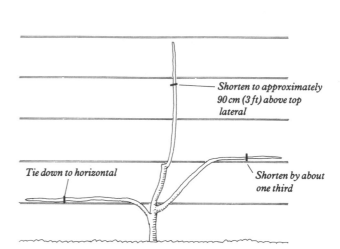

**Fig. 10.24** Wisteria. Training and pruning after first season's growth.

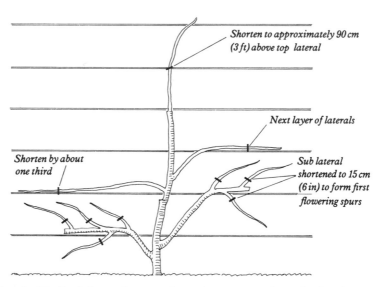

**Fig. 10.25** Wisteria. Idealized shape after second growing season and pruning in winter.

plant too much [Figs. 10.23 and 10.24].

The following season the same procedure is followed to produce further extension of the main vertical, another set of laterals, and the first of the flowering spurs [Fig. 10.25].

In this manner, over a number of years a formal espalier is produced. Since flowering spurs are not produced until two years after planting, this explains why a young plant can take so long to start flowering.

This pattern of lateral and spur production is continued until sufficient laterals are produced to fill the allotted space. If desired, a less formal system may be allowed to develop, perhaps with more than one basal shoot, but it is important that the laterals are eventually trained horizontally with sufficient space between them for flowering.

### Training as a free-standing shrub

A wisteria may be grown as a free-standing shrub suitable for use as a specimen in the centre of a lawn. After planting, the young plant is encouraged to produce several basal shoots. These will permanently require support from vertical posts. As these shoots thicken they will take on variously twisted shapes which add character to the plant.

### Training as a standard

Another method of training these plants is as a standard. The young plant has a single stem taken vertically up a post to the height required. Once this is reached, the stem is stopped and encouraged to produce a head that will eventually produce a profuse crop of flowers [Fig. 10.26].

### The pruning of mature plants

Once the plant, in whatever shape it has been

**Fig. 10.26**
Wisteria. Trained as a standard. Once the head is formed, pruning twice a year, as detailed in the text, will control growth and at the same time encourage profuse flowering.

Using this system of pruning twice a year, the plant is constrained and encouraged to flower freely. Gradually flower spurs are developed that are capable of bearing many racemes of flowers in a small area.

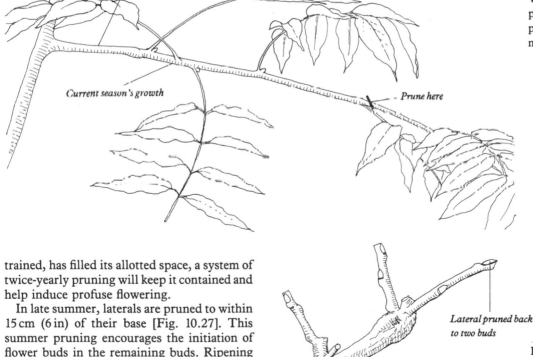

**Fig. 10.27**
Wisteria. Summer pruning. Laterals pruned to approximately 15 cm (6 in).

*Previous season's growth*

*Current season's growth*

*Prune here*

*Lateral pruned back to two buds*

**Fig. 10.28**
Wisteria. Winter pruning. Laterals pruned back to two or three buds.

trained, has filled its allotted space, a system of twice-yearly pruning will keep it contained and help induce profuse flowering.

In late summer, laterals are pruned to within 15 cm (6 in) of their base [Fig. 10.27]. This summer pruning encourages the initiation of flower buds in the remaining buds. Ripening of this wood is also encouraged by better air circulation and exposure to the sun.

In mid-winter these laterals are further pruned back to two or three buds [Fig. 10.28].

# CHAPTER 11
# *Roses*

## General principles

All roses, when growing wild, have the same basic pattern of growth. A strong new branch arises and begins to flower. Gradually, over several seasons, it loses vigour and eventually dies. As this original branch gets older, another new branch will appear to start the cycle again. This explains the appearance of roses in the wild with a mass of old, often dead wood, some flowering shoots, plus a few new shoots. The aim of pruning is to keep the plant young with a preponderance of young flowering wood. The importance of using the correct tools and cutting to a bud, as explained in Chapter 2, cannot be over-emphasized. Cutting too far above the bud must be avoided or else the disease complex causing die-back will become a serious problem [Fig. 11.1].

The general principles are as follows. Dead, diseased and damaged growth should be removed and burnt. Be sure to cut back into healthy wood; if the central pith is brown, cut back further until it is a healthy white. Try to produce an open-centred bush, with branches

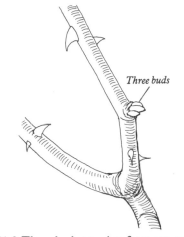

**Fig. 11.2** Three buds growing from one eye. If it is decided to prune to this eye, these buds will have to be reduced to one by pinching out the young growth as soon as possible.

regularly spaced around the bush. To this end, remove crossing or thin growth, pruning to an outward-facing bud. A good flow of air through the bush will help to reduce the incidence of the disease *Podospheara leucotricha* (rose mildew), *Phragmidium tuberculatum* (rose rust) and *Diplocarpon rosae* (black spot).

If a rose has a particularly spreading habit it may be correct to prune sometimes to an inward-facing bud to try to obtain more upright growth.

Modern hybrid roses may occasionally produce more than one bud from an eye. If this occurs, reduce the buds to one [Fig. 11.2].

## Seasons for pruning

### Early spring

The main pruning period for most roses is early spring. Timing is fairly critical and depends not on the calendar, but on the prevailing weather conditions and development of the roses.

Early to mid winter pruning is not generally

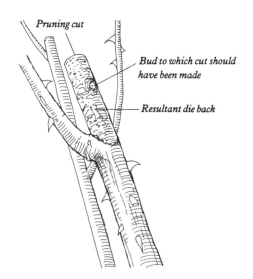

*Pruning cut*

*Bud to which cut should have been made*

*Resultant die back*

**Fig. 11.1** A rose that has been poorly pruned in the past, with die-back evident where a cut was made too far above a bud.

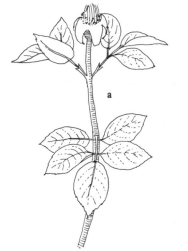
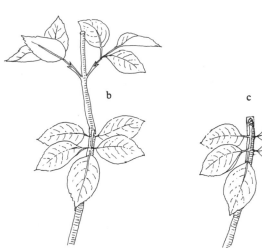

**Fig. 11.3** (*a*) Spent flower requring pruning. (*b*) Incorrect pruning cut not made to a bud. (*c*) Correct pruning cut made to the first bud.

recommended as it can lead to the precocious growing out of the buds that are then vulnerable to late frosts.

Prune when the buds half-way up the vigorous stems are beginning to swell. Waiting until later when all buds have broken results in wasting much of the plant energy. Pruning is also practically difficult as it is difficult to avoid accidentally brushing against and knocking off some of the young growths.

Despite this care, high day temperatures followed by night frost can result in late frost damage. Plants may then need extra pruning, in such problematic seasons, to remove frost damaged shoots back to undamaged, less advanced eyes.

## Summer pruning

Summer pruning is confined to the removal of spent flowers. This is done for several reasons. Old decaying petals can act as a disease focus, especially in wet seasons. It prevents the plant wasting its effort in seed production and encourages repeat, also known as recurrent, flowering. Note that spent flowers are not removed from roses such as *Rosa moyesii* and *Rosa rugosa*, where their large coloured hips in the late summer and autumn are another added attraction. Cut back to the first bud or young shoot immediately below the complete inflorescence [Fig. 11.3].

## Autumn pruning

In the autumn shorten longer growth by 15–30 cm (6–12 in). The rootstock only makes comparatively few coarse roots which afford

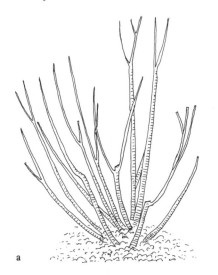
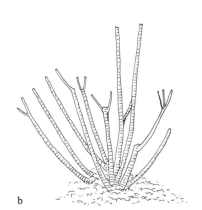

**Fig. 11.4** Autumn pruning of Large Flowered and Cluster Flowered roses. Long growths are reduced by 15–30 cm (6–12 in). This helps prevent wind rock. Heavily mildewed growth and leaves infected with black spot should also be removed. (*a*) Unpruned rose. (*b*) Rose pruned as for autumn.

poor root anchorage. If not done, the plant may suffer from wind rock through the winter. This is especially necessary with young roses in an exposed, windy situation [Fig. 11.4].

Autumn pruning also helps to break the life cycle and stop the carry-over of diseases, including rose mildew and black spot. Heavily mildewed growth and leaves infected with black spot should be removed and burnt. Shoots produced too late in the season, which

**Fig. 11.5** The Large Flowered rose 'Ballerina' with heavily mildewed growth that should be removed at the time of autumn pruning.

are still very soft at their tips, should be cut back to ripened wood to avoid winter injury [Fig. 11.5].

## Recent name changes

Roses formerly known as 'Hybrid Teas' should now be called 'Large Flowered' and those formerly called 'Floribunda' should now be described as 'Cluster Flowered'. These new names were introduced because it was felt they described the type of flower produced by each group better. The old names referred to grouping by breeding, but in recent years this grouping has largely been eroded.

Anyone interested in growing roses needs to know these four names and how they relate. The new names are now commonly used.

## Large Flowered (Hybrid tea) and Hybrid perpetuals

These two groups of roses are pruned in the same way. They flower on the current season's growth and are described as being recurrent flowering since flowering occurs continuously or in several flushes through the growing season.

They benefit from fairly severe pruning which, with adequate feeding, should ensure the production of plenty of new growth on which they flower.

The more vigorous cultivars, for example 'Peace', respond best to comparatively light pruning, heavy pruning resulting in a few very vigorous and, often flowerless shoots. Weak-growing cultivars, in contrast, respond well to comparatively hard pruning.

### Pruning new plants

Upon receipt of a new bare root rose in autumn or winter, trim any excessively long or damaged roots and cut back shoots lightly to a bud if not already done. A top-grade new rose should have three to four shoots coming from the point at which it was budded. Growth should be firm, with no signs of desiccation or buds beginning to grow out [Fig. 11.6].

In early spring, cut each growth back to two or four eyes above ground level.

Summer and autumn pruning is done as previously described.

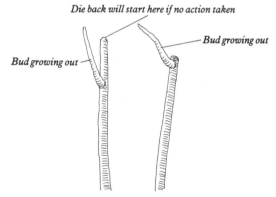

**Fig. 11.6** A poor new rose. Only two shoots coming from where budded on the briar (not in itself too much of a disadvantage.) The fact that buds have begun to grow out as shown is a sign of poor storage. If accepted, prune back to still dormant buds before planting.

### Treatment of 'blind' shoots

Some vigorous Large Flowered roses, for example 'Chicago Peace', occasionally produce so-called 'blind' shoots. These are very vigor-

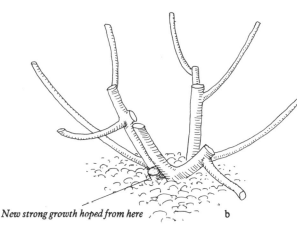

**Fig. 11.7 Spring
pruning of an
established
Large Flowered
rose.**
(*a*) Rose pruned as
for autumn.
(*b*) Rose after
spring pruning.

*New strong growth hoped from here*

a

b

ous, but unfortunately do not produce flowers,
they just abruptly stop growing. Prune these
shoots back as soon as recognized to encourage
new lateral growth which will then produce
flowers in the normal manner. Excessively
hard pruning of very vigorous cultivars tends
to exacerbate this problem.

### Disbudding for exhibition

This is only done with Large Flowered
cultivars. If growing for exhibition or show
work, the grower may disbud his roses, leaving
only one flower per stem. The remaining
flower should then be exceptionally large. This
specialized disbudding is usually coupled with
extra-hard pruning and heavy feeding.

### Pruning in subsequent years

The following spring the rose receives its next
severe pruning.

Dead, diseased, crossing and weak growth is
cut out. Prune back remaining shoots. Strong
growths are cut back to four to six eyes, but
weaker growths cut down to two to four eyes.
Remember weak-growing cultivars require
hard pruning, but those that are strong-
growing require lighter pruning.

In subsequent years prune as above, but also
remove a few of the oldest stems to ground
level. This is done to encourage new growth
from the base and keep the overall bush full of
new wood. Try to ensure that no wood within
the bush is more than three years old
[Fig. 11.7].

## Cluster Flowered (Floribunda) roses

The spring pruning of Cluster Flowered roses
is very similar to Large Flowered roses. Dead,
diseased, crossing, inward-growing and weak

**Fig. 11.8 Spring
pruning of an
established
Cluster Flowered
rose.**
(*a*) Rose pruned as
for autumn.
(*b*) Rose after
spring pruning.

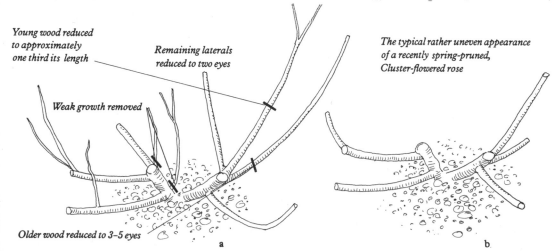

*Young wood reduced
to approximately
one third its length*

*Remaining laterals
reduced to two eyes*

*The typical rather uneven appearance
of a recently spring-pruned,
Cluster-flowered rose*

*Weak growth removed*

*Older wood reduced to 3–5 eyes*

a

b

growth should be removed.

Because of their generally greater vigour, slightly lighter pruning is done. Young wood is reduced by approximately one third of its length, older wood reduced to three to five eyes and any remaining laterals pruned to two or three eyes.

Once the bush is three or more years old, some of the oldest wood should be cut down to ground level or a promising bud low down. This is done to encourage strong renewal growth. After pruning, Cluster Flowered roses present a slightly more irregular appearance than Large Flowered roses, but this represents a good compromise between the aims of obtaining maximum flowers and sufficient renewal growth [Fig. 11.8].

### English roses

This is a new race of roses. Most people like the flower shape and form of Old Garden Roses, but their major disadvantage is that they are non-recurrent, flowering only once a season. The concept behind the breeding of English roses was to incorporate the shape of the Old Garden Rose flowers with the recurrent flowering nature of Large Flowered roses. Examples are the cultivars 'Jayne Austin' with rosette-shaped flowers and 'Graham Thomas' with flowers of a cupped shape.

Pruning may be as for Cluster Flowered roses when many, but smaller flowers will be produced, or as for Large Flowered roses when fewer, but larger flowers will be produced on a smaller shrub.

### Patio roses

These are a comparatively new type of rose, intermediate in size between miniature and Cluster Flowered roses. The idea behind their breeding was to provide roses that had masses of flowers on a comparatively small bush. As such, they should be ideal for the smaller garden. They have a very recurrent pattern of flowering, being in flower for most of the growing season.

Pruning is the same for Cluster Flowered roses.

### Miniature roses

These are a group of small-growing roses, only

growing to 30–60 cm (1–2 ft) in height.

Pruning is the same as for Large Flowered roses, but do not prune newly planted plants quite so hard. If a vigorous shoot is produced that unbalances the plant during the growing season, cut back to rebalance after flowering.

### Climbing and Rambling roses

Before separating Climbing and Rambling roses into their different groups, it is worth noting that all new growth except that required for extension growth should be tied into as near a horizontal position as possible. Such shoots will produce flowering laterals along their length and give a generous display. In contrast, vertical shoots will tend to grow and flower only at their tips.

### Rambling roses

Rambling roses can be separated from Climbing roses on the pattern of their flowering. In nearly all cases rambling roses are non-recurrent whereas climbing roses are recurrent. Rambling roses can be sub-divided into three groups according to their pruning needs.

*Group 1*

This first group includes those ramblers derived from *Rosa wichuraiana*. They flower on one-year-old wood. Long shoots produced from the base of the plant the previous growing season, flower in one flush in mid-summer. Examples of cultivars within this group include 'American Pillar', 'Dorothy Perkins' and 'Excelsa'.

A young, bare root plant should be hard-pruned to 23–38 cm (9–15 in) before planting. The following growing season vigorous growth will occur which should be trained horizontally onto wires. No flowers should be expected.

The next growing season profuse flowering will occur in mid summer. Strong young basal shoots will develop [Fig. 11.9].

In late summer or early autumn cut away the flowered growths at their base, then tie in new growth horizontally. If not enough growth has been produced for complete coverage, a few old canes may be retained [Fig. 11.10].

*Group 2*

This second group differs in that they produce

*Ceanothus arboreus*
'Trewithen Blue'
grown to
perfection. The
result of careful
training and
pruning after
flowering in early
summer.

Pyracantha pruned and trained informally.
Suitable pruning where growth needs to be
controlled, but where an informal effect is
desired.

Pyracantha pruned severely and trained in espalier manner. Suited to a garden formal in style.

*Wisteria sinensis* in full glory in early summer.
The culmination of correct siting and pruning.

Classic beauty brought about by correct pruning
and training.

Bougainvillea trained and pruned to clamber over
a conservatory pergola.

*Opposite:*
A well-shaped plant of *Pachystachys lutea*, full of
flowers; the result of appropriate and effective
pruning.

An effective way of ensuring that the scion shoot and rootstock are in a straight line.

*Below:*
A sorry and all-too-common sight that illustrates complete ignorance of why and how an apple tree should be pruned.

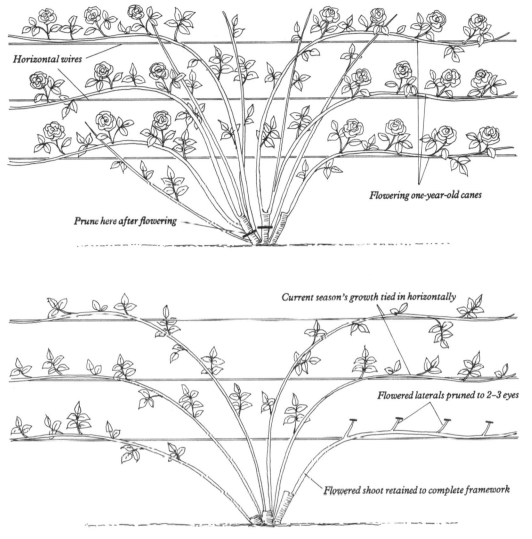

**Fig. 11.9** Rambler from Group 1 at first flowering.

*Horizontal wires*

*Flowering one-year-old canes*

*Prune here after flowering*

*Current season's growth tied in horizontally*

*Flowered laterals pruned to 2–3 eyes*

*Flowered shoot retained to complete framework*

**Fig. 11.10** Rambler from Group 1 after pruning and tying in of new growth in early autumn.

new canes, not principally from ground level, but from mid-way up on the old canes. They flower on one-year-old wood.

The new plant growth requires the same hard pruning as Group 1.

The aim of annual pruning done after flowering in early autumn is to tie in new growth and remove old wood in the same proportion [Figs. 11.11 and 11.12].

Examples of cultivars within this group are 'Albéric Barbier', 'Albertine', 'New Dawn', 'Paul's Scarlet Climber' and 'Veilchenblau'.

*Group 3*
Group 3 of the Rambling roses includes

climbing species, near species and hybrids with enormous vigour. These plants are well capable of growing 6 m (20 ft) in one growing season. Their use is best confined to growing up into trees or as ground cover over banks or ground. Do not try to grow these roses in a controlled manner on walls or fences.

The young plant requires no pruning, but if it is intended to grow up into a tree, initial training will be necessary.

Examples of roses within this group are *Rosa filipes* 'Kiftsgate', 'Francis E. Lester', 'Paul's Himalayan Musk' and 'Wedding Day'.

Best grown in the unrestricted manner suggested, very little pruning is necessary or practical. If possible, dead, diseased and weak wood should be removed. If the supporting tree is becoming overwhelmed, the rose will have to be reduced, whole branches being removed near the base. This can be done in early spring and will result in much regrowth from the rose near its base.

**Climbing roses**

Climbing roses flower on the current season's growth. The group includes climbing sports of Large Flowered and Cluster Flowered roses, plus climbers of the large flowered style. Most are recurrent flowering. Examples of cultivars within this group are 'Handel', 'Iceberg' (Climbing), 'Maigold', 'Masquerade' (Climbing), 'Meg' and 'Zéphirine Drouhin'.

Two other roses that fall within this group of climbing roses are *Rosa banksiae* of which the cultivar *Rosa banksiae* 'Lutea' (the yellow banksian rose) is the most common and *Rosa* 'Mermaid'. In both cases they are slightly tender and additional pruning may consist of cutting off winter damaged growth in spring.

Because of their moderate vigour and flexuous nature of their growth, climbing roses are ideal for growing on walls, fences, pergolas, etc.

On receipt of a new bare root plant, trim the root as for any other rose. Do not prune the shoots. This is especially important with climbing sports of Large Flowered roses, since pruning may cause them to revert to the bush form. At planting time, train in the shoots [Fig. 11.13].

Climbing roses are not particularly vigorous

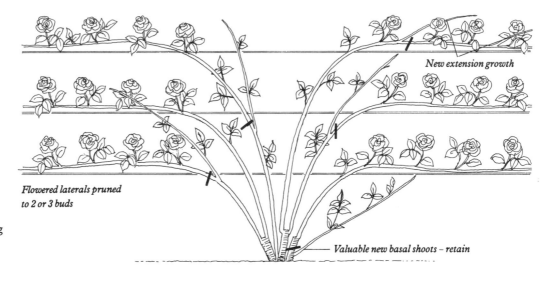

**Fig. 11.11**
Rambler from Group 2 at flowering. Pruning done soon after flowering.

*Flowered laterals pruned to 2 or 3 buds*

*New extension growth*

*Valuable new basal shoots – retain*

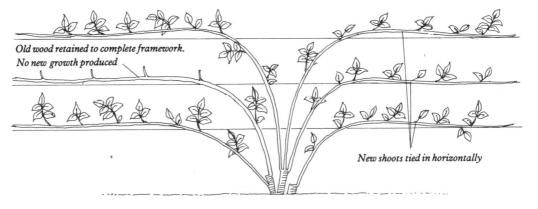

**Fig. 11.12**
Rambler from Group 2 after pruning.

*Old wood retained to complete framework. No new growth produced*

*New shoots tied in horizontally*

and little pruning is required. In the summer all that is required is to dead-head the laterals and tie in any new growth that may be made.

In the winter, shorten flowered laterals to three or four eyes (do not do this to *Rosa banksiae* 'Lutea' or *Rosa* 'Mermaid'). Cut out any weak growth and tie in new growth [Fig. 11.14].

After several years it will become necessary to remove some of the oldest wood right back to the base to encourage the rose to produce new vigorous growth from ground level [Fig. 11.15].

## Species and shrub roses

The group does not require as much pruning as the Large Flowered and Cluster Flowered roses. However, similar basic rules apply to keep the bush young and flowering well.

No pruning is required at planting. The aim

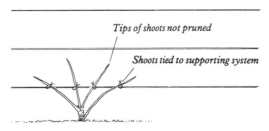

*Tips of shoots not pruned*

*Shoots tied to supporting system*

**Fig. 11.13** Newly planted climbing rose.

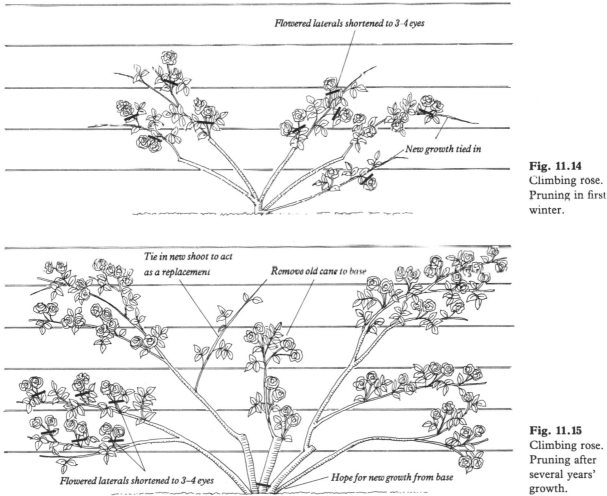

*Flowered laterals shortened to 3–4 eyes*

*New growth tied in*

**Fig. 11.14** Climbing rose. Pruning in first winter.

*Tie in new shoot to act as a replacement*

*Remove old cane to base*

*Flowered laterals shortened to 3–4 eyes*

*Hope for new growth from base*

**Fig. 11.15** Climbing rose. Pruning after several years' growth.

131

is to produce a framework upon which the flowers will be produced. As with all roses, dead, diseased and damaged wood should be removed.

Spent flowers should be removed, but not from those where the autumn display of hips is important, e.g. *Rosa moyesii*.

Within this large group there is some variation in growth pattern and this should be remembered with pruning.

Some produce very dense bushes which require very little pruning. Examples are many rose species including *Rosa pimpinellifolia* (Scotch rose or Burnet rose), *Rosa rugosa* (ramanas rose) and its cultivars, Gallica roses

and Burnet roses. Others produce a more open type of shrub with an arching habit growth. This arching habit is produced by vigorous shoots being sent up from ground level. These may need pruning by up to one third their length to prevent them arching over completely and their flowers falling into the mud. This arching habit is an attraction in itself and harder pruning would destroy this and be a mistake. Occasionally an old branch may be removed at ground level to encourage the production of new vigorous growth from the base.

Included in this group are the Alba, Centifolia and Moss roses, plus species such as *Rosa moyesii* and its cultivars, for instance *R. moyesii* 'Geranium' and its hybrids, for example *R.* 'Highdownensis'.

A third group tend to be recurrent in their flowering. They produce new flowering laterals in the summer and regular dead-heading is important to obtain continuity of flower. Because of this mass of flowering laterals, they tend to become thick in the head and these laterals need reducing to two or three buds during spring pruning. Examples within this group are many Bourbons, some Modern Shrub Roses and certain very vigorous Large-Flowered and Cluster Flowered roses [Fig. 11.16 and 11.17].

## Standard roses

### Plant selection

Standard roses are produced by taking up a single stem of a briar rose and budding the flowering cultivar at the required height. To produce a good balanced head to the standard two buds, one bud on either side of the briar stem is required.

When selecting a standard rose, ensure that it has been double-budded and the head is reasonably well balanced.

### Pruning

Large Flowered and Cluster Flowered cultivars are used to form standard roses. Pruning should be of the same type and done at the same time as described previously for these groups of roses when grown as shrubs.

*Weeping Standards*
Rambling roses derived from *Rosa*

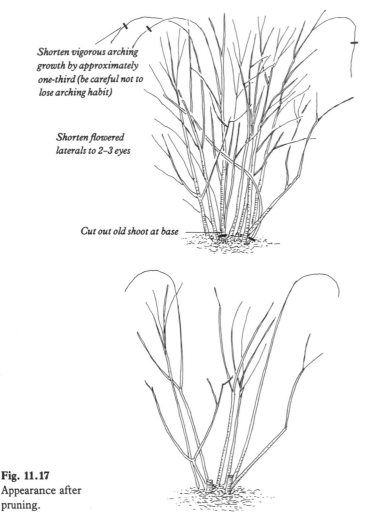

**Fig. 11.16**
Generalized pruning of an established shrub rose. Before pruning.

*Shorten vigorous arching growth by approximately one-third (be careful not to lose arching habit)*

*Shorten flowered laterals to 2–3 eyes*

*Cut out old shoot at base*

**Fig. 11.17**
Appearance after pruning.

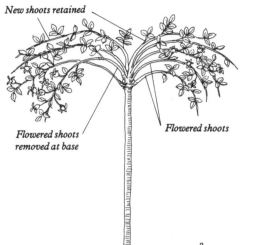

New shoots retained

Flowered shoots removed at base

Flowered shoots

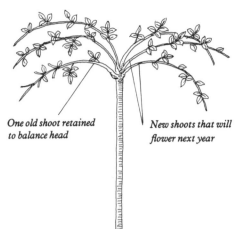

One old shoot retained to balance head

New shoots that will flower next year

a

b

**Fig. 11.18 Pruning of a weeping standard.**
(*a*) Young standard rose after flowering.
(*b*) Young standard rose after pruning.

*wichuraiana*, including cultivars such as 'Crimson Shower', 'Dorothy Perkins' and 'Excelsa' can be budded onto a stem of *Rosa rugosa* at a height of approximately 1.5 m (5 ft) in the same way as standard roses are produced.

Pruning consists of removing completely two-year-old flowered shoots in late summer or early autumn. This will leave vigorous shoots that have just been produced and will flower the following summer. If insufficient new growth has been made, then a few two-year-old shoots may be retained [Fig. 11.18].

## Ground cover and landscaping roses

Recent years have seen the introduction of many of these roses. The basic ideas behind their breeding and introduction was to produce roses that could provide colour for a long period, cover the ground to reduce weed growth, and require very little maintenance, this including pruning.

There are two distinct forms. One is prostrate, producing a low mat of vegetation over the soil. The 'Game Bird' series of roses are prostrate and examples of cultivars are 'Partridge' and 'Pheasant'. *Rosa* 'Paulii' is an ollder hybrid that also has a prostrate habit.

The second form comprises large arching shrubs up to 1 m (3 ft) high, but considerably wider. These taller roses can be used in large-scale landscaping to provide undulating beds of flowering ground cover. Examples are 'Red

Blanket' with vigorous arching growth, and 'Bonica' with slightly less vigorous arching growth. Others with a more upright habit, whilst still useful for mass planting, can also be used for hedging, examples being the cultivars 'Pink Meidiland' and 'Sevillana'.

### Pruning

*Prostrate and low growing*
Pruning is done in the winter. Shorten any growths that tend to grow vertically. Remove aged, unsightly growth. Remove some of the older growth upon which the new growth may tend to pile up.

*Taller, arching shrubs used in mass planting*
In many cases no pruning is recommended, but it may be necessary to control oversized plantations, this being carried out in the late winter.

*Taller, less-arching shrubs used for hedging*
Pruning to a required height can be done using a mechanical flail or reciprocating cutter bar equipment. Trimming is best done only on top of the hedge. This encourages flowering from the base and sides of the hedge.

Such a pruning technique is contrary to that recommended for all other roses. The innate vigour and disease resistance of these roses allows this simple and quick approach to be carried out successfully.

Many of the cultivars suitable for hedging

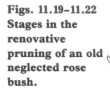

**Figs. 11.19–11.22 Stages in the renovative pruning of an old neglected rose bush.**

**Fig. 11.19** Neglected rose bush prior to pruning.

**Fig. 11.20** Rose after first renovative pruning.

**Fig. 11.21** Rose one year after first renovative pruning.

**Fig. 11.22** Rose after second renovative pruning.

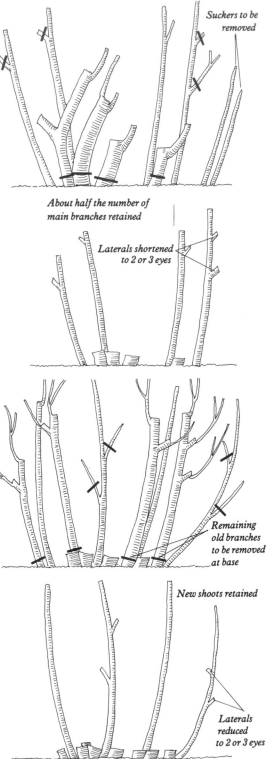

*Suckers to be removed*

*About half the number of main branches retained*

*Laterals shortened to 2 or 3 eyes*

*Remaining old branches to be removed at base*

*New shoots retained*

*Laterals reduced to 2 or 3 eyes*

also produce a good display of hips in the autumn, so pruning should be delayed until late winter.

*Suckers*

An increasing proportion of ground cover and landscaping roses are now being propagated on their own roots and with these roses suckering is no longer a problem.

## Renovation of shrub roses

On purchasing a house with an 'established' garden, the new owner may unfortunately find unpruned and neglected roses.

A choice has to be made. Either dig up the neglected roses, or attempt to renovate the existing plants. Provided they are not too old such roses usually respond rapidly and well to renovative pruning.

This form of pruning is done in early spring. A drastic approach is to cut the bush down completely to ground level. This usually works well and is simple, but not pleasing to the eye.

A less drastic approach is as follows. The first year, remove all dead, diseased, damaged, thin and tangled growth. All suckers that almost inevitably will be present must be removed as previously described. Next, remove down to ground level half the remaining shoots. Those main shoots left should have all weak growth removed and laterals cut back to two or three buds [Fig. 11.20].

Whether the drastic treatment or more subtle approach is used, pruning must be followed by an application of rose fertilizer plus a mulch that is at least 5 cm (2 in) thick.

A lack of response to this form of pruning may indicate that the bush is just too old, generally in excess of 10 years old, or has been weakened excessively by disease, generally black-spot and die-back.

The second early spring, all the remaining old shoots are removed at ground level. Several new strong growths should have appeared from at or near ground level. These are retained with any laterals being reduced to two to three eyes [Figs. 11.21 and 11.22].

By now the bush is essentially renovated. The new shoots form the framework of what is essentially a new bush rose. The rose should now be pruned as a young bush according to what type of bush rose it is.

# PART II

## ORNAMENTAL PLANTS UNDER GLASS

# CHAPTER 12

# *Shrubs Under Glass*

## Suiting the plant to the environment

The whole point of growing shrubs under glass in the UK is to give us the ability to grow those plants from warmer climates which we would not normally be able to grow. There are many reasons for this inability. In most cases, it is simply that the plants are just not hardy enough to withstand the coldness of our winters. However, it may also be that our summers are not long enough for a particular plant to produce a shoot which will grow and flower all in the same growing season. Then again, other plants require a higher temperature than we can provide outdoors.

Although lack of heat is the main reason for failure, it can also be the lack of a sufficiently long period of heat or a shortage of sunlight. This is not always a problem outside or in a greenhouse but, in a house, it can be serious in the winter.

There is another side to all this because we must not forget that these unreliably hardy plants vary in the degree to which they are unsuitable for growing outdoors. Some plants are simply less hardy than others because they come from a warmer climate.

As with all aspects of gardening, there are grey areas which are occupied by plants such as fuchsias and camellias. Whilst, generally speaking, these are hardy plants in the UK, they perform best in the extreme south and west where the temperature seldom drops below freezing. These make ideal subjects for cool greenhouses; they are easy to grow and merely require protection rather than extra heat.

This brings us on to the subject of choosing which plants we can grow in our greenhouse. The golden rules are, first, to establish just what degree of heat you are going to maintain in the greenhouse and then, second, to draw up a list of plants that will flourish in that temperature regime. Deciding what plants you want to grow and then trying to establish the conditions for them is a recipe for disaster. Not least because, within the list, there are usually plants that require totally different conditions. Likewise, if you have had no experience of this type of growing, then start with the easiest plants and those that require the least heat. One of the most common sources of plants suitable for growing in a greenhouse is a good garden centre. Most people on their first visit to the houseplant greenhouse are bewildered by the range to choose from. The first rule in these situations is that if you don't know what's suitable, ask.

## Greenhouse temperatures

Regarding the sort of heat achievable in greenhouses, there are three generally accepted temperature ranges for greenhouses in the UK.

### Cool

This refers to a greenhouse where the temperature is not allowed to fall below freezing. There is no upper limit but high temperatures are undesirable because many of the plants are on the borderline of hardiness.

The desirable minimum temperature for a cool house is 4–7°C (39–45°F) day and night mid autumn to early spring with a 3–5°C rise during the spring propagating period. No heating will be needed during the summer.

### Warm (temperate)

These house conditions are a minimum of 7–10°C (45–50°F) day and night in the winter. 10–13°C (50–55°F) minimum at night is about right for the spring and summer whilst, by day, it should be raised to 13–18°C (55–65°F).

### Stove (tropical)

These house conditions are for the tenderest plants and normally these are more of botanical rather than commercial horticultural or garden interest.

A night minimum of 15°C (59°F) in the winter and a range of 15–21°C (59–70°F) in spring and autumn, and 18–27°C (65–80°F) in the summer gives you a good idea as to why the stove house is rather special. It is the home of tropical and sub-tropical plants.

Although none of that has anything directly to do with pruning, it does lay down the ground rules for which plants do best where and, thus, will help you to avoid growing the wrong plants in any particular greenhouse or with unsuitable companions.

Besides the obvious reasons for matching the plants to the conditions, it must be realized that poorly grown plants will seldom answer satisfactorily to the recommended pruning treatment. Plants that are in cooler conditions than they need will usually grow in a stunted form, and those which are growing in too high a temperature will become weak and drawn. Naturally, both situations will influence the pruning.

One final point about choosing plants. If you are planning to plant them in the ground, remember that once planted and established, changing your mind won't do the plant any good. Make up your mind and stick with it.

## Training young greenhouse plants

Whilst pruning is generally taken to refer to woody perennial plants, such as shrubs and small trees, a young plant of any type may need training.

Training plants other than climbers will usually mean shaping the plant to the desired form. For example, some wall shrubs, such as *Tibouchina*, will need training against a frame or the greenhouse wall; it forms a far too lax and unstable shrub without support [Fig. 12.1]. It has the same sort of growth habit as the outdoor winter jasmine, though nothing else is remotely similar.

One point worth remembering about these wall shrubs (not climbers although they require support) is that siting the deciduous ones against the greenhouse wall is not always a good idea. As they mature, in the autumn many of their falling leaves can get trapped between the shrub and the glass and can present problems. For this reason, it is much

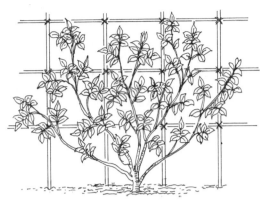

**Fig. 12.1** Shrubs that need some support should be trained either to a cane frame or the greenhouse side.

better to grow them either slightly away from the glass, or trained against something in the middle of the house.

The one thing that it is as well to remember is that plants truly needing artificial greenhouse conditions nearly always grow faster than outdoor plants in the UK. This can mean that a lot of growth appears in quite a short time and you must always bear in mind that it is far better for all concerned, not least the plant, to prune it in good time rather than leaving a shoot to grow into a branch before removing it.

On the whole, plants to be grown in a greenhouse or conservatory prosper far better when planted in the ground than when grown in a pot or some other suitably sized container. This is almost entirely because they have an unrestricted root run and an even supply of moisture and nutrients. This, in turn, results in better plants that give the grower more satisfaction.

However, it also means that most of the plants can be allowed to, and will, grow much larger. Remember this when deciding what to grow because it is never satisfactory having to undertake hard pruning simply to keep a plant to a manageable size.

## Choosing plants

When buying plants for growing under cover, always choose the actual specimens carefully and take particular care when examining for pests and disease. The shape can usually be improved but imported pests and diseases are no joke. The plants should also be pot-grown specimens. This may sound obvious but, even if a friend offers you a plant, it is seldom satisfactory if it is simply dragged off the parent plant as, say, a sucker with roots.

When raised in a pot, a plant will usually have an extensive root system already and will normally establish very quickly when either potted on into a larger container or planted out in the open ground.

In most instances, spring planting is preferable to autumn. The plants receive a minimal check and start growing almost at once. This leads to a well established plant by the following period of dormancy; it having had as long a growing season as possible.

As a rule, and because of their normally ample vigour, it is usually wise to hard prune a young plant on planting. This stimulates new growth so that the young plant is quickly furnished with young and healthy shoots. These, in turn, flourish and flower quickest.

In these early stages, it is important that all plants are trained into the shape suitable for their type. Spreading plants must have their shoots pegged or weighted down to encourage a creeping habit. This normally has to be done soon after growth starts because young shoots are always easier to bend than semi-mature ones. There is also less likelihood of breakages. It must be remembered, however, that horizontal shoots grow less vigorously. After the initial bending down, therefore, it is often better to leave the shoots to grow for a while in whichever direction they choose and then train them when they have achieved a good length but before the have hardened up.

Wall-type woody plants should be trained into their required shape as soon as there is enough material. If they are of a type that flowers on the current season's shoots, then clearly the framework has to be laid down first. Once this is established, you can encourage the growth of the flowering side shoots. Many of the honeysuckles are of this type. As with outdoor trees and shrubs, initial shaping and building has to take precedence over flowering.

## Pruning established plants

The reasons for and the principles of pruning woody plants under glass are exactly the same as for pruning those grown outdoors. Any differences that there are will be largely academic rather than practical. Thus, plants which flower on shoots that were produced on the previous growing season are pruned after flowering whether they are growing outside or in a greenhouse.

We can find differences, of course, and fuchsias are one. Whereas outdoors they are invariably killed back each winter, either to the ground or close to it, under glass they will seldom die back at all. This means that they are treated more as herbaceous plants outside but as deciduous shrubs under glass.

So it is not the principle that is changed so much as the degree to which it is carried out. This applies to a fair number of plants. The time of year or, rather, the stage of growth at which a given class of plant is pruned under glass remains the same. Thus, and this has already been mentioned, a shrub which flowers on shoots that grew in the previous season is, if necessary, pruned straight after flowering. This gives the new shoots (those which will flower next year) the whole of the rest of the growing season in which to grow.

Conversely, a shrub that flowers after, say, midsummer, on shoots that have just grown, is best cut in the spring at the start of the growing season. Here again, this gives the new shoots the longest period of growth before the onset of flowering. One might think that pruning after flowering, as with the previous group, would be a better system. However, the amount of growing time that exists between flowering and the winter is usually very small. This would result in very inferior shoots growing that would shortly stop.

It is far better to delay pruning until the following spring when the shoots can develop steadily, strongly and unchecked until they come into flower.

The main thing that one notices about flowering plants that are grown under glass is that the growing season and flowering season are usually much longer than with outdoor subjects. Many of the flowers last for several weeks instead of just blazing forth and then dying. This can confuse some people who are unwilling to prune away any flowers that are still there after the main flush. The temptation to leave them must be resisted as pruning of the early flowering shrubs can be delayed beyond the point when harm is being done.

The risk is not that you will kill the plant, but late pruning will mean that the growing season for the new shoots is late starting.

### Size of plant

One thing you must take into account when choosing a plant for your greenhouse, is its size. In fact although this is important when you buy the plant, you should also bear it in mind throughout the life of the plant. Always buy plants that are suitable for the size of your greenhouse. When you go into, say, the Palm House at Kew, or any other glasshouse that is managed by professionals, the first thing you will notice is that no plants have outgrown either their position or the greenhouse. They have been chosen for their size as much as for anything else. Pruning, of course, can be used to regulate the size of a tree or shrub but it should never be the main limiter of size. This will simply prevent the plant giving of its best.

However, certain plants can be pruned extremely hard without doing them any harm at all. Certain plants, in fact, benefit from extremely hard pruning; the acacias (mimosa) are some of them. It has to be admitted that this very hard pruning does nothing for the looks of the plant but, in this and most other cases, mimosa is a plant that is grown almost entirely for its cut flowers. It is seldom grown as a tree for the sake of it.

Finally, on this matter, it really is vital that the plants which you choose to grow will fit into the greenhouse, literally, and also into the temperature regime you intend to operate. You will have nothing but trouble if either of these factors are ignored. This is especially so with trees and climbers.

## Pruning tender trees and shrubs
### ABUTILON

The abutilons we are concerned with here are mainly *A. savitzii*, *A. pictum* (*striatum*) 'Thompsonii' and the large-flowered hybrids. Some, normally those with variegated foliage, are used in bedding schemes as dot plants. These are normally raised fresh each year and little pruning is needed after the initial stopping at, say, 15 cm (6 in) tall, which induces branching. Those grown for indoor or greenhouse display can be grown as bushes on a short leg, similar to the bedding ones or, more

usually, as taller plants along the lines of a 'standard'.

The initial cutting is allowed to grow unchecked until it reaches the desired height. All side shoots are pinched out during this time except any that form at the top of the stem towards the time at which it is stopped. Stopping the side shoots once, when they are some 15 cm (6 in) long, is normally sufficient to induce a satisfactory number of side shoots. These are left to flower.

The plants are kept from year to year and simply cut back as necessary in late winter to prevent them becoming straggly.

### ACACIA

The popular species are the fragrant flowering ones like *A. baileyana* and *A. dealbata*, the so-called 'mimosa'. These are vigorous growers and, in their native Australia, make large trees. Because of their size and vigour, they are only suitable for larger greenhouses were they would normally be grown in the ground.

We grow them almost entirely for their flowering shoots with virtually no thought for the appearance of the tree. This allows us to grow them more as a stool and more along the lines of pollarded willows.

A perfectly satisfactory way of treating them is to allow them to reach some 1.2 m (4 ft) in height and then take the tops out. This induces side shoots to form which will flower [Fig. 12.2]. If the flowering stems are cut for selling, that is normally enough pruning. The only additional treatment needed is to cut back any weak or sub-standard shoots after flowering. If the plants are left alone to flower, the spent

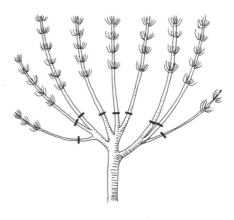

**Fig. 12.2** Trees, such as mimosa, respond best to 'pollarding', as it ensures long-flowering shoots.

shoots and all others are cut hard back after the flowers have faded.

Smaller species growing in pots are simply trimmed and tidied after flowering. In their early years, it is safer to keep them growing gently over winter rather than drying them off, as this regime is likely to damage them and cause an unacceptable amount of dieback.

## ALBIZIA
Closely related to *Acacia* and treated similarly.

## APHELANDRA (zebra plant)
With its striped leaves and brilliant yellow flower heads, this is not the sort of plant that you would normally associate with being pruned. However, it is a perfectly good perennial that will live for years, if given the right conditions.

The plants normally flower in the autumn, after which they should be gradually dried off to pass the winter more or less dormant but certainly not allowed to shrivel. In early spring, prune them and start them into growth again.

Pruning involves removing weak shoots completely – they will never make anything – and cutting back the strong shoots to within one or two pairs of leaves of the main stem. The aim is to prevent the plant getting leggy and to keep it bushy [Fig. 12.3]. Once the new shoots are a few centimetres or so long, knock the plant out of the pot, scrape away some of the old compost from around the rootball, trim back any pot-bound roots and repot in a smaller pot. Once the plant is over this trauma

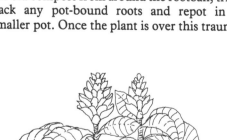

**Fig. 12.3**
Aphelandra, among others, can be kept for several years if pruned back in the early spring.

and growing again, pot it on into a large pot for the rest of the growing and flowering season.

Don't prune it again after this final repotting.

## ARALIA
Much confusion exists concerning the nomenclature of *Aralia*, *Dizygotheca* and even *Fatsia* and *Schefflera*.

The most popular is *Dizygotheca elegantissima* (see page 142).

## ARDISIA
This attractive pot shrub, which can carry fragrant white flowers and last year's red berries at the same time needs little routine pruning. The plant will in time, though, become leggy and leafless towards the base. When this happens, dry it off so that all growth stops and, in the early spring, cut the shoots down to within 5 cm (2 in) or so of the base.

## BELOPERONE (shrimp plant)
See **Justicia** on page 146.

## BORONIA
The most popular species of this Australian shrub is the sweetly scented, spring flowering *B. megastigma*. It makes a good houseplant because it seldom reaches more than 60 cm (2 ft) in height.

In their early life, the young plants should have the leaders stopped regularly to induce bushy growth. Little else will be needed. Once the plants have reached flowering age, they should be pruned quite hard back after flowering to tidy them up and further improve the bushiness.

## BRUNFELSIA
The commonly grown *B. pauciflora* (syn. *B. calycina*) is a charming evergreen, rather lax shrub that prefers a moist and warm atmosphere; stove conditions if it is grown in a greenhouse. The ultimate height of about 60 cm (2 ft) makes it a good subject for a houseplant.

There are several forms. The pretty and solitary purple flowers appear more or less all the year round. The only pruning required is to keep them reasonably upright and well shaped. This is best done before they start growth in the spring. Light pruning is preferred so the direction of growing shoots should be anticipated and any necessary action taken in good time.

## BUDDLEJA

No, not the familiar *B. davidii* but the sub-tropical *B. madagascariensis*. The inflorescenses are of the same shape but the individual flowers are orange/yellow and appear in late winter and spring.

The aim of pruning in the early years should be to build up a strong stool; thereafter, prune the flowering shoots hard back (in the same way as you would *B. davidii*) straight after flowering to maintain them in a stocky and tidy condition. Left unattended, they will soon become unruly.

## CALLISTEMON (bottle brush)

This is more of a conservatory plant than one for the house. Its lax and untidy growth is not easy to control. The pretty red (or yellow) flowers with their very long stamens appear in the summer on the growth that extends out of and beyond last year's flowers.

In the early years, the bushes should be kept stocky and well shaped, in much the same way as one would 'broom'. After that, pruning is restricted to a vain attempt at keeping the bushes compact and tidy. This is normally a losing battle as side shoots are formed only reluctantly, so pruning is best kept to the removal of shoots that are clearly out of place. The main problem is that the flowers are terminal on the shoots, so shortening back removes them.

## CAMELLIA

Although *C. japonica* can be considered hardy throughout England and Wales, the spring-flowering habit of most species means that the blooms are frequently lost to spring frosts. Growing these beautiful evergreen shrubs either in the ground, in a conservatory or in tubs, avoids this problem.

As is often the case, pruning is normally restricted to building up the plant in its early years by encouraging bushy growth by way of tipping branch leaders as and when required. Once flowering is established, the removal or cutting back of any wayward or over-vigorous shoot is usually all that is required.

Any pruning thought necessary should be done straight after flowering.

Plants in containers can spend the summer out of doors.

## CASSIA

More of a conservatory plant than for the house and, even then, succeeds best when planted in the ground. The only pruning necessary is in shaping the young bush and later in keeping the plant as bushy and as tidy as possible.

Prune in the early spring as growth starts.

## CITRUS

All forms of citrus are increasing in popularity as pot, house and conservatory plants. Fruiting oranges, lemons etc., are dealt with in the fruit section (see Chapter 15). Here we are concerned with the many and varied ornamental species and varieties.

Most are easy to grow and many thrive outside in a sunny position during the summer. Indeed, this is the best treatment they could get because they are largely Mediterranean plants and only object to our low winter temperatures.

All named varieties have to be budded or grafted; they do not come true from seed.

Pruning can usually be restricted to keeping the plants well shaped and bushy. No treatment is required to encourage flowering and fruiting; if these fail to occur and pruning has been kept to a minimum, there is something else wrong with the management of the plants. Any necessary pruning should be carried out in the early spring at the very first signs of new growth.

*C. mitis*, a small, shrubby pot plant, is one among a few citrus plants that is inclined to become leggy and needs harder pruning to prevent this.

## CODIAEUM (croton)

These are popular houseplants and give excellent results when planted in the conservatory. Their highly coloured evergreen foliage comes in a variety of shapes and colours and gives interest all the year round. The most normal leaf shape and size is similar to that of the hardy laurel.

The plants normally grow with a central leader but can be induced to be more bushy if this is stopped in the young plant and the subsequent laterals are also tipped. Later on this gives variable results as side shoots are less willing to appear. Any pruning should be done in the late winter when the plants are still dormant or excessive bleeding will occur.

### CYTISUS (broom)

All the half-hardy and tender brooms (mainly *Cytisus* and *Genista*) are pruned in just the same way as the hardy garden species.

After flowering, those shoots which have borne flowers are cut back. The hardness of pruning depends on the flowering intensity but the normal system is to shorten back the flowered shoots to the point where all the dead flowers have gone. Harder pruning is quite all right but never extend back into the old wood; this very seldom sends out new shoots so large gaps can be created.

Pruning will not only tidy up the plant but it will also ensure that it stays short, bushy and well clothed with leaves. Once a plant has become leggy, either through old age or neglect, it is best to discard it; as already mentioned, hard pruning never works [Fig. 12.4].

### DATURA (Angel's trumpet)

By nature, *D. sanguinea* and *D. suaveolens* are small trees but, in the UK they are best grown as standards planted in the conservatory border. They can also be grown in pots but are rather too big for comfort.

To form a standard, take a single stem up to the required height, at least 1.2 m (4 ft) tall, and

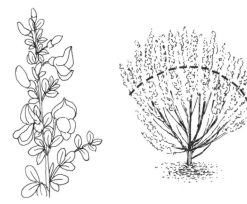

**Fig. 12.4** Mature cytisus should be lightly pruned after flowering, to remove the part of the shoots that carried the flowers. Occasionally remove leggy branches.

stop it during the dormant season. The subsequent shoots are allowed to grow, and possibly flower, unchecked. In the winter, these are cut hard back to their point of origin. This routine is repeated every year; the only refinement being to select and retain only the best placed and strongest shoots for flowering. All others are removed as early as possible.

Older plants flower the best.

### DIZYGOTHECA

The best known species that we grow is the delicate and graceful *D. elegantissima*. When grown in a pot, this will make a small, single-stemmed 'tree' without any side shoots. This is normally the best form in which to keep it. Because its juvenile form is the prettiest, it is the sort of plant that pays for occasional replacing. Once it becomes 1.2 m (4 ft) or so high and the bark loses its colour, it needs attention. The top can be taken out and rooted to form another tree whilst the remaining stem can be cut down to a few inches tall and the resulting shoots used for cuttings.

Taking a single shoot up from the cut back stem is never very satisfactory. See also **Aralia**, on page 140.

### DREJERELLA (shrimp plant)

See **Justicia** on page 146.

### ERICA

*E. canaliculata* is one of the South African heaths and is reasonably hardy outside in the south and west. Elsewhere, it is better as a conservatory plant.

There are now several other dwarfer species that make first rate pot plants; some, such as *E. hyemalis* (pink flowers), are winter flowering. They are quite widely available.

As with our own hardy heaths and heathers, no real pruning is needed but they should be trimmed over soon after flowering to tidy up the plants and keep them bushy.

Once they become leggy, replace them as they won't break out from old wood [Fig. 12.5].

### ESCALLONIA

Escallonias are perfectly hardy in milder areas, but are susceptible to cold winds and heavy frosts. *E. macrantha* is typical of this, and in an exposed site it can be killed back to quite thick wood in a sharp winter. In such districts, all species and hybrids make admirable conservatory and container shrubs. Most flower in mid-summer on long arching shoots that grew during the previous year. These flowered shoots are cut back selectively after flowering to induce more to replace them. Weak or over-vigorous shoots are cut back hard. Any shoots that are wanted to increase the size of the bush are cut back by half to two-thirds.

## EUCALYPTUS

We are looking here at the less hardy relatives of the almost hardy *E. gunnii*. All the 'gums' are Australian trees but this need not rule them out as many can be grown in a restricted form in conservatories here and some of the weaker growing in pots. In most cases, it is their juvenile foliage that is the attraction but some of them, such as *E. ficifolia*, have richly coloured flowers. *E. citriodora* makes a good pot plant on account of its size and lemon scented leaves.

The most successful way of growing them is from seed but, even if raised in this way, the plants can be kept from year to year. Prune them hard back in the late winter to ensure a good, annual supply of young shoots.

## EUPHORBIA

The main species that we are likely to come across in the home and greenhouse is the poinsettia, *E. pulcherrima*. Although normally thought of as a dwarfed, Christmas pot plant, they can be kept, potted on and grown quite easily more or less indefinitely. After flowering, cut off the dead heads and dry off the plants, but not completely. In mid spring, they can be watered to bring them into growth again and cut hard back. If the plants are single stems, this will mean to about 10 cm (4 in) high. The resulting breaks can be used either for cuttings or retained to make a bigger plant. These larger plants tend to be rather bare at the base and may well need up to a 20 cm (8 in) pot so they are not to everyone's liking. They will also be considerably taller than the treated originals. If kept for a further year, and more, they should be treated as before but just the current season's shoots are cut hard back. It

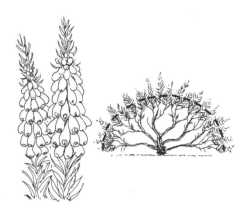

**Fig. 12.5** All low-growing heathers should be lightly clipped after flowering to encourage bushiness.

shouldn't be necessary to go back into older wood. Never cut poinsettias when they are growing, as they bleed profusely.

## × FATSHEDERA

×*Fatshedera lizei* is a cross between *Fatsia japonica* and *Hedera hibernica*. It has a variegated form. It forms an upright stem with few, if any, side shoots. As such, it needs support once it exceeds about 30 cm (12 in) tall.

When a plant becomes too tall for comfort and/or bare of leaves for some way up, it should be cut down to about 30 cm (12 in) high in the spring. The stump will send out up to three side shoots which can be taken up as fresh growth. The portion that was cut off can be used for propagation.

## FICUS (figs)

The genus *Ficus* contains plants of such a wide variety that it is quite impossible to standardize the pruning.

The three most popular species are *F. benjamina*, *Ficus elastica* and *F. pumila*, together with their varieties and cultivars. These three are representative of the main habits of growth and all require completely different pruning.

*F. benjamina* has an erect stem but slender and weeping shoots. Pruning for shape is the main task in the early years but, even so, a better plant is formed if pruning is kept to a minimum; merely the removal of out-of-place shoots and any side shoots that appear to be bidding for dominance.

Unless space is unimportant, *F. benjamina* is

best grown in a container rather than in the border, where it would soon need drastic, and damaging, treatment.

*F. elastica* (rubber plant) seldom needs pruning of any kind. After some years, its straight and rigid stem may become bare of leaves at the base. If this becomes serious, one solution is to cut the stem down to a sensible height and allow up to three side shoots to develop, from which is created a new and rejuvenated plant. The severed, leafy, top section can be used for propagation.

*F. elastica* is best grown in a pot; if planted in the greenhouse or conservatory border, it is likely to take over. A tight pot gives the best results as it reduces vigour, which gives a better plant with shorter internodes.

Other species of *Ficus* should be treated similarly to whichever of the above type they are most like.

*Ficus pumila* will be found under 'Climbers' (see page 151).

### FUCHSIA

A conservatory or cold greenhouse is the ideal place for fuchsias. Although they are almost hardy outside, in all but the mildest areas they are killed to the ground each winter so are more like herbaceous perennials than shrubs. Under cover, they are grown as pot plants in bush or standard form, or as trailing plants in hanging baskets.

To form a bush, and starting from scratch, the original rooted cutting is stopped when there are three pairs (or trios) of leaves. This

can result in as many as nine side shoots growing out; or six if the leaves are in pairs. Each of the side shoots is then stopped at two pairs of leaves; leading to a further four or six side shoots on each of the originals. You can see that this will result in 24–48 shoots. In most cases, this will be all the training and stopping that is needed but, if you want a really big plant, say for exhibition, a further stopping is done, again at two pairs of leaves. This will lead to a first-rate plant but you must be sure that there is enough time left in the season for the resulting shoots to mature and flower. An early start is therefore needed.

Standards can have various lengths of stem but, for most purposes, the stem of a full standard is 80–100 cm (30–40 in) tall.

First, choose a strong and well-rooted cutting; some varieties are certainly better than others as standards. As it grows, any side shoots are nipped out the moment they are large enough to handle. Be ready to pot on the plant as soon as the roots have filled the pot because any check can cause it to form flower buds and stop growing. When the stem is 30–45 cm (12–18 in) tall, serious fuchsia growers will leave in the top four pairs of side shoots in case something disastrous happens to the main growing point. In that event, one of the side shoots can be taken up in its place. (If you adopt this technique, remove the lowest pair of side shoots once a new top pair has started.)

Once the stem is as tall as you want, take out the growing point. If you have been keeping four pairs of side shoots in case of emergency, these can be used straight away to form the primary branches. These are then stopped at two or three pairs of leaves and, in most cases, this will take you to the end of the growing season. Overwinter the plants under cover and, in the spring, start up again as though you were growing a bush on top of a stem.

Fuchsias and hanging baskets go together like bread and butter but, as with standards, some varieties are better than others. By and large, the thinner and weaker-stemmed varieties are best. Start off in the same way as you would for bush plants and, if you have the choice, plant up the baskets after the second stopping. This will give you good plants with plenty of shoots will soon start flowering.

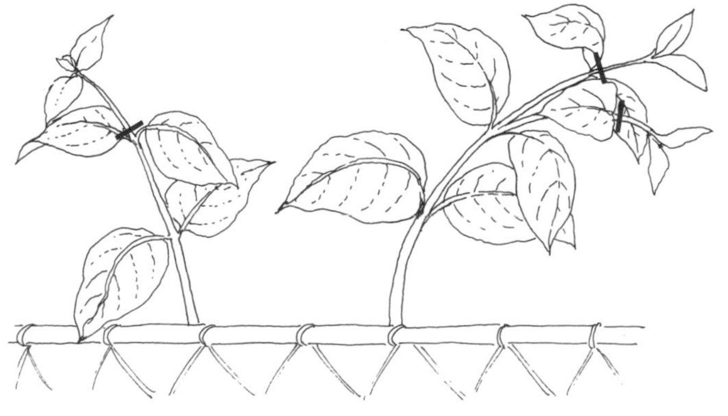

**Fig. 12.6** Only two stoppings are normally needed for fuchsias in hanging baskets. The first on the left; the second on the right.

Allow four plants to a 30 cm (12 in) diameter basket and proportionately more for larger ones. Stick to one variety per basket; it looks much better and you won't have dominant varieties striving to smother out weaker ones [Fig. 12.6].

## GARDENIA

This is not the easiest of plants to grow indoors but it is easier in a conservatory or greenhouse where the moister atmosphere is more to its liking. Gardenias need as even a temperature as possible; nor do they like it either too hot or too cold. Also, too much or too little water will cause the flower buds and flowers to drop.

The best plants are made up of three rooted cuttings per pot. No formal pruning is necessary, merely the nipping back or removal of over-vigorous and out-of-place shoots after flowering.

Remove dead flower heads as soon as they are seen.

## GREVILLEA

Two species are to be found in conservatories and greenhouses but neither makes a particularly good houseplant.

*G. juniperina* is sometimes grown successfully outside in the south and west but elsewhere needs conservatory protection. Pinching back the shoots in its early years encourages breaks to form but, after that, the occasional removal of old or sagging branch systems is all that is required.

*G. robusta* is essentially a foliage plant with finely cut leaves. It is often used as a dot plant up to about 80 cm (30 in) in summer bedding schemes. It is normally raised from seed each spring and is grown as a single stem plant. As such, any side shoots should be nipped out as soon as they are large enough to handle.

Treat it somewhat as you would rosemary.

## HEBE

Although most of the shrubby hebes are grown outdoors perfectly successfully, some are on the borderline of hardiness and are frequently knocked back in severe winter. Thus, they make excellent conservatory plants, especially when planted in the ground. The main point to watch is that the temperature should not rise unduly high or rank growth will be produced. Only the large-flowered summer flowering hybrids, some of which have variegated foliage, need this treatment; the species are hardy enough to be outside permanently, though even these can be knocked back by severe cold.

Judicious tipping of the shoots in the early years will ensure bushiness. Once flowering has started, the plants should be dead-headed and any wayward shoots cut back or removed.

## HIBISCUS

This is another plant that can be grown outdoors in the mildest parts of the UK but which is safer indoors, at least for most of the year, in the rest of the country.

*H. rosa-sinensis* is the most commonly cultivated tender species; *H. syriacus* is the perfectly hardy outdoor one.

When pruning the greenhouse *Hibiscus*, the main aim is to keep its size under control. This is best achieved by fairly hard pruning in early spring. A good way to treat them is similarly to the hardy, outdoor *Buddleja davidii* (see page 68); first build up a framework of sturdy branches and then cut hard back all the shoots that grew and/or flowered in the previous summer.

*Hibiscus* is usually grown as a pot plant but gives of its best when planted out.

## HYDRANGEA

Whilst most hydrangeas are grown outdoors, some of the showier and less reliably hardy species are better under cover, where they make excellent tub plants. Still more are grown as small, flowering pot plants. For the most part, these are the hardy 'Hortensis' type which, after flowering indoors, can be planted outside in a sheltered and not too cold position. Alternatively, they can be grown from year to year under cover in containers of some sort. They require very little pruning as they are naturally branching and bushy plants.

Beyond the removal of faded flowers and, at the same time, any light pruning to keep the plants neat and tidy, little should be needed.

## JACARANDA

In general appearance, this looks somewhat like *Grevillea robusta* (see left) and indeed it is normally grown as a single-stemmed dot plant for summer bedding schemes outdoors. However, the leaves are much more intricate and fern-like. The one normally grown has been given the specific name of *J. mimosifolia*.

If grown as a single-stemmed plant, the only attention needed is the removal of any side shoots. If you want a multi-stemmed plant, nip out the top when the young plant is some 30 cm (12 in) tall.

## JACOBINIA
See **Justicia** below.

## JUNIPERUS
*J. bermudiana* and the variety 'Bedfordiana' are occasionally seen in conservatories where they make good ornamental tub conifers. No regular pruning is needed beyond that necessary to maintain a good shape.

## JUSTICIA (shrimp plant)
Formerly *Beloperone*. The shrimp plant is known to most people who have a liking for houseplants. It is easily looked after and requires a minimum of pruning because it is a naturally bushy plant. However, once a plant becomes leggy, usually through lack of feeding or because it needs potting on, it should be cut hard back in the early spring into the old wood and be allowed to produce another crop of shoots. These are retained selectively with the shape of the plant in mind. They should need little, if any stopping as they break naturally.

*J. carnea* is the usual species grown. It makes a good pot plant that flowers with a pink, *Aphelandra*-like flower spike in the late summer.

After flowering, the one or two stems that flowered are cut back to a convenient point, usually about halfway down. Choose carefully the pair of leaves to which the shoots are cut back. The leaves are opposite and in alternate pairs so that each pair is at right-angles to the one above and below it. Be sure that you cut to pairs of leaves which give you a square shape, when seen from above. If the two pairs of leaves are at right-angles to each other or in a straight line, the plant will look awful.

Two years is about as long as you would keep this type of plant, because after that, it becomes leggy.

*J. pauciflora* is another species; it is pruned in the same way.

## LANTANA
*Lantana camara* is about the sole remaining species of what was once a popular pot plant, if not particularly exciting. Visitors to the Mediterranean will have seen it growing as an ornamental shrub. It is grown under cover in the UK and is pruned in much the same way as *Fuchsia*, frequent stopping being needed to create a bushy plant. It is partially dried off for the winter so that growth is stopped but wilting avoided.

In the spring, all strong shoots are cut back to within 7–8 cm (3 in) of their base. This results in a bushy plant with many shoots and flowers.

Beware of whitefly.

## LEPTOSPERMUM
*L. scoparium* is just about hardy in Cornwall and on the Devon coast but, elsewhere, needs the protection of a conservatory. It performs better when planted out than when grown in a pot.

Having a similar growth habit to the tree heathers, pruning is largely a matter of shaping, by light tipping, in the early years and the complete or partial removal (according to need) of the shoots that have flowered in the early summer.

## LIPPIA
Like the *Leptospermum*, Lemon verbena (*L. citriodora*, now rather boringly called *Aloysia triphylla*) is hardy outdoors in the south and south-west but only half-hardy elsewhere; though it can be grown on a sunny wall if covered for the winter.

It seldom needs pruning except for the removal of old stems that have become leggy and bare at the base. Do this in the spring as growth starts. It may also need to be kept to a smaller size than that to which it would naturally grow. This is best done by removing completely the taller branch systems rather than snipping at them piecemeal.

## MUSA

After fruiting or flowering, the main stem of all bananas (that which carried the flowers or fruit) is cut down completely and one of the sometimes numerous suckers is retained to form another plant.

When grown in the ground in a conservatory, keep a sucker that does not need to be lifted and planted elsewhere.

## MYRTUS

*M. communis* (myrtle) is normally grown in a pot under cover but it is largely hardy in the south and west. Inland in the south, it will need the protection of a warm wall but elsewhere a conservatory is safer.

The only pruning usually needed is in shaping the bush in its early years and the occasional removal of branches, or parts of branches, to restrict its height and spread. This should be done in the spring.

Any heavy pruning needed, such as for reducing the size drastically, should also be done in the spring when new shoots will readily appear from the old wood.

## NERIUM

*N. oleander* (oleander) is as common in the Mediterranean region as, for example, forsythia is in the UK.

Flowers are only produced on well-ripened shoots so the plants must be in full sun. After flowering, they should be kept partially dry until early autumn, when they can again be watered as required. It is during this semi-dormant spell that any pruning should take place. If the plants are getting too tall and leggy, they can be cut hard back to restore compactness. The tallest or most spreading branch systems are the ones to remove so that mainly compact growth is left.

Any shaping should be done at the same time. This drying off and pruning programme will lead to new shoot growth starting to develop before the winter comes, thus improving the look of the plant. Any small shoots that appear to be growing close to the developing flowers should be nipped out early on or the flowers will be partially hidden by the leaves.

All parts of the plant, but especially the flowers, are very poisonous [Fig. 12.7].

**Fig. 12.7** The oleander will stand hard pruning to prevent legginess. Shaping may also be needed.

## PELARGONIUM

The half-hardy 'geranium' is not the sort of plant that one usually associates with pruning but, when trained as a perennial against the sunny wall of a conservatory, it will need attention each spring if it is to stay in good shape and flower all over.

Once growth starts with the warmer weather, any tall and bare shoots that have developed during the back-end of the previous growing season should be cut back to an existing side shoot or, if none are there, back to its point of origin. This will encourage new side shoots to form and, thus, new flowering growth.

Any shoots that have died should also be removed. In fact, although the spring is the best time, pruning out unproductive shoots

**Fig. 12.8** In a conservatory, pelargoniums are grown to best effect on a wall. Fairly hard pruning in the spring may be needed to prevent legginess.

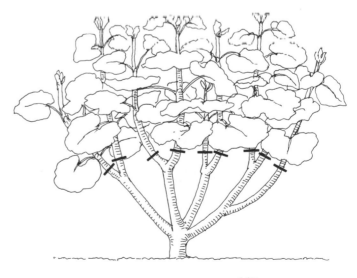

can be done at any time whenever you see them. The aim should be to have plenty of new growths covering the wall because it is only at the tip of growing shoots that the flowers are produced [Fig. 12.8].

## PUNICA

*P. granatum* is the common pomegranate and not a particularly attractive plant. However, *P.g.* 'Nana', the dwarf pomegranate, is completely different and makes a very good pot plant. Keep it in shape and well balanced by the occasional tipping of appropriate shoots. This will give you a good-looking, bushy plant.

## RICINUS

*R. communis gibsoni* is the castor oil plant so beloved by the designers of bedding schemes. Its dark red shoots and leaves, similar to sycamore, make a grand contrast to most bedding plants and add height to the display. It is normally allowed to grow as it wants, without either stopping it or removing side shoots.

## SCHEFFLERA

What little pruning will be found to be necessary is the same as for *Dizygotheca* (see page 142), except that cutting down leggy plants and allowing regrowth is more successful than with that genus.

## SOLANUM

*S. capsicastrum* (winter cherry) is a quick and easy pot plant to grow for the Christmas period. Virtually no pruning is needed beyond taking the top out of the seedling plant when it is 7–10 cm (3–4 in) high. This will encourage side shoots to form and a bushy plant. Occasionally tipping a leader and pinching back any shoot that grows too strongly is more or less all that is required. New plants are best raised from fresh seed taken direct from a mature (slightly wrinkled) berry.

## SPARMANNIA

*S. africana*, (African hemp), makes an attrac-

tive pot plant but it can become large and needs plenty of room. The best way of growing it is to prune it hard back each spring as growth starts. This is set in motion by pruning back a one-year-old plant to 7–10 cm (3–4 in) high at the start of its second growing season. This will lead to side shoots developing which are themselves cut back in the next spring. And so on.

## STREPTOSOLEN

This is an excellent greenhouse plant that is grown mainly as a loosely climbing shrub. It has no means itself of climbing so has to be tied or twined as it grows.

The only species in cultivation is *S. jamesonii*. Train and tie the growths to sticks or hoops and pinch back any straggling shoots. When grown in a pot, partially dry off the plant for the winter and cut back the shoots hard in the spring when growth restarts.

## TEUCRIUM

The most commonly grown species is *T. fruticans* (germander), a 90–120 cm (3–4 ft) high shrub. In the conservatory it will grow as a shrub but outside it is treated more like a half-hardy annual and replaced each year. It can also be lifted in the autumn and overwintered in a frost-free frame. In the spring it is cut hard back and brought into heat to grow again.

## TIBOUCHINA

Another plant that cannot work out if it is a shrub or a climber and, as such, it is best planted in the conservatory and supported by a wall or some cane structure. It can also be grown in a pot but is less successful there. The blue/violet flowers last only a short time but are formed almost continually during the growing season, though mainly in the autumn.

It is prone to get leggy and straggly so should be pruned hard back each spring as growth starts. Start by forming a framework of branches which will carry the temporary flowering shoots.

# CHAPTER 13

# Climbing Plants Under Glass

Much of what was said in the introduction to Chapter 12 on the pruning of shrubs under glass applies equally well to climbers. However it is generally agreed that climbers are less suited to being grown in pots than to being planted in the ground. This is because, on the whole, they are considerably more vigorous than shrubs and therefore appreciate the free root run afforded by being planted out. In general, most large-growing plants, whether climbing or shrubby, are better when planted. It is not a good idea, though, to adopt the grapevine technique in which the roots are outside and the top inside. This is tolerable for the grape because it is hardy enough for the roots to be largely unaffected. Less hardy plants won't like it.

There is no general rule about the best way to grow tender climbers but the vigour of any individual will have an important bearing on its cultivation and, in particular, its support and pruning. In the main, the less vigorous climbers are simply trained and tied onto some suitable structure and are lightly pruned to keep the growths young and flowering. Pruning is often, but by no means always, most appropriate at the end of the flowering period.

Vigorous climbers, for the most part, flower best on the current season's growth; the shoots growing and flowering in the same year. For these to give of their best, they should be pruned hard at the beginning of each growing season. This helps them to make vigorous shoots that flower all the better.

Deciduous climbers especially need harsh treatment or they are apt to become leggy at the base with most of their flowers high up.

Although not strictly speaking deciduous, the passifloras (passion-flowers) should receive this harsh treatment to encourage vigorous flowering shoots. Tender clematis are another example. Evergreen climbers, such as *Jasminum polyanthum*, operate perfectly well

when lightly pruned for a number of years and then given severe treatment to fetch out all the old growth and rejuvenate the whole plant. *Stephanotis* is another climber that responds to this treatment.

Although they seldom involve any pruning, annual climbers raised from seed or cuttings each spring are very useful and can be most effective. *Ipomoea* (morning glory) is one of the best. The supports we provide for tender climbers are important and, again, their vigour will influence the choice.

Purlin posts and cross members in the greenhouse and conservatory are very useful, especially for vigorous climbers in large structures. They are strong and extensive and will hold an enormous amount of growth.

Twiggy 'pea' sticks are good for the not-so-large climbers, especially those grown in pots.

As we discussed with tender shrubs, it is also very important to match the climber to the environment; never the reverse, as it seldom works and can be very frustrating and expensive. First, create an environment that you are happy with and are prepared to maintain and then choose the plants that will like it.

With very few exceptions, the attraction of tender climbers lies in their flowers. This in itself is fine but remember that many will be scented and that mixtures of smells are not always as pleasant as individual scents on their own. Remember also that not all the plants you might think of as being scented, are. Many of the tender honeysuckles are completely scentless. Good effects can often be had by training climbers over shrubs and small trees, even in conjunction with other climbers. Do not forget that some 'climbers' are, in fact, not climbers at all but wall shrubs. As such, they will need to be supported and tied to the support. The true climbers are what we call 'self-clinging'; in other words, they have their own system of hanging onto whatever they are climbing. This may be by twining stems (honeysuckle), by twisting leaf petioles (clematis), by adventitious roots (ivy), by tendrils (passiflora) or by thorns (roses). These climbers will simply need to be started off in the right direction and you then let Nature take over.

Before we look at the individual plants, you must understand that there is no hard and fast distinction between a climber and a wall shrub. We have just seen that climbers are generally considered to be plants that have a means of attaching themselves to some other plant or object. However, and to draw on a plant that everyone knows, the outdoor winter jasmine is neither one thing nor the other. Each plant will, therefore, be designated either SC (self-clinging or self-climbing) or WS (wall shrub). Even then, we may find some that are difficult to classify. *Abutilon megapotamicum*, for example, is classified as a wall shrub but *Clerodendrum thomsoniae* as a climber. Both are clearly treated as climbers and both need to be trained and yet they are not of the same botanical structure.

## A–Z of climbing plants and wall shrubs

### ABUTILON WS.

Most of the abutilons are perfectly normal shrubby plants but *A. megapotamicum* is immediately an example of a wall shrub that could easily be classed as a climber in the same way as winter jasmine.

Although it makes a good pot plant, it really shows off best when planted in the ground and trained up a purlin post and along cross members. It is certainly improved by pruning hard in the spring. As a pot plant, it will be cut back into old wood and then be encouraged, by feeding, to put out new flowering shoots each year. In the ground, you can usually leave it for a number of years and then cut it similarly hard back. This prevents it becoming bare and woody towards the base.

It is on the borderline of hardiness [Fig. 13.1].

### ALLEMANDA WS.

The most commonly grown species is *A. cathartica* and its improved form, *A.c. grandiflora*. It is a vigorous climber but needs support.

First, form a permanent framework or stool of established branches from which flowering shoots will grow. It flowers on the current season's growth so those shoots which have flowered are cut hard back to within a couple of buds of their base early the following spring.

### ARISTOLOCHIA SC.

These are represented by such species as the Dutchman's pipe, the swan flower and the pelican flower, hence the benefit of using a botanical name. Many are vigorous self-twining climbers.

*A. elegans* (Dutchman's pipe) is one of the commonly grown species. This is really a stove plant but it will survive quite readily in a warm conservatory. It is best planted in the ground at the base of a pillar, or something similar. This gives it its head and allows it to clamber at will.

It can become a bit overpowering and, if this is upsetting other plants, it should be cut back quite hard in the autumn. This will give its companions a fair share of what little winter light there is. Cutting it back to cover just the pillar and then thinning it out is the sort of treatment it needs.

### BOUGAINVILLEA Partially SC.

This brightly coloured sub-tropical climber must be known to anyone who has visited the Mediterranean and anywhere warmer.

It makes quite a good pot plant, when it should be trained gradually upwards, such as in a spiral around a hoop or globe. This will

**Fig. 13.1** In a pot, *Abutilon megapotamicum* should be cut quite hard back each spring to keep it young and flowering well.

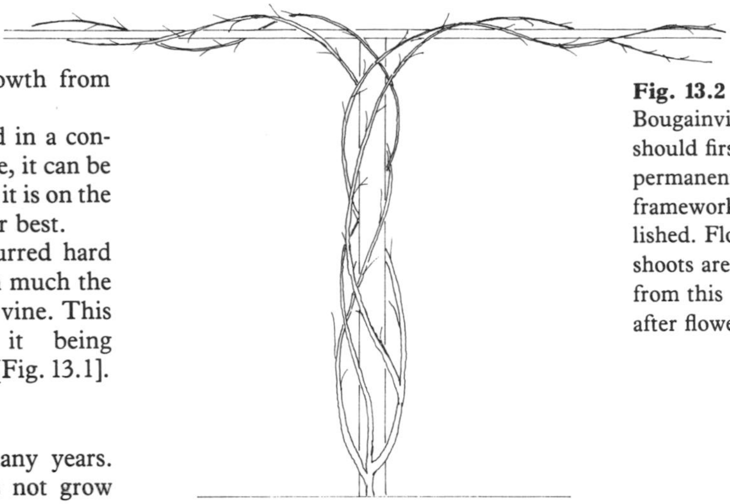

prevent the normally vigorous growth from becoming too much.

It is best, however, when planted in a conservatory at the base of a pillar. Here, it can be trained upwards and then along and it is on the horizontal lengths that it will flower best.

In the autumn, it should be spurred hard back to a few permanent 'canes'; in much the same way as one would deal with a vine. This encourages flowering without it being accompanied by too much growth [Fig. 13.1].

### CISSUS SC.

A very popular houseplant for many years. Excellent for pots because it does not grow excessively, though some shoots can develop to 1.8 m (6 ft) long. Best trained round hoops etc., which tend to control its vigour.

No regular pruning is necessary but any needed, such as to reduce its size or to remove bare stems, should be carried out in the spring when growth starts again.

### CLERODENDRUM SC.

*C. thomsoniae* is another in-between plant that is more of a climber than a wall shrub. Very little pruning is usually needed beyond the removal of old and worn-out shoots that are no longer producing the gorgeous white and scarlet flowers.

### DIOSCOREA SC.

No pruning required at all. The ornamental yam (*D. discolor*) is somewhat like our own runner bean in that it produces twining, climbing shoots in the spring that die down in the early winter.

### EPIPREMNUM

Formerly *Scindapsus*. A similar plant, in habit, to *Philodendron scandens* (see page 154), though considerably more vigorous and larger in every respect. It needs warm conditions and is happiest at stove temperatures. Encourage and train it to grow up a pillar, if possible; its aerial roots will soon take grip.

No regular pruning is needed but you may want to stop the plant early on to encourage more than one shoot to develop.

*E. aureus* is the original plant; *E.a.* 'Marble

**Fig. 13.2** Bougainvillea should first have a permanent framework established. Flowering shoots are removed from this annually after flowering.

Queen' is the more commonly grown variegated form.

### FICUS SC.

*Ficus pumila*. The neat and small-leaved creeping (or climbing) fig needs very little attention by way of pruning. In its early life, the main stems should be trained and held in the direction in which you want them to grow but little needs to be done beyond the training or removal of wayward shoots and any that have become bare towards the base. It makes an excellent climbing pot plant but, if appropriate, it is even better planted at the base of a shaded wall in a conservatory. It will soon start to climb and clothe it. For other (non-climbing) species of *Ficus* see pages 143–4.

### GLORIOSA SC.

*G. rothschildiana*, the glory vine, produces self-clinging, climbing shoots from a tuber annually, which then die down in the early winter. Cut down to ground level and remove dead growth.

### HEDERA SC.

Ivies are often treated as though they are far less hardy than they actually are. This probably arises from the fact that a great many are versatile and pretty enough to be grown equally well as indoor plants. However, nearly all are perfectly hardy and thrive when planted and grown permanently outdoors. The worst that normally happens is that there may be some leaf scorch to both the variegated and the large-leaved species and varieties in a bad winter. This, in fact, is when the main need for pruning outdoor ivies comes in (see page 117).

Under cover, they can be grown either in pots or planted in the ground. Little, if any, pruning is needed beyond the removal of those shoots that have reverted to wholly green on variegated varieties.

When the plants are young, training them to climb up wherever they are intended is achieved either by tying in the shoots as necessary or fastening them to walls with Blu-Tack, or something similar. It is also sometimes advisable to stop a limited number of shoots, to help them divide and produce a better furnished plant.

### HOYA SC. and trailing species

*H. carnosa* is a vigorous twining climber which, although sometimes grown as a pot plant, is better when planted. Alternatively, it can be grown in a large pot or tub and placed at the base of a purlin post in a conservatory. It is then trained up to wires, stretched in much the same manner as for grapevines, and tied to them. It enjoys full sun.

In late winter, any weak shoots are best removed along with any that are causing unnecessary overcrowding [Fig. 13.3].

### IPOMOEA SC.

The one that we grow in the UK either as a pot plant or planted in the greenhouse or conservatory is a half-hardy annual that is grown from seed every year. It requires no pruning at all.

### JASMINUM Climber but not SC.

There are several jasmines that make excellent conservatory plants and which, when young, are small enough to be grown in pots.

All those requiring protection are climbers and therefore need support. One of the most popular and vigorous is *J. polyanthum*. It is heavily scented and produces a succession of single white flowers, often tinged with pink, in the late winter. Although vigorous, it is usually bought as a two- or three-year-old pot plant and it can stay as such for another year or two. During that time, very little pruning is needed beyond shortening back any shoots that are clearly too vigorous and removing the dead flower panicles. However, once very vigorous shoots start to appear it is usually a sign that the plant is outgrowing its pot and needs either a larger one or to be planted in the ground.

After spring or summer planting, it will soon establish and put on a lot of growth. This should be trained up a post, or some similar structure, and then be allowed to run along cross members, bars etc. Training and tucking in wayward shoots is about all the treatment that is needed for the first few years, but ultimately, the time will come when something more drastic is necessary.

In the spring, therefore, you would untie and pull the whole plant away from the support. Cut out any dead or clearly too old (very woody) shoots and shorten back all the others to leave them no more than about 1.8 m (6 ft) long. Thin out the remainder and tie the whole thing back in place.

Other good jasmines include *J. sambac* and its double form, and *J. primulinum*.

### LAPAGERIA SC.

The only species in cultivation is *L. rosea*, a twining climber that is just about hardy in the south-west; it will even stand a touch of frost. They are not too vigorous and make excellent conservatory plants. For best results, they should be planted in prepared ground as the flowers are rather too large and wasted as a pot plant.

The magnolia-shaped crimson (or white)

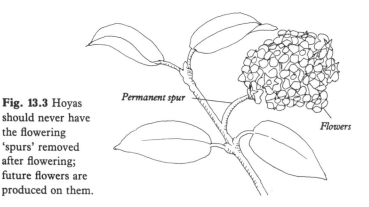

**Fig. 13.3** Hoyas should never have the flowering 'spurs' removed after flowering; future flowers are produced on them.

*Permanent spur*

*Flowers*

flowers are shown to perfection when the plant is trained along a cross member or horizontal wires. No pruning is needed beyond maintaining a good supply of new shoots and preventing overcrowding and legginess.

### LONICERA sc.

Several honeysuckles are not hardy enough to be grown outdoors but they make first rate conservatory plants. Most are vigorous, twining climbers and need to be planted.

One of the most showy, but scentless, is *L. sempervirens* (trumpet honeysuckle). It is just hardy in the south-west of Britain but needs protection elsewhere. A good way of growing it is up a single stake or post with the vigorous shoots tied in as they grow. The flowers are produced on laterals that grow from the shoots in their second year.

After flowering, the laterals can be cut hard back and more will be produced in the following year. However, once the plant is established and growing well, some of the older-flowered shoots should be cut back to the ground after flowering to allow fresh, young and better-flowering shoots to develop [Fig. 13.4].

### MANDEVILLA sc.

Another excellent plant for growing up a pillar in the greenhouse or conservatory but rather too strong for pot work once the plant is past its juvenile stage. *M. laxa* (Chilean jasmine) is the usual one grown. Keep the plant young and vigorous by removing very old shoots that have given up flowering as well as weak shoots. Don't prune the vigorous shoots but tuck them in at their full length as these produce the best flowers.

### PASSIFLORA sc.

Of the many species of *Passiflora*, the vast majority are ornamental, rather than fruitful. They are grown entirely for their decorative value. Their training and pruning is much the same as that for the fruiting species except that it need not be so regimented. They flower best with a restricted root to prevent excessive and unwanted growth forming at the expense of flowers. Planting them at the base of a pillar and training them up and along shows the flowers off well.

One would normally buy a young, pot-grown plant. Following, preferably, early spring planting in the greenhouse, the shoots are cut back to within a few centimetres of the ground. Of the resulting new growth, keep just the strongest shoots. How many this will be depends on the room available – remembering that they are vigorous, even with restricted roots. These are trained up the post and along cross members. Laterals will form and it is these that produce the flowers. It is usual to allow the growth to run unrestricted. Throughout the growing season, weak and unwanted shoots can be taken out to prevent

**Fig. 13.4**
Flowering laterals are best removed from honeysuckle after flowering. When old and woody, a complete section can be cut out.

**Fig. 13.5** The flowered laterals of plumbago are cut back after flowering and, occasionally, a complete branch system to keep the plant young.

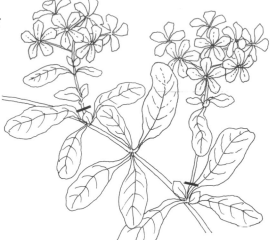

overcrowding. During the winter, all the lateral shoots are cut hard back to two or three buds from the parent stem. When growth starts in the spring, just the strongest one from each position is often retained to avoid overcrowding and to maintain the quality of the flowers. This, though, is a counsel of perfection; most people allow all that appears to continue growing and to flower.

## PHILODENDRON SC.

This is a group of mainly tropical plants, many of which are equipped for climbing. *P. scandens* (syn. *P. micans*) is the best known. Although it is technically a stove plant, it will grow quite satisfactorily in a warm greenhouse, but not in an unheated conservatory.

It is normal to plant it at the base of a pillar and leave it to climb upwards by itself after a tie or two to get it going. It puts out aerial roots that attach themselves to the pillar.

No pruning is normally needed but the top can be taken out when the plant is still very small to encourage more than one shoot to be produced. Although the plant will take longer to reach the top of the post, it will be better covered.

## PLUMBAGO WS.

This is another plant that grows so much better when planted than when growing in a pot, although the latter is perfectly possible. It can either be trained up a pillar or, preferably, be given more room and allowed to clothe a

wall. The pale blue flowers are produced throughout the summer.

Like many other wall shrubs, the best system is to train out young shoots over the first two or more growing seasons to create a semi-permanent framework of branches. These will produce the flowering shoots. After flowering, the plant is given much less water and, either then or in the early spring, the shoots that have flowered are cut back to within 10–13 cm (4–5 in) of the parent branch. This gives the whole growing season for the new flowering shoots to grow [Fig. 13.5].

## RHOICISSUS SC.

Although lightly less vigorous, the only significant difference between *R. rhomboidea* and *Cissus* is in the leaves. *Rhoicissus* has its leaves in groups of three; in *Cissus*, they are single and larger. It makes an excellent pot plant because it does not grow excessively. It climbs by means of tendrils. The new shoots are best trained round hoops etc., which also serve the purpose of containing the growth and keeping it within limits.

No regular pruning is necessary but any needed, such as to reduce its size or to remove bare stems, should be carried out in the spring when growth is starting.

## SCINDAPSUS SC.

See **Epipremnum** on page 151.

## STEPHANOTIS SC.

One of the most popular flowering, climbing pot plants and even better when planted in the greenhouse border. *S. floribunda* is easily grown and produces its beautifully scented, waxy, white flowers quite readily, provided that it has sufficient heat. This is a common fault amongst amateur gardeners; they keep the plant too cool and shady, which results in shy flowering.

Very little pruning is required beyond cutting out weak and dead shoots in the early spring. In a pot, train it around hoops; in the greenhouse, take it up a pillar and along the bars or over a frame close to the glass.

## SYNGONIUM SC.

Similar to *Epipremnum*, though not as vigorous. Treat it in the same way.

# PART III

## FRUIT TREES AND BUSHES

# CHAPTER 14

# *Nursery Training*

## What is a rootstock?

Most gardeners already know that fruit trees are not raised from seed or cuttings but by budding or grafting a portion of the required variety (the scion) onto a readymade set of roots (the rootstock or stock). This rootstock is normally of the same genus as the fruit itself so apple trees are grown on apple roots and cherries on cherry roots, but this is not always the case. The one prerequisite is that the scion variety is compatible with the rootstock.

## Why are rootstocks needed?

The cheapest and easiest way to propagate fruit trees, bushes, canes etc. would be from seed. However, this is quite impractical as they do not come true from seed; there is enormous variation amongst the offspring. The only way to produce progeny which are identical in every respect to the parent is to propagate vegetatively.

This would suggest cuttings but, unfortunately, most scion varieties are not yet either reliable or commercially viable because of the relatively low percentage of 'takes'. Many rootstocks, though, can and are propagated from cuttings; plum in particular.

For the most part, however, this leaves us with budding or grafting the scion variety onto a rootstock.

There are virtues possessed by rootstocks in their own right. They are cheap and easy to produce on a nursery; budding and grafting are also easy. With fruit trees, and principally apples because they are the major tree fruit of temperate regions, it is the rootstock, more than anything else, which determines the vigour and ultimate size of the tree; also, the speed with which it comes into bearing.

In a nutshell, then, we use rootstocks because they are the best way of producing a large number of trees that are identical to the 'parent', as well as each other, and whose size and vigour is predetermined.

Here are the main fruit rootstocks with which we are likely to be concerned.

## Apple rootstocks

Because apples are so widely grown, it follows that a lot of work has gone into the ever-continuing search for newer and better rootstocks. Research, though, is by no means confined to the factors already mentioned. It also has to take into account the amount of anchorage the roots will give, the rootstock's susceptibility or resistance to drought and/or water-logging, its tolerance of mineral deficiencies and its susceptibility to pests and diseases. Not all the rootstocks used by commercial fruit growers are available to gardeners but the most popular certainly are and there should be no problem in finding them. When you buy a fruit tree, it will not always be labelled with the rootstock on which it is growing. However, many nurseries are now doing this and all will certainly tell you in their catalogue.

The sort of thing you will see is 'All our apple trees are available on MM 106 and M9'. So what does this mean? Unlike other rootstocks, those for apples are numbered and not named but the modern ones always start with the prefix M or MM. This simply denotes the research station from which they originated; 'M' denotes Horticultural Research International (East Malling) and 'MM' refers to HRI in conjunction with John Innes Horticultural Institute. The number which follows is merely the serial number that the stock bore when it was under trial.

The three most popular and useful rootstocks for garden apple trees are:

### MM106

Described as 'semi-dwarfing', MM106 is the apple rootstock most used. It produces a medium-sized tree which starts cropping when only 3–4 years old. It is suitable for bush trees, dwarf pyramids, cordons, espaliers and spindles.

It is a good rootstock for producing a relatively small tree on a wide range of soil types.

### M26

This produces a tree slightly smaller than those on MM106. It is suitable for the same tree forms but, because it is less vigorous, the trees usually need staking for longer.

On poor land it is the best rootstock for producing a small tree and should be used instead of the dwarfer M9.

Cox isn't always successful on M26 but other varieties generally are.

### M9

This is a dwarfing stock which, until recently, produced the smallest apple trees. Although this distinction has now passed to M27, M9 is generally more suitable for gardens. The soil must be good for trees on M9 to give of their best and, where you are not certain about your soil's quality, it is safer to use M26.

Trees growing on M9 will normally need staking throughout their life. Suitable trees for growing on it are dwarf pyramids, cordons, dwarf bush, espaliers and spindles.

The trees crop very early in their life and the fruit tends to be larger and quicker ripening than from trees on other stocks. This is useful if you are growing early varieties.

There are a number of other excellent apple rootstocks if you want something out of the ordinary.

## Other apple rootstocks

### M27

This produces the smallest apple trees of all. So dwarfing, in fact, that it should only be used on good soil or your tree may never grow at all. Even in a pot, it tends to be too dwarfing but a tub or large trough suits it well.

### MM111

This gives a larger tree than any of the others mentioned and is a first rate stock for half-standards (and the almost extinct standards). The trees crop heavily and are resistant to drought, as well as potash and magnesium deficiency.

### M1

Similar in vigour to MM111 [Fig. 14.1] but rarely seen or used, though it does succeed on heavy and wet land where others may fail.

### M2

Considered now to be an inferior version of MM111.

## Rootstocks for other fruits

### Pear

The choice of pear rootstocks is limited to Quince A and Quince C, the latter being the less vigorous of the two and the one that crops soonest. In fact, unless one wants a relatively large and vigorous tree, Quince C is the one to choose for gardens.

An interesting point about quince rootstocks is that certain varieties of pear are, to a greater or lesser extent, incompatible with it. The best known of these are 'Williams' and 'Merton

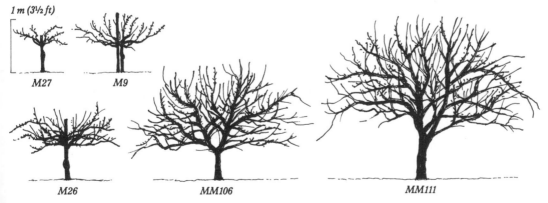

*1 m (3½ ft)*

M27    M9

M26    MM106    MM111

**Fig. 14.1** This illustrates the different vigour of trees on the main apple rootstocks.

**Fig. 14.2** Trees
with too angled a
union are best
avoided.

Pride'. This, fortunately, is well known by
nurserymen who introduce a sliver of a compatible variety (an interstock) between the
quince rootstock and the incompatible scion at
the time of budding or grafting.

### Plum

The number of plum rootstocks is as small as
that for pears. St. Julien A is used for
traditional-sized trees and Pixy for smaller
ones. Pixy produces a tree about two-thirds the
size of those growing on St. Julien A. Even this,
though, is a far larger tree than an apple on M9.

### Peaches and Nectarines

Most peaches and nectarines are grown on St.
Julien A, although one or two specialist fruit
nurseries are using Pixy with an interstock
between the rootstock and the peach. This
results in a smaller tree than average.

### Cherry

The only other important tree fruit needing a
rootstock is the cherry. Whilst the sour morello
makes only a small tree anyway, the semi-sour

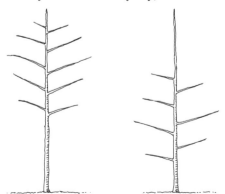

**Fig. 14.3 and 14.4**
Feathers that are
well up the stem of
maiden fruit trees
are normally more
use than those low
down.

Dukes and sweet cherries tend to be huge; far
too big for gardens.

The most widely available semi-vigorous
stock is Colt and most nurseries are now using
this. However, there is also an extremely
dwarfing one from Belgium called Inmil. This
leads to a tree only some 2.4 m (8 ft) tall so it is
clearly in a class of its own, though long-term
results are still inconclusive.

Those, then, are the most important and
popular rootstocks used today for raising fruit
trees. Now we come to the early and formative
pruning of young fruit trees.

## The initial pruning and training of fruit trees

The training and formation work that a young
fruit tree receives in its first two or three years
sets the pattern for the rest of its life. If it is
carried out properly, the tree will thrive and
prosper; if it is carried out badly, the tree is
seldom a success. This is particularly true of
young apple trees. A well feathered and
strongly growing tree will be years ahead of a
feeble maiden whip.

An important point early on is the union; the
point at which the rootstock and the scion
variety are joined, whether by budding or
grafting. This should be such that the stock
and the scion are in as straight a line as possible. A union that looks like a bent knee is
never satisfactory. Either the stock is upright
or the stem of the tree is [Fig. 14.2].

This sort of thing can only be overcome in
the tree's first year or so; after that, the damage
is done. An even better starting point, of
course, is during propagation.

This sort of fault is more likely with a grafted
tree than with one that has been budded. It
happens when a bud from the wrong side of the
scion (the side away from the stock) is allowed
to form the main stem of the tree.

This is why budding produces a straighter
stem, especially when a snag is left to which
the young shoot can be tied during its first
year.

The height of the feathers on young fruit
trees is also important. Those that form early
in the season are too near the ground to be of
any use so have to be removed. However, if the
side shoots that invariably form on the root-

stock in the first year after budding are allowed to attain 30 cm (12 in) in length before they are removed, the lowest feathers are considerably higher and the stem of the tree is taller [Figs. 14.3 and 14.4]. This is because the formation of feathers on the whip is delayed until those on the stock are removed.

Whether you are raising trees commercially or at home for the fun of it, the actual shape into which the tree is trained in the early years is the same; the only difference is the way in which it is done.

## Bush trees

The commonest tree form in gardens, though not necessarily the most appropriate, is an open-centre bush tree. This should have 50–60 cm (20–24 in) of clear trunk below the bottom branches and it is formed, initially, by cutting back a feathered maiden or a maiden whip (unfeathered maiden) to 75–85 cm (30–33 in) tall after planting. Pruning during the first few years must be to build up the main branches that will form the tree.

This first pruning will lead to the formation of up to about eight side shoots and it is from these that the main branches will be formed. If you started off with a well-feathered maiden tree, you will already have the first side shoots, the feathers. This illustrates the advantages of a feathered tree; it starts a year ahead of a whip [Fig. 14.5].

From these feathers or side shoots, four are selected and retained. They should be at a wide angle to the central stem, to add strength to the joint, and, looked at from above, they should be at close to right-angles with their neighbours. These are cut back a third to half, harder for the weaker shoots, and all others are cut clean off. This will lead to the formation of up to eight new shoots. The leader (the shoot at the end) on each of these is cut back by about a third, to, usually, an outward-pointing bud to induce more side shoots to develop. If a shoot is produced where it is not wanted, it can be left intact to fruit or, if it is in the way, shortened back or removed altogether.

A variation on the open-centre tree is the delayed open-centre which, as the name implies, involves keeping the upright central leader until, normally, three tiers of branches have been formed. This results in a central

trunk 1.2–1.8 m (4–6 ft) tall.

## Half-standards and standards

These are formed in just the same way except that the trunk should be 1.2–1.5 m (4–5 ft) or 1.5–1.8 m (5–6 ft) tall respectively. (Incidentally, these measurements, and those for bush trees, refer to trees of any kind of fruit that are being raised.)

## Pyramids

Apples and pears can be grown as dwarf pyramids and, less usually, plums are grown as pyramids. The shape, hardly surprisingly, is roughly a tall pyramid. It is usual to restrict their height to about 2 m (6 ft 6 ins).

The initial pruning is to about 50 cm (20 in) tall or higher if the one-year-old tree (maiden) has side shoots (feathers). The following winter (the one after planting) the extension growth on the central stem is cut back to leave 20 cm (8 in) of new growth. Cut it to a bud that faces in the opposite direction to that in which the shoot was cut last year. This will maintain an upright, if not completely straight, stem. Any new side shoots are cut back to about 13 cm (5 in) long [Fig. 14.6].

A year later, the branch leaders (the new growth at the end of each proposed branch) are cut back to 13 cm (5 in) long to a downward outward-pointing bud. Side shoots (laterals) arising directly from the branches are cut back

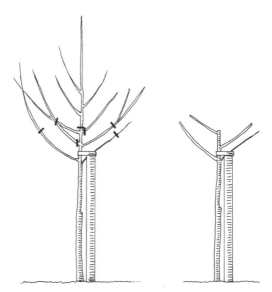

**Fig. 14.5** Pruning a feathered maiden or two-year-old bush apple tree. The same system is used for half-standards and standards; only the height of the stem differs.

**Fig. 14.6** Feathers or side shoots are cut back to 13 cm (5 in) long to form a pyramid.

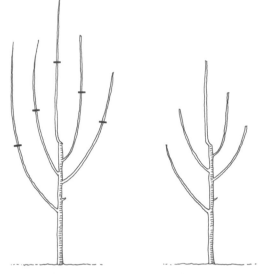

to 8 cm (3 in) long. This is usually about three leaves beyond the basal cluster.

Those arising from a previously pruned spur are cut back to 2–3 cm (1 in).

## Cordons

Apples, pears and, less usually, plums are all suitable fruits for cordons.

These single-stemmed trees are grown on dwarfing or semi-dwarfing rootstocks to restrict their vigour and size.

As a rule, the leader is left unpruned until it reaches the top wire. The exception to this is if you are growing a tip-bearing variety of apple; then, you should cut it back annually in the winter by a quarter to a half (the greater amount for trees lacking in vigour). This will encourage the formation of the characteristic short, fruit-bearing shoots. No other pruning

*Leader not usually cut*

*Cut to three buds*

**Fig. 14.7** Any feathers or side shoots longer than 10 cm (4 in) on maiden or older cordons are cut back to three buds.

is needed until longer side shoots have started to form.

A great help in producing a straight stem is to tie strong canes to the wires at the tree positions and tie the developing trees to these rather than directly to the wires [Fig. 14.7].

## Espaliers

Suitable for apples and pears.

Starting with a maiden tree, an espalier is formed by cutting it back to 5–8 cm (2–3 in) above the bottom training wire. The exact position of the cut will depend on the bud layout. The object is to find two buds pointing in opposite directions along the line of the bottom wire. These will form the first tier of branches [Fig. 14.8].

Other things allowing, the cut is then made above the bud immediately above the two selected to become branches.

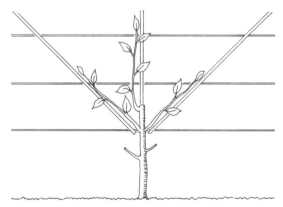

**Fig. 14.8** The starting point with an espalier.

A system of notching and nicking the branch buds will help to ensure that they do what you want. Notching encourages the treated bud to grow out into a shoot. A centimetre or so above the bud, a notch is made in the shoot so that a shallow piece of bark and wood falls away [Fig. 14.9]. If the notch is made any closer to the bud, it usually causes the resulting shoot to grow out at too acute an angle to the stem. A wide angle will give strong branch unions along with branches that are closer to the horizontal, and therefore earlier fruiting and less vigorous.

Nicking is done with the opposite effect in

**Fig. 14.9** Notching buds on a maiden tree intended for an espalier to induce the right buds to grow out.

mind, but at this early stage in the tree's life, the actual removal of the bud is easier and more effective. Nicking is useful later on, though, as it encourages a growth bud to change into a fruit bud.

Thus is initiated the bottom pair of horizontal branches. The bud above them, the top bud, will grow upwards to continue the main stem. From then on, the system is roughly the same each winter. The top bud being retained for extension growth, the two beneath it, if suitable, for the next tier of branches.

Stopping any of the branches is usually unnecessary; they are seldom vigorous and normally form fruit buds quite readily. If you find that one of a pair is lagging behind the other, cut it loose and raise its angle. This will automatically increase its vigour. It can be bent down and tied in again when it has caught up the other.

## Fan-trained trees

This is the most suitable training method for stone fruit (peaches, plums, cherries, apricots etc.). Some also recommend it for apples and pears. These trees, though, tend to be harder to manage because the branches nearer the vertical always grow more vigorously and, certainly to start with, crop less heavily. This doesn't happen to quite the same extent with stone fruit because the main rays of the fan, especially those of peaches and nectarines, are less permanent than they are with apples and pears. The latter can still be grown as fans but,

on the whole, they are less satisfactory and are better as espaliers.

For fan trees you will start by needing wires stretched either along a suitable wall or fence, if they are to be planted in their final position, or in the open ground if they are to be moved.

At this stage (for young trees), only three wires will be needed at, say, 45 cm (18 in),

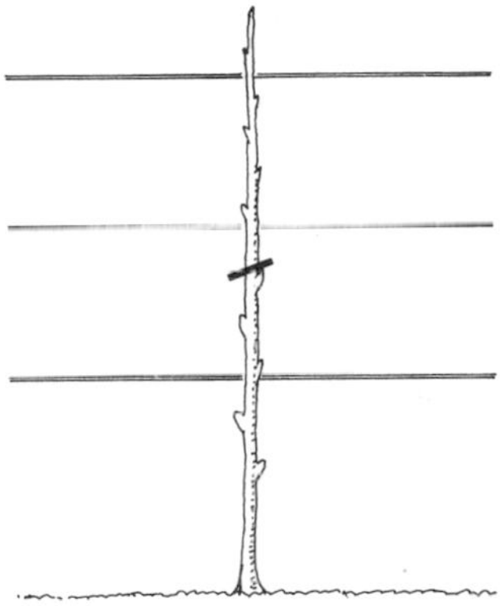

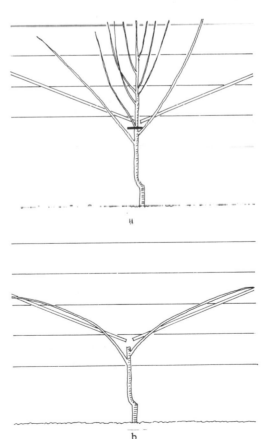

**Fig. 14.10** Starting off a maiden whip as a fan.

**Fig. 14.11** If there are one or more suitably placed side shoots/feathers, they can be used as the basis of the fan.

150 cm (5 ft) and the third midway between. The future shoots are not tied to these wires but to canes attached to them.

For older trees, more horizontal wires will be needed, say every 15 cm (6 in).

The spring after planting, maiden trees for fan training should be cut back to 60 cm (24 in) tall. The aim is to produce two good laterals on opposite sides of the main stem no more than 30 cm (12 in) from the ground. If there are already either one or two side shoots 30–60 cm (12–24 in) up the stem suitable for branches, keep them and cut the main stem back to immediately above the top one [Figs. 14.10 and 14.11].

If there are no shoots but only buds, wait until two suitable shoots have started to grow out; the main stem above them is cut back to the top one in the summer. These shoots are then loosely tied to two canes attached to the wires for this purpose. Any other shoots that grow out during that season are pinched back to one leaf beyond the basal cluster when they are large enough to handle.

Towards the end of the following winter, shorten back the two laterals to 30–45 cm (12–18 in) long.

In the following summer, the leading extension growth on each is tied to the wire to extend that particular ray of the fan. At the same time, two shoots growing from the upper surface of the shoot are selected and retained together with one from the lower surface. The upper two should be from 10–15 cm (4–6 in) apart.

Any shoots that grow straight towards the wall should be rubbed out as soon as possible. With trees in the open, however, they can be retained but pinched back to one leaf, along with any others not wanted for branch formation.

In the following spring, the new shoots and the extension growth on the leader are all cut back to 45 cm (18 in) long and tied to the same, or additional canes as necessary.

Fan trained figs are slightly different as nowhere near so much regimentation is possible, or needed, once the framework branches have been laid down. However, in their early life we should at least start them off in the right direction, even if they break away in later years.

Starting with a single shoot, a one-year-old tree, this is cut back to a point about 40 cm (16 in) from the ground. This will result in at least two shoots in the following summer.

These two, which should be pointing in as near opposite directions as you can find, are retained. They are shortened by no more than one quarter. Any other shoots are cut out.

From then on the system is the same as the standard formation of a fan tree, which has just been described.

With all fan-trained trees, the important thing is to start with the lowest rays of the fan first and work upwards into the centre.

The reason for this is that, at the centre of the fan, the upright branches grow much faster than the lower ones, so they soon catch them up to complete the fan. If the centre branches were formed first, they would dominate the lower ones completely and scarcely allow them to grow.

## Spindlebush

This system is suitable for apples and pears. The equivalent for plums is hooping or festooning. It is the latest important system of training and pruning and is much used by commercial growers. It is based on the fact that lightly pruned trees carry fruit earlier in their life than do hard pruned trees. It also brings the benefit of 'minimum maintenance'.

To form a spindle, a maiden whip is cut back to 90 cm (3 ft) tall after planting.

The starting point for a feathered maiden is 60 cm (2 ft) above the ground; any feathers below that are cut right out. The next three or four above that, depending on their suitability as branches, are shortened by about half to a bud pointing downwards. The central stem is cut back to three buds above the top lateral [Fig. 14.12].

The next move depends on the vigour of the tree in the following summer. If, by the time growth has stopped in late summer, it has been good, then the originally retained side shoots, and their extension growth, are tied down to near horizontal. Twine, secured at one end to either a peg in the ground or to the base of the central stem, is attached at the other end to the lateral, which is thus pulled down. This further reduces the vigour of the shoot and encourages fruit buds to form from growth

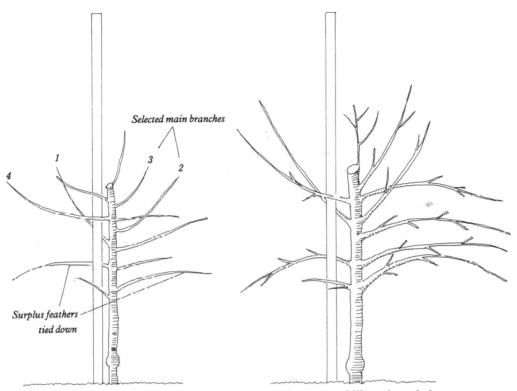

*Selected main branches*

*1*  *3*  *2*

*4*

*Surplus feathers
tied down*

**Fig. 14.12** Initial pruning of a feathered maiden apple or pear to form a spindle-bush.

buds. In trees that were originally unfeathered, some of the laterals could be rather too upright for bending down with comfort; these are best cut right out. Apart from that, the routine is the same. However, it does again illustrate the benefits of having a strong and well feathered maiden tree to start off with; it saves at least a year.

The formation pruning of what might be called miscellaneous fruit trees is largely a matter of common sense. It follows very general rules, rather than specific instructions.

If a tree is to have an open centre then, clearly, the one-year-old central stem must be stopped at the required height to ensure the formation of side shoots.

On the other hand, if a tree is to be grown with a central leader, then either the main stem is left intact or, after stopping (as with a spindlebush), the topmost lateral is trained up as a new leader. This serves the threefold purpose of limiting upward growth, encouraging laterals to form but maintaining an upright tree.

The only other point that has to be considered is the height of the trunk. This does not require great skill or knowledge; one wants either a tree of standard, half-standard or bush height, and we already know the approximate trunk height for all three.

Nor is there a great variation in the routines adopted for maiden fruit trees in the home garden and those growing in containers in the nursery. The ultimate tree size and shape are to be the same so the methods of attaining them are also the same. The only differences occur with other aspects of management.

Where specific fruits (including nuts) haven't already been mentioned, they can either be worked out by matching the type of fruit – for example an almond tree is formed in just the same way as any other stone fruit tree – or, if there is some specialist method required, it will be found in the main text.

Young cobnuts are a good example of this. Although it would have been perfectly possible to have included them in this section, it is neater if the whole process, from cradle to grave, as it were, is covered together.

A walnut, on the other hand, is formed in much the same way as any other standard fruit tree.

## The initial pruning and training of soft fruits

The pruning of soft fruit in their nursery years is just as important as it is for top fruit if successful fruit growing is to follow. It may not have such lasting effects when compared to tree fruits but good treatment is equally vital.

### Bilberries, blueberries and cranberries

Bilberries and cranberries pretty well look after themselves in their early years. About all they will need is clipping in the autumn to maintain them as low-growing shrubby plants and to prevent them becoming tall and leggy.

Highbush blueberries need virtually no pruning at all during their first few years, beyond the removal of any shoots that are dead, broken or clearly upsetting the shape of the bush.

This minimum upkeep can continue until about the third winter after planting the bushes. During that period, they should not be allowed to carry fruit as this can seriously reduce the vigour of the developing bush.

### Cane fruits

Broadly speaking, these are all treated the same in their early life. This is not because the actual fruits are similar, although they are, but because, with the exception of autumn-fruiting raspberries, they all operate on a biennial system. The canes grow in the first year and fruit in the next.

Following dormant season planting, either in nursery rows or in their fruiting position, all canes fruits are cut down to within about 20 cm (8 in) of the ground. This encourages the production of new canes from at or below ground level in the following growing season. The short length of stem that is left will produce a few shoots and leaves that will act as sap drawers but it will not allow the production of enough blossom or fruit to weaken the new canes to any extent.

It should be noted that cane fruit plants older than one year are not recommended for transplanting. A plant that has had just one growing season after propagation is the only sort that should be bought. For that matter, it is also the only sort that should be sold. For this reason, the only form of support that is necessary is an individual bamboo cane for blackberries and the hybrids.

If any support is deemed necessary for young raspberry canes, twine down each side of the rows is normally enough. The same can be said for autumn-fruiting raspberries.

All that has been said refers to the pruning of young canes that have been propagated and planted out in the open round.

A new system has grown up as a result of the introduction some years ago of micro-propagation. Because of the small size of the plants during their first year, they are almost always grown and sold in pots. If they have not been sold (or planted) by the end of that year, they are then planted in nursery rows and cut down as previously recommended. Whilst in pots, there is seldom any need for support. If there is, it probably means that the plants are in need of planting out anyway.

## Currants

Because of the way in which they flower, black currants, red currants and white currants cannot all be pruned in the same way. This is because black currants produce their best fruit on young shoots whereas red currants fruit best on spurs that are built up on a semi-permanent framework of branches. This reflects in the way they are pruned throughout their life and the difference starts in the very first year after propagation.

To achieve the best results, black currants are grown as a stool with many of the new branches originating from at or below ground level. Red currant bushes are on a short leg and consist mainly of mature branches furnished with fruiting spurs.

### Black currants

The aim here is to build up a strong stool quickly so that heavy crops are carried from an early age. If the propagation was carried out correctly, two or three shoots will have grown from the cutting by the autumn after propagation. They will normally be shooting from the few buds that remained above ground but they could also be from below the soil surface.

Whatever their origin, they are cut back to leave just one strong bud per shoot beyond the cluster around the base.

This pruning is normally done with the

rooted cutting still in its original position [Fig. 14.13]. A year later, when the bushes will need to be planted out further apart, all the strong shoots are cut back to 5–8 cm (2–3 in) long. Weak shoots are cut out completely.

No tipping of shoots is normally required at any time because, if well grown and fed, plenty of growth will come naturally.

### Red and white currants

The white currant is treated in every respect in exactly the same way as the red currant. As such, their pruning is also identical. For this reason, only the red currant will be spoken about but it can be taken to apply equally to white currants. Whereas black currants fruit best on the younger shoots, red currants produce better fruit on spurs borne on older branches.

When being grown as traditional bushes, and provided that they have been propagated correctly, there should be some 13 cm (5 in) of clear stem below the bottom shoot at the end of the first year after propagation. Any shoots that are closer than that to the soil are removed. Any obviously weak shoots are also removed. The remainder of the new shoots are then cut back by a third to a half (hardest for the weakest) to build up a good framework of strong branches. However, any very strong shoots that are growing straight up are best removed as they tend to become too dominant [Fig. 14.14].

In the following winter, the bush can be lifted and planted in its final position.

Its worth noting that the actual planting is an inducement to the formation of fruit buds. It is, after all, a form of root pruning.

When growing the bushes as standards, you must start with a one-year-old bush carrying a vigorous and unpruned shoot as near to vertical as possible. All others are removed and the retained shoot is tied to a cane in the ground beside it to maintain the straight and untipped stem.

A year later, this single stem is cut back to 90–120 cm (3–4 ft) tall, according to the height you want the stem of the standard.

After another year, as many strong new shoots as may be suitable are retained and cut back by a third to a half to form the main framework branches. These should be evenly

**Fig. 14.13** The first year's shoots of black currants are pruned very hard so that more are encouraged to form.

spaced around the stem, of approximately equal vigour and close together.

This will give you the rudiments of the standard. Red currants can be grown very effectively and economically as single, double ('U') [Fig. 14.15] or triple vertical cordons.

A single cordon is formed in a similar way to a standard except that, each autumn, the extension growth is shortened by a quarter to induce side shoots to grow out.

In the formative years, the resulting shoots are winter pruned by shortening them, back to two buds. To form cordons with two or three upright stems, the original young plant is allowed to produce two shoots. These are carefully bent down and tied to a horizontal cane. As they grow in the following year, they are trained outwards and then upwards so that they form vertical shoots 30 cm (12 in) apart. From then on, they are treated in the same way as the single cordon.

A three-stem cordon is started off just like a

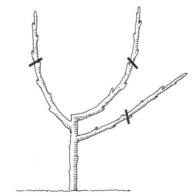

**Fig. 14.14** Red currants have a very different starting point to black currants. The bushes are grown on a leg and the first shoots are pruned less hard.

two-stem except that a third shoot is then taken up the middle from the base of one of the other two.

Each upright is to be 30 cm (1 ft) apart, resulting in a 60 cm (2 ft) wide plant.

### Gooseberries

Because the gooseberry fruits best in the same way as the red currant, that is upon spurs borne on semi-permanent branches, the pruning is done in much the same way.

An open centre to the bush is important; both to make picking easier and also to discourage the 'gooseberry sawfly', which lays its eggs in the sheltered centre of the bushes. Gooseberries should be pruned slightly harder early in their life years because their shoots are more supple and the bushes naturally adopt a weeping habit. The bushes are normally grown on a short leg and the new shoots are cut back by half (not a third, as for red currants) for the first few years. This gives a more rigid framework of branches. The buds to which you cut are selected on the basis of the direction in which you want the future shoot to grow. If you want the branch to stay reasonably straight, you must alternate the buds from year to year. Thus, if you choose a left-pointing bud one year, you should normally choose a right-pointing one in the following year. Side shoots are pruned in winter by cutting back all those that are not required to form extension growth to 7–8 cm (3 in) long. This builds up

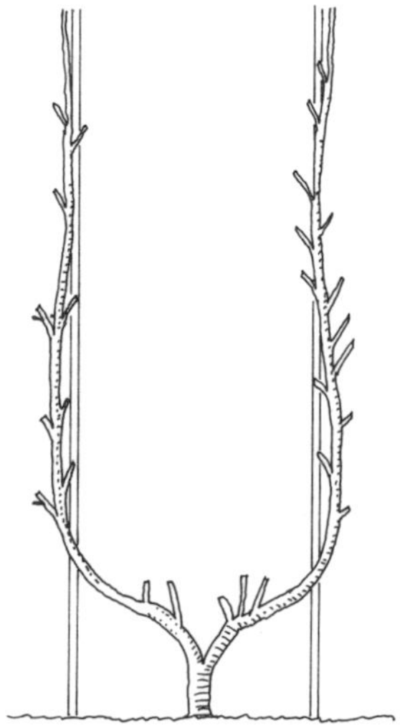

**Fig. 14.15** A gooseberry double 'U' cordon.

the spur system.

Gooseberries can also be grown as cordons and standards, as described above for red currants.

### Grapes

Regardless of how a vine is going to be grown after permanent planting, and whether it is going to be planted and grown in the greenhouse or outside, its initial pruning after the original cutting has taken and grown out, is exactly the same.

Most vines will start life in a pot. This is far better for them because they don't like root disturbance during the growing season and it means that they can be bought and planted when the gardener, rather than the plant, wants. The only pruning required by the vine eyes, once they have rooted, is to make sure that only one shoot develops and that any laterals which grow out from it are stopped at one leaf. It is important, though, to make sure that they don't become pot-bound either.

If the vine is not for your own growing, it will need to be potted on during the next winter. In addition, the cane should be shortened back when it is thoroughly dormant. 90 cm (3 ft) would be a convenient height to bring it back to.

This routine can be used for all vines, whatever method of training and pruning is to be carried out later.

If the vine is subsequently planted inside a greenhouse, it is then cut back to two or three buds.

If it is planted outside, it is led through the wall and cut back so that there are just two buds inside.

*Grapes in pots*

Layering is not a particularly good method of propagation but it does have one interesting and profitable application; that of growing grapes in pots.

During the growing season, a first-year cane is retained and trained upwards from a bud low down on an established greenhouse vine.

Once dormant, the cane is shortened to 2.5–3 m (8–10 ft). All laterals are cut hard back.

The rest of the operation is given in detail on pages 205–8.

# CHAPTER 15

# Tree Fruits Outdoors and Under Glass

## OUTDOORS

The important thing to remember about pruning fruit trees is that there are several ways of doing it, depending on the kind of fruit, the specific shape or form of tree you are growing and what you want to end up with. There is no simple answer to the question, 'How should I prune a fruit tree?'

This may sound obvious to the initiated but you would be surprised at how many new-comers to pruning think that 'a fruit tree is a fruit tree is a fruit tree' and that all are dealt with in the same way. There are certainly basic principles that can be applied to most fruit trees but these are designed more to maintain their shape and restrict their size rather than to increase the quantity and improve the quality of the fruit.

### Apples and pears

Broadly speaking, these are pruned in exactly the same ways. Where there is a difference, it will be mentioned. One peculiarity of apples, though not pears, is that all varieties fall into one of two types as regards the way in which the fruits are borne. By far the larger group is what are called 'spur bearers', that is, the majority of the fruit buds (flower buds) form, initially, directly from two-year-old shoots. They develop from what were previously growth buds.

Once a flower has formed and a fruit has been produced and picked, the swollen woody stem that is left behind will usually be seen to be carrying one or more fat fruit buds for the coming year. This organ is called a 'spur' and spurs tend to go on producing fruit buds on successive swellings. After a number of years, a fruiting spur can be quite a complicated piece of growth. Almost all pears are spur bearers. A few apple varieties, though, produce most of

their fruits, not from buds actually on the shoots or older spurs but at the end of very dwarf shoots, usually less than about 15 cm (6 in) in length. These varieties are called 'tip bearers'. Some of the commoner ones include 'Worcester Pearmain', 'Bramley', 'Jonathan', 'Blenheim Orange' and 'Tydeman's Early'.

We will see later how their pruning differs from that of spur bearers.

With free-standing trees (ordinary trees which are not trained in an intensive way), virtually all the pruning is carried out during the dormant season from early winter to early spring. This reduces the risk of most fungal diseases infecting the wood through wounds and it also makes it far easier to see what needs to be done by way of shaping and balancing the tree. It may also make it slightly harder to distinguish living shoots and branches from dead ones but this is soon overcome.

Intensively grown trees, though (meaning those which are trained into rigid shapes), such as cordons and espaliers, respond better to being pruned in the summer. There are three main reasons for this.

First, it reduces the vigour of the tree and, thus, directs more energy into the developing fruits. This clearly benefits the present crop but it also encourages the production of fruit buds for the future.

Second, it removes a lot of the leaves that would otherwise shade the developing fruits. This improves the appearance of coloured varieties and brings out the true flavour of all varieties.

Thirdly, in some cases summer pruning can almost replace winter pruning.

There is a fourth, though rather peripheral, advantage which is not always appreciated until you actually come to do the job. It is far more pleasant to be out in the fresh air and sunshine in late summer than in the biting wind and freezing cold of midwinter!

Choosing the correct time to summer prune apples and pears is one of those instances when it is more important to go by the stage of growth of the tree than by what the calendar says. The correct time is when the current season's shoots are just hardening (ripening) at their base. By that time, they would be about as thick as a pencil. If some shoots are still immature when you start summer pruning, leave them for about a month and then come back to them, or leave them until the winter.

In some years, the cessation of growth in mid summer, with the formation of the fatter terminal bud, is an indication that it is time to prune. This, though, cannot always be relied upon because a tree will sometimes stop growing in the summer, if there is a shortage of water, and then start up again after a period of irrigation or prolonged rain.

It is safer to go by the stage of growth and size. Remember, however, that summer pruning apples and pears is only applicable to trees which are trained and grown intensively. Traditionally shaped trees derive no benefit from it at all; largely because it takes no account of the need to shape a tree or where the fruit buds are produced on non-trained trees. Besides that, it would be very difficult to do and would take an extremely long time.

The nearest we can get to creating in winter the same effect as summer pruning is by 'established spur' pruning certain varieties. This is discussed later (see page 170).

We saw in the last chapter that standards, half-standards and bush trees are really just different sizes of the same sort of tree. The rootstocks used are normally different as well, but otherwise the main distinguishing feature is the height of the trunk.

Standard trees are very seldom planted these days, as they are far too big for gardens, but everything that is said about half-standards can be taken to refer equally to standards.

With this in mind, it is safe to deduce that the same pruning methods can be adopted (though sometimes adapted) for all three sizes. These are 'regulated' pruning, the 'renewal' method and, much less commonly, 'established spur' pruning. All three are carried out during the dormant season.

## Regulated pruning

The name is somewhat misleading because it implies that the system has more effect on the tree than in fact it does. It is the simplest and least fussy of the three methods and is the very least that one should do to maintain an apple or pear tree in good shape and cropping in a garden.

It is about as simple as you can get and much of the work can be carried out with a pruning saw, rather than secateurs. Indeed, secateurs should be used as little as possible as they do away with much of the simplicity of regulated pruning. The whole idea of the system is to make as few cuts as possible with greatest effect. Time should be taken to look at the tree and decide what has to be removed. The main aim is to keep branches away from each other, thus giving them light and space, and to make picking, spraying and other management easy to carry out.

In the early life of a tree, all that needs doing is for a few shoots to be shortened to help in the formation of the main branches. This light pruning also encourages the early formation of blossom buds so that the trees come into cropping earlier than those receiving more complicated pruning. The system thrives on the fact that unpruned shoots crop earlier than pruned ones. It is not always suitable for very heavily cropping trees because it can encourage the formation of small fruits. Nor do trees lacking in vigour always respond well; they frequently stop growing altogether or may develop a biennial cropping habit (fruiting in alternate years). The system's main disadvantage, when carried out strictly 'by the book', is that, as the tree gets older, so the fruiting shoots get further from the ground.

The actual pruning involves the removal or shortening of all shoots and branches that are dead or diseased or which are broken or in the way. This last category usually means those which are crossing from one side of the tree to the other or those which cause overcrowding. Similarly, all branches that are either too high, too low or too spreading should also go [Fig. 15.1]. When we consider a tree that has been appropriately and sensibly pruned to the regulated system from the start, even the largest specimen can usually be pruned in less than an hour; simply because it is already the

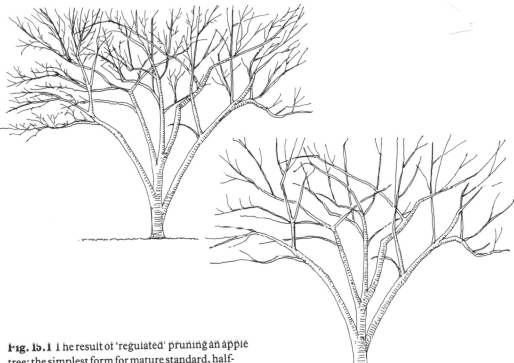

**Fig. 15.1** The result of 'regulated' pruning an apple tree; the simplest form for mature standard, half-standard and bush trees.

right shape and size. Standard, half-standard and bush trees can all be pruned in this way and it makes no difference whether apples are spur or tip bearers.

## The renewal system

With the renewal system, the same general rules still apply with regard to the removal of unwanted branches but it is carried a stage further. In this way it leads to more and better fruit than does regulated pruning.

All fruit trees produce their finest crops (both quantity and quality) on relatively young branches; certainly not more than about 10

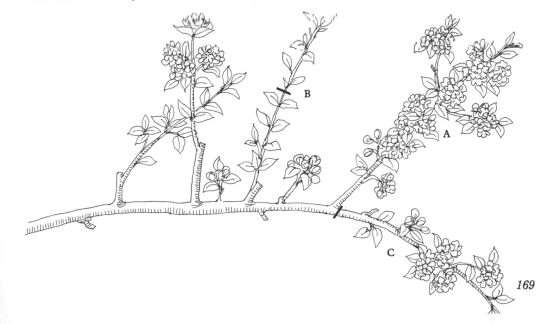

**Fig. 15.2** A single apple branch pruned by the 'renewal' method. (A) is a productive and well-placed fruiting lateral. (B) will take its place. (C) has become too low and is taken out.

years old. You must not take this to mean that any branch over ten years old has to be removed. It is the actual fruit-bearing branches which should be kept young; not those that form the framework of the tree.

The aim of the renewal system is to produce a succession of young shoots, spurs and branches every year on mainly permanent and mature branches so that the cropping element of the tree is kept young, active and efficient. That being the aim of renewal pruning, we can say that the art of carrying it out is the ability to recognize whether a shoot should be cut out completely or used for the production of blossom buds, further young shoots or in the formation of a new branch [Fig. 15.2]. When, eventually, these new branches get too large, out of place or too old to fruit properly, they are removed.

Whilst this is going on, the smaller branches that are to replace them are built up in the course of three to four years for this specific purpose. However, provided that there is room, the new shoots produced which are not wanted for branch production can be left unpruned to form young, temporary fruiting units. Once they begin to crowd the more permanent branches, they are cut out or shortened back, as appropriate. When you shorten them back, always do so to a replacement shoot which can be developed into a fruiting shoot.

Thus we have a tree that is furnished with main branches, fruiting branches and developing branches.

Both these systems are fine for extensively grown, free-standing trees, though clearly the renewal system is more efficient.

## The established spur system

Many years ago and, unfortunately, still today in some gardens, all apple and pear trees were pruned in the same way. The method was known as 'tipping and spurring' and it was done primarily to make the trees neat and tidy and only secondarily with a view to producing good fruit.

As luck would have it, some of the better known and more pronouncedly spur-bearing varieties were admirably suited and, even as recently as the 1960s, varieties like 'Lord Derby', 'Miller's Seedling' and 'Early Victoria'

were still being spur pruned in commercial orchards. Indeed, it is really only the supersedence of these varieties that has put a stop to the practice.

Whilst the system was, and still is fine in the hands of someone who knows what they are doing, it can be devastating if carried out incorrectly.

The suitability of spur-bearing varieties to this system was mentioned just then but, as we have seen, other quite commonly grown varieties, such as 'Worcester Pearmain', 'Tydeman's Worcester', 'Blenheim Orange', 'Bramley's Seedling' and 'Jonathan', are tip-bearers. Spur pruning these in the same way that you would treat spur bearers would remove up to three-quarters of the fruit buds because they tend to form on the end of shoots up to about 15 cm (6 in) long. Although the modern way of spur pruning is not as harsh as it was in the past, it is still the most savage system and the one that requires the least intelligence but the most time.

It has a similar visual effect to summer pruning but is carried out during the winter instead of later summer. Thus, it has few of the benefits. Although largely forgotten now, spur pruning can still be very effective when carried out on spur-bearing varieties, where a simple method of pruning is required to keep trees strictly within bounds and yet still productive.

In essence, a spur-pruned tree consists of a convenient number of permanent branches (up to perhaps ten) from which, lateral (secondary) branches are trained out. All these branches carry a spur system on which the fruit is carried. Extension growth on the end of the main branches is cut back by a half to a third each year, depending on the vigour of the shoot; the weaker the shoot, the harder it is pruned. More branches may be formed as, when and where required.

One-year-old shoots not wanted for extension growths and which are growing directly from the framework branches are cut hard back to 8–10 cm (3–4 in) long. Those growing from shoots previously shortened are cut back to 2–3 cm (1 in) or removed altogether. In this way a fruiting spur system is built up [Fig. 15.3].

Vigorous varieties like 'Bramley's Seedling'

**Fig. 15.3** A young
Cox tree pruned to
the renewal
method.

are unsuitable for spur pruning whilst, on tip bearers (see above), any shoot less than 15 cm (6 in) long should be left unpruned as it will usually have a fruit bud on the end.

On the whole, the established spur system is the least recommended of the three methods covered so far. It is a specialized system of pruning that only suits a small number of varieties.

Summer pruning is never carried out on these large tree forms; it would take far too long and be of little benefit.

Going a stage further, therefore, new gardens are becoming increasingly smaller and, thus, there is a greater need for smaller trees. This is where the more intensive systems of fruit growing become applicable. Most of them have been developed over the years, mainly for commercial growers.

A slightly different arrangement exists with the smaller trees. With standard, half-standard and bush trees, we have been able to choose one of three different pruning methods. With the smaller types of tree, they have their own

method of pruning because it is largely the pruning that creates them. Thus we find that there is a method of pruning which, when applied to a one-year-old tree, leads to a dwarf pyramid.

The type of tree you want and the method of pruning required to maintain it therefore go together.

## Dwarf pyramids

This was the first of what we might call the modern dwarf trees. It was probably developed from certain French systems; at least, they all have a lot in common.

In ease and intensity of pruning, it comes somewhere between a cordon (see page 160) and a bush tree in that it is largely summer pruned and yet it is three-dimensional; as opposed to cordons, espaliers and fans, which are two-dimensional. The shape, hardly surprisingly, is roughly a tall pyramid; the outline being something like a Christmas tree.

As little as 1–1.2 m (3–4 ft) is required between trees in a row, when grown on a dwarfing rootstock, though 1.5–1.8 m (5–6 ft) is more normal on, say, MM106. It is usual practice to restrict their height to about 2 m (7 ft). We saw earlier that the initial pruning was to about 50 cm (20 in) high, or higher if the one-year-old tree (maiden) had side shoots (feathers). This was done straight after planting (see page 159).

In winter, after planting, the extension growth on the central stem is cut back to leave 20 cm (8 in) of new growth. Cut it to a bud that faces in the opposite direction to that in which the shoot was cut last year. This will maintain an upright, if not completely straight, stem. Any new side shoots are cut back to 13 cm (5 in) long. Starting around midsummer, the branch leaders (the new growth at the end of each proposed branch) are cut back to 13 cm (5 in) long to a downward or outward pointing bud. Side shoots (laterals) arising directly from the branches are cut back to 7–8 cm (3 in) long. This is usually about three leaves beyond the basal cluster. Those arising from a previously pruned spur are cut back to 2–3 cm (1 in) [Fig. 15.4].

Any fresh growth coming from the cut shoots is removed in early autumn or in the winter. From then on, the main central leader is always pruned in the winter but the branch leaders and all new shoots are dealt with in summer as already described.

As with all styles of pruning, it must be re-membered that these are only, if you like, the principles. You still have to use common sense to cater for the unexpected. If for example, and this frequently happens, a particular shoot does not develop in the way you wanted, you have to be ready to find a substitute or take whatever other course you think appropriate.

## Cordons

These are single-stemmed trees grown on dwarfing or semi-dwarfing rootstocks to restrict their vigour and size. As a further inducement to fruit, the trees are almost invari-ably, and certainly should be, planted at an angle of 45°. This has the effect of channelling more energy into a production of fruit buds and less into unwanted, upward growth. These trees are called 'oblique cordons'. Although 'vertical cordons' are sometimes grown against, for example, house walls of sufficient height, they are difficult to control and manage and much of the fruit is out of reach from the ground.

Although cordons can be grown against walls and fences or in the open garden, sup-porting system of wires is always necessary. Three wires are enough and these are stretched horizontally 70, 130 and 200 cm (2½, 4½ and 6½ ft) above the ground. You may have them higher but it means that the top of the tree will be out of reach from the ground.

When the trees are in the open garden, the wires should be stretched between stout posts driven 45–60 cm (1½–2 ft) into the ground and 2–2.1 m (6½–7 ft) high.

As a rule, no pruning is needed until side shoots have formed and the central leader is left unpruned until it reaches the top wire. Once that has been reached, a further induce-ment to fruit is to cut the tree away from the supporting wires and bend it down further to approximately 30°.

A great help in producing a straight stem is to tie strong canes to the wires at the tree positions and tie the developing trees to these rather than directly to the wires. Once the top wire has been reached for the second time, the central stem is pruned to a few inches above the wire and any further shoots from the top are treated as ordinary side shoots and pruned back accordingly.

There is an exception to the rule of leaving

**Fig. 15.4** Pruning pyramids and dwarf pyramids is blissfully simple but it has to be done properly to achieve these results.

the leading shoot unpruned until it reaches the top wire. If you are growing a tip-bearing variety, you should cut back the leading shoot annually in the winter by a quarter to a half (the greater amount for trees lacking in vigour). This will encourage the formation of the characteristic short, fruit-bearing shoots.

Though leader pruning is carried out in the winter, all other pruning is done in the summer at the stage of growth described for dwarf pyramids. Side shoots that are growing directly from the central stem are cut back to three leaves beyond the basal cluster of leaves [Fig. 15.5]. This is normally to about 8 cm (3 in) long. If the new shoots are growing from growth pruned in earlier years, they are cut back to one leaf (2–3 cm/1 in) beyond the basal cluster. Thus, once established, a cordon can be pruned almost entirely in the summer.

The exception lies in the case of relatively old trees which have developed large and complicated spur systems. These tend to produce small and few fruits because the sap has difficulties in reaching the extremities. Simplification and a reduction in size of these spurs is therefore essential [Fig. 15.6]. It is quite easily done, the only problem is steeling yourself to do it.

There is no rule about thinning out old spur systems but you should reduce their size so that each one has two, or at the most three, fruit buds on them. These should be close to

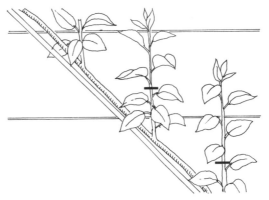

**Fig. 15.5** Cordons and espaliers are best pruned in the summer as it has the greatest influence on fruit bud formation.

the parent branch so that there is very little non-productive woody material.

Do this in the winter and, even as soon as the following year, you will see a great improvement in fruit size.

## The espalier

As the name will suggest to you, this tree form is of French origin. It has very little in common with the cordon as far as shape is concerned but a great deal in the way in which it is managed. The tree consists of a central, vertical stem from which, at regular intervals, pairs of horizontal and opposite branches are trained out sideways. This is carried on upwards until either the tree is as tall as you

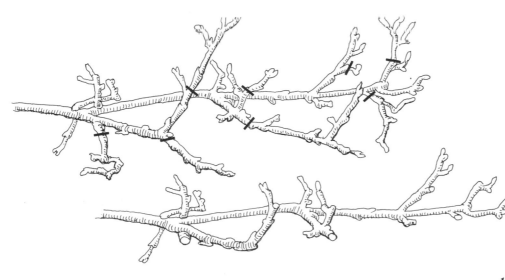

**Fig. 15.6** When spur systems on cordons, espaliers and fans become large and complicated, they must be thinned out.

want or it has reached the top of the wall.

Many different formations and arrangements can be worked out using the same basic design and they can be trained, like the cordon, either to walls or fences or to wires in the open garden. One attractive system for the open garden is the three-dimensional espalier in which each pair of branches is at right-angles to the one beneath. Thus, if the bottom pair point east-west, the one above runs north-south and the third one, east-west.

Both the espalier and the cordon are perfect for small gardens where every square inch counts because they occupy little ground space but produce very worthwhile crops. Although the trees are formed in a very different way, once that is done, the annual pruning is virtually identical to that of cordons so no fresh system needs to be learned.

The recommended distance between each tier of branches varies but is usually 40–45 cm (15–18 in). However, with the weaker varieties and with the more dwarfing rootstocks, 30 cm (12 in) is normally adequate. This is also the approximate height of four rows of bricks, which is handy when you come to put up the supporting wires.

Vigorous trees should be planted up to 5.5 m (18 ft) apart; average strength, 4.6 m (15 ft) and weak growers, 3.7 m (12 ft). The horizontal supporting wires should be at the appropriate distance apart with the lowest one 45 cm (18 in) from the ground.

After planting a maiden tree, cut the central stem back to a few inches above the bottom wire. The exact position of the cut will depend on the layout of the buds. What you should be looking for are two buds pointing in opposite directions along the line of the bottom wire. These will grow into the first tier of branches. Of course, it really is quite important that at this stage everything should go as you intend; simply because you can lose a year if it doesn't. To help with this, a system of 'notching and nicking' can be used.

Notching is the more useful of the two because it encourages the required buds to grow out into shoots. A centimetre or so above the bud that you want to grow out, a notch is made in the bark so that a shallow piece of bark and wood falls away. If the notch is made any closer to the bud, it usually causes the resulting shoot to grow out at too acute an angle to the stem. A wide angle is what is wanted as this leads to strong branch unions and branches that are closer to the horizontal, and therefore earlier fruiting.

Nicking a bud has the opposite effect; it is done to prevent it growing out. Instead of removing a wedge of bark from above the bud, a short cut is made from below the bud, upwards and under it. This will induce either dormancy or a fruit bud to form.

Of course, during the early stages of a tree's formation, one would normally remove a bud completely if a side shoot was not wanted; it has a more definite result than nicking does. Notching and nicking can, though, be very useful in later years when the tree is nearing its maximum size and the end of its shaping.

To return to the young tree; when the two shoots of the first tier are about 30 cm (1 ft) long, canes are tied to the wires behind them at an angle of 45°. The shoots are then bent down and tied to them. This would normally be done in midsummer [Fig. 15.7]. Another cane is tied in behind the central leader to which the new growth at the top is secured. In the winter, the two lateral shoots are further bent down to 30° above the horizontal. At the same time, the central leader is cut back to somewhere above the second wire.

Once again, the exact position of the cut depends on the layout of the buds. As before, you should select a pair which are close to the wire and which are pointing in opposite directions along the line of the wire. Choose another suitably placed bud close to and above

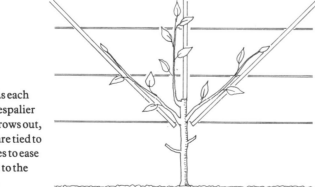

**Fig. 15.7** As each new tier of espalier branches grows out, the shoots are tied to angled canes to ease them down to the horizontal.

these for the upward extension of the central leader. Cut immediately above this bud. In the following (second) summer, the two resulting side shoots are tied down to 45°, as before, and the leader is once again tied to the vertical cane to maintain its straightness. In the winter (second), the two original and lowest 'branches' are freed from their canes and tied direct to the lowest wire. The second pair of lateral shoots are bent down to 30° and the extension on the central leader is treated as previously. This routine is carried out every year until the espalier reaches the required height [Fig. 15.8].

A word of explanation is needed here about the reasons for angling the shoots first instead of tying them straight down to the wire. The main object is so that growth will continue at a fairly good rate on the lateral. If it were bent down to the horizontal in its youth, it would take a long time to reach its proposed length. At the same time, we can use the angle to increase or decrease the rate of growth of a specific shoot if its companion is growing faster or slower.

If, for example, one shoot is growing much slower than its opposite number, the angle can be raised to nearer the vertical to increase its vigour. Once the shoots are of roughly equal length again, they can be restored to the same angle. Remember; raising a shoot increases its vigour; lowering it to nearer the horizontal decreases it. Of course, whilst all this is going on, new shoots are appearing from what is already there and the main branches are growing outwards.

There is no reason why you should not have fruit spurs on the central stem, but any shoots produced must not be allowed to develop. For this reason, they are cut back to 7–8 cm (3 in) long in the winter following their appearance.

During the formative years, extension growth on the tiers of branches should be adequate but not excessive; this is controlled by the angle at which they are tied in. Once they have been secured to their horizontal wires, they will still continue to grow but at a far slower rate. If this is too slow and a branch is taking a long while to reach maximum size, a new growth on the end can be cut back by a third to a half to induce greater vigour. If, after a year, vigour has not increased, the branch can

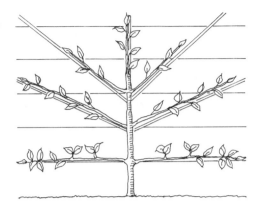

**Fig. 15.8** Repeat the procedure with the second and subsequent tiers.

be released from the wire and held in a more upright position. Keep it like this until growth has been restored. It is simply applying the previous principle to an older branch.

Once a branch has reached the end of its wire, it is simply stopped an inch or so beyond it. Subsequent shoots developing from it are cut hard back each year in late spring. This late pruning after growth has started reduces its vigour by giving it a severe check.

When pruning apple and pear espaliers, it must always be borne in mind that it is being done with two totally different aims. One is the formation and maintenance of the tree shape, the other is for fruit production.

We have looked at the shaping side of the operation; pruning for fruit is exactly the same as that described for cordons in that it all takes place towards mid to late summer, according to your location. Then, briefly, all new shoots that are growing directly from the central stem or horizontal branches are cut back to three leaves beyond the basal cluster. Those that are growing from previously cut shoots are shortened back to one leaf from the basal cluster (see also page 173).

Whilst espaliers are certainly the preferred shape for large, intensively grown apple and pear trees, fan-trained trees are sometimes seen in large gardens of the past. Whilst there is no overwhelming reason for not growing them as fans, there are certain disadvantages.

We have seen that the horizontal arms of espaliers keep a very well balanced tree made up of permanent branches bearing fruiting spurs. By and large, all the branches grow at the same rate and are of similar vigour. Everything, in fact, that encourages apples and pears to perform to the best of their ability. The system suits them.

With a fan-trained tree, you have branches of different length and different vigour growing out at different angles. Not an ideal arrangement and one which can, if not managed properly, lead to fruit-forming towards the end of the more upright branches and a considerable amount of bare wood. Oddly enough, this shape suits stone fruits well and that is where we shall be discussing the system; specifically, under Peaches (see page 184).

That leaves us with just one tree form to describe.

## The spindlebush

This used to be, and largely still is, a method of tree training that is essentially aimed at the commercial fruit grower. It is easy to carry out, requires a minimum of work and results in a tree that starts cropping very early in its life. The spindlebush is a restricted form of tree but not to the extent of requiring training wires so that it is grown two-dimensionally. It is grown three-dimensionally around a central stem. It is well known that most fruit trees will bear fruit at a considerably earlier age if they are left largely unpruned. This is the principle of the spindlebush.

In essence, it is a single-stemmed (central leader) tree carrying fruiting laterals. It needs the support of a stake throughout its life because it will crop heavily on slender branches. The fruiting laterals are of two types. The lower ones are more or less permanent and carry fruiting sub-laterals that are pruned on the renewal system. Both the laterals and sub-laterals are allowed to remain until they are broken, diseased, too long or are simply not carrying good crops; they are then cut back to a replacement or removed completely.

The branches higher up are treated roughly the same as the lower sub-laterals in that they are semi-permanent fruiting branches which are removed and replaced as and when necessary; usually at 3 years old.

Using the principal of the espalier, in that horizontal branches fruit more readily than vertical ones, we can help the young tree come

into cropping sooner by tying down its branches to near the horizontal. This encourages the formation of blossom buds and reduces vigour. This technique can also be used to control the vigour and cropping of the tree. In addition, once a spindlebush starts to fruit, the weight of the fruit bends down the branches and the crop imposes a check on its own vigour that will encourage it to continue fruiting.

In a nutshell, cropping is the greatest encouragement to further crops.

The glory of the spindlebush system is its simplicity; the aim is to keep a young, open (uncrowded) and fully cropping tree. Pruning is carried out in the following manner.

First, if you are planting a maiden 'whip' (a single-stemmed one-year-old with no side shoots/feathers), cut the stem back to a bud to leave it some 90 cm (3 ft) tall. You may start forming the tree during the first summer if growth is strong enough but, more usually, you will have to wait until the second summer. In either event, after growth has stopped (usually in late summer) choose four strong shoots, the lowest being no less than 60 cm (2 ft) from the ground.

If you are planting a one-year-old tree already well equipped with side shoots (a feathered maiden) you will be gaining a year and will be starting at this stage. Select and keep three or four of the feathers; with the lowest no closer than 60 cm (2 ft) from the ground.

From now on, whichever kind of tree you started with, both types are treated the same.

The one-year-old shoots must be growing at a wide angle from the stem and, when viewed from above, they should be nearly at right angles to each other, i.e. pointing roughly north, east, south and west. This results in a well-balanced tree. These four shoots can be tied down to about 20° above the horizontal. Strong twine is perfect and this should be tied at one end to halfway along the shoot and at the other end to low down on the trunk. If there are any strongly growing, narrow-angled side shoots coming from the central stem, usually from immediately under the leader, remove them completely.

Tie the central leader upright to the stake [Fig. 15.9]. In the winter, the new growth on the central leader is cut back by a third to encourage more side shoots to grow out. Cut to a bud pointing in the opposite direction to that in which the leader is growing; this will keep the tree straighter. In the following growing season, you should see the first crop. This will help to hold down some of the previously tied branches and, where this happens, the ties can be removed. New side shoots which have appeared further up the tree should be tied down, as before.

Little, if any pruning should be necessary in the winter beyond shortening the new growth on the central leader. The more vigorous it is, the less it should be pruned. After that, cropping will be building up to a maximum which will make pruning even less necessary; the curb on vigour being exerted by the fruits. If the upper branches start to overshadow those lower down, cut them back, where necessary, to a fruit bud. Similarly, those fruiting sub-laterals on the lower branches which have become too large or out of place should be cut back or removed. When doing this, always leave a small stump a couple of centimetres or so long to act as a source for future fruiting shoots [Fig. 15.10].

You will probably have realized by now that pruning an established and fruiting spindle-bush is more a matter of common sense – of knowing what is needed and knowing how to achieve it – than of slavishly following a given system, such as renewal pruning. It is more a case of tree management; balancing the production of high quality fruit with that of maintaining growth. After the formative years, the only real pruning is connected with the central leader, which should never be allowed to dominate the tree. If it does, you will have to remove the vigorous leader completely by cutting the central stem back to a suitably placed and younger branch beneath the wayward leader.

## Apricots

The apricot is not nearly as tender a fruit as most gardeners imagine. However, away from warmer climates they always succeed best when grown fan-trained against a warm wall or fence. In colder areas where spring frost is likely to destroy the blossom they can still be grown under unheated glass. They are ideally

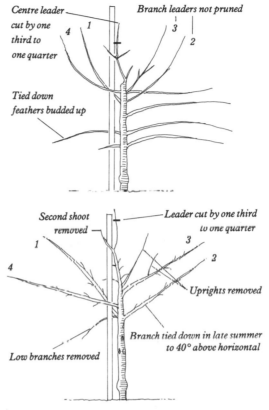

Fig. 15.9 After the first full year of growth, the lowest tier of branches on a spindlebush apple or pear should be tied or weighted down.

*Centre leader cut by one third to one quarter*

*Branch leaders not pruned*

*Tied down feathers budded up*

*Second shoot removed*

*Leader cut by one third to one quarter*

*Uprights removed*

*Branch tied down in late summer to 40° above horizontal*

*Low branches removed*

Fig. 15.10 Once the tree is cropping, keep it young and open by the judicious removal of whole, or part, of the oldest branches.

suited to being grown in pots as this makes it possible to bring the trees under cover when they are in flower and a frost threatens.

Their mode of fruiting is similar to that of plums in that they produce most of the best fruits on two-year-old and older shoots, as well as on older fruiting spurs. However, the fruiting laterals do not stay in efficient bearing for more than three or four years. They are not long-lived. We need not spend time on the actual pruning here because a fan-trained tree is formed and subsequently pruned in the same way as a peach (page 184) whilst the pruning of a bush tree in the open garden, during its formative years, is the same as for a bush plum (pages 186–7).

Once a bush tree is established and cropping, a form of renewal pruning is best so that the tree stays young. This gives rise to the best fruits and takes into account the fact that fruiting shoots on apricots need to be replaced.

Another aspect of pruning apricots concerns a particularly nasty fungus disease, dieback (*Sclerotinia laxa*). This often attacks apricots and can greatly influence the pruning operation. It normally enters the tree via the flowers (blossom wilt) and, from these, spreads back into the spurs (spur blight) and, thence, into the shoot and branch (dieback). As the name suggests, the fungus kills anything from small shoots to quite large branches. As well as removing the individual victims, pruning fan-trained trees will also involve replacing dead branches with other and younger shoots and branches.

So severe can the disease be that, sometimes, removal of the dead shoots and branches is all the pruning that is necessary.

Although the benefits of painting over pruning cuts are seriously questioned these days, there is no doubt that when the cut is made to remove a dead or diseased bough, then a pruning paint containing a fungicide is clearly an advantage.

If the disease is regular and serious, routine spraying, say monthly during the growing season, with Bordeaux mixture or another copper fungicide is a great help.

# Cherries

Cherries belong to one of two different groups. In one group are the sweet (dessert) cherries and 'Duke' varieties whilst, in the other, are acid ('Morello') cherries. 'Duke' cherries are sweet × acid hybrids. The main distinguishing feature is the difference in size of the trees. Sweet and Duke cherries traditionally make enormous trees; Morellos, on the other hand, grow to little more than 3.6 m (12 ft) high and have a much more twiggy growth than the stiff and erect shoots of sweet cherries.

Cherries have, in recent years, undergone more changes for the better than probably any other fruit. In the past, sweet cherries were confined mainly to commercial orchards of enormous standard trees and were hardly ever seen in gardens. Now, commercial orchards contain trees of half their original size and they are finding their way into private gardens, albeit gardens of above-average size. There are two reasons for this rise in popularity: the ability to grow much smaller trees and the appearance of varieties that do not need cross-pollination.

Traditional rootstocks gave rise to enormous trees. However more modern and dwarfing

rootstocks, such as Colt in the UK, result in a tree about two-thirds of the size; whilst Inmil, an arrival from Belgium some years ago as GM19, will give a tree that can be held to no taller than 3 m (10 ft). These smaller trees led to the development of new methods of pruning to suit them. Further, the breeding of self-fertile varieties of sweet cherry at once made it possible to grow just one tree in a garden rather than two compatible varieties that were hitherto needed.

These two factors coupled together give you a much smaller tree that is self-fertile; ideal for gardens, in fact.

## Acid varieties

These would normally be grown as bush trees on a trunk about 60 cm (2 ft) tall. When dealing with a 'whip' tree (one-year-old with no feathers), cut it back to a bud 1 m (3 ft 3 in) high. This will result in side shoots, in a year's time, which can be used for the initial branches. When buying a feathered maiden, cut out the central leader at about the same height (1 m/3 ft 3 in) and treat the best placed and strongest feathers as the basis for the branches. You will need four or five of these and they should be at roughly the same angle to each other so that, from above, the layout looks roughly like the spokes of a wheel. Cut each lateral back by two-thirds to, usually, an outward pointing bud. This initial pruning will lead to a good framework of branches and it is from this that the tree is built up.

The important thing to remember about acid cherries is that they fruit mainly on the previous season's shoots; similar to the peach. The aim is to produce a tree that is continually producing strong new growths to carry the fruit. Therefore once the tree is cropping, a small proportion, say a quarter, of the shoots that have fruited should be completely cut out or cut back to a suitable one-year-old replacement. Obviously the tree must be kept in an attractive and businesslike shape but this is simply a question of removing out-of-place or crowded shoots and branches.

Because the demand for acid cherries is somewhat limited, many gardeners would be happier if the tree took up less room in the garden than does a bush tree. To meet this need, it is often a better idea to have a fan-trained tree against a wall, fence or wires in the open garden. One of the virtues of acid cherries is that they can be perfectly happy on a sunless, north-facing wall. All they ask is that they are planted about 15 cm (6 in) away from the base of the wall so that they have adequately moist soil. Their tolerance of a sunless position is probably due to the lack of sugar in the fruits. A sweet fruit needs sunshine to convert much of the starch into sugar; an acid fruit does not. The northern aspect does have a definite advantage as well. Because cherries flower in the early spring, they run the risk of having the blossoms killed by a night frost. The damage is always worse if the morning sun strikes the flowers whilst they are still frosted.

As with apricots, the system for building up a fan-trained tree is the same as for a peach (page 184). The wires support system, whether against a wall or in the open, should consist of horizontal wires stretched along the wall 15 cm (6 in) apart. Once the tree is established in the basic fan shape, pruning a trained tree is along the same principles as the bush tree in that a continuous supply of young shoots is the aim. We thereby establish a semi-permanent frame, the rays of the fan, which is furnished with temporary, fruiting, lateral shoots.

From mid spring to early summer, select new shoots that grow out from the branches and retain enough to result in one new shoot every 5–7 cm (2–3 in). Tie these into the wires and they will fruit during the following summer. Once there are enough replacement shoots, any more that appear should be pinched out as soon as they are large enough to handle. Pruning takes place straight after fruiting when all the shoots which have fruited are cut out. If you have made a good job of selecting and retaining replacement shoots, you should end up with approximately the same number of fruiting shoots next year. As a rule, the fruited shoots are cut out to leave a stub carrying one bud, which will grow out in the following year to form a fruiting shoot in the following.

Older branch systems tend, with age, to develop bare stretches of wood towards the base. Once this starts to happen a proportion of the older branches should be completely removed and younger systems spread out and tied in to fill the gap. If this is carried out on a regular basis, there will be no reduction in cropping.

## Sweet and Duke cherries

One very old authority on cherries used to recommend that they be pruned at planting time and never again. We can do rather better than that now but it does illustrate that pruning is not vital to their wellbeing; it merely improves their shape and efficiency.

As with acid cherries, sweet and 'Duke' varieties may be grown as either bush trees or fan-trained. The important thing is to grow them on either Colt or Inmil rootstocks so that they can be kept within bounds.

Several self-fertile varieties are now available, the best known being 'Stella' and, more recently, 'Sunburst'. However, as with all fruit trees, the heaviest crops are still only obtained when cross-pollination has taken place.

With the advent of small trees on Inmil rootstock, bush trees can now be grown quite easily in even the smallest garden and it means that we are no longer tied to self-fertile varieties.

### Bush trees

To form a bush tree, a maiden whip is cut back to about 75 cm (30 in) tall. Late in the next winter, three or four of the best placed resulting shoots are retained; the rest are cut clean out. The retained shoots should be at a wide angle to the stem to make a strong joint. If enough new shoots are present, it is often wise to remove the top one; it is normally too upright and vigorous for best results. The retained shoots are cut back to outward pointing buds to leave 30–45 cm (12–18 in). By the following winter, there will be a good head of up to ten strong, young branches. These are again pruned back to 30–45 cm (12–18 in). It is unlikely that any more leader pruning will be needed as this is only done to encourage side shoots to form on the main framework branches. The first crops should appear in the following year and this is normally enough to establish a fruiting pattern.

A useful tip at this stage is to carry out hand pollination, just to make sure that all is well. Of course, when the tree gets larger, this is impossible.

From then on, the only pruning is likely to be the removal of dead, diseased, broken, crowded, crossing or otherwise out-of-place branches. Get into the habit of pruning very late in the winter; even to the extent of waiting until the first signs of growth appear. This will go a long way towards keeping 'silver leaf' fungus disease at bay.

### Fan-trained cherries

Sweet cherries have, for many years, been grown fan-trained against walls or to wires in the open garden. Apart from the comparatively little space they occupy, the trees are also quite easily protected from birds by throwing nets over them at the appropriate time. Starlings are the main culprits and will strip a tree once the fruit starts to colour up. It is also possible to throw old bed-sheets over them to keep spring frosts at bay during the blossom period.

Partly trained fan trees can sometimes be bought at the better garden centres but one would normally have to buy one from a specialized fruit nursery. Fan-trained cherries are formed in exactly the same way as fan-trained peaches (see page 184). Keep the central part of the fan open until the side branches are well established as those in the middle always grow vigorously and will soon catch up. In addition, by leaving them until last, the other branches will give them a significant check. Most of the leading shoots will need tipping to induce them to break out but this should only be light

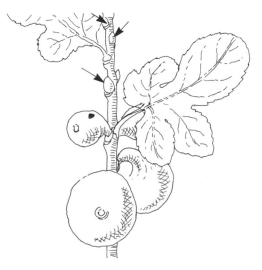

**Fig. 15.11** Only those fig fruitlets small enough to withstand the winter should be allowed to remain after mid-autumn.

to avoid encouraging excessive growth from them.

### Pyramids

With the ability to grow much smaller trees now, even dwarf pyramid cherries are perfectly feasible. The central leader, or the maiden whip, is cut back to about 50 cm (20 in). This will result in a number of side shoots growing out plus extension growth on the leader itself. The following spring, the leader is trained and tied upright to a cane or stake and cut back to leave 45 cm (18 in).

If the side shoots are carrying fruit buds, they can be left unpruned. If, though, they are rather too upright and seem reluctant to form fruit buds, they should have the tips cut out to encourage them to branch. Don't prune them hard or they will simply grow furiously and you will be no better off.

It could even be worthwhile tying down the shoots to nearer the horizontal to encourage fruiting. This routine is continued until the tree is of the required height and as many branches as you want have formed. Once the branches have reached the required length, they are tipped in the summer to discourage growth.

If, after some years, the lower branches become bare and unfruitful, they should be cut out and replaced with younger ones.

## Figs

Figs are Mediterranean plants and, as such, are questionably hardy in more temperate climates. Another important thing about them is that, rather oddly, the fruits form one year, overwinter on the trees and then ripen late in the following summer. The situation is further complicated by the fact that the embryo figs appear in the axils of the leaves and are produced more or less continuously throughout the growing season; not just in the spring as with other fruits. Whilst this may not appear to have anything to do with pruning, you will see that it is upon this strange fruiting habit that the pruning system is largely based.

It is only those fruitlets which form towards the end of the growing season that we are interested in. Those appearing earlier in the year are too small to develop and ripen during the current season but are too large to withstand the cold of the winter [Fig. 15.11].

We cannot leave the whole lot on the tree and let Nature take its course; although this is what most gardeners do, simply through ignorance. By allowing the unwanted early fruits to remain, the formation of more is discouraged and it is the later ones which we want.

The fruitlets must, therefore, be removed throughout the greater part of the growing season as soon as they are large enough to handle. This should continue until late summer so that only one or two embryo fruits remain on the end of each shoot at the onset of winter. Any that are as large as a pea should have been nipped out because they will not survive the cold.

This may sound a complicated routine but it is no more so than disbudding perpetual-flowering strawberries up to the end of spring so that they concentrate their efforts on an autumn crop. Whilst few people have the time or enthusiasm to lavish much attention on a free-standing fig tree in the open garden, it is essential to look after one which is trained against a wall if good results are to be had and the whole thing is not to get completely out of hand. A consequence of the fig's doubtfully complete hardiness, and its Mediterranean origin, is that it crops far better in temperate climates when grown against a sunny wall or fence.

A fully grown and well managed fan-trained tree can occupy as little as 3.6 m (12 ft) length of wall. Although larger trees exist, these are often bare at the base and much of the wood is unproductive. When planting a fan-trained tree, the first necessity is to fix wires on the wall. For the first few years, horizontal wires about 23 cm (9 in) apart are sufficient for support. To these are tied canes roughly in the positions that you want the main branches. Later, because of the large number of young shoots that are to be retained, the wires are supplemented with vertical twine tied in when and where required. Thus, the new shoots have plenty of wire or twine to which they may be tied.

To form the fan-trained tree from a single-shoot, dormant, one-year-old, pot-grown tree, first prune it back to 30–40 cm (12–15 in) high to induce side shoots to form. Do this in late winter. A year later, the best two shoots are selected that grow out on opposite sides of the stem along the line of the wall. These are tied to canes and cut back to 45–60 cm (18–24 in) long to encourage further breaks. For the next few years, the pruning is largely a question of training and tying in those shoots that you wish to make into branches whilst filling up the gaps between the branches with renewable young fruiting shoots.

As with cherries, fill the centre of the fan last.

A good tree size to aim for is one with five or six main branches. Once these have been established, the art of pruning outdoor fan-trained figs is to maintain a balance between young and old branches.

During the early part of the growing season, all new growths should be stopped as soon as they have produced five or six leaves. This should continue until the end of early summer. It will encourage more shoots to form and, at the same time, reduce the number of unwanted embryo fruits.

During mid summer, all the retained shoots are tied in to the wires. It is these which will carry the fruitlets that will ultimately ripen the following late summer/early autumn.

You may notice, but certainly not on every tree, that embryo figs have formed towards the base of some of the one- or two-year-old shoots. So long as these are of the required size at the onset of winter, they will usually survive. Indeed, in cold gardens and where winter protection has not been given, these could be the ones that provide the bulk of the crop. Thus, you may well have ripening, growing and embryonic fruits at the same time.

Because of the fig's doubtful hardiness, winter pruning is best delayed until early to mid spring; by which time any frost-damaged or diseased shoots can be seen more clearly and cut out. Also, thin out all the young and future fruiting shoots to 23–30 cm (9–12 in) apart.

Once a tree has been fruiting for a few years, you will see that certain shoots stop bearing fruit whilst others clearly outgrow their position. Both these should either be shortened back to a younger shoot or removed completely. Which you choose will depend on the space available. In addition, because fruiting is almost exclusively on one- and two-year-old shoots, even the main framework of a fan tree can only be regarded as temporary.

By the time a tree is about ten years old, therefore, some of the original branch systems will be bare lower down with fruiting shoots mainly towards the extremities. That is the time at which to start removing some of the oldest branches early each spring. Provided that a living and healthy stump is left, this will soon send out more shoots that can be trained and tied in to fill any gap. Two or three of these could be cut back or completely removed each year once bareness starts to appear. Much will depend on the size, age and fruitfulness of the tree, though; you cannot make any hard and fast roles.

In cold areas, even those trees trained to a sunny wall will benefit from winter protection. This is best provided by covering the whole thing with bracken or straw and tying it in place to stop it blowing away during the winter. Once the weather starts to warm up in early spring, keep an eye on the tree and uncover it the moment there are signs of growth.

## Medlars

These are strange fruits; part rosehip, part hawthorn, and part quince. All these are *Rosaceae*, as are medlars (*Mespilus germanica*).

The fruits are 4–5 cm (about 2 in) across and have rather a distinctive taste. They are best left uneaten until around Christmas time. This allows them to go well past what would normally be regarded as ripe and actually turn brown inside. It is a process known as bletting and only after this are they fit to eat. Indeed, many people think that, even then, they are still pretty frightful. Although the fruits contain pips, these are unsuitable for propagation as, like other named varieties of fruit tree, they do not give rise to true-to-type plants.

The pips can, though, be used to produce rootstocks onto which true varieties may be budded or grafted.

If left to itself the medlar plant would make a small, untidy tree or bush with twisted and twiggy growth very much along the lines of the hawthorn. As such, it looks a mess with very little form or structure. It can, though, be grown more like a tree with a well-defined leg. This is certainly the tidiest way to grow

medlars because, having naturally straggly growth, the branches need to be kept well off the ground if you wish to work under the tree.

This being so, the simplest formative pruning is along the lines of developing a half-standard apple tree. This is done by cutting back the central stem of the young medlar to approximately 1.2 m (4 ft) high.

Nothing else need be done that year unless the tree already has side shoots. If it does, four or five of the best placed of these are selected and retained to form the main branches. They should be strong shoots forming wide angles with the central stem and spaced as evenly as possible around the stem. These shoots are cut back by a third to a half according to their vigour; the stronger they are, the less they should be cut.

This is also the treatment that a two-year-old tree should receive a year after the initial cutting back of the central stem to 1.2 m (4 ft) tall. The following winter, a choice again has to be made as to which new shoots are to be retained as branches. As before, they should be strong growers and pointing in as near the required direction as possible.

These selected shoots are again lightly pruned to induce further breaks. Those not required for branches can be either left unpruned to fruit, cut back as necessary or removed completely. As a general rule, the less a tree is pruned, the better it is and the more likely it is to fruit soon.

From that point on, very little pruning will be needed at all. The size and shape should be controlled by cutting out or shortening back those shoots and branches which, for one reason or another need treatment. These would include branches that are dead, diseased, or broken together with growth that is too high, too low or simply out of place. It is very much a case of keeping the tree to the shape and size you want it together with maintaining an open and uncluttered habit.

## Mulberries

In spite of the traditional nursery rhyme that encourages us to go round the mulberry bush, the mulberry is, in fact, a very handsome tree that can live to an extremely ripe old age and reach some 6–7.5 m (20–30 ft) high.

Whilst the uses for the actual crop of berries

are limited (except, apparently, where blackbirds are concerned), it can make an excellent specimen tree in a lawn or border.

It is very long lived; there are references to trees of 400 years old. By the time they reach maturity, many of the lower branches need to be supported with props to keep them off the ground and stop them breaking under the weight of foliage and fruit.

There are actually two different mulberries commonly cultivated; *Morus nigra* (black mulberry) and *M. alba* (white mulberry). It is the black mulberry that is grown for its berries; the white mulberry provides leaves for feeding silkworms. Both, though, make grand ornamental trees. The fruits, which appear in late summer, are not in the least like what you would expect to come from a large tree; they are very similar in shape and size to a loganberry or tayberry; very dark red when fully ripe. They have a sharp flavour and large pips. Like the loganberry, the mulberry is better in pies and tarts than eaten raw.

Although it makes a large and attractive standard tree, it can also be grown as a dwarf pyramid or bush tree along exactly the same lines as an apple. It is also an excellent subject for a pot; mainly on account of its slow growth. The fruits of the white mulberry are paler and virtually useless.

Mulberries fruit on the current season's shoots as well as on spurs borne on older wood. Pruning is not necessary nor to be encouraged because the trees tend to bleed sap whenever cut so it should really be limited to shaping the tree in its early years.

The main characteristics of a mature mulberry tree are the low-growing habit and oddly shaped branches, frequently in need of propping up. Although this looks very attractive, it should not be encouraged. For this reason, a standard tree is the best sort to buy and maintain because the branches are naturally high off the ground and will take many years to develop the weeping habit. To encourage this upright shape still further, the central leader should be retained and kept dominant for as long as possible. Tying the leader to a tall cane up the middle of the tree will help with this.

When shaping a standard, the lowest branches should be around 1.8 m (6 ft) from the ground. All shoots that are put out below this height should be rubbed out when they are large enough to handle. Also, of course, any that grow out below the lowest branches after they have been established should be similarly treated. Retain and support the central leader. If any of the early main branches appear to be dominating and growing too upright and strongly, they can be bent down nearer to the horizontal and lightly tipped to curb their vigour.

When remedial work has to be carried out on mature and possibly deteriorating trees, it should be done in the early winter. A careful thinning out of the branches when there is the first sign of overcrowding and before specimens start to deteriorate is always advisable. Not only does it improve the appearance of the tree but it also delays ageing. It must be done thoughtfully and carefully, though, with the appearance and wellbeing of the tree taking precedence over all else.

## Peaches and nectarines

First, and to avoid the need to refer to both fruits throughout, all that is going to be said is just as applicable to nectarines as it is to peaches. After all, the former originated as a smooth-skinned form of the latter. The only significant difference is that the nectarine makes a slightly larger tree than the peach.

More than any other tree fruits, these lend themselves to being trained against walls and fences. Indeed, because, like the fig, they are Mediterranean in origin, they really only give of their best when given the shelter and warmth of a sunny wall or fence.

### Bush peaches

Although there are several schools of thought regarding the best time to prune bush peaches, straight after fruiting is as good as any. The main reason is that it is still during the growing season and, thus, a great help in avoiding infection by the silver leaf fungus. Like other fruit trees, year-old peach trees may be either feathered or whip maidens. In either event, the central leader is cut back to leave 45–60 cm (18–24 in) between the lowest required feathers or selected buds and the ground.

If four or five good side shoots can be retained to form the lowest branches, they should be cut back to 15 cm (6 in) long and all others removed. This should be done either in the early autumn or, if the tree is planted in the winter, the following spring.

A year later, the branch leaders are pruned back to suitably placed buds so that the resulting shoots grow out in the required direction. This would normally be outwards but it could be that you need two shoots to fill up a gap. In that case, two buds will need to be selected accordingly.

The leaders are cut back to leave approximately 30 cm (12 in) of strong growth. This is repeated a year later so that up to a dozen shoots are suitable for branches. This is really the end of the formal shaping phase because, from then on, the tree will start to produce blossoms and fruit.

Something to remember is that peaches only produce their flowers on the previous year's growth and, whilst this won't have as much influence on the pruning of bush trees as it does on fan trees, it is, nonetheless, relevant. The aim from now on is to maintain a good balance between fruit production and new growth.

Pruning is normally preferred in autumn straight after fruiting as you can see better any shoots and branches which are dead or diseased, crossing from one side of the tree to the other or which are causing overcrowding. All these must obviously be removed.

In cold districts, spring pruning may be wiser so that any dieback from the cold can be taken into account.

Another purpose of pruning is to reduce the number of new shoots (which will fruit next year) so that the crop is kept at a sustainable level and shading is reduced.

When correcting overcrowding, it is clearly better to remove fruited shoots instead of those that will fruit next year. However, one would normally reckon on having the new fruiting shoots about 15 cm (6 in) apart along a branch when pruning is finished. Unlike fan pruning, there is no need to remove most of the fruited shoots. Very little tipping will be necessary but it should be carried out when you want to fill up a gap with new growth.

Any large (saw) cuts should be painted over to exclude the spores of the silver leaf fungus.

**Fan-trained Peaches**

Whether against a wall or in the open garden, these will need the permanent support of horizontal wires stretched 15 cm (6 in) apart with the lowest one 40 cm (15 in) from the ground. If you have a tree that has already been part-trained by the nursery, then all well and good. It certainly saves a year or two's training but, of course, you pay more for it. You may, though, buy a one-year-old feathered maiden or a maiden whip.

1. Before planting a feathered maiden, look at the feathers and select two strong ones, pointing in opposite directions, more or less opposite each other and forming a wide angle with the central stem. If they are 30–60 cm (1–2 ft) above the proposed planting depth, they can be used as the lowest main branches of the fan. The tree can then be planted with this in mind.

Cut out the central leader immediately above the top one together with any other feathers so that just the two chosen ones are left. These are shortened to 45–60 cm (18–24 in) long [Fig. 15.12].

2. Sometimes, one is lucky enough to find a tree with more than just two suitable feathers for branch formation. In this case, you could consider retaining four feathers, but they must be close together. Also, you should only select an even number so that the tree is equally balanced on either side. When four are kept, the upper two are pruned harder (to about 15 cm/6 in) than the lower two. This will prevent the upper pair dominating the lower pair.

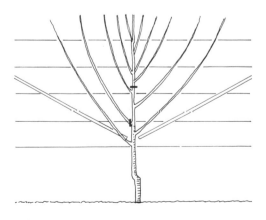

**Fig. 15.12** Well-placed feathers can save you a year when forming a fan peach. Keep up to four and cut out the rest.

3. A third permutation is that, although there are feathers, no two are sufficiently strong or suitably placed to form the initial pair of branches.

When this happens, cut the central stem back to a feather that is immediately above a pair of strong growth buds pointing in opposite directions along the line of the wall suitable for branch formation.

After the first growing season, the part above the two resulting shoots is cut back to the top shoot of the pair.

4. When the tree to be planted is a maiden whip, select two strong buds with similar specifications to the two feathers first mentioned above; i.e. pointing in opposite directions and with the top one 60 cm (2 ft) or so above the ground. Cut the stem down to the top bud.

During the following summer, canes can be tied to the wires at 45° and the growing shoots tied to them.

At the end of the summer, cut these back to 45–60 cm (18–24 in), completely remove all others and lower the canes to about 30° above the horizontal.

This form of support is necessary for all fan-trained peaches when the first pair of branches are growing.

We should now have reached the stage at which all the young trees, however they started off, are of the same shape; i.e. with the initial two ribs of the fan tied to canes and all other side shoots removed.

Late in the winter, the two shoots are cut back to 45–60 cm (18–24 in) long (if this has not already been done). When growth is going well in the summer, three or four suitably placed shoots growing from each of the originals are selected and tied in; once again, all others are removed [Fig. 15.13]. 'Suitably placed' means that they should be on the upper or lower surface of the parent branch; not growing directly towards or away from the wall, where they would be difficult to train back into the same place as the wall and hard to tie in. Just one of the new shoots should also be on the lower surface of the parent, all others on the upper. This process of retaining and tying in selected new shoots is carried out every summer whilst, where necessary, some are shortened to 30–45 cm (12–18 in) to induce side shoots which will help to fill the gaps.

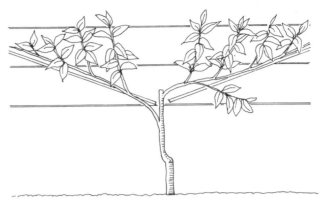

**Fig. 15.13** During the following summer, retain only those shoots that you want for further branches.

During this later formative pruning period, we can allow an increasing number of fruits to develop and ripen but it should never be overdone or the growth of the tree could suffer. Once the major part of the allotted space has been filled, we can start pruning for fruit. The two important things to remember are, first, that the fruit is only carried on last year's shoots and, second, that there are two different types of bud.

Once a tree is two or three years old, you will notice, on the one-year-old shoots, that the buds are in groups of up to three and are of two distinct shapes. There are plump ones and thin ones. The plump ones are flower (fruit) buds, the others are growth buds and they can be present as anything from single buds to groups of two fruit buds with a single growth bud between them. When pruning to produce a shoot, therefore, you must cut to a single growth bud or a cluster containing a growth bud. Ideally, you should also rub out any accompanying fruit buds.

Pruning a fan-trained peach for fruit is based on encouraging a succession of temporary fruiting shoots to form on the framework branches. During the spring, it will be seen that many young shoots start to grow out from those shoots and branches already tied in. These new ones will bear fruit in the next (not current) summer. Here again, only those new shoots growing from the upper or lower surface of the branches are kept; all others are pinched out.

A further thinning of the retained shoots may be needed so that you end up with one every 15 cm (6 in) along the top and bottom of the branch. Those to go are cut back to one leaf; those to stay are tied in towards the end of the summer and, should they reach 45 cm (18 in) or so long in the meantime, the tops are pinched out. This pinching out and tying in each spring and summer continues.

When a tree is fruiting well, we have to turn our attention to those shoots which have fruited; remembering that they won't fruit again on the section that has already done so. This is carried out straight after fruiting and the rule is that, if there is room for a fruited shoot to be tied in to fill a gap, then this is done and it is treated as a new branch. If, though, there is no room, they should be cut back to the cluster of buds at their base and be allowed to produce more flowering shoots the following year [Fig. 15.14].

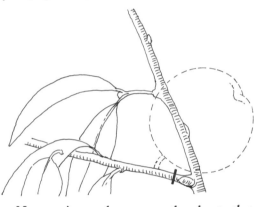

**Fig. 15.14** After fruiting, the shoots that carried fruits are normally cut back to the buds at their base.

Next spring and summer, the shoots that grow from the cluster are reduced to one or two and tied in for fruiting in the following year.

Another kind of pruning that might be needed from time to time is the removal of dead, diseased, old or broken shoots and branches. This is best done in the early spring so that those which need to be removed can be seen quite easily whilst, at the same time, it avoids the main infection period of silver leaf. When a large branch has to be cut out, the wound is painted and the gap left is filled in over the next few years by retaining, tipping and tying in the necessary shoots.

Although not strictly part of the pruning operation, fruit thinning is nearly always needed on peaches; provided, of course, that hand or natural pollination was adequate. A strong and healthy tree will be able to carry fruit on the basis of one to every 23 cm (9 in) or so of fruiting shoot. Thus, a shoot 30 cm (12 in)

long will support one fruit whilst one 50 cm (20 in) long will manage two. A preliminary selection and thinning should take place when the fruitlets are a centimetre or so across. This will involve the removal of any that are small, diseased, damaged, misshapen or trapped behind a branch or wire. A second thinning is done when they are about 2.5 cm (1 in) across; only the best specimens are retained.

## Plums

Plums can be grown as standards (rarely) half-standards and bush trees, pyramids, cordons and fan-trained.

The free-standing standards, half-standards and bush trees are pruned largely on the lines of the 'regulated' system that is used for apples and pears (see page 168) but, generally speaking, plums need far less attention than apples and pears and perform all the better for being left alone. In fact, once plums are cropping, the less they are pruned, the better. Also, whereas apples and pears are pruned in the winter, plums should not be.

It has already been explained for peaches that stone fruits are much more susceptible to the potentially fatal silver leaf fungus disease than are pome fruits. The fungus releases its spores during the winter and it is through any kind of wound, such as pruning, that the disease gains entry to the new victim. Pruning at a time other than in the winter, therefore, considerably reduces the risk of infection.

We can say that, for trees which are passed the formative stage, it is possible to prune at any time from the start of growth until about the end of summer. Commercially, it is often done in the summer in conjunction with fruit thinning or immediately after picking.

Because of the plum's acute sensitivity to silver leaf, large (saw) cuts should always be painted. Very young trees that are still being shaped are best pruned in the winter to get the correct response from the buds that you want to grow out. However, the small size of the wounds makes it most unlikely that they will pick up silver leaf.

### Standard, Half-standard and Bush Trees

The rules for pruning these are very simple; only prune when you have to. This is mainly because pruning usually encourages growth and excessive growth often depresses fruiting in plums. Unnecessary pruning, therefore, can reduce crops. There are, of course, important exceptions to this sweeping generalization and they are the same as those already covered for the regulated system of pruning apples and pears. After the tree has been built up and is cropping, pruning is restricted to the removal of dead, dying, badly diseased (silver leaf etc.), broken, crossing, too high, too spreading, too low and too vigorous branches together with any which are causing overcrowding. 'Crossing' branches are those which originate on one side of a tree, cross over the centre and finish up on the other side. This will have a shading effect on the centre of the tree, to the detriment of the fruit, and, if the tree is large, these branches are usually impossible to reach. Their removal at source will lighten the whole tree and make it easier to manage.

The formation of these free-standing trees is also very much along the same lines as for apples and pears.

Standard trees can be largely ignored for gardens, they are far too big. However, their formation is the same as for a half-standard except that the central stem is cut back to about 2 m (6 ft 6 in) high.

The half-standard is started by cutting back the stem of a one-year-old tree to 1.3 m (4 ft 6 ins); a bush tree is cut back to 90 cm (3 ft). Incidentally, none of these heights have to be exact. It can be taken to mean the nearest suitable and strong bud or shoot to that height. Many maiden trees will have feathers (side shoots) on the main stem. If any are sufficiently strong and growing in the right direction, they can be used as the start of main branches. They are retained and cut back by two-thirds to an outward or upward pointing bud.

Feathers have the distinct advantage of being set at a very good angle, often at right-angles, to the main stem. This gives a very strong junction that is most unlikely to break under the weight of crops in later years. It is also less susceptible to infection by bacterial canker because there are few wrinkles and crevices in which the bacteria can shelter and develop.

Any feathers not wanted for branches are cut out. In a year's time, whether feathers were used or not, there will be up to about five strong new shoots. From these, choose and retain as many as are suitable to form the main branches. They should be of approximately equal vigour, must be set at a wide angle to the stem, be growing in the right direction and should radiate roughly evenly when looked at from above.

Also, the shorter the length of stem that they grow from, the better; i.e. if all start from a section of stem 30 cm (1 ft) in length, it is preferable to a 60 cm (2 ft) section. It makes a better shaped tree with more even growth. Those shoots which match up to this specification are shortened back by half to two-thirds; the weaker ones being pruned the hardest.

Other side shoots can be allowed to remain if they are not too vigorous and likely to compete with the main ones.

This treatment should give rise to about double the number of branches in a year's time, which will normally form the basis of the tree. From then on, pruning is largely governed by the shape, size, habit and needs of the tree. For instance, an upright variety like 'Marjorie's Seeding' will need encouragement to spread rather than grow vertically. This will normally be achieved most simply by pruning to outward pointing buds.

On the other hand, 'Warwickshire Drooper', and others of a weeping habit, should be pruned to upward pointing buds with a view to making them more upright. Where a space exists, shoots can be tipped lightly to fill it. But remember, although plums are naturally of a more twiggy nature than apples and pears, they can still get clogged up with excessive growth. If a strong shoot suddenly appears from a branch, it can be kept and tamed, if there is room for it, by tying it down to near horizontal. If it is not wanted, cut it out completely; shortening it merely strengthens it and makes it grow all the more.

### Pyramid Plums

Moving down in tree size, pyramids are a real possibility with the wide availability of trees growing on the less vigorous Pixy rootstock. Even so, careful attention to detail has to be paid if the tree is to be kept within bounds and yet still fruitful.

To start with, the central leader of a maiden tree is cut back to 1.5 m (5 ft) high in mid spring. Any feathers less than 45 cm (18 in)

**Fig. 15.15** Cordon plums should be cut back after planting and any side shoots shortened.

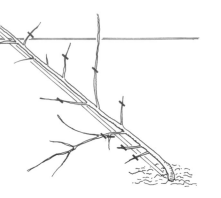

from the ground are removed; the remainder are cut back by about half to an upward pointing bud.

By mid to late summer, growth will have stopped and the new shoots are cut back to about 20 cm (8 in) long to an outward or downward pointing bud. This will prevent the young branches growing too strongly and straight upwards. The central leader is left unpruned then but is shortened back the following mid spring by two-thirds.

Once the tree has reached the height you want, usually about 2.75 m (9 ft) for plums, the new growth on the central leader is pruned hard back each late spring to 2–3 cm (1 in).

The branches are only pruned during mid summer. This reduces the risk of silver leaf infection and, once the tree is cropping, it also helps to reduce the shading effect of the leaves and discourages the mealy plum aphid.

**Fig. 15.16** Because of their greater vigour, plum trees often produce a lot of feathers; use all that you can.

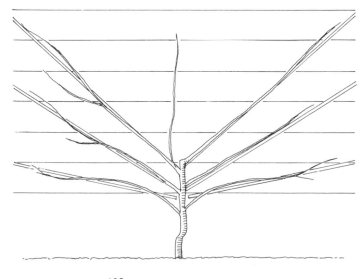

The new growth on the branch leaders is cut back to 20 cm (8 in), whilst new laterals (side shoots) on the branches are shortened to 15 cm (6 in); in both cases to an outward or downward pointing bud. Any upright and vigorous shoots that are likely to compete with existing branches are cut out completely. We saw earlier what happens if this is not done.

### Cordons

Plums can make good oblique cordons but, unless there is unlimited space, it is most important that they are on Pixy rootstock or they are soon likely to take charge. Also, naturally spur-forming varieties, such as 'Coes Golden Drop', are preferred as they fruit more readily, which itself is a further curb on vigour. At first, they may dislike being restricted but, once fruiting starts, life becomes easier. The other thing about cordon, and also fan-trained plums is that the space should be used for choice gage varieties, not wasted on cooking or dual-purpose.

Besides 'Coe's', suitable varieties would be 'Old Greengage', 'Oullin's Golden' gage, 'Reine Claude de Bavay' and the 'Transparent' gages (Early, Late and Golden).

The planting and wiring is just the same as for apples and pears; plant at 45° with the scion part of the union uppermost. In the early spring after planting, though, the trees are headed back to about 90 cm (3 ft) high instead of being left unpruned. Any side shoots are shortened by half [Fig. 15.15]. In mid to late summer, after growth has stopped, the extension growth on the central leader is cut back to 20 cm (8 in) and all laterals to 15 cm (6 in); virtually the same as one does with pyramids. Thenceforth, the leader is cut back by two-thirds every early spring until it has reached the desired height. Extension growth on the side shoots, and on the leader after the desired height is reached, is cut back to 15 cm (6 in) in mid to late summer.

### Fan-trained

With this intensive system of training, it is, again, important that the tree is growing on Pixy rootstock. The preliminary pruning to establish the basic 'Y' shape together with the first generation of shoots on the upper and lower surfaces of the 'Y' is broadly the same as for peaches (page 184) [Fig. 15.16]. A slight difference is that you allow just two shoots to remain on the upper surface with one on the lower. This allows for the greater size and vigour of plums over peaches.

All eight shoots are again cut back in the autumn; this time to an upward pointing bud 60–75 cm (2–2½ ft) from their point of origin. The same summer and autumn routine can be followed for another year, by which time the main framework will have been formed and you can start thinking about fruit production.

The main thing to remember is that, instead of being cut out, those new shoots that are not wanted for extensions or as fillers are kept pinched back to about six leaves throughout the growing season [Fig. 15.17]. In the autumn, the sometimes complicated systems are cut back to either spurs or fruit buds near their base. If they are cut out completely in the first instance, much useless growth would result without any chance of encouraging fruit buds to form. The other difference concerns the number of fruiting shoots retained. In peaches, the recommendation is for one every 15 cm (6 in) along the top and bottom of the branch; in plums, it can be reduced to one every 10 cm (4 in) because the fruits are smaller.

## Quinces

Quinces are botanically close to pears, but there the similarity ends, apart from the shape of the fruit.

Like the medlar, it is inclined to be an untidy grower with a lot of twiggy growth that sometimes needs thinning out. The natural habit is somewhat compact and slow growing so it is suitable, if kept under control, for a small garden. All pruning can be done in the winter. Bush trees and half-standards are the most commonly grown forms but, in descending order of suitability, espaliers, fans and cordons are also grown.

Half-standard and bush trees are formed in just the same way as apples and pears in that the maiden tree is cut back to 1.2 m (4 ft) or 75 cm (30 in) respectively. A year later, those of the resulting shoots which are suitable for forming main branches, are retained and cut back by a third to a half, depending on their vigour (the weakest are cut hardest).

For the next two years or so, a similar routine is followed with selecting and lightly tipping those growths which are suitable to form main branches. The tipping will strengthen them and encourage more side shoots.

Once the skeleton of the tree is formed, the only pruning needed will be to keep it open and within its intended space, together with the removal of dead, diseased, broken and crowded branches. As with the medlar, the only pruning needed once the tree has been formed is that necessary to keep it in good shape, open and productive.

An espalier and cordon are formed and then pruned in the same way as an apple and pear (pages 172–6) whilst fans are built up in the same way as plums (page 188) but are then pruned as pears.

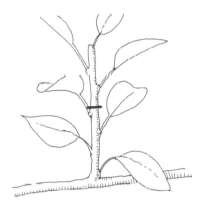

**Fig. 15.17** Unlike the technique with peaches, new side shoots on plum fans not wanted for fruiting laterals are spurred back.

## Restoring neglected trees

Something that often causes a sinking of the heart of anyone taking on a new garden is that venerable old fruit tree that the former occupant thinks is the cat's whiskers but which is clearly nearing the end of its days. However, provided that the problem is tackled logically, it really shouldn't hold the fears that it so often seems to.

First, though, and most important, the decision has to be taken as to whether or not the tree is actually worth saving.

One so often hears of people spending hours and much money on dragging some gnarled old ancient back from the jaws of death only to have it die of natural causes a couple of years later. It is therefore well worth spending a little time first on looking at the points that must be considered when deciding on the future of the tree.

Incidentally, with any fruit plant other than a tree, the chances are that it is seldom worth spending on it any time or money. On the whole, the maximum useful life of bush fruits is around 20 years, with 15 more likely. In these cases, the veterans are far better pulled out and replaced with either the same or better varieties. If a particular bush or other plant cannot be replaced with the same variety, then you may need to propagate from it.

In fact, a wise precaution with fruit trees, bushes, canes etc. of actual or sentimental value is to propagate from them well in advance of their expected demise to ensure their continuation and a good overlap. This is what is being done with the original 'Bramley's Seedling' apple tree. First, though, there are questions that you have to ask yourself; though not in any particular order.

1. Is the tree old and neglected or young and neglected? It makes a big difference; not only to the treatment but also because an old tree is possibly not worth keeping whereas a young one may be.

2. Does it take up a lot of room? Where some trees are concerned, their space is often worth more than their presence. You may want to have something else in the same position or it could be that the tree is shading other plants or starving the ground around it.

3. Is the tree good looking and improving the appearance of the garden? Some trees form the focal point of a garden and their removal could be criminal. Then again, it could be hideous and you can't wait to get rid of it.

4. An important thing to remember is that old and or neglected trees are usually riddled with pests and diseases. This is one of the prices you pay for neglect. If these are simply aphids, caterpillars and the like, you can get rid of them very easily. On the other hand, if the tree is carrying some foul and potentially lethal disease like silver leaf, then it is a very different matter.

Similarly, some of the older varieties, and indeed a few new ones as well, are riddled with either apple canker or bacterial canker, as appropriate.

5. Some trees will be so full of dead wood that, after its removal, there is very little left.

6. The variety. It is pretty safe to say that more than 50% of the old (50 years or more) varieties have been superseded by newer ones.

For the most part these are better, but certainly not always.

The present interest in, and enthusiasm for, old varieties of fruit has led to many old trees being saved from the axe. However, keeping the old variety simply because it is old is asking rather a lot when space is limited and you cannot grow anything under it. Another point about variety is that an enormous number of these very old trees are unnamed seedlings which are neither use nor ornament. If the tree is of unknown variety, therefore, wait until it next fruits and decide for yourself whether or not it is worth keeping. It doesn't matter whether it is an unknown seedling or a famous variety, if you don't like it . . . .

It could be that you like a particular tree but that it is hopelessly out of control. Then, buying a replacement or getting someone to grow a new tree from your old one is well worth considering. The best thing to do is to plant the new one well away from the old one and take that out when the youngster has started fruiting. Never get rid of the original too soon; fate can play nasty tricks sometimes.

Nor should you grub a tree simply because it is neglected, any more than you should hang on to it just because it is either old or large or both. Every case must be judged on its merits and it usually pays to draw up a balance sheet and then go in the opposite direction to that which it indicates!

Never decide in a hurry to pull out a tree. You can always do it in a month's or a year's time but you can never put it back.

Let us assume then that, after consideration, you decide to keep the tree. Whilst a great many other things will need to be done, we are only going to consider the pruning here.

The first part of restoration, and it is most certainly a skill, is really a refinement of the regulated system of pruning apples and pears. If the tree is old, it has probably stopped growing so the first essential is to encourage new shoots to form that can be built into young and fruitful branches. If the tree is an apple or pear, this is done in the winter once the leaves are off. It is the safest time to prune and you will be able to see much better exactly what needs to be taken out. If the tree is a stone fruit, wait until early or mid spring to reduce the risk of silver leaf infection.

First, get rid of any dead, dying, diseased or broken branches. These are followed by branches that are too high, too low or spreading too far out.

With the tree now roughly the right size, cut out any branches that are crossing from one side to the other together with those which are clearly causing overcrowding. You should not be frightened of taking out quite large branches if they need to go; but branches can cause big problems. Not only will the removal of all this unwanted wood stimulate the tree to grow but it will make sure that the new growth will flourish in the more open environment that you have created within the tree.

A lot of the time should be spent on the ground just looking at the tree and judging just which branches are the best to remove. This is much easier than when you are up a ladder or climbing about the branches.

Primary and hard pruning like this should be done almost entirely with a saw. Secateurs are used for the detailed work with which we are not yet concerned. All we want to do is clean up the tree and get it growing again.

It is also worth noting that, if the tree is very large and obviously needs a great deal of wood taking away, it is often worth spreading the job over two winters. It also allows the tree to adjust better to the sudden change and reduces the explosion of growth that invariably follows hard pruning.

This sort of work invites the question as to whether or not the wounds should be painted. Much the same applies to fruit trees as to ornamentals in that, on the whole, healing without painting is usually perfectly satisfactory and can even be better than when painting has been carried out.

However, there are still occasions when it is preferable to paint over a saw cut. These mainly occur when stone fruits are involved because of their acute susceptibility to silver leaf. At worst, painting a wound will delay its healing so, on balance, it is safer to paint over saw cuts on plums, cherries, peaches, apricots and any other stone fruits, including almonds. If the sealant or paint contains a thiophanate-methyl fungicide, this will kill any fungal spores that land on it.

So much for 'helping the aged'. With younger trees that have simply been allowed to grow unchecked and unpruned, the task of bringing them to heel is a great deal easier.

The main problems will be connected with excessive height and spread and probably some overcrowding. The trees could be fruiting quite well. All that normally needs to be done is to cut back the branches that are growing beyond their bounds as well as any that are crossing the centre or spoiling the shape of the tree. Here again, it is usually possible to see all these from the ground.

The same decision as before has to be taken as regards the number of winters over which the job should be spread; remembering that hard pruning in a single year will lead to a lot of growth. With the primary work out of the way, there will probably be little to do until the same time next year. However, trees that have had their middle cleared out will usually put forth a great number of strongly growing shoots from near to the points where branches were removed. Whilst these water shoots are frequently suitable for building up new branches, clearly not all are needed so a preliminary selection and thinning can be made during mid summer.

It is as well to leave this late because, before then, the shoots are still growing and their ultimate size and quality are still uncertain. By mid summer you will be able to see quite clearly what there is and growth may well have stopped.

Select and retain any shoots that look as though they could be suitable for branch formation and cut out the rest. In fact, they will often pull out and this has the advantage that it discourages more growing from the same point. The retained shoots have to be strong, healthy and normally growing from the upper surface of the branch.

If, of course, a branch is required to come out at an angle to fill a particular space, then a suitable shoot originating from the side of a branch could be better. It depends what you want and where you want it.

Don't cut out too many shoots at this stage because you may change your mind when the proper pruning is done. You can always take out more but you cannot put them back.

No tipping is done in the summer; you are merely removing clearly inferior or unwanted new shoots so that those remaining will benefit by ripening better.

A year after the initial treatment, a more critical selection is made when only those shoots that you definitely want for branches are kept. All the others are usually cut right out but, as appropriate, some may be cut back to a few inches long to form fruiting spurs. The retained shoots are cut back by a quarter to a third to a bud pointing in the required direction. This will lead to sufficient strong side shoots without encouraging excessive growth.

From then on, the new branches are built up in exactly the same way as one normally would when pruning apples or pears by the renewal method. You are, after all, simply renewing those branches which have been cut out.

Stone fuits would be pruned less severely and in accordance with the normal procedure.

## 'Ballerina' apples

The very nature of these unique trees makes it somewhat unnecessary to discuss their pruning. Described technically as 'compact columnar' apple trees, pruning is normally not needed at all. 'Ballerina' is the generic trade name for this type of apple tree, all varieties of which carry the dominant gene that imparts the compact columnar characteristic.

This gene originally came from a sport of the cultivar 'Mackintosh' in Canada in 1960, and from this single tree, named 'Wijcik' after the finder, all other cultivars have been bred. The growth of Ballerinas is such that few, if any, side shoots are put forth in the early years and it is only when they have reached their maximum expected height of 3.6–4.5 m (12–15 ft) that they will appear in any quantity. Because the appearance and habit of growth of a Ballerina is very similar to that of a cordon, any pruning that becomes necessary is also along the same lines.

Around midsummer any side shoots are cut back to 7–8 cm (3 in) long, if they are growing directly from the main stem, or 2.5 cm (1 in) if they are from previously pruned spurs. Alternatively, this can be left until the winter. The advantage of summer pruning is that the pruned shoot is more likely to form flower buds instead of further growth buds.

Once a Ballerina has reached its maximum height, an alternative to pruning is to allow a side shoot to grow up from near the base to form a twin stem. This has the effect of depressing other would-be laterals.

On no account should the growing point of a Ballerina tree be removed; branching will almost certainly follow.

## Pruning trees in pots

With the smaller gardens that seem to be the norm these days, space is often at a premium. This is particularly important where fruit trees are concerned as, in the minds of many new gardeners, fruit trees need a lot of room to grow satisfactorily.

This is not so, as nearly all the different kinds of fruit that can be grown outdoors in Britain have appropriately dwarfing rootstocks to go with them. The ultimate in miniature fruit trees is surely to grow them in pots?

This is neither the time nor the place to go into the subject in depth; we are, after all, concerned here with pruning. However, one important fact is that trees to be grown in pots seldom need a dwarfing rootstock to prevent them getting too large; the pot provides all the restraint on growth that is necessary. One big benefit that pot-trees have is that they are automatically subjected to the restricting action of the pot. This makes sure that the tree, or any other fruit plant, comes into bearing at an early age. We do not, therefore, have to worry about encouraging fruiting through appropriate pruning.

The main aims are to keep the tree in an attractive shape, to avoid lengths of branch devoid of laterals or fruit buds and to keep the tree producing new growth as well as fruit. In a nutshell, more or less what we prune anything for. In addition, and because we are dealing with a very small tree, we must also keep the fruit buds close to the main central stem so that no space is wasted. This is usually achieved by maintaining a roughly pyramidal shape.

It is seldom possible to prune rigidly to a defined system or shape; it is more a question of shaping the tree continually and keeping a good balance between growth and fruiting.

As well as the pyramid for stone fruits, you

Apples and pears perform best when trained as espaliers.

A small pear
espalier flowering
well against a shed
wall in a private
garden.

The spindlebush
system of training
and pruning apples
and pears
combines early
cropping with a
minimum of
maintenance.

'Katy' is one of the relatively new apples that succeeds admirably as a spindlebush.

*Below:*
A beautifully trained and pruned Morello cherry fan at the Royal Horticultural Society's Wisley Garden.

Even the smallest
tree, 'Greensleeves'
in this case, has
the potential to
carry heavy crops.

Vigorous cane fruits with supple canes, such as the tayberry, are best trained by the 'weave' system.

*Opposite:*
This standard gooseberry in the R.H.S. Wisley Garden shows that bush fruit can be decorative as well as functional.

Grapes at the R.H.S. Wisley Garden trained by the cordon method.

The Guyot system of training a grape vine.

can also grow cordons and fans. For apples and pears, the dwarf bush and pyramid are the most suitable, but cordons and espaliers are also perfectly possible.

As regards the best time of year to prune; cherries, plums and peaches are still pruned in the summer to reduce the risk of infection by silver leaf. Summer pruning apples and pears in late summer is useful as an additional means of controlling vigour and encouraging fruiting. Then again, some tying down of branches to near horizontal can also bring on fruiting. The control of vigour is, without a doubt, what beginners find the most worrying aspect and it seems instinctive to use pruning as the solution. One would hope that, by now, those ideas have been dispelled.

The pot itself is the major restriction whilst its effect can be augmented by judicious watering and feeding. You must not carry this to extremes, though, or fruiting, as well as growth, will suffer.

The next thing to try, if all else has failed, is root pruning. Although it is quite a specialized job for trees in the open ground (see page 194), when they are in pots, it is relatively simple.

It is carried out during the dormant period, preferably towards the end, and simply involves lifting the tree out of the pot and slicing away the side and base of the root ball about an inch from the outside. This will effectively remove the young and active roots.

The tree is then repotted and the extra space made good with fresh compost; not forgetting to start by putting a layer in the bottom.

As a last resort, bark ringing may be undertaken when the trees are in flower. It should only be carried out on apple and pear trees, no other kind of fruit. When done correctly, it will reduce the upward flow of sap, thereby slowing down the tree's rate of growth. When done incorrectly, it can kill it. So be warned.

For pot trees, remove with a sharp knife a partial ring of bark 0.75 cm ($\frac{1}{4}$ in) wide and three-quarters of the way round the trunk. The wound must be taped over at once to prevent both drying out and infection.

Bark ringing, however, is very seldom necessary if all the other things have been carried out correctly and have been given time to take effect.

## Bark ringing

This operation is also an effective method of vigour control for apple and pear trees planted in the ground. Although not strictly speaking a method of pruning, it is an important part of tree management when a young or teenage tree stubbornly refuses to start bearing fruit. Unlike the situation with pot trees, it is the less vicious of the two surgical operations that can be used to reduce a tree's vigour and, thus, induce it to begin fruiting. It is done after pruning and soil management have failed to have the desired effect.

As with root pruning (see below), the effect of bark ringing is to reduce the amount of nitrogen and water being carried up into the tree and, thus, to allow the carbohydrates, as manufactured by the leaves, to exercise their full effect on the production of fruit buds. Not only is the urge to grow curbed, but the carbohydrates etc. are held in the top of the tree and are prevented from passing down into the roots.

It is carried out during the blossom period (mid to late spring).

With trees of, say, seven years and more, a complete ring of bark is removed from around the trunk below the lowest branches. Even with older trees, this should never be wider than 1 cm ($\frac{1}{2}$ in) and these younger trees will respond to 0.75 cm ($\frac{1}{4}$ in) ring of bark being removed.

For the least effect and for younger trees (say, three to five years), a single cut without the removal of any bark often has the desired effect.

After the operation, the wound is immediately covered with sticky tape to prevent

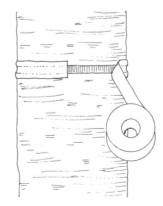

**Fig. 15.18** Bark ringing to reduce the vigour of a fruit tree.

drying out and infection by fungal disease spores [Fig. 15.18].

The tape is normally removed in the autumn after callusing has occurred.

## Root pruning

The sole purpose of root pruning is to bring a reluctant fruit tree into bearing when all else has failed. It can be of great value but should only be carried out after all the other methods, including bark ringing, have been unsuccessful in curbing its vigour and inducing it to fruit.

It involves removing much of the supporting system of the tree so most trees that have been root pruned will need a stake for a good few years afterwards.

It is normally carried out on fruit trees of up to around 15 years old. Over this age, a tree is unlikely to develop the sudden need for a powerful check and, anyway, the other methods of reducing vigour are more appropriate.

With trees less than about six years old, the best way of root pruning is just to dig up the tree and replant it; even in the same place. This will have just the same effect as it will sever a large number of roots.

One other point when root pruning is contemplated is that you should check that scion rooting is not the cause of the excessive growth. If you see that the union is buried, even for a very little depth, you must dig away the soil and sever any roots coming from the scion. If this has been necessary, leave the tree for another year and see if it has done the trick.

Root pruning is best undertaken in the autumn soon after leaf-fall.

First, scratch a circle not less than 90 cm (3 ft) from the trunk of smaller trees and up to 2.4 m (8 ft) for larger trees. You can do this best with a loop of string of appropriate length that goes round the trunk and has a stick to hold it tight and mark out the circle.

Unfortunately, there is no hard and fast rule about the optimum radius of the circle but it is far better to err on the generous side, by making the circle large, than by making it too small and possibly killing the tree. If you take half the radius of the branch spread, you shouldn't be far out.

The mark that you made around the tree represents the inside of the trench that is then dug around the tree two spade widths wide and 90 cm (3 ft) deep [Fig. 15.19].

Whenever a clearly main and vigorous root is found, a section is cut from it with a pruning saw. Likewise, any strong roots growing down under the tree also have to be cut.

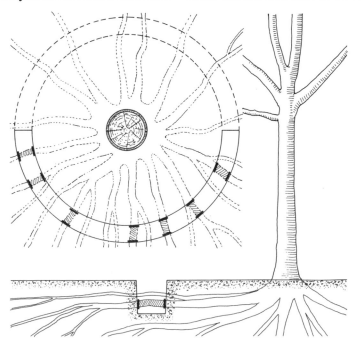

**Fig. 15.19** Only carry out root pruning when all else has failed.

You must never, though, cut through so many roots that it makes the tree so unsteady that even a stake is unable to hold it.

You must also leave the finer and smaller roots in place because it is these that will sustain and partially support the tree. The temptation, and easy way, is to cut through all the small roots and leave the large; don't, as this is the very opposite of what is required.

When you are satisfied that there are only enough major roots left to hold up the tree, put the removed soil back into the trench and carefully but firmly tread it down with your feet. Carefully, because it is important that all the retained roots are in working order and not broken and trodden on more than can be helped. Stake the tree firmly. If necessary, use two stakes, one on each side.

Because an enormous amount of root will have been severed from the tree, you must keep an eye on the tree in the following summer and be ready to give it water if the soil shows any sign of drying out. Never wait until the tree is clearly in distress before you water; it will probably be too late. Don't expect the tree to carry a full crop in the year following root pruning; it is in that year that the fruit buds for the following year are laid down.

In other words, it will be at least the second growing season after treatment that an improvement will be seen in cropping.

## TREE FRUITS UNDER GLASS

### The principles

Although the subject of this book is pruning, a certain amount of knowledge about the growth of plants and ways in which we manage them is essential if pruning is to be carried out successfully. You must know why you are pruning and what the response will be before you can hope to carry it out effectively and gain the required results.

We have discussed the pruning of tree fruits in the open air at length and, armed with this knowledge, there really is no reason at all why we should not adapt what we have learned to enable us to prune trees growing under glass. First, though, we have to draw a distinction between 'growing' under glass and, if you like, 'sheltering' under glass.

This latter category covers, in the main, fruit grown in one sort or another of container and which then spend a small part of each year in the protection of a greenhouse etc.

Fruit trees in pots and strawberries in tower-pots or growing-bags are examples of these and we have covered the pruning of fruit trees in pots elsewhere (see pages 192–3).

Now we are concerned with fruit that is grown throughout its life in a greenhouse. Nine times out of ten, it will be planted in the greenhouse border. In this way, growing conditions will be similar to what would be experienced in a warmer climate. For our purposes here, a cold greenhouse is the one most usually recommended. That is, one with either no artificial heat at all or simply a paraffin stove, or its equivalent, to stop the temperature falling too low. It is not necessarily frost-free.

Perhaps surprisingly to some, this will give the UK something pretty close to a Mediterranean climate. As such, the sorts of fruit that we could expect to grow would include grapes, peaches, nectarines, apricots, figs, citrus, granadilla (passion fruit), pomegranate, guava, pineapple guava (feijoa), Natal plum (carissa), kiwi fruit.

To these can be added melons; tender annuals grown from seed. They are perfectly easy but require a fair bit of pruning if they are to give of their best.

Fruits with which we are not really concerned here are more the exotics which require higher temperatures and little, if any, pruning. These would include bananas and pineapples.

Others in which we are not interested are the fully hardy fruits like apples, pears, plums and cherries. Apart from bringing into the greenhouse during blossom time those which are growing in pots, we should keep them outside the whole time.

### Citrus fruits

This covers oranges, lemons, grapefruit, tangerines and all the other hybrids that appear from time to time. Incidentally, the hybrids very seldom reproduce true from seed so, if you want a particular one, it is much better to buy a young plant from a reputable nursery, which will probably have been propagated from semi-ripe cuttings in the late summer.

In any event, thc chances are that you will buy a bush of two or more years old which will already have the makings of a branch system.

If, however, you acquire just a rooted cutting or a very young plant with just a central stem, this should be stopped at 10–15 cm (4–6 in) high to induce side shoots to form in the same or the following year.

Most citrus plants form what, in apple terms, is a delayed open centre (see page 159). Although the central leader has been stopped, a strong side shoot will usually take over. This is fine because the vigour of an unstopped central leader is often so great that you end up with a tall and thin plant. With a side shoot taking over as leader, the branches that develop below it are stronger and more of a bush develops.

After the first, and maybe second, year, the only pruning required will be to maintain the shape of the bush and to reduce the vigour of any shoot that grows too strongly. If these are allowed to remain, the shape of the plant will suffer along with the fruiting.

The best approach is to nip out the tops just as soon as it is seen that an over-vigorous shoot is developing, or to wait until the following spring and, as growth starts, remove the whole shoot completely. All citrus plants which are grown for their edible fruit can be treated in this way. Those growing in pots can be moved outside to a warm, sunny and sheltered spot for the summer, if desired.

## Figs

Although varieties such as the usual 'Brown Turkey' are normally hardy outside in all but the coldest districts, the choicer-flavoured varieties, like 'Bourjasotte Grise' and 'Negro Largo', will only give of their best under glass.

This is the main benefit of growing figs in a protected environment.

Another is that, properly managed, they will give two crops a year. With sufficient heat and feeding, they may even give three. Although some form of root restriction is desirable for figs grown in the open, it is vital for those under cover or they will grow far too strongly at the expense of fruit.

The best times for winter-pruning figs under glass are immediately after leaf-fall or at the first sign of growth in the spring. Sap move-

ment is at a minimum then and bleeding is less likely. The trees, whether in pots or planted direct in the greenhouse soil, are normally grown fan-trained. It gives you good control over them. However, you can also grow them as pyramids in pots. This makes them more three-dimensional but the greater space they occupy may be important. If grown fan-trained in pots, a cane frame will be needed to which the main branches are tied. The fruiting shoots that will follow can be allowed to stand out from the fan rather than being tied in, as one would with a larger fan.

The frame may be either in the pot itself, pushed into the ground behind it or even on a sunny wall with the pot placed against it.

Pyramid trees in pots are grown as follows. The young tree is planted in a 18–25 cm (7–10 in) pot, according to its size, and, in the first winter, is stopped at about 60 cm (2 ft) tall. This will lead to side shoots (laterals) growing in the following spring which, in turn, are stopped when about 15 cm (6 in) long. A refinement is to stop the upper shoots shorter than the lower ones so that a roughly pyramid shape is created, with the lower branches longer than the upper. It is from these stopped laterals that the fruiting shoots will grow.

Once it is seen that two or three fruitlets on a shoot are sufficiently large to ripen later in the same year, the tip of the shoot and any embryo figs beyond the ripening ones are taken out. This will induce more shoots to appear further back down the main branches. These are left unpruned and it is the youngest and smallest embryos at their tip which are allowed to over-winter and form next year's first crop.

With a fan-trained tree planted in the ground, wires are needed on the wall behind it. Here again, they are of the same layout as those outdoors.

The formation of the fan is also done similarly in that the young growing shoots are nipped back to induce branching. This continues with successional shoots until the fan is as large as you want.

Once the tree is of fruiting age, it is up to the grower to judge which shoots with embryo fruits on are to be retained and which are to be stopped. If you think that the fruits will ripen in the current season, leave them, but if too large to overwinter, stop them.

With these fan-trained trees planted in the greenhouse border, the first summer crop, like outdoor trees, is from embryo figs that have overwintered. This is followed by one, or even two, more crops that develop from embryos formed in the current year.

It follows, therefore that, unlike outdoor figs, constant tipping of the shoots during growth is undesirable as it removes the very embryos that we want for crops. The aim is to produce strong and stocky shoots where we want them on the tree. First, therefore, unwanted shoots near the base of the branches, or further along them, are rubbed out throughout the growing season as soon as they are large enough to handle. Those which are wanted for replacements or to fill gaps are retained. These are seldom used as fruiting shoots.

Once the main branches become too long and uneconomical to keep through lack of new fruiting shoots, they are cut out in the autumn and those that have been built up to replace them are tied in instead.

The routine that was recommended for outdoor fan-trained figs, whereby young shoots were encouraged to form and were then stopped during the early part of the growing season, is inappropriate for figs under glass.

Outdoors, we wanted a large number of small fruits to overwinter for the coming year's single crop. Under glass, we will be using the embryos to form the second and, possibly, third crops. Thus, instead of tipping the young shoots, they are left alone. All that is necessary is to keep an eye on their number and to nip out any more that form after what you judge to be the optimum number have developed into fruiting shoots. This is a matter of judgement rather than following a rule.

With the approach of autumn, though, the same job of removing the largest fruitlets is still necessary so that only the smallest remain for the winter once all the leaves have fallen.

As you will have gathered, whether they are grown outdoors against a sunny wall or fan-trained in the greenhouse, figs require a lot of attention and should not be attempted if you feel that there might not be enough time to do the job properly. If you still want to grow figs, an ordinary free-standing tree in a sunny border is likely to be the answer.

## Peaches and nectarines

In just the same way that these fruits grow and crop best outdoors when fan-trained against a sunny wall (see page 184), they are always a greater success when grown in the same way under glass.

As with figs, the main benefits of protected cultivation are that the choicer varieties can be grown and that the season can be extended in both directions; earlier and later. Unlike figs, though, you will not get more than one crop a year! A godsend that is sometimes ignored by authors is that the dreaded peach leaf curl disease is virtually unheard of in a greenhouse. This is because the fungus is spread by raindrops carrying and splashing it from infected to clean foliage. Remember this if you do have the mischance to see any, because overhead damping down in the summer will have the same effect as rain.

Although 'Peregrine' and 'Rochester' are the standard outdoor varieties, they can be grown to absolute perfection under glass. You might, though, like to grow a late variety which would be difficult to ripen properly outdoors, except in a brilliant summer. 'Bellgarde' falls into this category and has a first rate flavour too.

With thought, therefore, you can have fresh peaches throughout the summer; the earliest and latest under glass and the maincrop outside. Much the same applies to nectarines, with a succession of fruits during the late summer and early autumn from, in this order, 'Lord Napier', 'Elruge' and 'Pineapple'.

As with their outdoor cultivation, peaches and nectarines are treated similarly except that nectarines are more likely to suffer from a water shortage when the fruits are swelling. This doesn't always matter outdoors but it is important under glass where all the water is given by the grower.

Just as the general cultivation of peaches under glass is virtually identical to that of outdoor trees, so is the pruning.

Any difference is not in the method of pruning and training but in its timing and frequency. Indoor trees are naturally going to require attention earlier in the spring and more often during the growing season. They may also require it later in the autumn because of the extended growing season.

# CHAPTER 16

# Soft Fruits Outdoors and Under Glass

## OUTDOORS

### Bilberries, blueberries and cranberries

These three berries are all of the genus *Vaccineum* (*Ericaceae*) and require extremely acidic soil conditions.

### Bilberries

A dwarf shrub of similar growth habit to heather and grows wild on many moors. No regular pruning is either needed or desirable. Occasional clipping with shears after the fruit has been picked will keep the plants compact and prevent them becoming straggly.

### Blueberries

The cultivated form most widely grown is the 'high bush blueberry'. It is grown commercially on a small scale in acid sandy areas.

It is a deciduous bush, eventually reaching some 1.5 m (5 ft) high. It fruits in a similar way to black currants, producing most of its crop on young lateral shoots arising from older wood and on new vigorous shoots growing from the base of the plant.

Like the black currant, it is best grown as a stool so that there is a continual supply of new wood coming from lower down. This means that any pruning, and little is needed, must be aimed at keeping the bushes young and vigorous.

This is achieved by the occasional removal of older branch systems that are clearly past their best. These will have stopped producing new side shoots and crops are well below par. Obviously, any damaged, dead and crowded shoots and branches must go, along with any that are out of place.

Young bushes will require a little shaping and tipping of vigorous shoots to encourage branching but this should not be overdone as it is on these young shoots that the crop is borne. The emphasis is on producing new growth by feeding properly rather than by heavy pruning. Once the leaves have fallen in the early winter, pruning can start.

### Cranberries

These prefer poor, acidic soils but, unlike the previous two fruits, are quite at home on swampy and poorly drained ground.

The cranberry is a trailing plant that forms a mat on the ground with 15–20 cm (6–8 in) tall shoots growing up from it. As with the bilberry, the only pruning required is to keep it within bounds and to stop it getting lanky.

### Blackberries and hybrid cane fruits

The term 'hybrid cane fruits' covers a multitude of sins but, for the most part, it refers to loganberries, tayberries, sunberries and any thornless sports. Other less important ones include the boysenberry, marionberry and, more recently, hildaberry.

All the hybrids are crosses between blackberries and raspberries, of one sort or another, and exhibit growth habits varying between the two. All, including the blackberry, operate on a biennial system with the canes growing up from the crown of the plant (a stool) in the first year and then fruiting in the second; after which they are cut out. That, in essence, covers the pruning of these fruits but, clearly there is more to it than that.

The main variations are connected with the number of new canes produced by the different kinds and varieties. Some blackberries, for example 'Himalaya Giant' and 'Fantasia', produce very few; maybe only one in some

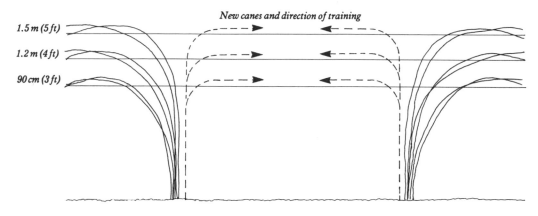

New canes and direction of training

1.5 m (5 ft)

1.2 m (4 ft)

90 cm (3 ft)

years, and this will have an important influence on pruning.

However, at the start of it all, planting is normally recommended for the autumn and, following this, all these cane fruits are cut down to within 20 cm (8 in) or so of the ground to encourage the production of new canes from buds at and below ground level in the following growing season. This short length of old stem is left to produce some shoots which will act as sap drawers to keep the plant growing.

Because of the vigour and length of the canes, a permanent system of support is needed and this usually takes the form of four horizontal wires stretched 0.9, 1.2, 1.5 and 1.8 m (3, 4, 5 and 6 ft) above the ground between stout posts.

During the first year of growth, the new canes are tied loosely to the wires for support but are not normally tied into their final positions until growth has stopped in the autumn. Then they are cut loose and are trained and tied to the three lower wires. There are several methods of training; the most appropriate one for a particular fruit depending on the number and vigour of the canes.

Blackberries tend to have the fewest canes but they are thicker and less flexible so the method most commonly adopted is the one-way or two-way rope system.

The one-way is used when there are very few new canes, three or less, because in the autumn these are trained to the lower three wires on one side only of the stool. They are trained up and then along at one cane per wire [Fig. 16.1]. During the following summer, the new growing canes are loosely tied to the wires on the other side of the stool. This is not only convenient and easier, more importantly it isolates the new canes from possible fungal infection from the older fruiting canes.

With the two-way rope system, the fruiting canes are trained and tied to the lower three wires on both sides of the stool. Thus, you can have six canes, all with a wire to themselves, or more if you want to double up. The new canes, as they grow, are taken straight up the middle from the stool until they reach the top wire, when they are trained along it on one or both sides. Here again, this keeps them apart from the fruiting canes, thus reducing the risk of cane infection.

For hybrid cane fruits with vigorous, thin and supple canes, such as the sunberry, the weaving system is better than the rope. With this, the fruiting canes are taken out on each side of the stool but, instead of each cane being trained along one wire, they are woven up and down between the three. In this way, each cane takes up very much less sideways space because its horizontal spread is greatly reduced.

As with the rope systems, the growing canes are taken up from the centre of the stool and loosely tied to the top wire.

With varieties that have more canes but less vigorous ones, such as 'Loch Ness' blackberry, the fan system of training is more appropriate. Here, the fruiting canes are taken out on each side of the stool in the form of a fan. A gap is left in the middle, up which the new canes are trained and tied during the growing season. Once again, the new ones are not mixed with the older fruiting canes.

Another training system is useful for taming very vigorous blackberries, like 'Himalaya'

**Fig. 16.1** The one-way rope system keeps the fruiting and growing canes of blackberry and hybrid cane fruits well apart. The new canes are taken in the opposite direction to those fruiting.

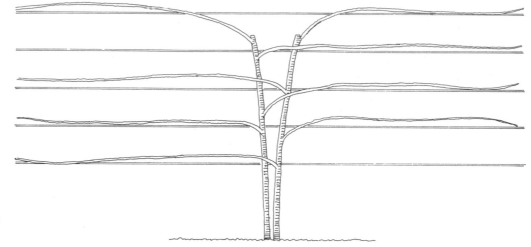

**Fig. 16.2** When canes are few but extremely vigorous, tip them and later tie in the laterals.

and 'Fantasia', which produce only perhaps one or two new canes each year. The growing cane or canes are trained vertically until they reach, say, 1.8 m (6 ft) high or the top of the fence or wall to which they are tied, whichever is less. The tops are then cut out so that laterals develop which are trained out horizontally and tied to the wires [Fig. 16.2]. This effectively covers the desired area but there is much less bending of the canes than with the rope system and so, less danger to yourself and of damaging the canes.

The main problem is that it is difficult to keep the new canes apart from those fruiting and, when pruning, there is rather a lot of cane to tackle. As has already been mentioned, pruning takes place as soon as convenient after the fruit has been picked. This removes any pests and diseases that might be on the fruited canes and also ensures that the new canes ripen fully.

With vigorous blackberries, the old canes are best cut out in short sections. This is easier for the grower and avoids any damage to the new canes; such as they would suffer if the old canes were torn out whole in one operation.

In nearly every case, the fruited cane is cut out at its point of origin. However, where the length of new cane is hardly enough to cover the allotted area, and this sometimes happens with vigorous blackberries, you can make use of one or more of the strong side canes that often grow out from towards the base of the

fruiting canes [Fig. 16.3]. If the fruited cane is cut back to one of these, it will fruit perfectly satisfactorily in the following year; after which, it is cut right out in the normal way. Staying with strong growing blackberries, a pair of secateurs is pretty useless for pruning them; the main stem can, on occasions, be as much as 5 cm (2 in) thick. A pair of loppers or a pruning saw are what are needed.

Another difficulty that might arise is disposing of the old fruited shoots. If left as they are, they are no good for anything but they are first rate if put through a shredder; it also effectively disarms the thorns. The only alternative is a bonfire, but this is a waste of excellent raw material for composting.

Although all blackberry varieties are extremely hardy, the same cannot be said of the hybrid cane fruits. This has always been a problem with the loganberry in either a particularly bad winter or, more frequently, in cold northern districts.

Although the tayberry and sunberry are much hardier, to be on the safe side it is wise to bundle up the new canes of the hybrids into one bundle per plant and tie this to the wires for the duration of the winter.

If this is felt necessary, pruning is usually delayed until the early winter so that most of the leaves will have fallen. The bundles are normally cut loose and the canes tied into their fruiting position during early spring, before, or immediately after, growth has started.

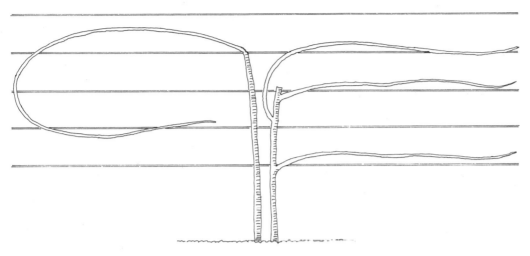

**Fig. 16.3** If there are too few new canes to fill the allotted space, one or more of the fruited canes can be cut back rather than removed completely.

## Currants

We cannot couple black currants together with red currants from the pruning angle because they are treated completely differently. This is because black currants produce their best fruit on shoots younger than about four years old whereas red currants fruit best on spurs that are built up, by appropriate pruning, on semi-permanent branches. As such, black currants must be encouraged to grow as well as fruit by applying adequate fertilizer each spring.

Another difference, not unconnected, is that black currants are grown as a stool with many of the new branches originating from a point at or below ground level.

Red currant bushes are grown on a short leg, or trunk, with the bush itself consisting mainly of mature branches furnished with fruiting spurs. From this, it will be apparent that completely different pruning techniques are required. The actual time at which winter pruning takes place is somewhat immaterial. The old recommendation was to prune black currants as soon as picking was over, or soon after. This allowed time for the retained shoots to ripen properly. Then favour passed to the autumn as soon as the leaves had started to fall. This, too, is now largely ignored but it is a good idea to prune as soon as you can after leaf-fall.

Most authorities prune when the bushes are bare because it is much easier to see the overall picture and what needs to be taken out.

### Black currants

The pruning of the young bushes is designed to encourage the quick appearance and growth of strong young shoots from at or below ground level. Two-year-old bushes are the best to buy but, whether they are one or two, immediately after autumn planting, all strong shoots are cut back to leave just 5–8 cm (2–3 in) above the ground. Weak shoots are cut out completely.

No tipping of shoots is normally required at any time because, if well fed, plenty of growth will come naturally. For this reason, pruning throughout most of the bushes' life is aimed mainly at shaping and encouraging growth. If growth is good, fruiting is a natural consequence.

Weak shoots need to come out together with any that are clearly out of place or causing crowding. The bushes will start fruiting in about their third year but the process of building them up will continue.

After four or five years, it has always been traditional to remove those oldest branch systems which have stopped producing good quality berries. This timing is fairly fluid because the fruiting efficiency is far more important than the age of the branches. However, it is certainly true that, once the quality and quantity of fruit produced starts to deteriorate, it is time to start removing the oldest branches [Fig. 16.4].

If a bush has been built up satisfactorily,

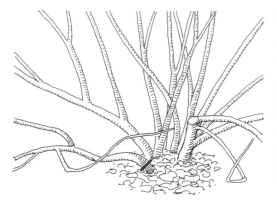

**Fig. 16.4** Once branches, or a whole branch system, stops fruiting properly, remove it.

there will be ample new branches to take the place of those removed and crops will improve at once. What it really boils down to is that, once the efficiency of an older branch slips below that of a younger one, it should be removed. It will normally involve cutting out the branch right back to its point of origin. Very little is ever gained simply by cutting it back to a younger side branch. A good pair of loppers and a thin-bladed pruning saw are normally of more use than secateurs in pruning black currants.

Heading back a branch system is never done to induce more growth from a particular branch. Once a branch has deteriorated, remove it completely. Side shoots and the tops of branches are only removed to reduce overcrowding; never to induce growth.

### Red and white currants
The white currant is a colourless form of the red. As such, their pruning is exactly the same. For simplicity, therefore, white currants will not be mentioned again as all that is said about reds applies equally well to them.

We have seen that, whereas black currants fruit best on the younger shoots, red currants carry their best crops on spurs borne on older branches. This is an important difference because it means that they are best grown as either traditional bushes or as cordons.

When grown as bushes, they should have a short trunk and are made up of semi-perm-

anent branches carrying fruiting spurs.

Before planting, any shoots are removed that are growing from below what you intend to use as the lowest branch. This should leave about 15 cm (6 in) of clear leg between the roots and the lowest branch; some 13 cm (5 in) of clear stem after planting. Once planted, any obviously weak shoots are removed. The remainder of the current season's new shoots are then cut back by a third to a half (hardest for the weakest) to build up a good framework of strong branches.

When up to a dozen semi-formed branches exist, you can begin to think more about pruning for fruit. This is done by shortening back all new side shoots in the early winter to two buds (about 3 cm/1 in). In this way, a fruiting spur system is built up.

Once the branches have reached the required length, extension shoots on the ends are treated as though they are new side shoots and are cut back similarly.

As an alternative, summer pruning can be carried out in early summer when the new shoots are cut back to about five leaves. This is followed by winter pruning as just described.

Summer pruning has the same benefits as it does for apples and pears. It encourages quicker ripening by removing a lot of leaf shading. The berries are bigger because more sap goes into them.

After seven to ten years, some of the main branches are likely to start deteriorating. These are cut out to make room for younger ones when the quality and quantity of their spurs and fruit is clearly not as good as previously.

From growing red currant bushes on a short leg just a few inches in length, it is only a small cultural step to extending the leg to up to 90 cm (3 ft) high and growing the bushes as standards. This not only adds interest to them but it also means that you do not have to attend to them on your knees.

They can just as well be grown in tubs or half barrels.

The method of building up the stem is perfectly simple but it does help to start with a one-year-old bush, rather than an older one. This allows you to choose a young, vigorous and unpruned shoot as near to vertical as possible. All others are removed and the chosen shoot is tied to a cane in the ground beside it so that a straight stem is created. Don't tip it at this stage.

After the next growing season, you will have a tall single stem and, in the early winter, this is cut back to 90–120 cm (3–4 ft) tall.

A year later, as many strong new shoots as may be suitable are chosen, retained and cut back by a third to a half to form the main framework branches. These should be evenly spaced around the stem, be of approximately equal vigour and close together, covering only a short section of stem.

After another year, there will probably be enough new shoots for the full compliment of branches. These should also be cut back as were the previous year's but with the main aim of encouraging side shoots to form further back.

When these have formed, they are cut back as was described for normal bushes and, indeed, all further pruning, both summer and winter, is the same as for normal bushes.

Bearing in mind that red currants fruit on carried on established branches, it follows that they can be grown very effectively and economically of space in gardens by training them against walls, fences or simply canes in the open ground.

The normal systems of training are single, double ('U') or triple-vertical cordons.

Single cordons are the least economical, because you only end up with one stem per bush, but they do reach their required height quickest and start cropping earlier than the multi-stemmed cordons. Two- or three-stemmed cordons are more satisfactory on the grounds of economy and also because they are easier to control once they have reached their desired size; their energies are expended on more stems.

A single cordon is formed in a similar way to a standard except that, each autumn, the extension growth is shortened by a quarter to induce side shoots to grow out.

These are subsequently either winter pruned alone, by shortening back all new side shoots to two buds (about 3 cm/1 in), or, greatly to be preferred, by summer and winter pruning, when the new shoots are cut back to about five leaves in early summer, to be followed by winter pruning as just described [Fig. 16.5].

**Fig. 16.5** Summer pruning red currants is especially beneficial for ripening the berries.

To form cordons with two or three upright stems, the original young plant is allowed to produce two shoots, instead of just the one. These are very carefully bent down and tied to a stout, horizontal cane. As they grow in the following year, they are trained outwards and then upwards so that they form vertical shoots 30 cm (1 ft) apart. From then on, they are treated in the same way as the single cordon.

To form a three-stem cordon, start off with a two- and take a third one up the middle, originating from the base of one of the others. The side verticals must each be 30 cm (1 ft) away from the central one. Thus, the whole plant is 60 cm (2 ft) wide whilst the two-stem cordon is just 30 cm (1 ft) wide.

## Gooseberries

The best time to winter prune gooseberries rather depends on the circumstances. The general rule is to prune in the early winter but, in rural areas where bullfinches are much in evidence, it is far wiser to wait until the spring. Then, any damage by way of bud stripping can be taken into account when choosing the severity of pruning needed.

Because the gooseberry fruits best in the same way as the red currant – upon spurs borne on semi-permanent branches – the pruning is done in much the same way. The main differences are refinements rather than important changes.

It is important to keep the bush with an open

centre so that you will not have to pick the fruit by stretching through the outer branches; which normally results in getting torn to shreds. Another reason is that the worst pest of gooseberries, the gooseberry sawfly, lays its eggs in the sheltered centre of the bushes. Anything that can be done to discourage it is worthwhile.

For these reasons, any shoot threatening to cross right over the centre is always cut hard back and never retained as a future branch.

Gooseberries need to be pruned slightly harder in the early years because their shoots are more supple and the bushes naturally adopt a weeping habit.

Whilst the starting point is the same as for red currants, in that the bushes are normally grown on a short leg, the new shoots are cut back by half and not a third, for the first few years. This leads to a more rigid framework of branches. You also have to pay more attention to the buds to which the shoots are cut back.

You select these on the basis of the direction in which you want the future shoot to grow. However, if you want the branch to stay reasonably straight, and this is always easier to manage, you must alternate the buds from year to year. That is, if you chose a left-pointing bud one year, you should (other things being equal) choose a right-pointing one in the following year. Side shoots can be pruned in winter by cutting back all those that are not required to form extension growth to 8 cm (3 in) long. Over the years, this builds up the

spur system.

Early to mid summer pruning has many advantages and is a perfectly simple job to undertake. The side shoots not wanted are cut back to five leaves and then to three buds in the winter. The more important benefits of summer pruning are that:

(*a*) many possibly mildewed tips are removed and, by also cutting out those that are not diseased, the risk of the mildew spreading is greatly reduced;

(*b*) more energy is put into berry production than into new growth;

(*c*) removal of all those leaves lets in the sun and light to help the berries ripen;

(*d*) a small point, but important, is that it makes it easier to see and pick the berries besides reducing the number of thorns.

An even more effective way of growing gooseberries, and of avoiding actual bodily harm by way of the thorns, is to grow them as cordons; as has just been described for red currants. The formation of the one-, two- and three-stem cordons is just the same. It is, though, most important that summer pruning is carried out because this is half the object of growing cordons. As with bushes, cut the side shoots back to 13 cm (5 in) in early to mid summer, then to 8 cm (3 in) in early winter.

Leave the leader unpruned in the summer but cut it back by one quarter every winter. It need not be pruned hard to stiffen it because, being a cordon, the leader(s) is/are always tied to canes. Once traditionally pruned bushes are approaching 10 years old, it will become necessary, as it is with red currants, to remove one or more branch systems in most winters to make room for young and more actively growing replacements.

Finally, on the pruning side, it is quite possible and fully in order to grow gooseberries as standards. This is done in the same way as was described for red currants (pages 202–3) except that the pruning of the branches in the formative years, after the stem has been developed, is lighter than is the case with a traditional bush because the weeping habit is no disadvantage in a standard [Fig. 16.6].

By the way, much of the one-year-old wood that is pruned out in winter from both red currants and gooseberries makes perfect material for cuttings.

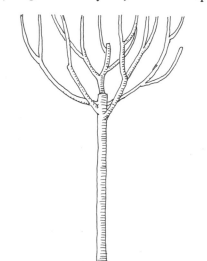

**Fig. 16.6**
Gooseberries make excellent standards, which are pruned more lightly than normal bushes.

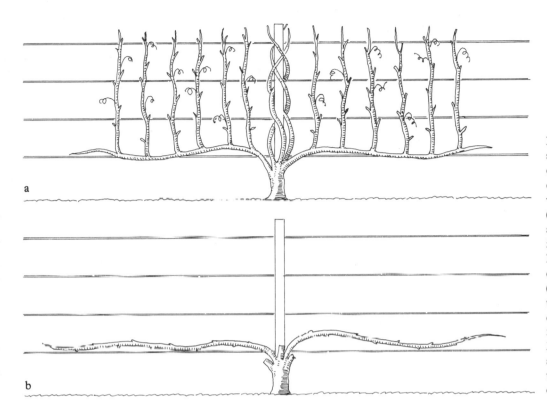

**Fig. 16.7** Guyot system of training outdoor grapes, especially wine varieties.
(*a*) A Guyot vine as it would appear in early winter, leafless and dormant.
(*b*) After pruning: the two horizontal canes and their fruited laterals have been cut out and replaced by the best one-year-old canes.

## Grapes

On the whole, it is the wine grapes that succeed best outdoors in temperate climates but, in a sunny spot in a warm district, dessert varieties can be grown perfectly satisfactorily in summer. Make sure, though, that you plant a true outdoor variety and one locally recommended for your area. If possible, buy one-year-old pot-grown plants for planting in the dormant season. Tease the rootball apart and spread out the roots. Plant with the roots about 15 cm (6 in) deep.

The distance between plants will vary with the method of training. For example, if you intend to have a permanent cane framework trained to a wall or wires, 1.5 m (5 ft) would be about right. Training and pruning are really quite easy so don't let it put you off.

The Guyot method comes near the top for all-round ease and efficiency, especially for wine grapes; nor do the vines take up too much room. The support needed for this system consists of a horizontal wire 15–20 cm (6–8 in) from the ground to which will be tied the fruit-

ing cane. You will also need a vertical bamboo to which to tie the two canes as they grow. However, we can make more economical use of the space if, instead of just one wire, another is stretched a foot above the first.

If the vines are then planted 45 cm (18 in) apart, instead of 90 cm (3 ft), double the crop can be had by training alternate plants to the top wire. Following winter planting, the vine is cut down to no more than three buds from the ground. In the first growing season, just one shoot is allowed to develop. In the winter, this is cut back to about four buds.

During the next growing season, just the two top buds are allowed to grow out into shoots. From here on, each shoot is pruned differently. One is cut back to two buds; the other is to produce fruiting laterals next year so is shortened to six buds. It is then bent down and tied to the supporting wire.

Shoots will grow from most of the buds on this longer cane. These laterals will produce flower trusses and are stopped at two leaves beyond the truss. Any other shoots that appear on them, or on their parent cane, are pinched back to one leaf.

The cane that was reduced to two buds in the winter will send out a shoot from each. These are allowed to grow unhindered but any others are removed.

In the winter, the laterals that have fruited, together with their parent cane, are removed completely. The other two are treated as were the original two in the previous winter [Fig 16.7].

From then on, simply follow the same routine each year; cutting out the fruited laterals and parent and shortening back one of the two others to two buds and the other to six.

Another method of training is very similar to that used under glass and is a better one for dessert grapes.

You will need supporting wires but, in this case, they are stretched horizontally along a sunny wall or fence or between firm posts in the open garden. A convenient distance between the wires is 23–30 cm (9–12 in) especially on a brick wall because the two extremes represent three and four courses of bricks respectively. With this cordon type of training, you may have anything from one to six or more vertical stems coming from each vine. It mainly depends in how long you are prepared to wait until the allotted area is full.

One stem per vine is obviously quicker but, of course, it costs proportionately more to establish a planting than when growing multi-stem cordons. After planting, and if there are no suitably strong shoots to keep, cut the vine down to within a few buds of the ground.

In the early summer, when you can see which resulting shoot is clearly the strongest, nip out all the others and tie the retained one vertically to a cane.

If the original plant has an appropriately strong shoot when planted, keep it and cut out all the rest. Tie the retained shoot to a cane. Although a year apart, the two vines are now at the same stage.

This vine should be cut back to about 60 cm (2 ft) tall. What is more important, though, is that the wood is firm and ripe with a strong bud at the required place. Side shoots are cut back to two strong buds from their point of origin. The leader is extended upwards in the same way each year; growing in the summer

and being shortened in the winter. It is finally stopped when it reaches just above the top wire. At the same time, any side shoots that grow directly from the main stem are cut back to two buds. Those that are growing from previously pruned spurs, are cut hard back to the cluster of buds at their base.

During this time, there is no reason at all why grapes should not be allowed to grow on the laterals, which are, after all, there to carry fruit.

If you are growing a cordon with two or more vertical stems (there should be an even number), then the first step involves training out a horizontal shoot on each side.

After planting, only the strongest shoot is retained and this is cut back to about 30 cm (1 ft) high. More important than the height is that the top bud should be pointing along the line of the wires and that another, very close to it, is pointing in the opposite direction. In the spring, allow the shoots from these two selected buds to grow out but pinch out all others as they appear.

Train these two out at 45° and, in early winter, bend them down to the horizontal and tie them in to the wire. The soft tips of the canes are then cut back to ripe wood so that they are approximately the same length.

Most of the buds on these two canes will grow into shoots in the following spring and summer. They should be trained up vertically. The recommended space that should exist between these new canes is 90 cm (3 ft). This means that the first one on each side should be 45 cm (18 in) out from the central trunk. Thereafter, one should be left every 90 cm (3 ft). If, at this stage, there are not enough vertical rods to fill the intended space, the end rod can be bent down and tied to the bottom wire. This will extend the horizontal branch and, in twelve months time, there will be a fresh lot of vertical rods to choose from.

If the vertical rods have reached the highest point that you want them to, they are stopped. If not, they are left to grow on.

You now have two horizontal branches furnished with upright rods every 90 cm (3 ft); this is the permanent framework of the vine. There may also be some shoots on the rods. If so, these are taken hard back to the rod.

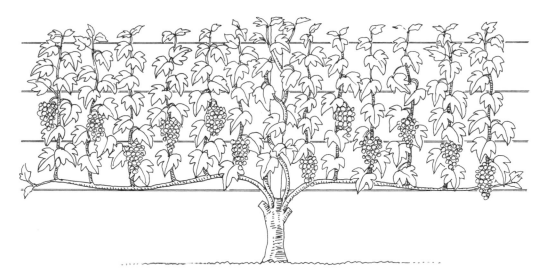

**Fig. 16.8** The complete Guyot vine with its two temporary horizontal rods with fruiting laterals growing from them.

In the following growing season, side shoots will form. With a vigorous vine, you may not need all these so they should be thinned out to leave one every 30–35 cm (12–14 in) on each side of the rods. All others are pinched out as soon as they are large enough to handle. Only one shoot must be allowed to grow per spur. If two or more appear, wait until one is clearly dominant and remove the rest.

The spaced and retained rods will shortly produce flower trusses. At one leaf beyond the truss, the shoots are stopped. Only one truss per shoot must be allowed.

Any subsequent shoots that arise from the fruiting laterals or the vertical rods are stopped at one leaf. This is carried on throughout the summer whilst the grapes are developing. The next pruning needed is the main winter treatment that is carried out during early winter after leaf-fall. The important thing about pruning grapes is that they must be completely dormant so that no bleeding follows cutting. Then, all the fruited canes are cut hard back to within one bud of the vertical rod. Any shoots which grew during the summer and which were, as previously instructed, cut back to one leaf are now cut hard back to the rod or the horizontal branch at the bottom.

At the same time that you are winter pruning, it is a good habit to get into to look at all the ties holding the branches and rods to the wires. If any are tight or broken, replace them.

Yet another way of growing grapes outdoors, and the method that takes up the least room, is what is called the 'spurred stump' method. This is mainly used for wine grapes.

After planting, the vine is allowed to grow for a year without disturbance to build up a strong root system. In fact, this can be done with all outdoor vines and it is well worth it. However, there are few of us who can either be bothered or who have the time. After the year, the cane is cut back to a strong bud some 20 cm (8 in) from the ground and all other shoots are removed.

In the following summer, two or three shoots may develop, and there could even be some fruit. By the way, mention is continually being made of a 'strong' bud. This is important because it is only from a strong bud that a strong shoot will grow and fruit is only carried on strong shoots. The stump will send out a varying number of shoots each spring. Four to six of the strongest are allowed to grow and bear fruit; the rest are rubbed out early on.

There is no firm ruling no this, but the shoots are stopped at some distance beyond the fruit truss, say six to eight leaves. A cane is then pushed in beside the vine and the 'tent' of fruiting shoots is tied to it for support. For something different and a bit of amusement, vines can also be grown as standards in much the same way as is done with gooseberries. They are normally grown in pots for 'show-off' value but it is perfectly easy to grow them in the open ground. Following planting, a single shoot is trained vertically up a cane. In the winter, it is cut back to a bud 90–120 cm (3–4 ft) high; the actual height is unimportant.

In the spring, several shoots will grow out and the best five or six of these are stopped at five or six leaves. If any shoots other than the chosen few appear, rub them out at once along with any flower trusses.

In early winter, the shoots are taken back to one strong bud.

In the following year, the vine can be allowed to produce its first fruit. The shoot bearing it is stopped at two leaves beyond the flower truss. From then on, the system is more or less the same as for grapes grown in any other way. Only the strongest canes are kept and only one bunch per cane is permitted to grow. These are cut hard back in early winter.

Of course, the number of canes you grow can be increased as the vine gets older and as you feel more confident in being able to judge its capacity.

One difference is important and that concerns supporting the bunches.

The cane or stake to which the vine is tied should be somewhat taller than the uppermost shoots. Soft twine is led from the top of the

stake and tied to the shoot carrying a bunch so that the weight is taken off the shoot.

The one thing about grapes is their versatility; once you have the system under control, your imagination is the only limiting factor as to the number of different ways of growing them. Some will be successful, others will not be; but experimenting is half the fun.

## Kiwi fruits

The main thing about growing kiwi fruits outdoors is that you should be ready to protect them for the winter; they are not 100% hardy, especially when young.

Because of this lack of hardiness, it is also good practice to plant them in the spring rather than in the autumn, and then site them against a warm and sunny wall.

There are two main ways of training and pruning kiwi fruits; one (the espalier method) can be used both outdoors and under glass, the other (the New Zealand system) is essentially for outdoors as it takes up too much room for the average amateur greenhouse.

For the New Zealand way, you first need to put up a wire support system. Stakes 2.5 m (8 ft) long are driven into the ground 60 cm (2 ft) deep. A T-piece 1m (3 ft) long is nailed to the top of each stake. Wires are fastened to the two ends of one T-piece and are taken along to the other T-piece where they are drawn taut and nailed to the corresponding ends. A third wire is stretched down the middle between the top of each stake. 6 m (20 ft) between posts is normal.

The plants are put in under the centre wire with a cane next to each; the top of which is secured to the wire. Only one shoot is allowed to grow from the plant and, when this reaches the wire, the top is nipped out.

When two strong and well-placed shoots appear, one is taken in each direction along the centre wire and is tied to it. Don't allow the shoot to twine round the wire, though. The object is then to create a system of permanent laterals growing from the two main shoots to the outer wires. The permanent laterals are best kept in opposite pairs about 50 cm (20 in) apart. When a lateral reaches its outer wire, it is stopped and tied to it [Fig. 16.9].

Building up the skeleton of permanent branches in this way is continued until the

**Fig. 16.9** The customary way of training kiwi fruits outdoors.

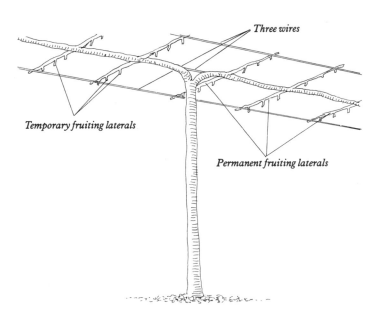

Three wires

Temporary fruiting laterals

Permanent fruiting laterals

plant is complete. It is from the permanent laterals that fruiting laterals will grow.

Selection and treatment of these fruiting laterals is important if overcrowding is to he avoided. One would normally reckon on three fruiting laterals per shoot and they should be growing from the underside of the permanent laterals. Any that are not are pinched back to leave a 2–3 cm (1 in) spur.

Similarly, the fruiting laterals should be kept pinched back to six leaves beyond the last developing fruit in the summer. Because the fruiting laterals are renewed each year, a replacement either at the base of each fruiting lateral, or on the permanent lateral close to it, is retained each year.

In the following late winter, any fruiting spurs are cut back to a couple of buds beyond where the last fruit was and the spent fruiting laterals are cut back to their replacement.

## Raspberries

Until relatively recently, all the raspberries that were grown in gardens and commercially fruited in the summer on canes which had grown in the previous growing season.

Then, along came a completely different type whose canes grew and fruited in the same year. This kind of raspberry is called a 'primocane' and all our autumn fruiting varieties are of this type; the canes grow from ground level in the spring and fruit in the autumn.

It follows that these two kinds need entirely different pruning.

When dealing with blackberries and the hybrid cane fruits, we saw that they operated on a biennial system with the canes growing during the first year and flowering and fruiting during the second. After that, they were cut out to make room for the new ones.

That is the case with the summer-fruiting varieties of raspberry. Once fruiting has finished and all have been picked, the fruited canes are cut clean back to the ground. With the autumn fruiting varieties, the primocanes, all the canes grow and fruit in the same year.

They normally finish fruiting during late autumn but, instead of cutting them down immediately afterwards, they are left until shortly before growth starts again in early spring.

Besides there being no particular need to cut

them down after fruiting, it has been found that the canes afford a certain amount of protection from the worst of the winter weather to the underground buds that will be emerging in the spring.

In early spring therefore, the whole bed is cut to the ground, treated with fertilizer and/or a good mulch of manure or compost and left to break into growth again.

Surely this must be the easiest fruit there is to prune!

However, pruning is one thing but all raspberries need to be supported, as their canes are simply not strong enough to remain upright and tidy unaided. For summer fruiting varieties, there are several recognized systems; all based on horizontal wires stretched between firmly bedded posts.

The simplest consists of two horizontal wires. One is stretched 60 cm (2 ft) above the ground and the other above it, 1.2–1.5 m (4–5 ft) from the ground; the actual height of the upper one depending on the vigour of the variety. Once the row of plants is established, the canes are tied to the wires so that, along the top wire, they are some 10 cm (4 in) apart. Although it was said earlier that all fruited canes are removed after fruiting, this can be extended to include any of the new canes which are lacking in vigour or are, for any other reason, not worth keeping.

The simplest way of carrying out this selection is, first, to tie in all the strongest canes and then, if necessary, work in those slightly weaker to bring the average distance between them to 10 cm (4 in). Once complete, cut out any that are left over and tie in the retained canes to the lower wire.

The rows of canes can be up to 18–19 m (20 yd) long without requiring intermediate posts.

Another method sometimes used consists of two parallel wires secured to a T-piece of wood, a metre/yd long, attached to the top of each post. The canes are tied to one or other of the wires so that they are roughly evenly distributed between the two.

When carrying fruit, this hangs down outside the row of plants and is easier to see and pick. If this is combined with one of the modern thornless varieties, like 'Glen Moy' or 'Glen Prosen', picking raspberries has lost any of the minor discomforts it used to have.

With both systems, the canes are left extending above the top wire for the winter. In the spring, they are either cut back to 15–20 cm (6–8 in) above the top wire or they are bent over and tied to it. Tying down the tops will lead to a slightly heavier crop but the topmost berries are smaller than average.

Several other training systems exist but none has any distinct advantage over the two described. For autumn fruiting varieties, a simpler system can be used because support is only needed once the canes begin to bend over during the summer. As before, a stake is driven in at each end of the row but, instead of one or two wires being drawn between them, strong twine is tied to one and is then led down the outside of the row. This is firmly attached to the stake at the far end and is then led back down the other side. Thus, the row of growing canes is supported round the outside.

If it is found that this is not sufficient for the height of the crop, another length of twine can be brought round the outside of the row above the first.

Alternatively, and this is normally enough, cross-strings can be introduced to hold the two lines of twine together and stop them from spreading apart.

**Fig. 16.10** In the first winter, the vine is cut back by two thirds and any laterals on the retained section to one strong bud.

# SOFT FRUITS UNDER GLASS

## Grapes

Grapes in a greenhouse should be pruned soon after leaf-fall in late autumn. If it is left until the late winter, the canes will bleed profusely when growth starts in the spring, to the detriment of the vine.

There are many systems of pruning a vine; in fact, each system of training has its own appropriate method of pruning.

### Cordons (rod and spur)

This method can be used in the open and in the greenhouse. It is also easy to carry out. In essence, it involves having either one or two permanent canes per vine (usually one) from which fruiting laterals grow out annually.

If the vine is planted inside, after winter planting it is cut back to two or three buds. If it is planted outside, it is led through the wall and then cut back so that the length remaining inside is just two buds long.

Just one cane is allowed to grow in the first year after planting. It grows vigorously and can reach up to 3 m (10 ft) in length.

Any laterals that form on it during that first year are stopped at five or six leaves. Any sublaterals growing from these are stopped at one leaf. This encourages a strong main cane. In the winter, the cane is cut back by two-thirds of its length and the laterals upon it to one good bud from their point of origin. These should be spaced at up to 30 cm (1 ft) apart along the central rod [Fig. 16.10].

This routine is carried out each year, with the new growth on the central canes being cut back by two-thirds, until the vine reaches the desired size. During these formative years, you can allow fruiting canes to form on the previous years' sections.

Once established, the annual winter pruning involves cutting back to within a couple of buds of the mature parent cane all the laterals that have just fruited. Cutting back to two buds allows you to choose just the better of the two shoots that will grow out in the following year. This is not the end of pruning because it is also carried out during the growing season to prevent the vine getting out of hand and to channel most of the energy into the fruits.

Growth is encouraged to start in late winter

by giving the vine heat and spraying the rod with plain water. When two or more shoots have grown out from each spur and are long enough to see which is the strongest, all others are nipped out. When a flower truss has formed, the growth is normally stopped at two leaves beyond the truss; this can vary a little with the variety, though, as weak growers tend to need three or four to pass back sufficient 'food' into the bunch to sustain the developing fruitlets. Any side shoots that subsequently grow from the fruiting cane are stopped at one leaf. All tendrils should be removed.

As soon as the fruiting shoots have been stopped at two (or more) leaves beyond the flower truss, they are tied in to the wires. This has to be done gently so that there are no breakages and one of the best ways is to tie down the shoots halfway at first with some thin twine or raffia and then complete the tying a few weeks later.

That brings us back to pruning the vine in the early winter.

A winter job under glass that can be carried out at the same time as the pruning is to strip off all the old bark from the permanent main canes. This bark provides shelter for many pests during the winter; the worst one is red spider mite.

By stripping off all the old loose bark after pruning, much of the shelter is removed, along with a great many of the mites themselves, or their eggs. Be sure, though, only to remove the old brown bark and take care not to penetrate into the underlying green tissue. It isn't an essential job but it's a useful one and it tidies up the vine.

### Grapes in pots

Layering is not a particularly good method of propagation but it does have one interesting and profitable application; that of growing grapes in pots.

A first-year cane is retained and trained upwards from a bud low down on an established greenhouse vine. Straight after leaf-fall in late autumn, the cane is cut free from the training wires and shortened to 2.4–2.7 m (8–9 ft). All laterals are cut hard back. The cane is then pushed carefully through the carefully enlarged hole in the base of a 25 cm (10 in) pot.

An upward slanting cut is made in the cane just below a node; it should go about a third of the way through. Moss is then tied loosely round the cut and in it to keep it open.

With this portion of the cane towards the bottom of the pot, John Innes Potting Compost No. 2 is then put in and pressed firmly in. Roots will form in the pot during the following growing season along with several bunches of grapes.

When these are nearly ripe, the new 'vine' can be severed from the parent immediately outside the bottom hole of the pot. Do this in easy stages by making a slanting cut a third of the way through, another third further a week later and the final severence a week after that.

### Kiwi fruit under glass

We have already seen that it is more reliable to grow kiwis under glass than in the open (see page 208) but, whereas two systems of training are available for outdoors, the espalier method is certainly the most commonly used under glass. However, it is not the sort of plant to start growing in a greenhouse unless you are fully aware of its vigour and also that you will need at least two plants; one male, one female. It is all too easy to bite off more than you can chew, because a small domestic greenhouse is no place for a kiwi fruit vine.

For the espalier system, horizontal wires are stretched along the inside greenhouse wall 45 cm (18 in) apart with the lowest 45 cm (18 in) from the ground. Have as many wires as are necessary for the height you want the kiwi to occupy. Push in a suitable length cane behind the plant to reach the eave with another to the ridge and cut back the plant to just below the bottom wire. When growth starts, retain only three strong and suitably placed shoots; nip out all the others. The middle one is tied to the cane and the two others are trained out on each side along the bottom wire.

When the upright shoot reaches the second wire, nip out the top again and, when three more shoots have grown, repeat the process (central shoot upwards and one out on each side). Carry on like this until all the wires are occupied.

When the laterals (side shoots) reach about 90 cm (3 ft) long, nip out the tops to encourage side shoots to grow out from them; these sub-

**Fig. 16.11** A trained kiwi plant in a greenhouse should look something like this.

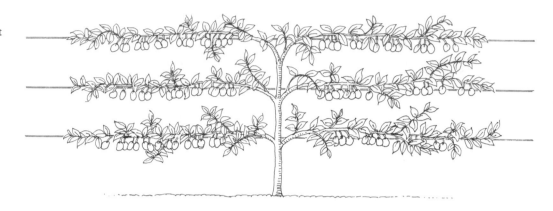

laterals will ultimately develop into fruiting spurs. The spurs are formed by keeping the sub-laterals pinched back to five leaves. Any shoots that develop on these later in the summer are nipped out when you see them [Fig. 16.11].

The spurs will soon start fruiting and, once they do, any shoots growing from them are stopped at seven leaves.

In the winter, after fruiting, cut back all the spurs to just two buds beyond where the last fruit was.

You will no doubt be pleased to hear that this sounds a great deal more complicated than it actually is. Once you are faced with a growing plant, you will see that it all makes sense; or you should.

### Passion fruit and granadilla

Although there are some 400 species of *Passiflora*, very few have edible fruits. Of these, the passion fruit, the banana passion fruit, the sweet granadilla and the giant granadilla are the most important and the only ones that we would consider growing for their edible fruit in temperate climates. Our outdoor passionflower with the dry, orange, egg shaped fruits can hardly be regarded as edible. The best that one can say is that it is not poisonous.

All those grown for their fruits are natives of the tropics and sub-tropics and need greenhouse treatment here. They do not require excessive warmth but it must be frost free. They are grown entirely for pleasure.

The training and pruning of these fruiting

passifloras is much the same as that of the ornamental species. The main difference is that the edible ones are not required to look decorative so are treated in the best way for flower and fruit production rather than decoration.

Both kinds must have a restricted root run to prevent excessive and unwanted growth forming at the expense of flowers and, where applicable, fruits.

There is no firm recommendation for the shape into which the plant is trained but something along the lines of a greenhouse grape serves well. Following, preferably, early spring planting in the greenhouse, the shoots are cut back to within a few inches of the ground.

Of the resulting new growth, only one or two of the strongest shoots are kept. It really depends on how many you have room for; remembering that they are very vigorous. These are trained up and tied to wires in much the same way as grapes are. When laterals form, they are trained out sideways where they will flower and fruit [Fig 16.12].

For the decorative species, it is usual to allow the growth to run unrestricted but the fruiting ones should have the laterals stopped when six or so flowers have set fruit, though this, again, depends on the room available. Throughout the growing season, weak and unwanted shoots must be taken out 'at birth' to prevent overcrowding.

During the winter, all the lateral shoots are cut hard back to two or three buds from the central stem. When growth starts in the spring, only the strongest one from each position is re-

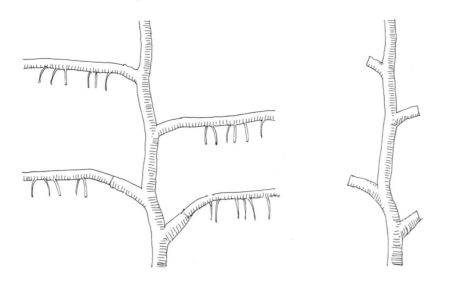

tained. Once again, we see the similarity with grapes [Fig. 16.10].

## Soft fruit in containers

Just as it is perfectly possible to grow tree fruits in containers of one sort or another, so it is quite feasible to grow soft fruits in the same way.

In many respects, it is a great deal easier because, on the whole, soft fruits take up far less root and top room. There are obvious exceptions, such as kiwi fruits, but even these can be grown in containers; it's just that it takes more work and skill to do it well.

For bush fruits, the system is based on growing them in more or less the same way that you would use if they were in the ground. All the check on growth comes from the container, which obviously places a severe restriction on the root system. As far as pruning soft fruit growing in containers is concerned, there are no special requirements beyond keeping the plants at a convenient size and shape with a balance between new growth and fruitfulness.

Don't forget, either, that 'containers' can refer to anything from traditional clay pots to plastic troughs or even growing-bags. All have their virtues and vices but this is neither the time nor the place to discuss them. Suffice it to say that no container should be ruled out as long as it is large enough and, preferably, capable of being drained.

# CHAPTER 17

# *Nuts*

## Almonds

The almond is a close relative of the peach. As such, its cultivation is more akin to a fruit than a nut. So like a peach is it that it is one of only three trees that are susceptible to peach leaf curl; the other two being peach and nectarine.

On the whole, they are grown more successfully in the UK as ornamental trees than for the nuts. The one to grow for nuts is *Prunus dulcis* 'Macrocarpa'. Most of the nuts on sale in the UK come from the Mediterranean region.

The nuts from the more ornamental varieties of almond are very variable and may well be thick shelled and often empty. This may also be because they are seedlings rather than proper almond trees raised in and bought from a reliable nursery.

The main problem with growing almonds in the UK is that, like the peach, they flower very early in the year (early spring, or even late winter in an advanced year) and the blossoms are, more often than not, caught by spring frosts.

As to pruning almonds; the less, the better. When necessary, they should be treated as peaches. When forming a young half-standard almond tree, one would usually buy one that is older than a maiden.

However, if it is a feathered maiden or a two-year-old and largely unpruned, cut the central stem back to about 1.2 m (4 ft) high; or whatever other height you want the trunk to be. If four or five good side shoots can be retained to form the lowest branches, cut them back to about 15 cm (6 in) long and remove all the others.

This should be done in the early autumn or, if the tree was planted in the winter, the following spring.

In a year's time the new branch leaders are pruned back to about 30 cm (12 in) long to suitably placed buds so that the resulting shoots grow in the required direction. This is repeated a year later so that there are up to a dozen shoots suitable for forming into branches.

That just about covers the formal and formative pruning.

Once the tree has been shaped and formed, all that has to be done is to keep an eye on the shape and remove any shoots or small branches that are dead or dying and clearly either too high, too low, too spreading or causing overcrowding. In fact, exactly the same as is recommended for plums and bush peaches.

Similarly, all pruning should be done at a time other than during the winter, to reduce the risk of infection by silver leaf. In practice, this usually means during early spring or in early autumn. The exact time may be influenced to a certain extent by the state of the crop but it is usually quite easy to prune out any unwanted branches at the same time as a crop is picked.

## Cobnuts and filberts

Now we come to what might be called proper nuts. Cobs and filberts are not the same as the wild hazels of our hedgerows, they are much larger and are immigrants from the Continent. The difference between the two is simply in the length of the husk that covers the nut.

In the filbert, the husk is the same length, or longer than, the nut, which is consequently hidden.

In the cobnut, the husk is shorter and the nut is visible.

The exception to this is the main commercial nut, the Kentish Cob which, by the classification, is a filbert.

Cobs and filberts are pruned exactly the same and there are two main ways. The first is the easy method in which the nut tree is allowed to grow pretty well at will.

As with any cropping tree that is given its

head, the problem here is that, after a few years, most of the crop is being produced on the end of the branches and way out of reach from the ground. This is not always as awkward as it sounds because the branches can be shaken in the autumn and the nuts, if the squirrels have left any, will fall to the ground.

These large bushes can be formed into excellent and profitable windbreaks for exposed places and visual barriers to hide factories and the like. The main pruning done to trees of this free-growing type (when their height is not wanted) is to remove the tallest branches in an effort to keep them reasonably within bounds and easy to pick.

One useful tip if you grow the trees in this way is to leave one tall branch system in the middle of each tree. You may know that many nuts are wind pollinated by pollen from the catkins and this is carried by gravity and the wind. Sweet corn works in the same way. By having a branch in the middle and higher than the rest of the tree, the pollen from its catkins will be well distributed to the female flowers beneath it.

The other way of pruning cobs and filberts is exactly the opposite, into a tightly controlled and severely pruned vase shape.

After planting in the winter what is often just a single-stemmed sucker, and allowing it to grow on for a year, it is cut down to within 30 cm (1 ft) of the ground. from the resulting new shoots that will grow in the spring, three or four of the strongest and most evenly spaced are retained to form the main branches. All the other are pinched out.

In the winter, the retained shoots are shortened back to about 23 cm (9 in).

Remembering the open-centre shape that you are aiming for, from the new shoots that develop from these in the spring, two or three of the stoutest and best placed are retained and allowed to grow on; all the others are pinched out.

Thus is formed the basis of the vase; up to a dozen strong shoots, roughly in the form of a circle. It is not these that will carry the crops but the twiggy side shoots that grow out from them. These main branches must, therefore, be kept short and stocky so that the bush is of a convenient height and carrying lots of twiggy shoots full of catkins (male), female flowers and

later, one hopes, nuts. Once the ultimate height has been reached, any extension growth on the leaders is cut hard back each winter.

The twiggy, cropping growths are fairly short-lived as far as nut production is concerned and have to be thinned out and or replaced each winter. This reduces overcrowding, encourages the production of more young shoots and, thus, improves the quality of the crops. A good time to do the pruning is straight after 'flowering', as this allows you to see which shoots are producing catkins and flowers and which are not. The exact time is judged by shaking the shoots carrying the catkins. If no more pollen falls from them, pruning can start.

As a rule, only the twiggy growths are bearing shoots, the vigorous straight ones are not and should be cut right out or hard back [Fig. 17.1].

Of course, a naturally vigorous bush will not put up with this harsh treatment without protest and the form it usually takes with a cobnut is a rash of strong water shoots from around the base. These must not be allowed to remain or they will quickly dominate the bush, take a lot of energy from the existing flowering shoots and prevent the formation of more. Like rose suckers, they should be pulled off or dug up, not cut off with secateurs as this simply leads to even more.

An odd practice used to exist whereby a form of summer pruning was carried out.

During the summer, the strong water shoots were snapped by hand about 15 cm (6 in) from their point of origin but, instead of being

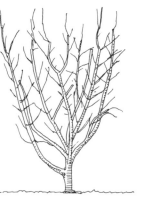

**Fig. 17.1** If you want a cobnut to remain compact, it will need hard pruning. The twiggy, flowering shoots are constantly being replaced.

broken clean off, the end was left hanging there. The idea was that this inflicted a greater check on the bush's growth than if the shoot was completely severed. The dead end was removed during the next winter pruning.

It might have been effective but it couldn't have done much for the appearance of the bushes. Nowadays, pruning is largely carried out in the winter or straight after flowering, which is much the same thing.

## Sweet chestnuts

In all honesty one cannot say that sweet chestnuts are a worthwhile crop in Britain. As with almonds, those we buy in the shops come mainly from warmer countries normally bordering the Mediterranean. Occasionally, however, trees in the UK carry a very useful crop but these usually follow a good summer and cannot always be relied upon. One cannot be more definite about this because there are plantings of mature trees which crop heavily every year. These, though, are the exception rather than the rule.

The chestnut that supplies the nuts is the Spanish chestnut, *Castanea sativa*; the best variety is 'Maroon de Lyon' (Hilliers), which carries nuts from an early age.

For best results, the nuts are normally singled to one per cluster (burr) to improve the size and uniformity.

Picking the nuts is unnecessary because, when mature, they drop to the ground in their burrs. They are then usually trodden on to expel the nuts from the prickly husks.

Pruning is virtually non-existent after the early years. Then, though, it is as well to prevent a leader dominating the tree or its eventual height will be enormous. Likewise, an extra strong lateral will create a lopsided tree. A standard is the best shape so that initial stopping of the main stem should be at about 1.8 m (6 ft) high.

After another year's growth and from the resulting shoots, the leader is maintained and the best of the remainder are selected to form the main branches. These are looked after for the next few years to make sure that they thrive and build up into a well-shaped tree. This treatment will keep the tree well balanced and without a tendency for any shoot to dominate. Beyond this, only undesirable branches need

to be removed.

This is the same type of chestnut that is used for tree stakes and fencing. It is notoriously bad firewood, spitting and banging like a firecracker. This is worth knowing if you are tempted to use removed branches or felled trees for logs.

## Walnuts

The walnut grown for nuts is *Juglans regia* not *J. nigra* (black walnut), whose nuts are useless. Further than this, not all *J. regia* trees are of equal quality, some producing good nuts and others bad. It is most important, therefore, that you only buy walnut trees from reliable nurseries or grow your own trees by budding or grafting scion material from a known and high quality tree.

Once again, the best nuts come from the Mediterranean region but very acceptable crops are had from mature trees of the right variety in Britain. The quality of nuts is slightly inferior to the imported ones and the crops are lighter but, provided they are only wanted for home consumption and not for selling, they are perfectly adequate.

If possible, buy a three- or four-year-old tree that has already been shaped and which has a good, straight trunk and graft union and a well-balanced top. This is important because trees grown for nuts (as opposed to timber) are often grafted and there is a risk of a kink between the seedling rootstock and the scion.

Budded trees are not so liable to this as a good nursery will grow a straight-trunked tree.

The trees may be planted in their final position as little as a year after budding or grafting. As the trees form a good head of branches naturally, little pruning is needed, even in the early years. It is merely desirable to keep a straight stem by cutting off any side shoots until it has reached the required height for stopping; usually about 1.8 m (6 ft) to form a standard tree (the best).

Crossing branches have to be sorted out and any dead or dying branches must be removed.

Pruning in the spring can lead to copious bleeding and must be avoided. The best time to prune is after growth has stopped in the late summer. The sap flow will be at a minimum and the comparative warmth will encourage the wounds to dry quickly.

Something to be aware of is that the shoot tips of young walnut trees are frequently killed by frost. If this should happen, care must be taken to ensure that the subsequent growths are suitable. If left unattended, it is possible to end up with the wrong shoot gaining dominance, thus ruining the shape of the tree. A well-shaped tree is achieved in the usual way by selecting and tipping suitably placed shoots in the first three or four winters to build up a strong and well-shaped branch framework. As always, the aim must be to have angled junctions between the branches and the trunk so that breakages in later years are kept to a minimum.

As with the sweet chestnut, very little pruning is needed after the formation of the main branches.

# Legal Aspects of Pruning

*Note to readers*: Laws will vary from country to country: the legal aspects described in this chapter reflect the law as applied in the United Kingdom.

## Introduction

Disputes between neighbours often bring out the very worst in human nature. It is a sad fact that trees and shrubs planted near garden boundaries with the intention of giving pleasure frequently give rise to bitter disagreement. It is an act of good neighbourliness to make every effort to avoid such problems by considerate planting and not permitting branches to overhang a neighbour's garden. In cases of minor disagreement sensible discussion and negotiation should always be the first course of action. In the UK if this fails the local Citizen's Advice Bureau can offer helpful guidance and will certainly assist in deciding whether or not a solicitor should be consulted. Civil action in the courts should be viewed as a last resort. Legal action is an expensive business and judges usually are of the opinion that disputes between neighbours are best kept out of the courts. Even if legal action is successful there will be little hope of any future good relations between the neighbours involved. If the action is unsuccessful the plaintiff can face the additional humiliation of having to pay the defendant's legal costs.

There is one instance when it is foolish not to consult a solicitor. If someone claims that a tree or branch from your garden has caused a serious accident you should contact a solicitor at once. The implications of this situation are severe and only a solicitor is properly qualified to deal with it.

## Overhanging branches

The usual owner of a tree or shrub is the owner of the land on which it is planted, even if its roots and branches extend onto a neighbour's property. Any such roots and branches are also the property of the owner of the tree. If such growths overhang or encroach onto your property they may be said to constitute a nuisance. This is one of the rare occasions when direct action can legally be taken to abate the nuisance. You may cut off the shoots or sever any roots without notifying your neighbour but you must not cut anything on his side of the boundary or enter his land to effect your action without his permission. As the tree or shrub is his property any prunings taken and any fruit that they may carry remain his and should be offered back to him in an undamaged condition. Merely throwing them over the fence without his consent is not appropriate. You also have no entitlement to pick and retain fruit that grows on branches that overhang your land without your neighbour's agreement. In law even windfalls from such branches should be offered back to the owner of the tree. A case in Kent was brought by a landowner against a neighbour who picked and sold Bramley apples from his . trees where branches overhung. The landowner won his case and secured damages to the estimated value of the 'stolen' crop.

Resorting to unagreed direct action to alleviate the nuisance of overhanging branches does carry a disadvantage. Apart from the loss of a potential friendship with your neighbour you will also forfeit any right to bring a civil action in a county court for damages; you cannot resort to self remedy and claim damages for past nuisance as well.

## Obstruction of light or view

Under normal circumstances the planting of trees or shrubs is not subject to planning regulations and neither does anyone have a legal right not to have the view from his premises blocked. If a neighbour's tree grows to obscure a view that you previously enjoyed, unless you can amicably persuade him to prune or remove it, there is nothing that can be done. The problem of shading caused by neighbouring trees has been increased by the popularity of large conifer hedges in recent years. A garden owner has no legal right not to have his garden shaded by a neighbour's trees so, once again, unless a negotiated solution can be found nothing can be done. The windows of a dwelling house or greenhouse, however, so long as they have enjoyed uninterrupted light for at least 20 years, or if such light has been granted by a deed are legally entitled to a continued right to light. In such a case a civil court may order the defendant's trees to be removed or cut back and maintained to a stated height. In reaching such a decision the court will not base judgement on whether light levels have been reduced by the offending trees but rather on whether or not there is sufficient light left for the normal comfort of the dwelling house or whether the greenhouse is still usable as such.

In view of the fact that so little can legally be done to remedy problems caused by shading from a neighbour's tree, the importance of sensible discussion with the neighbour cannot be over emphasized. Many gardeners who have planted a leyland cypress hedge have had a limited knowledge of final growth potential and are not best pleased with the ultimate effect. This could be your opportunity to help your neighbour to take down his hedge and advise him on the selection of a more suitable replacement!

## Threat to buildings or property

Injury and damage caused by fallen trees is regrettably common. That a landowner should take all reasonable care to prevent this from happening is a moral and legal obligation.

If injury or damage is caused by a tree or branch fall, any liability would rest with the tree's owner only if he was aware, or could reasonably be expected to have been aware, of the tree's unsafe condition. If a tree has had any obvious signs of ill health such as poor leaf colour, branches dying back or water seeping from the bark of the trunk or major limbs, this would certainly constitute grounds for awareness of a potential safety problem. If you believe that such a neighbour's tree is threatening your property or safety your first course of action should be to discuss the matter with him. He may well agree and be happy to implement a satisfactory remedy. If he disagrees you could contact your local council who will arrange for the tree to be inspected. Should their inspector agree that the tree is dangerous they will serve an order requiring the tree's owner to make it safe. If he does not comply or does not successfully appeal against the order the council may take the work in hand to make the tree safe. When this is completed they will usually proceed to recover their expenses from the owner. Local councils have similar powers to cut back or remove trees which threaten the general public. This may occur if a tree appears to be in danger of collapsing over a road or public walkway. The obstruction of view at a road junction or the obscuring of street lights or road signs would similarly qualify. Electricity distribution companies have similar powers concerning trees that may foul overhead power lines.

## Laws prohibiting pruning

It is an offence to cut down, top, lop or otherwise damage a healthy tree which is covered by a tree preservation order. Tree preservation orders are made by local councils under the Town and Country Planning Act 1971. Their function is to protect trees that may be in danger for the enjoyment of the public. Orders may cover individual or groups of trees. A local council will inform a landowner of its intention to place a tree preservation order and also offer him guidance should he wish to appeal against it. If no successful appeal is made an order will be confirmed and last indefinitely. On purchasing a property an official search should reveal the existence of any tree preservation orders. The buyer is subsequently bound by the same limitations as the seller had been. Any intentions to work on trees covered by preservation orders must be discussed with and approved by the local council. Failure to comply with this can result in heavy fines.

Conservation areas are designated by local councils to protect the character of particular settlements or small areas of historical interest. They are most numerous in rural areas and landowners or dwellers within a proposed conservation area are notified by the council.

The fact that a property is within a conservation area will be indicated to a new buyer in a search. Any work within such an area that adversely affects its character is discouraged. To this end planning regulations are more stringent and trees with a trunk diameter of more than 7.5 cm at breast height must not be pruned or felled without the permission of the council. Offenders are liable to the same penalties as those who disregard tree preservation orders.

In some leases or tenancy agreements there is a clause to the effect that the landlord's permission is required before trees or shrubs can be pruned or removed. If a dwelling is to be sold it is a normal condition that garden plants are regarded as 'fixtures' and must not be interfered with or removed by the vendor after the contracts have been signed. Any deviation from this must be made clear to the buyer before signing. Failure to comply with this could jeopardize a potential sale.

## Summary

You may prune or remove any plant in your own garden unless:

1. it is a tree covered by a tree preservation order;
2. it is a tree with a trunk diameter greater than 7.5 cm (3 in) at breast height and in a designated conservation area;
3. you are a tenant and there is a restrictive clause such that the landlord's permission is required;
4. you have signed a contract which agrees the sale of your property.

You may prune back branches or roots on a neighbour's tree or shrub but only if they overhang or grow under your land. If this is done you may only cut back as far as the boundary and must offer any prunings and fruit back to the neighbour.

You are liable for any damage to people or property caused by trees or branches falling from your land but only if such trees were in an apparently unsafe condition before the accident. If you are accused of having a tree that has caused serious damage or an accident, it would be best to seek the advice of a solicitor immediately.

# Index